Introduction to

Introduction to Cognitive Cultural Studies

EDITED BY LISA ZUNSHINE

The Johns Hopkins University Press

Baltimore

The Johns Hopkins University Press
2715 North Charles Street
Baltimore, Maryland 21218-4363
www.press.jhu.edu

Library of Congress Cataloging-in-Publication Data

Introduction to cognitive cultural studies / edited by Lisa Zunshine.
    p. cm.
    Includes bibliographical references and index.
    ISBN-13: 978-0-8018-9487-9 (acid-free paper)
    ISBN-10: 0-8018-9487-5 (acid-free paper)
    ISBN-13: 978-0-8018-9488-6 (pbk. : acid-free paper)
    ISBN-10: 0-8018-9488-3 (pbk. : acid-free paper)
    1. Psychology and literature. 2. Cognitive science—Philosophy. 3. Characters and characteristics in literature. 4. Discourse analysis, Narrative. 5. Influence (Literary, artistic, etc.). 6. Reader-response criticism. I. Zunshine, Lisa.
    PN56.P93I58 2010
    801'.92—dc22   2009039363

A catalog record for this book is available from the British Library.

Special discounts are available for bulk purchases of this book. For more information, please contact Special Sales at 410-516-6936 or specialsales@press.jhu.edu.

The Johns Hopkins University Press uses environmentally friendly book materials, including recycled text paper that is composed of at least 30 percent post-consumer waste, whenever possible. All of our book papers are acid-free, and our jackets and covers are printed on paper with recycled content.

If we understand the relations between nature and culture as a relation of ramification and elaboration, or in the language of science, as a form of emergence or complexity, rather than that of opposition, the one, nature, providing both the means and the material for the other's elaboration, and the other, culture, providing the latest torsions, vectors, and forces in the operations of an ever-changing, temporally sensitive nature, cultural studies can no longer afford to ignore the inputs of the natural sciences if they are to become self-aware.

Elizabeth Grosz, *Time Travels: Feminism, Nature, Power*

CONTENTS

ACKNOWLEDGMENTS

Out of the fifteen essays appearing in this collection, three have been published previously. Their authors are grateful to the editors of *Narrative* and *Poetics Today* for letting them include Patrick Colm Hogan's "Literary Universals" (*Poetics Today* 18.2 [1997]: 223–49), Ellen Spolsky's "Darwin and Derrida: Cognitive Literary Theory as a Species of Post-structuralism" (*Poetics Today* 23.1 [2002]: 43–62), and Lisa Zunshine's "Theory of Mind and Experimental Representations of Fictional Consciousness" (*Narrative* 11.3 [2003]: 270–91).

The editor is grateful to Porter Abbott for his thoughtful and detailed comments on earlier versions of this volume; to Michael Lonegro, an editor at the Johns Hopkins University Press, for his expertise in and long-standing encouragement of the work in cognitive cultural studies; to Trevor Lipscombe, JHU Press's editor-in-chief, for seeing the manuscript through to press in the final stages; to MJ Devaney for her careful and insightful editing; and to the contributors to this volume, for their patience, good humor, and professionalism. David Herman, Patrick Colm Hogan, Suzanne Keen, Alan Richardson, and Ellen Spolsky have been particularly helpful in their comments and suggestions regarding various parts of this collection.

Introduction to Cognitive Cultural Studies

What Is Cognitive Cultural Studies?

LISA ZUNSHINE

Introduction

This volume brings together fourteen essays representing the rapidly growing interdisciplinary field of cognitive approaches to literature and culture. Reflecting the explosion of academic and public interest in cognitive science in the last two decades, it features work that combines literary and cultural analysis with insights from neuroscience, discursive psychology, cognitive evolutionary psychology and anthropology, cognitive linguistics, and philosophy of mind. That readers, both specialist and nonspecialist, are eager for an informed and sustained conversation about literature, culture, and cognition is apparent from the stream of conferences, essays, monographs, and World Wide Web discussions on the subject. To mention just one example that demonstrates the interest it elicits, the membership in the MLA official discussion group on cognitive approaches to literature has grown from 250 in 1999, the year it was organized, to over 1,221 in 2009.

The present volume seeks to build on that interest and to shape the field for the coming decade. Oriented toward students in a broad variety of literature and cultural studies courses, *Introduction to Cognitive Cultural Studies* works simultaneously on three levels. First, it provides its readers with grounding in several major areas of cognitive science. Second, it presents new interpretations resulting from applying insights from cognitive science to cultural representations. Third, it considers these new interpretations in the context of the commitment of those who have adopted cognitive approaches to seeking common ground with existing literary-theoretical paradigms, a development that marks decisively the field's entrance into mainstream literary and cultural studies. Writing in 2001, cognitive literary theorist F. Elizabeth Hart noted that a position "of inclusiveness toward a full array of contemporary literary approaches" is "productive" ("Epistemology," 329) yet uncommon among cognitive literary critics; today this position has become one of the key features of the field.

The wide range of approaches represented by the collection underscores both the theoretical coherence and methodological eclecticism of cognitive cultural studies. The authors share the crucial theoretical assumption that the contemporary sciences of the mind destabilize the old division between "nature" and "nurture" and open new venues for investigating the role of universally shared features of human cognition in historically specific forms of cultural production. As one of the contributors to the present volume, Ellen Spolsky, puts it in the preface to *The Work of Fiction* (2004), an important earlier collection of essays representing the field:

> Cognitive literary theory is . . . well positioned to provide insights into a question that has been occluded by the well-deserved successes of the reemergent historical and multifaceted cultural studies that have proliferated after the New Criticism in the twentieth century. That question is this: how does the evolved architecture that grounds human cognitive processing, especially as it manifests itself in the universality of storytelling and the production of visual art, interact with the apparently open-ended set of cultural and historical contexts in which humans find themselves, so as to produce the variety of social constructions that are historically distinctive, yet also often translatable across the boundaries of time and place? It is the job [of cognitive literary theory] to begin to chart the emergence, manifestation, and readability of these only temporarily stable relationships between the humanly universal and the culturally and individually specific, as coded and recorded in cultural artifacts. (viii)

Moreover, because the relationships between the humanly universal and the culturally specific are only "temporarily stable," the investigation of these relationships is itself open ended on several counts. First, we don't know a priori what form of cognitive-cultural interplay we will uncover as a result of our analysis. Second, we are not constrained in choice of methodology by a consideration of boundaries between different subfields. The same cultural phenomenon can be approached from a variety of cognitive-theoretical perspectives; sometimes the best strategy is a combination of methodologies.

The fuzziness of boundaries is, in fact, an important feature of cognitive cultural studies. The present volume is organized around several distinct rubrics, including cognitive historicism, cognitive narratology, cognitive ecocriticism, literary universals, and so forth, yet this categorization is more a matter of editorial convenience than evidence of fault lines dividing the field. For example, an essay on cognitive ecocriticism would also fit comfortably in the section on cognitive historicism; an essay on cognition and emotion in literature and film could easily fall under the rubric of cognitive narratology or aesthetics. This compatibility stems directly from the goal of the cognitive cultural project, which is to understand the evolving relationship between two immensely complex, historically situated systems—the human mind and cultural artifacts, such as novels, poems, or paintings—and not to merely use such artifacts to illustrate a particular scientific hypothesis about one particular feature of human cognition.

A student of cognitive cultural studies would thus do well to think of herself as a *bricoleur* who reaches out for the best mix of insights that cognitive theory as a whole has to offer without worrying about blurring lines between its various domains. Cognitive scientists themselves cross disciplinary boundaries daily, attracting new academic fields into their orbit. If the traditional cognitive sciences drew on neuroscience, philosophy of mind, artificial intelligence, linguistics, evolutionary anthropology, and cognitive, developmental, and clinical psychology, today this list has expanded to include work done in comparative psychology (i.e., study of nonhuman animals), law, economics, music, engineering, and political science. For instance, a conference organized by the cognitive science program at Yale University, entitled "The Evolution of Social Psychology" (7–9 November 2008), brought together psychologists studying nonhuman primates with scholars from philosophy, computer science, law, and behavioral economics. Until recently, these fields would have been thought of as having nothing in common with comparative psychology, yet today they are engaged in the common project of understanding how the mind works.

Note, too, that, while participating in this project and thus becoming, in effect, cognitive sciences in their own right, philosophy, law, computer science, and other disciplines do not risk losing their autonomy by being subsumed by psychology. Clearly, scholars working in some areas within these disciplines benefit from this kind of conceptual integration, while for other areas it is irrelevant. The situation is similar in our own field of literary and cultural studies. Some domains of literary criticism develop in exciting new directions by integrating work from cognitive psychology with our long-standing interest in how the mind works (for we, too, have been grappling with this issue, using variously the framework of psychoanalysis, phenomenology, deconstruction, and cultural studies). Others don't need it (the thriving field of contextual historicism being one immediate example[1]).

The boundaries between various subfields of cognitive cultural studies thus remain fluid as a function of the opportunistic nature of cognitive science, that is, of its tendency to grow and change by complementing and enhancing various aspects of other disciplines. To foreground this fluidity, the concluding part of this introduction maps out connections between individual essays across several subfields (brief overviews of these subfields are left to headnotes preceding each section in the body of the volume). Similarly, the suggestions for further reading that conclude this introduction are organized alphabetically rather than by category since very few books and essays on this list fall naturally into any one discrete category.

Finally, because our goal is to offer the reader an introduction to cognitive approaches to literature with an emphasis on cultural studies, this volume does not feature work on other aspects of cognitive literary studies, such as conceptual blending theory, cognitive poetics, and empirical studies of literature. An overview of these important areas of research can be found in Alan Richardson's "Studies in Literature and Cognition: A Field Map" (2004); foundational texts include Mark Turner's *The Literary Mind* (1996), Rueven Tsur's *Toward a Theory of Cognitive Poetics* (1992), and David Miall's *Literary Reading: Empirical and Theoretical Studies* (2006).

Cognitive Cultural Studies: Definition and Legacy of the Term

The term "cultural studies" has a long and complicated history, referring to both a particular school of thought (or several related schools) and an ever-expanding set of academic research programs. "Cognitive cultural studies" most commonly evokes the second, broad meaning of the term, thus connoting the incorporation of insights from cognitive science into the study of cultural practices. Yet the first, more specific, meaning turns out to be also directly relevant, in fact, crucially so, as the field of cognitive cultural studies seeks to position itself inside mainstream cultural theory. For, even though only one essay in the present collection, Bruce McConachie's "Toward a Cognitive Cultural Hegemony," explicitly revisits the work of a founder of cultural studies, Raymond Williams, the volume as a whole is compatible with Williams's original vision of cultural studies, articulated in *The Long Revolution* as exploring the relationship between the "evolution of the human brain [and] the particular interpretation carried by particular cultures" (18).

The legacy of Williams's work and its relation to the project of cognitive cultural studies is worth discussing at length here, for there is a misconception that still haunts cognitive approaches to literature and culture, although it has become less widespread during the past several years. According to this view, by making a "cognitive turn," a literary critic abandons the traditional paradigms of her own field, be it gender studies, feminist criticism, postcolonial theory, poststructuralism, performance theory, psychoanalysis, or cultural studies. In reality, there is neither reason nor obligation for her to abandon them; no more than there is reason or obligation for a scholar who develops interest in media studies to give up her commitment to feminist or postcolonial theory.

In fact, just as in the case of other interdisciplinary fields, some of the most exciting research in cognitive approaches to literature and culture comes from scholars who develop interfaces between cognitive science and more established literary and cultural theories. Nor should that be surprising. Given that the "human mind in its numerous complex environments has been the object of study of literary critics for longer than it has been the object of study of cognitive scientists," we should expect and welcome cognitive readings that resonate with existing literary and cultural theory.[2] Several essays in this volume, such as Spolsky's "Darwin and Derrida: Cognitive Literary Theory as a Species of Post-structuralism," argue that there is a good deal of consonance between cognitive approaches and various aspects of traditional literary theory.

Consider the opening argument of Williams's *The Long Revolution*:

> The central fact of [the] new account of the activity of our brains is that each one of us *has to learn to see*. . . . There is no reality of familiar shapes, colours, and sounds, to which we merely open our eyes. The information that we receive through our senses from the material world around us has to be interpreted, according to certain human rules, before what we ordinarily call "reality" forms. The human brain has to perform this "creative" activity before we can, as normal human beings, see at all.
>
> . . . [Reality] as we experience it in this sense is a human creation; . . . all our experience is a human version of the world we inhabit. This version has two main sources: the human brain as it has evolved, and the interpretations carried by our cultures. Man's version of the world he inhabits has a central biological function: it is a form of interaction with his environment which allows him to maintain his life and to achieve greater control over the environment in which this must be done. We "see" in certain ways—that is, we interpret sensory information according to certain rules—as a way of living. But these ways—these rules and interpretations—are, as a whole, neither fixed nor constant. We can learn new rules and new interpretations, as a result of which we shall literally see in new ways. There are thus two senses in which we can speak of this activity as "creative." The evolution of the human brain, and then the particular interpretation carried by particular cultures, give us certain "rules" or "models," without which no human being can "see" in the ordinary sense at all. In each individual, the learning of these rules, through inheritance and culture, is a kind of creation, in that the distinctively human world, the ordinary "reality" that his culture defines, forms only as the rules are learned. Particular cultures carry particular versions of reality, which they can be said to create, in the sense that cultures carrying different rules (though on a common basis of the evolved human brain) create their own worlds which their bearers ordinarily experience. But,

further, there is not only variation between cultures, but the individuals who bear these particular cultural rules are capable of altering and extending them, bringing in new or modified rules by which an extended or different reality can be experienced. Thus, new areas of reality can be "revealed" or "created," and these need not be limited to any one individual, but can, in certain interesting ways, be communicated, thus adding to the set of rules carried by the particular culture.

The effect of the new knowledge seems to me to be of the greatest importance, but I know from my own attempts to absorb it that it is so difficult to grasp, in any substantial sense, that its application must meet with all kinds of resistance and confusion. (18)

Writing in 1961, Williams expected that attempts to integrate the science of the "evolved human brain" with cultural interpretations would meet with "resistance and confusion." His expectation has been confirmed insofar as ignoring a difficult concept constitutes a form of resistance to it. During the last forty years, cultural studies has thrived and expanded, but its explicit cognitive-evolutionary component, as articulated by Williams, has been ignored.

It is significant, for example, that when cultural studies is defined today, in its broadest incarnation, as "an unstable meeting point for various combinations of critics and specialists," the list of its affiliate approaches includes "Marxist theory and criticism, feminist theory and criticism, literary and media studies, postmodernism, anthropological theory and criticism, social semiotics, postcolonial cultural studies, rhetoric, race and ethnicity, visual culture, gender theory and criticism and body theory, and the sociology and history of culture and science" but not cognitive science.[3] It is also significant that when a cultural theorist, such as Cary Nelson, wants to counterbalance "the widespread belief that cultural studies [is] anything that an intellectual happened to be investigating" and thus calls for a reengagement with the work of Williams, cognitive science is absent from his conceptual horizon. Attempting to define "what cultural studies is and what it is not," Nelson lists fourteen points, ranging from cultural studies' grounding in "contemporary life and current politics" to its resistance to unreflexive historicizing, but there are no references of any kind to the human mind or brain.[4]

Such omissions are striking because they obscure the theoretical foundation of the project of cultural studies as formulated by Williams. Crucial precepts of the field—its resistance to a narrow understanding of culture and art and hence its radical broadening of the range of objects of critical analysis—are grounded in Williams's cognitive-evolutionary take on human creativity.

But it wouldn't do merely to acknowledge that the "new account of the activity of our brains" constitutes an original conceptual mainstay of cultural studies. Williams's prescient argument also reminds us that when literary theorists today turn to cognitive science they in fact commit themselves to a more integrated cultural and historical analysis. Just as he needed studies of "a common basis of the evolved human brain" to develop his theory of individual and cultural change, so do contemporary critics need such studies, enriched, of course, by the new work done in the intervening years, to analyze specific cultural formations in their specific historical moments.

And this is why cognitive cultural studies *is* cultural studies as originally conceptualized by Williams. It is an interdisciplinary field that studies the relationship between the "evolved human brain" and "the particular interpretations carried by particular cultures." The reason that now we must call it *cognitive* cultural studies is to underline the cognitive-evolutionary aspect that for the last forty years has remained dormant. One hopes that the publication of the present volume will hasten the day when the qualifier "cognitive" can be dropped again—that once cognitive approaches are no longer excluded from cultural studies, the cultural will simply be understood as being in part constituted by the cognitive. For just as the concept of the human brain becomes meaningless once we attempt to separate it from the culture in which it develops, so the concept of human culture becomes meaningless once we try to extract the human brain from it.

Cognitive Foundations of the View of Culture as a "Whole Way of Life"

Among Williams's lasting contributions to contemporary critical thought is his view of culture as "a whole way of life" (*Long Revolution*, 40) and of art as not separate from but continuous with our social institutions and everyday practices. Today these are founding principles of cultural studies, yet nobody seems to remember that these insights grew out of Williams's belief that the new "work on perception, as a process of the brain and the nervous system," finally allowed cultural critics to "take a decisive step forward" in clarifying what art entails and what the word "creative" really means (*Long Revolution*, 16). In what follows, I consider Williams's arguments in the first chapter of *The Long Revolution* that lead up to his assertion that "we are in a position to reconcile the meanings of culture as 'creative activity' and 'a whole way of life'" and then compare these arguments with those developed by Spolsky, a leading theorist of contemporary cognitive cultural criticism. My goal here is not so much to establish Williams as one of the early cognitive critics (although it begins to feel strange *not* to consider him one) as to articulate the grounds for the claim that recent cognitive cultural theory is continuous with the original cultural studies.

Williams opens the first chapter of *The Long Revolution*, tellingly named "The Creative Mind," with a critique of dualism that informs our attitude toward art. "Plato or a Puritan or a modern Practical Man can dismiss art as inferior. Aristotle or a Renaissance theorist or a modern Romantic or aesthete can praise art as superior" (22). What underlies these seemingly disparate positions, however, is the same "assumed duality: the separation of art and reality, or of man and the world he observes" (22).

Building on the work of neurobiologists, such as Sir Russell Brain, and neurophysiologists, such as John Zachary Young, Williams then suggests that "what we now know about perception . . . opens the way to ending this duality, and thus transforming our thinking about art" and creativity (22). We begin to realize that it is "man's nature, and the history of his evolution, to be continually learning" (22) to see the world and by learning to see it, to transform himself. Moreover, since "this continuing organization and reorganization of consciousness is, for man, the organization and reorganization of reality—consciousness as a way of learning to control his environment—it is clear that there is a real sense in which man can be called a creator" (22).

And the reason that "man" (to stay with Williams's antiquated gendering of his subjects) can be considered truly creative is that the process of human learning and self-reorganization is profoundly communicative:

All living forms have communication systems of a kind, but again, in man, the process of learning and relearning, which is made possible by social organization and tradition, has led to a number of communication-systems of great complexity and power. Gesture, language, music, mathematics are all systems of this kind. We can think of them as separate systems, yet to understand their nature in any depth, we must see them in their context of the whole process of social learning.

(22)

Hence, instead of being treated as a separate system, art becomes a form of communication:

The artist shares with other men what is usually called "the creative imagination": that is to say, the capacity to find and organize new descriptions of experience. Other men share with the artist the capacity to transmit these descriptions, which are only in the full sense descriptions when they are in a communicable form. The special nature of the artist's work is his use of a learned skill in a particular kind of a transmission of experience. (26)[5]

And just as the success of any act of communication is judged by its effects—did what you learned yesterday transform your personal organization, your experience, of the world?—so the success of art is judged by its ability to transform its recipients. In fact, the word "recipient" is misleading because it does not convey the deeply participatory nature of the interaction between the artist and his audience. For to "succeed in art is to convey an experience to others in such a form that the experience is actively re-created—not 'contemplated,' not 'examined,' not passively received, but by response to the means, actually lived through, by those to whom it is offered" (34).

Thinking of art as a form of communication predicated on the living organism's need to adapt to its constantly changing environment or to find a way to modify that environment—given that our species' environment is most and foremost *other minds*—has two immediate implications. First, we cannot continue to see art as qualitatively special and thus discontinuous with everyday practices, a perspective that has historically led to either extolling art as a superior version of reality or denigrating it as its inferior imitation. Thus Williams:

The abstraction of art has been its promotion or relegation to an area of special experience (emotion, beauty, phantasy, the imagination, the unconscious), which art in practice has never confined itself to, ranging in fact from the most ordinary daily activities to exceptional crises and intensities, and using a range of means from the words of the street and common popular stories to strange systems and images which it has yet been able to make common property.   (39)

Second, we can now link individual cognitive development with the functioning of social institutions, for, viewed from a cognitive perspective, an institution can be sustained only as long as it successfully communicates, that is, changes the way people see the world. As Williams puts it, "If people have lived together, and come to share a certain kind of organization by which their minds have been trained to activity, we shall find that the processes of organization are in fact institutions, of which art is usually one" (31).[6]

We are now nearing the concluding point of Williams's opening chapter: his view of culture as "a whole way of life." If art is one of the institutions that emerge out of a shared cognitive entraining of people who live together, then there is no neat separation between art and other forms of communication that sustain a given society. "The fatally wrong approach" to art thus stems "from the assumption of separate orders, as when we ordinarily assume that political institutions and conventions are of a different and separate order from artistic institutions and conventions" (39). By contrast, once we posit "learning to see" as the condition of our being in the world, and once we consider art as an innovative way of seeing that has to be communicated, and once we envision our society as a network of institutions that facilitate all kinds of communication, we "are in the position to reconcile the meanings of culture as 'creative activity' and 'a whole way of life,' and this reconciliation is then a real extension of our powers to understand ourselves and our societies" (40).[7]

Thus Williams in 1961. When we look for work in cultural studies done between then and now that builds on his remarkable endeavor to factor the "evolved human brain" into cultural critique, we do not find anything. But if we look at contemporary cognitive literary theory—particularly those subfields within it that integrate insights from poststructuralism, cultural historicism, feminism, and performance studies—we discover a striking compatibility between their and Williams's conceptual frameworks. What it means is not just that the original project of cultural studies might be carried on today by cognitive cultural critics but that insights from cognitive evolutionary science might be a necessary component—it was so in 1961 and remains so in 2009—of cultural critique that is self-aware—aware, that is, of its goals, methodology, and ideology. To put it differently, we may not need cognitive science for every bit of cultural analysis we perform, but if we want to be aware of the epistemological foundations of what we do, we have to go back, or forward, to the "evolved human brain."

Consider again the work of Spolsky, whose pioneering books, *Gaps in Nature* (1993), *Satisfying Skepticism* (2001), and *Word vs. Image* (2007) exemplify cognitive approaches to literature that are fully engaged both with cognitive science and contemporary critical theory. Like Williams, Spolsky views art as a cognitive tool integrated with other systems of communication. Williams observes that "the artist shares with other men . . . the capacity to find and organize new descriptions of experience" and that for "members of the audience, as for artists, communication is a way of living: to receive and live an artist's experience is no casual activity, but an actual living change" (35). Spolsky makes a similar case in one of her essays in the present volume, "Making 'Quite Anew': Brain Modularity and Creativity" (chap. 3):

> Human cultures are not inert but dynamic; they aren't marble-chambered museums through which intimidated neophytes walk silently, receiving impressions. A culture is more like a force field with no shelter from challenge, no permit for passivity. Like the rest of us, artists have no choice but to be engaged in our shared space. But, also like the rest of us, they have the chance to be active tool makers. Particularly successful works of art, like other enabling innovations, are engines, not reflections, of culture. The most successful of them have the potential to bring audiences to new understanding.

Spolsky also shares Williams's belief in the reconciliation "between the meanings of culture as 'creative activity' and 'a whole way of life.'" As she puts it, "Seeing stories and paintings as artifacts on a par with arrowheads and antibiotics rather than as messengers from a privileged if useless aesthetic realm prompts us to investigate the hypothesis that the work of artists has work to do." And that work consists in enabling "audiences to recognize and understand something new and then use that new understanding, at least occasionally, to renew the world around them." Such an argument is congenial to Williams's assertion that we constantly need to "learn new rules and new interpretations, as a result of which we shall literally see in new ways."[8]

The confluence between Williams's and Spolsky's views would not be interesting if it were simply a result of intellectual influence—for example, Spolsky reading Williams and taking his insights to heart. Spolsky, however, arrived at her concept of creativity via a completely different route: building on studies of relationships between literary and oral narratives, on cognitive philosopher Andy Clark's exploration of "representationally hungry" cultural problems, and, most centrally, on recent research in cognitive modularity. According to Spolsky, "human cognition is enabled by a collection of specialist sensory intake modules, each of which does a different job, each of which is responsive to a different kind of energy" in one's environment. Since these modules (the visual system and the language system, for example) speak different languages and yet must communicate with each other if we are to be able to speak about what we see, a modular mind must perforce be a creative mind: modularity itself demands constant translation, constant remapping of communication among modules, an ongoing recategorization and re-representation of experience.

Using Raphael's *Transfiguration* of 1520 as her case study, Spolsky demonstrates how an artist can re-present a counterintuitive idea—"that a man could simultaneously appear as a god"—in a way that makes it easier to accept. The *Transfiguration* may enable its viewers to bridge "the gap between the categories of humanity and divinity," and in so doing, to quote Williams again, it may help them to "literally see" these categories "in new ways."

Spolsky's essay seems to illustrate most strikingly the convergence between early cultural studies and recent cognitive theory, but there are other examples of such a convergence throughout this volume. What this demonstrates is that the grounding assumptions of cognitive evolutionary science—its denial of teleology, its emphasis on indeterminacy and on ongoing, mutually goading transformations of individuals and their environments—make this science indispensable to a nonreductive cultural analysis.

For, as feminist philosopher Elizabeth Grosz has shown in *Time Travels: Feminism, Nature, Power* (2005), excluding evolutionary science from cultural theory perpetuates the intellectually and politically crippling dichotomous thinking about nature as "passive, inert, unchanging, ahistorical" (45)—a mere "background" for cultural elaboration (46)—and culture as "changing, the historical, the unpredictable" (49), creatively expanding nature in new directions. Grosz observes that this "nature/culture opposition seems foundational to cultural analysis, which defines itself by excluding the natural from its considerations. If nature is not the other, the opposite, of culture, but its condition, then the relations between them are much more complicated than a binary division implies" (46). And this binary division is what Williams wanted to destabilize by binding "biology" and "ways of seeing" the world into a unified yet open-ended system in which nature necessarily exceeds culture and thus makes it possible.

Consider again Williams's assertion that our reality is but one possible version of endless realities, constructed to serve our specific survival needs:

> The information that we receive through our senses from the material world around us has to be interpreted, according to certain human rules. . . . [Reality] *as we experience it* in this sense a human creation; . . . all our experience is a human version of the world we inhabit. . . . Man's version of the world he inhabits has a central biological function: it is a form of interaction with his environment which allows him to maintain his life and to achieve greater control over the environment in which this must be done.   (18)[9]

To understand what is at stake here, that is, to understand what ground-breaking and underappreciated philosophical assumptions early cultural studies was built on, see how the same argument—that culture limits nature and not vice versa—is rearticulated today by thinkers committed to Darwinian epistemology. Grosz suggests that culture actualizes only a tiny subset of possibilities latent in nature, narrowing it down to make it relevant to the needs of a specific human moment:

> If culture does not so much add activity to nature's passivity, then perhaps we may understand culture as subtractive: culture diminishes,

selects, reduces nature rather than making nature over, or adding to it social relevance, significance, and the capacity for variation. Nature itself may be understood as perpetual variation, and life as the evolutionary playing out of maximal variation or difference, as Darwin's own understanding of evolutionary processes implies. If biological evolution is the generation of an immensely productive machinery for the creation of maximal difference[,] . . . then culture rather than nature is what impoverishes nature's capacity for self-variation and becoming, by tying the natural to what culture can render controllable and what it sees as desirable. Perhaps Bergson, following Darwin, is right to claim that our human activities diminish rather than augment the effects of the natural world in order that we can discriminate its features and highlight only those that interest us. Culture is not the magnification of nature and its animation through human effort, but the selection of only some elements or facets of the natural, and the casting of the rest of it into shadow, a kind of diminution of the complexity and openness of the natural order. (48)

See too how Spolsky captures this important reversal of the traditional understanding of the relationship between the cultural and the natural in her *Satisfying Skepticism,* when she suggests that the "theoretically infinite number of creative possibilities will in practice always be channeled and restricted by the cultural surround" even if "those restrictions are themselves often negotiable" (4).

This is what it means, then, to say that a cognitive-evolutionary perspective commits cultural critics to a more rigorous historicizing than a perspective that ignores human evolved cognition. Williams argued that "we interpret sensory information according to certain rules—as a way of living" but that "these rules and interpretations" are "neither fixed nor constant," which means that we can both learn and invent "new rules and new interpretations, as a result of which we shall literally see in new ways." As one of many systems that enable new ways of seeing, art is thus profoundly historically contingent. To understand why a certain new interpretation of "sensory information," say a movie about Prohibition-era gangsters made in the 1990s, becomes, or does not become, particularly relevant and appealing (or, as Williams would say, communicable), we have to situate it in its rich historical context. We have to ask what specific challenges of this moment—economic, theological, sexual, political, emotional, linguistic, ecological, personal (and so forth: ways of framing these challenges are infinite)—this way of seeing the world engages. But at the same time we also have to ask how it engages them so as to be relevant (again: communicable) to specifically human cognition; for example, how it interacts with our theory of mind, with our tendency to engage in analogical thinking, with our embodied perception of the world, with particularities of our emotional response to representations and how it forges (or severs) connections between our sensory modules. This volume builds on research into these and other aspects of cognition that were not available to Williams in his day. Still, his insistence on seeing "art as a particular process in the general human process of creative discovery and communication" and culture as "a whole way of life" offers an expanded and enriched conceptual framework for scholars in the humanities interested in cognitive science and thus allows them to reclaim early cultural studies as cognitive cultural studies.

Volume Overview

Patrick Colm Hogan's classic essay "Literary Universals" (1997) (chap. 1) sets the overall tenor for the volume by arguing that a study of universals (a term that can be extended, in the case of other essays, to aspects of cognition ranging from the capacity for attributing mental states to analogical thinking) does not foreclose responsible historicist analysis but rather makes it possible. As Hogan puts it:

> The proponents of cultural and historical study are mistaken . . . in seeing the study of universals as somehow opposed to or contradictory of cultural study, in believing that the examination of universals somehow precludes historical research. . . . [The] study of universals and the study of cultural and historical particularity are mutually necessary. Like laws of nature, cultural universals are instantiated variously, particularized in specific circumstances.

An antiuniversalist stance handicaps the cultural critic (that is, if she actually follows it through instead of merely paying lip service to it). If a student of Sanskrit literature does not consider allusion a literary universal, she will not look for it in *Ramayana*, will fail to recognize its importance in that text, and thus will be "unlikely to advance a culturalist or interpretive project." Moreover, one should differentiate between "empirical universalism (the isolation of genuine cross-cultural invariants) and normative absolutism (the cross-cultural imposition of a culturally non-universal idea of practice)."[10] The latter represents pseudouniversalism: a creed that "derive[s] from and seek[s] to further colonial, patriarchal, or other ideologies supporting unjust domination." By contrast,

> no racist ever justified the enslavement of Africans or colonial rule in India on the basis of a claim that whites and nonwhites share universal human properties. Rather, they based their justification on presumed differences among Europeans, Africans, and Indians, usually biological differences, but often cultural differences as well. Indeed, "liberal" racism and colonialism—with their paternalistic emphasis on leading the native out of primitive ways and into civilization— were always based on specifically culturalist differentialism. . . . A universalist program that succeeds in uncovering genuinely universal principles of human thought and human society, principles that are not relative to race and culture, necessarily runs contrary to racism and ethnocentrism.

In discussing such cross-culturally recurring features of literary texts as symbolism, imagery, assonance, foreshadowing, plot circularity, and image patterns, Hogan confronts two common misconceptions about literary universals. The first is that they must be present in *all* literary works and the second is that they should take the same forms across different cultures. But to count as universals they merely have to appear "with greater frequency than would be predicted by chance alone," and the forms that they take are always specific to their environments.

Hogan's second essay in the volume, "On Being Moved: Cognition and Emotion in Literature and Film" (chap. 11), takes up the difficult issue of our strong yet peculiarly limited emotional engagement with fictional representations. What cognitive factors, asks Hogan, inhibit "our actional response to fictionally or imaginatively produced emotions"? Why, for example, when we read about a rapidly approaching lion, do we not put down the book and start running away? His answer is that what checks this fight-or-flight response to fictional scenarios is "our direct engagement with critically proximate egocentric space." We constantly recalibrate our actual physical position "in relation to [the] subjectively fixed space" of a movie or a book.

Hogan's discussion of emotions builds on his argument in "Literary Universals," emphasizing the crucial difference between the project of studying cross-cultural emotional patterns and assuming "a high degree of uniformity within cultures, particularly within foreign cultures." Focusing on a set of our innate sensitivities "to other people's emotion expressions," Hogan suggests that cultural differences in representing such "consequential" phenomena as human emotions "will be largely a matter of variations within parametric or other constraints," variations deriving "from accidents of history, group dynamics, physical environment, and related factors." His case study, Hindi film *Yathharth* (*The Truth*), depicts a little girl whose particular circumstances prompt her to dance with joy every time a funeral procession approaches the place where she lives. She responds to corpses with joy because her father, an untouchable, can provide food for her only when somebody dies and he receives payment for cremation. The girl's reaction thus suggests the plasticity of human emotions and their dependence on specific personal histories and cultural contexts. But the movie also exploits our perennial fascination with mental states as performed and betrayed by the body—we follow eagerly both the spectacle of the little girl's incongruous jubilation and of other villagers' shocked reaction to it. Moreover, for viewers immersed in Hindi culture, this fascination will be further layered by the awareness that the little girl's dance is unmistakably reminiscent of the dance performed by the goddess Kali on the cremation grounds.

What Hogan calls our innate sensitivity to "facial expressions, tones of voice, postures, and so forth" is further explored in the essays by Alan Richardson, Alan Palmer, Blakey Vermeule, and Lisa Zunshine. They consider the implications for literary and cultural studies of the work on theory of mind, the term used by psychologists to describe "our awareness of the existence of other minds, our knowledge of how to interpret other people's thought processes, our mind-reading abilities in the real world" (Palmer, "Storyworlds and Groups" [chap. 8]). Zunshine's "Theory of Mind and Experimental Representations of Fictional Consciousness" (chap. 9) draws on the work of cognitive evolutionary psychologist Simon Baron-Cohen to suggest that fiction engages, teases, and pushes to its tentative limits our mind-reading capacity. Building further on the recent research of Robin Dunbar and his colleagues, she considers a passage from Woolf's *Mrs. Dalloway* as an example of spectacular literary experimentation with our theory of mind.

The starting point of Palmer's essay is that any fictional narrative is the "description of fictional mental functioning" and hence that spaces and objects evoked by a given story "usually only have significance in so far as they affect the mental functioning of the characters in the storyworld." Moreover, specific fictional characters are not the only ones whose thoughts, beliefs, and desires drive the plot: "Just as in real life, where much of our thinking is done in groups, a good deal of fictional thinking is done by large organizations, small groups, families, couples, friends, and other *intermental units*." Hence fictional towns can be shown to have mental states, although different genres use very different representational techniques to portray towns as intermental units. Novels, such as *Middlemarch*, explored by Palmer in detail elsewhere, construct the minds of their towns quite differently from musicals, such as *Chicago*, or anime movies, such as *Metropolis*. (Note that these examples, *Chicago* and *Metropolis*, come not from Palmer's essay, but from discussions, inspired by his work, in graduate seminars.[11] For it turns out that Palmer's concept of intermental thinking applies to moving images as well; a city's current state of mind can be represented via close-ups of newspaper headlines: "Roxie Rocks Chicago!")

To show how a town can function as an intermental unit—that is, how it can have a mind of its own—Palmer turns to a passage Evelyn Waugh's *Men at Arms*. We learn on the first pages of that novel that Santa Dulcina, a small city in Italy, considers simpatico, that is, likes, many of its inhabitants, be they bores, gross vulgarians, or even criminals. Surprisingly, one person whom the town does not consider simpatico is the educated, open-handed, and upright protagonist, Guy Crouchback. As Palmer demonstrates, representing the town as having a broad array of mental states—capable of liking some people but not others, of grieving and rejoicing with some of them, of gleefully observing them, and so forth—is an important rhetorical move on the part of the author. For the passage Palmer analyzes is "not just about the intramental functioning of one individual and not just about the intermental functioning of the town: it is about the complex, dialogical relationship between the two." What the town thinks about Guy, and how it came to think it, is crucial for our understanding of the psychological dynamic of the story. Although not all works of fiction cultivate intermental units, those that do use them in striking and specific ways, and now with the benefit of Palmer's insights we can begin to trace the effects of intermental thinking in a broad variety of texts.

Vermeule's essay, "Machiavellian Narratives" (chap. 10), builds on cognitive evolutionary research in theory of mind to reengage a question that has preoccupied literary theorists since Plato, namely, "why literary experience feels so rich and vivid." Vermeule's answer is that "moments that we consider especially literary, and that therefore have attracted intense critical scrutiny, tend to reflect a special—and especially intense—kind of reasoning." This reasoning, which she calls Machiavellian, "is especially intense because it engages something we care about most—the extremely complicated dynamics of social interactions." Redefining in cognitive terms our traditional intuition that some fictional characters are flatter than others—as she sees it, flat characters are those less capable of complex, reflexive states of mind—Vermeule offers the following socio-cognitive account of scenes experienced by readers as "especially literary":

> When flat characters interact with round characters, they mine a rich vein of theory of mind. In literary narratives from ancient to modern times, some version of the following pattern repeats itself over and over again: a flat or minor character provokes a fit of reflection in a round or major character. The fit of reflection enlarges the scene and the minds of the people in it, who engage in elaborate rituals of shared attention and eye contact. The scene itself becomes soaked in mindfulness, increasing the sense of self-consciousness all around.

Using examples that range from Virgil's the *Aeneid* and Spenser's *The Faerie Queene* to Thackeray's *Vanity Fair*, Poe's "The Purloined Letter," and Thomas Mann's *The Magic Mountain*, Vermeule shows that "round" or "Machiavellian" narratives typically feature complex interplays of mental states while also exploiting a series of tropes, such as chess, tennis, gambling, games of chance, and labyrinths, that signal "the presence of high narrative reflexivity."

Vermeule's overarching argument, that the attraction of fictional cognitive complexity is directly related to our unquenchable fascination with social complexity, complements David Herman's emphasis on the socially situated mind. In his essay, "Narrative Theory after the Second Cognitive Revolution" (chap. 7), Herman introduces the field of cognitive narratology, defining it as an approach that builds on the work of classical narratologists by supplementing it with discursive-psychological research—"research premised on the idea that minds are always already grounded in discourse." Herman's essay develops a compelling model of interdisciplinary exchange, showing how by integrating insights from the "second cognitive revolution," narrative theory can in turn influence social psychology. In particular, Herman demonstrates that fictional "scenes of talk"—when readers are called on to engage with sparsely annotated dialogue—"bear importantly on the tradition(s) of research that locate cognitive processes not in the heads of solitary thinkers but rather in sociocommunicative processes unfolding within richly material settings."

Herman begins with an exposition of earlier conceptions of the mind, grounded in Cartesianism, introspectionism, behaviorism, and the first cognitive revolution. He then contrasts them with discursive psychology's emphasis on the mind that "does not preexist discourse" but, as an "ongoing construction," emerges and changes along with it. Using as his case study Hemingway's short story "Hills Like White Elephants," Herman shows that "cognitive processes can be lodged not just in reports about characters' behaviors, utterances, and experiences but also in modes of narration, types of perspective, and details about the spatial and temporal contexts of narrated situations and events."

Note too how Herman's view of a fictional mind in progress, a mind as constructed via specific communicative and material contexts, amplifies Williams's earlier insight that we create the world by learning new ways of seeing it. Hemingway's story, Herman demonstrates, constitutes its two protagonists as embodied by implying the physical situatedness of their views of the white "hills across the valley" and of each other. As Herman puts it,

> Not only does "Hills" suggests that what can be seen, what is known about the world, alters with the spatial coordinates of the embodied self that is doing the looking; more than this, it suggests that a self is in part constituted by what it sees and by when and where it sees it—with narrative being one of the principal means for tracing this perceptual flux.

Hence it is not just that the construction of fictional worlds is contiguous with our ongoing construction of reality (which supports Williams's view of "art as a particular process in the general human process of creative discovery and communication"). It might also be that our constructions of reality—our "ways of seeing"—are actualized through the processes best captured by cognitive narratologists when they discuss "modes of narration, types of perspective, and details about the spatial and temporal contexts." Newly refocused on the social mind, narrative theory can indeed "inform discursive-psychological research," making communication between literary critics and cognitive psychologists a two-way street.

The social mind remains the focus in Nancy Easterlin's essay, "Cognitive Ecocriticism: Human Wayfinding, Sociality, and Literary Interpretation" (chap. 12), which introduces the field of cognitive ecocriticism, with a particular emphasis on gender and social cognition. Easterlin begins her discussion of the relationship between cognitive evolutionary psychology and ecocriticism by observing that by excluding evolutionary science, conventional ecocritical thinking encourages us to "conceptualize 'nature' or 'environment' as fixed and bounded entities excluding humanity." Conventional ecocriticism is thus teleological, despite its invocation of process; its desire to posit the existence of a benign interrelationship among "all elements of the natural order" leads it to gloss over such uncomfortable facts as "the operation of chance" and the "incredible variety" and "frequently conflicting interests normal science continues to discover in nature."

Taking as her starting point the importance of wayfinding for our "knowledge-seeking species," Easterlin then demonstrates that environment is always constructed via networks of social and emotional relevance (a "specifically human version of the environment," as Williams would put it, or the "selection" of only those features that "interest us," as Grosz would).[12] Our wayfinding abilities, Easterlin argues, "depend on an emotional connection to the environment, for it is such a connection that promotes interest." Moreover, the "affective charges" connected in our evolutionary past to "specific environmental features still resonate with humans today, whether or not we have any conscious knowledge of the evolved basis of our predilections (for mountains, for instance, from which visual advantage could be secured) or aversions."

The notion of "specifically human" relevance does not imply normativity in representations of nature, such as the privileging of specific genres or perspectives. Like Williams and Spolsky (and Herman in "Stories as a Tool for Thinking"), Easterlin considers art a "way of knowing and coping with the world—of exercising problem-solving skills, of imagining alternatives." In this view, the ecocritical predilection for literary modes and genres that manifest environmental correctness is fundamentally misguided: "Realism in this perspective is neither good nor bad; it is one mode of response, and not necessarily one that will establish an affective connection between the reader and the nonhuman natural world; it is in any case a human fashioning of perceived actuality, since an evolutionary perspective renders obsolete the infatuation with grasping the thing-in-itself."

Easterlin's take on literary realism in the context of ecocriticism dovetails with that of Alan Richardson in his recent comprehensive review "Studies in Literature and Cognition" and that of Suzanne Keen in her groundbreaking study *Empathy and the Novel* (2007). Discussing the work of scholars who use evolutionary epistemology to posit the superiority of a "direct correlation between literary representation and patterns of behavior in the lived world," Richardson emphasizes that cognitive literary criticism rejects this kind of "naïve realism" and keeps sight of "the fantastic or 'off-line' character of fictional representations" (12). Similarly, Keen's view of character identification "runs counter to common assumptions" that "complex or realistic characterization" is necessary to eliciting readers' empathy (69). Hence the case studies used by Easterlin to show how fictional narratives build on the excitement and anxiety attendant on human wayfinding span a variety of genres and representational traditions, from nature writing in prose and poetry and chronicles of sci-fi journeys to stories of physical and mental confinement in novels and on stage.

For Easterlin, gender often comes to the forefront of "literary depictions of wayfinders in a democratized, industrialized world." As her ecofeminist analysis shows, such narratives as Charlotte Brontë's *Jane Eyre*, Katherine Mansfield's "The Little Governess," Alice Munro's "Wild Swans," and Henry James's *Daisy Miller* use female protagonists to embody the clash between wayfinding and social knowledge. Women who travel alone (and are assumed to have led a sheltered existence prior) might be thrilled by "physical movement and discovery," yet they are dangerously lacking in social competency and struggle and often fail to make inferences about various people they encounter "based on knowledge of behavior." (Note, too, that large and small breakdowns in communication have long been a subject of particular interest to cognitive literary critics: as Spolsky puts it elsewhere, "failures are more tellable.")[13]

Bruce McConachie's essay, "Toward a Cognitive Cultural Hegemony" (chap. 6), works toward reconciling Williams's rethinking of Antonio Gramsci's concept of cultural hegemony with a notion of embodied cognition as developed by cognitive linguist George Lakoff and philosopher Mark Johnson. To show "how external cultural practices get processed and reproduced in the internal workings of the mind/brain," McConachie begins by revisiting Williams's suggestive but underappreciated term "structure of feeling," arguing that recent work in cognitive linguistics and cognitive anthropology allows us to finally tackle the difficult issue of the relationship between culture and cognition that Williams wanted to capture with that term. According to McConachie, when Williams first introduced the phrase in the 1950s, he used it "to correlate the form and emotional power of an artistic product with the general psychology of a culture" in an attempt to work out a conceptual framework that would clarify how culture gets below what he called the "top of our minds." Subsequently, however, he narrowed the meaning of the term "to refer primarily to the innovative forms and new psychology of emergent cultures of opposition," and later yet, he stopped using it altogether.

What McConachie suggests is that the work of contemporary cognitive anthropologists that investigates how "external culture" gets linked to "internal minding" allows us not only to revisit and elaborate Williams's "structure of feeling" but also to clarify its connections with the concept of cultural hegemony. Fusing cognitive anthropologist Bradd Shore's insights with those of Lakoff and Johnson, McConachie argues that over time individuals in a given culture build up "a large stock of conventional schemas"—for example, spatial and social schemas involved in understanding a baseball game—that get invested with a variety of emotions and can then be "drawn on to understand unfamiliar events." A dominant culture (to come back to Gramsci's discussion of cultural hegemony) thus "reproduces itself, in part, by analogically transferring concepts and schemas to a network of cultural practices." As in McConachie's baseball example, some of the "same internal concepts will be brought into consciousness when the individual wants to recall a certain game or decides to project an idea of baseball onto another area of life through metaphor. 'He pitched me that sale, but I wasn't swinging.'"

But this process of transferal also opens up opportunities for challenging a dominant culture: representatives of oppositional groups can reframe old metaphors and project various established schemas onto "historically new fields." McConachie's example of a body-based conceptual metaphor that informed the perpetuation of a specific political paradigm is containment: a figure involving "necessary relations among an inside, an outside, and a boundary between them." McConachie demonstrates that as an embodied spatial concept, containment "structured much of the dominant culture" of the Cold War era. It shaped not only political endeavors, such as the passing of the National Security Act of 1947, but also aspects of popular psychology (such as the anxiety about the effects of advertising) and theater productions (for example, "all of Rodgers and Hammerstein's Asian musicals"). At the same time, oppositional playwrights, such as Tennessee Williams in *Cat on a Hot Tin Roof* and Lorraine Hansberry in *A Raisin in the Sun*, intuitively exploited the fact that "the cognitive logic of containment required an outside Other to delimit an inside Same," their plays giving voice to "abject Others" often silenced by dominant cultural discourse.

Lakoff and Johnson's work on embodied cognition also constitutes the starting point of Mary Thomas Crane's essay, "Analogy, Metaphor, and the New Science: Cognitive Science and Early Modern Epistemology" (chap. 4). Crane uses cognitive studies of analogy to challenge the currently accepted narrative of the epistemological shift that "accompanied, and made possible, the 'scientific revolution' of the seventeenth century." According to this narrative, analogy functioned "as the central structuring mechanism of the old epistemological system but was replaced, in the seventeenth century, by variously, 'identity,' 'difference,' or 'mechanism,' depending on who is telling the story." However, Crane suggests, if, "as Lakoff and Johnson have argued, all human thought is built up metaphorically from the basic kinesthetic experiences of living in a body, no scientific system could dispense completely with analogy." Instead, analogical thinking would take different forms and structure different systems of relationships. To uncover this process we need to look at a broad spectrum of contemporary cultural representations and social institutions.

And so analogical thinking was not abandoned during the Renaissance—it was transformed. In traditional Aristotelian philosophy, Crane demonstrates, analogy was equated with identity. For example, the "alchemical symbol for gold . . . was a circle, because both the circle and the gold were considered to be perfect: the perfection of the symbol was thought to reflect in essence the perfection of its referent." In contrast, in the new science, analogy indicated a structural relationship between two entities. The idea of such a structural relationship made it possible to imagine a larger system within which these two entities interacted with each other and other phenomena.

Moreover, by sponsoring alternative ways of conceiving of the natural world, analogical reasoning also opened new venues for poetic imagery. Hence John Donne's poem "A Valediction: Forbidding Mourning." Donne speaks of the separated lovers' souls as the connected feet of a compass (one moves when the other does), but he does not, as some scholars have suggested, posit "an essential similarity" between the two unlike things, a pair of human souls and a mathematical instrument. Instead, influenced by the new style of analogical thinking, he envisions a "structural relationship between two joined yet divided poles"—a more complex "concept of circular perfection" than the one enabled by the classical Aristotelian use of analogy. In other words, as Crane argues compellingly, poetry participated in the new epistemology, but to become aware of this dynamic interaction between poetic images and natural philosophy, we need both cognitive and historical perspectives.

The essays by Crane, McConachie, Richardson, Spolsky, and Zunshine exemplify a subfield of cognitive cultural studies known as cognitive historicism. As Richardson explains in his essay, "Facial Expression Theory from Romanticism to the Present and Beyond" (chap. 2),

Cognitive historicism retains the emphasis on specific sociocultural environments, on common discursive strategies linking, say, the poetry of an earlier era with its jurisprudence and its botany, and the acknowledgment of the impossibility of any objective, transcendent historical perspective that marks other "new" literary historicisms. In addition, however, it recruits and selectively adapts theories, methods, and findings from the sciences of mind and brain, partly in the hope these will provide suggestive (though, it is understood, necessarily imperfect) analogies with past models and partly in hope that cultural and historical differences will emerge *more* clearly and cleanly when set against what appear to be stable and invariant aspects of human cognition and behavior.

Richardson's essay brings together studies of the universal human capacity for "gauging the emotions and intentions of others through reading their faces" with the investigation of cultural representations and institutions that were informed by and in turn gave form to this capacity in the Romantic era. His larger argument is that "the study of human expression has played a key role both in the development of a cognitive neuroscience of human behavior and in the resurgence of intellectual interest in stable and universal aspects of human nature." An important early nineteenth-century specimen of the neurological approach to the study of emotions is Charles Bell's *Anatomy and Philosophy of Human Expression* (1806), a precursor of Darwin's *The Expression of the Emotions in Man and Animals* (1872) and, in some respects, "*more* forward looking" than the later treatise. For instance, Bell emphasized the "communicative role of facial expressions," a concept crucial for our contemporary "neurocultural" perspective but one that was underplayed by Darwin. It is not accidental, then, that to underscore the role of expressions in social communication, Bell turned to theater, using, for example, Sarah Siddons's performance of Shakespeare for his neurological analysis.

Taking as his starting point Bell's interest in the "multimedia art of theater," Richardson demonstrates that "the science of facial expression has been bound up with literature all along." For instance, Bell's contemporary, Johanna Baillie, a poet and playwright, explored various developmental aspects of the "universal fascination with human expression" in the "Introductory Discourse" to her *Plays on the Passions* (1798). Richardson's other examples range from Baillie's *Count Basil* and Keats's *Isabella* to Austen's *Emma*, as he shows that a "keen interest in how the body manifests emotions and intentions—and in how a given human mind attempts to extrapolate from these manifestations the mental dispositions, conscious or not, of others—made for a central rather than peripheral aspect of Romantic-era literary life."

Zunshine's essay, "Lying Bodies of the Enlightenment: Theory of Mind and Cultural Historicism" (chap. 5), shares with Richardson's its emphasis on specific cultural forms assumed by our "fascination with human expression," although she mainly focuses on the period between the 1720 and 1790. She suggests that there is an important overlap between the fields of inquiry of cultural studies and cognitive evolutionary psychology—both want to know why and how bodies "perform" minds—and that this overlapping interest provides the ground for a long-term dialogue between the two disciplines.

Zunshine begins by registering a paradoxical position occupied by the body in eighteenth-century discourse, which treated body language (including facial expressions) as simultaneously a highly valuable and quite unreliable source of information about a person's mind. She then uses research on theory of mind to explain this double view of the body in novels ranging from Eliza Haywood's *Love in Excess* and Samuel Richardson's *Clarissa* to Henry Fielding's *Tom Jones* and Thomas Holcroft's *Hugh Trevor*. Like Alan Richardson, Zunshine is interested in using cognitive theory to trace new connections between different cultural discourses of the period. Moving backward from Henry Siddons's *Practical Illustrations of Rhetorical Gesture and Action* (1807) to eighteenth-century acting manuals and novels, she explores the double perspective of the body in the Enlightenment's obsession with measuring gaps between people's body language and their actual feelings on stage and in print.

Like Spolsky, who draws on cognitive neuroscience in her analysis of visual representations, Gabrielle Starr ("Multisensory Imagery" [chap. 13]) believes that "the architecture of the mind . . . has much to say about the architecture of art." Her focus, however, is on "cognitive principles governing nonvisual mental imagery." Starr opens her essay by suggesting that poets from Horace on evoke not merely different kinds of sensory imagery, including olfactory, haptic, motor, and gustatory, but "multisensory imagery, fundamentally," thus making available to us the "subjective experience of sensation without corresponding sensory input." Traditionally, studies of such an experience dealt with visual images, reflecting the crucial role of the human visual system, but the situation is changing now as "an increasing amount of research addresses imagery from the other senses." Starr's focus is on these other senses as engaged by poetry (particularly motor images), her case studies ranging from Bishop's "At the Fishhouses" and Hopkins's "Pied Beauty" to Dryden's "Alexander's Feast" and Keats's "The Eve of St. Agnes."

After considering possible neural bases for motor, auditory, olfactory, and gustatory imagery as well as for imagery of touch, grasping, and feeling, Starr suggests that poetry forges "new connections between the senses, which push beyond the mimesis of the natural world" and thus induce aesthetic pleasure in listeners and readers. For example,

> Work on memory has demonstrated . . . [that] people tend to remember a tone and image presented together much better than either alone; more than this, when data from one sense is presented, the entire multisensory image is triggered. The connections that multisensory imagery can form are rapid and strong. A cognitive approach to multisensory imagery may give us a window on aesthetics as the study not just of sensation (*aesthesis*) but also of imagined sensation. . . . I believe that motor imagery, in part because it is peculiarly multisensory, may have the most powerful potential for evoking and structuring aesthetic pleasures.

Starr further demonstrates that as a poem develops, it may reorder and recombine sensory modes that it has originally evoked and, in doing so, literally inhabit and change the body of the reader. For instance, an evoked motion may emerge "not just as . . . described" but as experienced "in mind, or hands, or tongue."

That the pleasure of reading poetry is an embodied pleasure rings intuitively true to literary critics and cultural historians. Indeed, Williams saw rhythm as "a way of transmitting a description of experience, in such a way that the experience is re-created in the person receiving it, not merely as an 'abstraction' or an 'emotion' but as physical effect on the organism—on the blood, on the breathing, on the physical patterns of the brain" (*Long Revolution*, 24). What Starr demonstrates, however, is that we need research in cognitive neuroscience to see how what Williams called the "physical effect"—the embodied experience of poetry—is made possible by our neural architecture. Moreover, although Starr's tour-de-force analysis of multisensory imagery centers on poetry, classroom practice shows that her conceptual framework can be productively extended to the study of prose fiction. For instance, it turns out writers such as Joyce cultivated images that forcefully juxtaposed different sensory modes, making the evolution of such images throughout the narrative into a story in its own right.[14]

Concluding the volume is Spolsky's essay "Darwin and Derrida: Cognitive Literary Theory as a Species of Post-structuralism" (chap. 14), an early articulation of the view that "the assumptions that emerge from the study of evolved human brains in their successive contexts, far from being inconsistent with post-structuralist thought, actually extend and enrich it." According to F. Elizabeth Hart, Spolsky's essay demonstrates that "the materialist ontology of Charles Darwin is every bit as relevant to understanding postmodernism as are the materialist epistemologies of Jacques Derrida, Jacques Lacan, or other of the thinkers at the foundations of literary poststructuralism" ("Embodied Literature," 88).

Using as her theoretical mainstay the modular theory of cognition, Spolsky shows how an evolutionary framework affirms and regrounds the poststructuralist insight that the "functioning of human language depends on both its iterability *and* its instability." As she puts it:

> Precisely because the human species and its ways of knowing are evolved by the accumulation of random mutations, in interactions with changing environments, rather than genetically engineered for the task of knowing, it is not at all surprising that they are unstable. They were not purpose designed and are always vulnerable to further environmental change. It is just this instability, however, that provides the possibility for advantageous flexibility. People, then, and their ways of knowing, and their languages, are *responsive* (a word that doesn't have the negative connotation of *un*reliable or *un*stable), that is, adaptable within a changing environment.

Thus, in Spolsky's view, "nothing could be more adaptationist, more Darwinian, than deconstruction and post-structuralism, since both understand structuration—the production of structures (and this is the same thing as the production of theories of structures, ad infinitum)—as an activity that happens within and in response to a specific environment." In fact, Spolsky argues that a number of twentieth-century influential theoretical frameworks, from Wittgenstein's "model of language games" to Stephen Greenblatt's "view of the circulation of social energy in a dynamic of challenge and containment," are Darwinian because they seek to "account for systematicity—that is, for stability and predictability—while allowing for the possibility of adaptive change."

Suggestions for Further Reading

The list below includes only works of cognitive literary/cultural criticism. The references to foundational studies in respective parent fields of cognitive science, such as discourse psychology, cognitive linguistics, cognitive neuroscience, and evolutionary psychology, can be found in the essays themselves and in the list of works cited at the end of the volume.

Abbott, Porter. "Narrative and Emergent Behavior." *Poetics Today* 29.2 (2008): 227–44.

Aldama, Frederick Luis. "Race, Cognition, and Emotion: Shakespeare on Film." *College Literature* 33:1 (Winter 2006): 197–98.

———. *A User's Guide to Postcolonial and Latino Borderland Fiction.* Austin: University of Texas Press, 2009.

———, ed. *Toward a Theory of Narrative Acts.* Austin: University of Texas Press, 2010.

Crane, Mary Thomas. *Shakespeare's Brain: Reading with Cognitive Theory.* Princeton: Princeton University Press, 2001.

Easterlin, Nancy. "Voyages in the Verbal Universe: The Role of Speculation in Darwinian Literary Criticism." *Interdisciplinary Literary Studies* 2.2 (2001): 59–73.

———. *What Is Literature For? Biocultural Criticism and Theory.* Baltimore: Johns Hopkins University Press, forthcoming.

Esrock, Ellen J. *The Reader's Eye: Visual Imaging as Reader Response.* Baltimore: Johns Hopkins University Press, 1994.

Grosz, Elizabeth. *Time Travels: Feminism, Nature, Power.* Durham: Duke University Press, 2005.

Hart, F. Elizabeth. "The Epistemology of Cognitive Literary Studies." *Philosophy and Literature* 25 (2001): 314–34.

Herman, David. *Story Logic: Problems and Possibilities of Narrative.* Lincoln: University of Nebraska Press, 2002.

———, ed. *Narrative Theory and the Cognitive Sciences.* Stanford, CA: Publications of the Center for the Study of Language and Information Publications, 2003.

Hogan, Patrick Colm. *Empire and Poetic Voice: Cognitive and Cultural Studies of Literary Tradition and Colonialism*. Albany: State University of New York Press, 2004.

——. *The Mind and Its Stories: Narrative Universals and Human Emotion*. Cambridge: Cambridge University Press, 2003.

——. *Understanding Indian Movies: Indian Culture, the Human Brain, and Cinematic Imagination*. Austin: University of Texas Press, 2008.

——. *Understanding Nationalism: On Narrative, Neuroscience, and Identity*. Columbus: Ohio State University Press, 2009.

Keen, Suzanne. *Empathy and the Novel*. Oxford: Oxford University Press, 2007.

McConachie, Bruce. *American Theater in the Culture of the Cold War: Producing and Contesting Containment, 1947–1962*. Iowa City: University of Iowa Press, 2003.

——. *Engaging Audiences: A Cognitive Approach to Spectating in the Theatre*. Houndmills, UK: Palgrave, 2008.

McConachie, Bruce, and F. Elizabeth Hart, eds. *Performance and Cognition: Theatre Studies and the Cognitive Turn*. London: Routledge, 2006.

Palmer, Alan. *Fictional Minds*. Lincoln: University of Nebraska Press, 2004.

——. *Social Minds in the Novel*. Columbus: Ohio State University Press, 2010.

Persson, Per. *Understanding Cinema: A Psychological Theory of Moving Imagery*. Cambridge: Cambridge University Press, 2003.

Richardson, Alan. *British Romanticism and the Science of the Mind*. Cambridge: Cambridge University Press, 2001.

——. *The Neural Sublime: Cognitive Theories and Romantic Texts*. Baltimore: Johns Hopkins University Press, forthcoming.

Richardson, Alan, and Ellen Spolsky, eds. *The Work of Fiction: Cognition, Culture, and Complexity*. Aldershot, UK: Ashgate, 2004.

Scarry, Elaine. *Dreaming by the Book*. New York: Farrar, Straus and Giroux, 1999.

Spolsky, Ellen. *Gaps in Nature: Literary Interpretation and the Modular Mind*. Albany: State University of New York Press, 1993.

——. *Satisfying Skepticism: Embodied Knowledge in the Early Modern World*. Aldershot, UK: Ashgate, 2001.

——. *Word vs. Image: Cognitive Hunger in Shakespeare's England*. Houndmills, UK: Palgrave, 2007.

Stafford, Barbara Maria. *Echo Objects: The Cognitive Work of Images*. Chicago: University of Chicago Press, 2007.

Starr, G. Gabrielle. "Poetic Subjects and Grecian Urns: Close Reading and the Tools of Cognitive Science." *Modern Philology* 105.1 (2007): 48–61.

Vermeule, Blakey. *The Party of Humanity: Writing Moral Psychology in Eighteenth-Century Britain.* Baltimore: Johns Hopkins University Press, 2001.

———. *Why Do We Care about Literary Characters?* Baltimore: Johns Hopkins University Press, 2010.

Zunshine, Lisa. *Strange Concepts and the Stories They Make Possible: Cognition, Culture, Narrative.* Baltimore: Johns Hopkins University Press, 2008.

———. *Why We Read Fiction: Theory of Mind and the Novel.* Columbus: Ohio State University Press, 2006.

PART ONE

Literary Universals

The study of cross-cultural patterns has a long history. Even in the modern period, it precedes the emergence of cognitive science by many decades. Patrick Colm Hogan's work is a prime instance of the evolution of the study of literary universals within a cognitive framework. Further developments of Hogan's own ideas may be found in articles such as "The Possibility of Aesthetics" and "Of Literary Universals: Ninety-Five Theses" and, most importantly, his books, *The Mind and Its Stories: Narrative Universals and Human Emotion* and *Understanding Nationalism: Narrative, Identity, and Cognitive Science.*

Hogan adopts an approach to universals based on standard aspects of cognitive and neurocognitive architecture, stressing semantic structures (such as prototypes) and emotion systems. The other main approaches to universals have drawn on language study. To a certain extent Hogan's work may be seen as following from the Chomskyan/generativist tradition of universalist study and perhaps even more so from the tradition of research associated with Joseph Greenberg. Others have drawn on cognitive linguistics or on research in pragmatics. Cognitive linguistic work on universals has focused on metaphors or other figures of speech (see Zoltán Kövecses's "Metaphor"). Work in pragmatics has been more wide ranging (see Stephen Levinson's "Pragmatics"). The linguistic orientation of these researchers often means that their work is not specifically literary. However, there have been more narrowly focused literary studies that have adopted a linguistic approach (see, for example, Vito Evola's "Cognitive Semiotics").

CHAPTER ONE

Literary Universals

PATRICK COLM HOGAN

Ideology and Universalism

Today, there is little enthusiasm among humanists for the study of universals. Indeed, it is barely even a concept within the humanities, where the focus of both theory and practice tends to be on "difference," "cultural and historical specificity," and so on. What Carl Plantinga said recently of film theorists applies equally to literary theorists: they tend to seek "explicit ways to link" literary phenomena "to particular historical conditions and to ideology" (450). In keeping with this trend, a 1993 self-evaluation by the American Comparative Literature Association worries that comparative literature "may well be left behind on the dust pile of academic history" if it does not incorporate the current trends variously referred to as "culture studies," "cultural critique," and "cultural theory." Indeed, they insist that all work in comparative literature "should take account of the ideological, cultural, and institutional contexts in which . . . meanings are produced," which amounts to an insistence that all comparativist study be focused on historical and cultural particularities.[1] When universalism is mentioned at all in humanistic writing, it is most often denounced as a tool of oppression. For example, in their influential volume *The Empire Writes Back*, Bill Ashcroft, Gareth Griffiths, and Helen Tiffin maintain that the notion of universality is "a hegemonic European critical tool" (149). There are exceptions, certainly, such as the Kenyan Marxist novelist Ngũgĩ wa Thiong'o, who recently proclaimed himself "an unrepentant universalist" (xvii). However, the general trend is clear.

Part of the resistance to the study of universals derives from the politics, or rather the pseudopolitics, that vitiates much debate in the humanities today—the labeling of dominant theoretical views as "progressive" and the denigration of all alternatives as "reactionary" while showing relatively little concern for the political intentions of the theorists or the political consequences of the theories. In the case of universals, one might have expected some hesitation about such generalizations. After all, the major exponent of universals in our own day has been Noam Chomsky, a writer whose politics might be fruitfully contrasted with those of, say, Paul de Man or Martin Heidegger, the latter's work forming the background for much of the recent emphasis on difference. More importantly, no racist ever justified the enslavement of Africans or colonial rule in India on the basis of a claim that whites and nonwhites share universal human properties. Rather, they based their justifications on presumed differences among Europeans, Africans, and Indians, usually biological differences, but often cultural differences as well. Indeed, "liberal" racism and colonialism—with their paternalistic emphasis on leading the native out of primitive ways and into civilization—were always based on specifically culturalist differentialism.

This is not to say that antiuniversalist views are based on nothing. It has indeed happened that apparently universalist claims have been used to support some forms of oppression. Typically, humanist criticisms of universalism refer back to those putative universals that derive from and serve to further colonial, patriarchal, or other ideologies supporting unjust domination. However, as Kwame Appiah has noted, what anticolonial opponents of universals "are objecting to" in these cases "is the posture that conceals [the] privileging of one national (or racial) tradition against others in false talk of the Human Condition" (58). In other words, they are objecting to false and duplicitous universalism, claims of universality that are untrue and are, in addition, offered in bad faith. Appiah continues, "Antiuniversalists . . . use the term *universalism* as if it meant *pseudouniversalism*, and the fact is that their complaint is not with universalism at all. What they truly object to—and who would not?—is Eurocentric hegemony *posing* as universalism" (58).

Lalita Pandit has nicely defined this difference in an ethical context through her suggestive distinction between "hegemonic" and "empathic" universals ("Caste," 207). Hegemonic universalism involves the imposition of one set of local interests, beliefs, standard practices, and so forth, on everyone else, the absolutizing of a local law or custom, in such a way as to express and foster domination. Empathic universalism, in contrast, is based on the assumption that all people share ethical and experiential subjectivity and that universality must both derive from and contribute to this sense of shared subjectivity, with all that it entails in terms of allowing each set of subjective experiences equal weight. My only disagreement with Pandit is that, in my view, "hegemonic universalism" is not universalism at all, and would more appropriately be called hegemonic absolutism. I say this because "hegemonic universals" or "pseudouniversals" (in Appiah's term) are not merely false. They also do not even satisfy minimal formal criteria for defining universals.

Regina Barreca, elaborating on an observation by Joanna Russ, provides a fine example of a hegemonic "universal" from humor: "When a man looks you in the eye after telling you an offensive and not even particularly funny story, and says 'It was only a joke,' what he is really saying, according to Joanna Russ, is 'I find jokes about you funny. Why don't *you* find jokes about you funny?'" (71) The presupposition of the sexist joke teller is the sort of universal claim to which humanists typically object. This claim perfectly illustrates Pandit's division, for it is an imposition of one group's views on all humanity—an absolutizing of local preferences—and it is at the same time straightforwardly antiempathic.

But, again, it is more appropriate to refer to this as a hegemonic absolute, for, strictly speaking, it is not a universal at all. Specifically, it is a formal property of universals that their universality is maintained at higher levels of explanatory generalization. Clearly, a more abstract explanatory generalization must have at least as broad a scope as any less abstract generalization that it subsumes. If the explanatory generalization is not universal, then the lower-level generalization is not universal either. Hegemonic "universals" lack this criterial property. In other words, they are not, ultimately, claims of universal commonality. Rather, they are claims of group difference made to appear as universals.

Consider again the sort of sexist joke just mentioned. Barreca stresses that such demeaning jokes come from men who "bite their lower lips and drop their hands quickly" when they hear a similarly demeaning joke about men (71). Thus they fully recognize that men do not enjoy jokes demeaning to men. In other words, these joke tellers tacitly hold to a theory in which the lower-level universal, "jokes demeaning to women are funny for everyone," is explained by a generalization to the effect that "men are offended—and thus not amused—by statements demeaning to themselves, but women are not offended by statements demeaning to themselves." This is a strongly differentialist claim. Thus, the "universalist" theory that men and women like to laugh at women is not universalist at all. It appears to involve a universal claim, but this "universality" is only the superficial manifestation of an underlying (presupposed) difference. The genuine universal here would be, in Barreca's words, "we don't like to laugh at hostile jokes directed at groups of which we are part" (72). And the strict implications of this genuine universal directly contradict the presupposed "universal" or hegemonic absolute of the sexist joke teller. Thus, even in such paradigmatic cases of politically objectionable "universalism," it turns out that the objectionable claims are ultimately claims of difference—not universals but the antithesis of universals.

It is important to stress that this conclusion in no way detracts from the standard forms of particularist literary study. It responds not to their positive worth but to their exclusivity. More exactly, the proponents of cultural and historical study are mistaken not only in their condemnation of universalism but in seeing the study of universals as somehow opposed to or contradictory of cultural study, in believing that the examination of universals somehow precludes historical research. To argue for the study of universals is not at all to argue against the study of culture and history. All reasonable students of literature—including those engaged in universalist projects—recognize that particularist research and interpretation are extremely valuable. Indeed, it is the opponents of universalism who are most likely to limit our cultural and historical understanding, for the study of universals and the study of cultural and historical particularity are mutually necessary. Like laws of nature, cultural universals are instantiated variously, particularized in specific circumstances.[2] Thus, to isolate and test universal patterns, we often require a good deal of cultural and historical knowledge. At the same time, however, in order to gain any understanding of cultural particularity, we necessarily have to presuppose a background of commonality (as Donald Davidson, for example, has forcefully argued).[3]

Consider allusion, which appears to be a universal literary technique used to enhance the aesthetic effect of a new work by invoking in the reader associations with a prior work. Clearly, if we lack knowledge of the tradition in which a work is written, we will be unable to recognize its allusions. Conversely, if we fail to recognize that allusion is a universal technique, we will not look for allusions in particular works; in consequence, we will fail to understand those particular works, at least insofar as they rely on allusion. For example, a reader unfamiliar with the *Ramayana* will not recognize that Sakuntala's call for the earth to take her alludes to Sita's parallel call and subsequent descent into the earth when she refuses final reconciliation with Rama. Thus, on the one hand, the reader will not recognize the use of allusion as a significant literary technique here—and, presumably, elsewhere in Sanskrit literature. In other words, she will not be able to advance a universalist project. On the other hand, a reader who does not recognize that allusion is a universal technique is unlikely to look for such connections and thus is unlikely to advance a culturalist or interpretive project. Indeed, he will have a culturally impoverished experience of Kalidasa's *Sakuntala*, probably interpreting Sakuntala's appeal as an Indian version of the English cliché "I wish the earth would open up and swallow me," thus trivializing the scene, stripping the event of mythic resonance, masking the defiance of Sakuntala's act, occluding the play's implicit social criticism, and so forth.

The case of symbolism is the same. For example, particular types of birds have culturally specific associations in India, China, and elsewhere. When such birds appear in literature they are likely to have a symbolic function, which we can only recognize if we are familiar with those culturally specific associations. But we will only consider and interpret such an image symbolically if we recognize that symbolism is a universal literary technique.

Here too, then, the antiuniversalists have things backward. It is not universalism but antiuniversalism that occludes cultural particularity, blocking historical research and contextualization, just as it is not universalism but antiuniversalism (sometimes masquerading as universalism) that manifests and fosters patriarchal, colonial, and other oppressive ideologies.

In the following pages, I take up and reconsider the neglected and misunderstood topic of literary universals. In the first section, I articulate and illustrate with literary instances the various types and relations of universals. In the second section, I discuss two sets of literary universals in more detail, considering how they might be systematized and how they might be explained by reference to broader principles of literature and cognition. The first section seeks to clarify the nature of cultural universals in general and to sketch out some representative universals of literature in particular. The purpose of the second section is to indicate how a research program in literary universals—a cooperative project of isolating, refining, systematizing, and explaining literary universals—can proceed, and what some of its principles might be.

The Structure of a Theory of Universals

The first important point about universals is that they are not necessarily properties of all literary works. Indeed, such properties are rare and often trivial (i.e., a mere residue of our definition of a literary work). Rather, literary universals are properties and relations that are found across a range of genetically and geographically distinct literatures, which is to say literatures that have arisen and developed separately at least with respect to those properties and relations. More exactly, a property or relation may be considered a universal only if it is found in distinct bodies of literature that do not share a common ancestor having that property or relation. (Actually, things are slightly more complicated than this definition suggests. For example, borrowing across traditions may contribute to an understanding of universals insofar as such borrowing is selective and thus indicates that readers across traditions are sensitive to some techniques but not to others, prone to internalize and use some techniques but not others, and so on.)

It not only is unnecessary for universals to apply to all works; they also need not apply to all traditions. Linguists use the term "universal" to refer to any property or relation that occurs across (genetically and areally unrelated) languages with greater frequency than would be predicted by chance alone.[4] An *absolute* universal is merely a special case—a property or relation that occurs across traditions with a frequency of one. Universals with a frequency below one are referred to as *statistical* universals. On the whole, we should expect to find a limited number of hierarchies of statistically universal properties and relations, ordered according to abstraction and thus according to frequency (again, as abstraction increases, frequency can only increase or remain the same), with a few absolute universals at the apex of these hierarchies.

This extension of "universal" to statistically unexpected properties may seem odd, even misleading. However, it is perfectly in keeping with standard practices and definitions in all sciences and is inconsistent only with common prejudices about the nature of literary or, more broadly, cultural universals. An example from the field of medicine may help to clarify things. It is a universal principle of medicine that secondhand smoke causes lung cancer, despite the fact that most people who have inhaled secondhand smoke never develop lung cancer. It is a universal principle because there is a statistically significant correlation between inhaling secondhand smoke and developing lung cancer (or, rather, there is a statistically significant correlation that cannot be explained by other factors—obviously it is important to distinguish between correlations that are primary, or causal, and those that are derivative, or noncausal). Statistical universals of literature, as well as of linguistics, anthropology, and so forth, are no different.

More exactly, a theory of literary universals would describe a *repertoire of techniques* available to authors and a range of *nontechnical correlations* derived from broad statistical patterns. Nontechnical correlations comprise universal principles that are not, so to speak, devices or elements or structures that can be taken up and used in the making of literature, though they may define a range of or limits on usable devices. For example, standard line lengths appear to fall regularly between five and nine words. Clearly, a range of standard line lengths across different traditions is not a technique available to authors. Rather, it is a broad correlation across literatures. On the other hand, this universal correlation does presumably indicate a constraint on the techniques available to poets cross-culturally—or, if not a constraint, at least some sort of default tendency.

Techniques include all universal matters of "form" and "content"—including poetic meters, rhetorical devices, and so forth—that an author may draw on in composing a literary work. Many if not most basic techniques used in English literature appear to be universal. A partial list would include symbolism and imagery (discussed below); assonance, which is found not only in Indo-European works but in Japanese, Babylonian, and other verse as well; alliteration, which is important in Sanskrit, Japanese, Ainu, and so on; and verbal parallelism, which is found in Tikopia, Igbo, Basotho, Kuna, Chinese, Babylonian, Hebrew, and so forth.[5] Certain broader organizational devices appear to be universal as well—for example, foreshadowing and plot circularity, that is, beginning and ending a plot in the same place or situation or in closely analogous places or situations, often with the repetition of specific phrases concerning those places or situations.[6]

These techniques are organized into (explicit or implicit) *schemata* defining literary types and subtypes, such as "sonnet" in English. Within schemata, techniques may be *obligatory* or *optional*. If a certain poetic genre requires the use of end rhyme, then end rhyme is obligatory in the schema for that genre. On the other hand, the sonnet permits but does not require alliteration; thus alliteration is an optional technique available to a poet in composing a sonnet. We may also distinguish techniques that are not strictly obligatory but are nevertheless standard and may be understood as the highest or default cases within a schema. Thus a standard technique is employed unless the author explicitly chooses otherwise or some concurrently operating principle or schema prevents the implementation of the default.

Perhaps the best way to conceive of schemata is as cross-indexed lexical entries, wherein some techniques are specified and others are made accessible indirectly by reference to distinct lexical entries. These other entries may simply be coordinated (i.e., fully distinct, though cross-indexed), but they may also be superordinate (encompassing the entry in question) or subordinate (encompassed by the entry in question). Thus the schema for "sonnet" might list features specific to the sonnet (number of lines, rhyme scheme), then add some reference to the overarching category "poem" (we could think of it as a "see 'poem'" instruction). The entry for "poem" would be a superordinate category to "sonnet" and would include a list of techniques standard in poetry and available for use in sonnets (e.g., alliteration). The precise nature of each of these techniques could be viewed as defined in coordinate categories that are also cross-indexed (with, for instance, a "see 'alliteration'" instruction). (Obviously, I do not mean that there is literally a "see 'alliteration'" instruction in a lexical entry. Rather, I mean that there are specifiable links between entries, which it is convenient for us to represent in this way.)[7]

The most broadly encompassing schema, which is itself an absolute universal, is the minimally specified schema of verbal art itself. As Paul Kiparsky has pointed out, all societies have verbal art ("On Theory," 193–96). This may seem a mere triviality, but it is not. There is no logical necessity in the existence of verbal art, and in our own society very few people actually produce it. Why, then, should we expect it to appear in every society? As Chomsky has emphasized, one of the first tasks for researchers who study universals is to overcome habituation and to recognize how surprising universals are. We often "lose sight of the need for explanation when phenomena are too familiar and 'obvious' " (*Language and Mind*, 25). Once we have recognized that our expectation of verbal art is a mere matter of habit, we come to see that, far from being trivial, it is in fact highly surprising that verbal art is produced in small nomadic groups as well as in vast, highly urbanized nations.

In their most general forms, the three major genres of European literature—poetry, prose fiction, and drama—appear to be instances of larger universal categories as well. Thus it appears to be a universal that all or almost all societies have verse, which is to say a verbal art involving formalize cyclical patterning of speech based on acoustic properties. Tale telling also appears to be a literary universal. Probably in all societies, people articulate causal sequences of nonbanal events involving human agency (with banality defined relative to culturally specific expectations), and they do so at least in part for aesthetic enjoyment, itself based on identification, the patterned variation of emotional intensity, and so forth. Finally, some form of enactment for such tales seems to be universal as well, though in a more limited way. In many societies, such enactments may be confined to brief, farcical episodes on the one hand and ritual on the other. However, most literate societies have also developed some form of extended, nonritual theater; thus we find such theater in Europe, India, Southeast Asia, China, Japan, and the Middle East.[8]

More specific schematic patterns are isolable as well. Perhaps every tradition—and certainly every literate tradition—tells tales of conflict in two areas, love and political power, and produces tragedic and comedic sequences in each genre. Moreover, these tales involve a wide range of common character types, motifs, and subgenres across cultures. Consider, for example, love stories. A romantic comedy, in its most minimal form, typically involves two lovers who are separated, then reunited after a period of uncertainty. It is already surprising that this structure should be found in drama from Greece, Rome, India, China, and Japan and in stories from other regions as well. More surprising still is the fact that more particular patterns in this genre are also widely shared. For example, the separation is typically a matter of conflict with social expectations and structures, often manifest in a conflict with parents. It is frequently resolved by some sort of recognition, leading to a reversal, in the standard Aristotelian manner. Moreover, this recognition not only reunites the lovers but often involves the unexpected reunion of parents and children as well. Love stories typically include such characters as a hero, a heroine, a hero's companion, a hero's parasite, a heroine's confidant, and so on. Indeed, the character typologies set out by Sanskrit literary theorists two millennia ago (e.g., in Bharatamuni's *Natya Sastra*) and those drawn from New Comedy by Northrop Frye are similar to each other, and widely applicable beyond their own traditions, because of this cross-cultural consistency.

Perhaps the most cross-culturally widespread version (or subgenre) of the love plot is a particular variation on the comic love story. This variation, the "romantic tragicomedy," in effect incorporates the tragic love story, in which the lovers are separated, typically by death, and in which there is often the suggestion of literal or metaphorical reunion after death—as in Arabic and Persian retelling of the Laila and Majnun story (e.g., Nizami's twelfth-century poem), the *Ramayana* (100 BCE), and the love suicide plays of Chikamatsu (e.g., *Love Suicides in the Women's Temple* of 1708). Specifically, in romantic tragicomedy lovers are almost joined, then separated in a way that suggests death, then reunited in a sort of resurrection. The separation at the very least threatens not only to keep the lovers apart but to prevent them from ever hearing of each other again (as in Zeami's early fifteenth-century *Lady Han* and *The Reed Cutter*). This sort of separation is already akin to death, but the link with death is typically made more explicit. Thus, the separation often involves an apparent death (as in Chariton's *Chaereas and Callirhoe* [the earliest extant Greek romance]; Shakespeare's *The Winter's Tale*; Bhasa's fourth-century *Vision of Vasavadatta*; Bhavabhuti's eighth-century *Uttaramacarita*; the Thai *lakon jatri, Manohra*) or is represented in imagery closely associated with death (as in Sakuntala's assumption into the heavens or Chien-nu's "soul leaving her body" in Cheng's fourteenth-century play).[9] In any case, the link with death is clear, consistent, and important in a wide range of literary traditions. Similarly, these works regularly associate the separation of the lovers with imagery of winter and their reunion with imagery of spring. Moreover, the more general comic universals—conflict with society, recognition, reversal, reunion of separated parents and children—carry over, giving this schema remarkable cross-cultural consistency. In

Europe this sort of story most obviously reminds us of Shakespeare, but it has been a standard part of European literature since at least the "Erotici Graeci" of the early centuries of the common era. Outside Europe, beyond the works already mentioned, we could list the first-century *Toy Cart* and the seventh-century *Ratnavali* from India; the thirteenth-century *Chang Boils the Sea* and the roughly contemporary story of Cui Hu from China; the final voyage of Sindbad and the story of Aladdin from the Middle East; and Kanami's fourteenth-century *Hanakatami* and the eighteenth-century *Love Letter from the Licensed Quarter* from Japan—to take just two examples from each region that has produced a major written tradition.[10]

It is important to point out that the universality of either a (general) technique or a nontechnical correlation in no way implies the universality of any specification or instantiation of that technique or correlation, nor is putative universality falsified by differences in such specifications or instantiations. For example, the patterning of images seems to be a universal technique. It is certainly found in the genetically and in part geographically distinct written traditions of Europe, the Middle East, India, China, and Japan; it is also found in the unrelated oral poetries of the southern African Basotho, the Polynesian Tikopia, the Yirrkalla of Arnhem Land, and so forth.[11] This patterning does not, in and of itself, imply that implementations of the technique share further universal properties. For instance, it may be a universal that love is commonly associated with images of birds, as it seems to be in the various written traditions. Yet, if so, it is a distinct universal. Even if different cultures used widely different image patterns—some linking love with birds, others with tubers, others with types of fabric—the use of image patterns would still be universal.

Note also that each level of a hierarchy of abstraction serves as a partial explanatory generalization of all elements on lower levels. Thus we may find that the use of bird images for romantic love and the use of seasonal images for human life are far more common than chance but not at all absolute. We may then find the more general use of image patterns to be very widespread, perhaps absolute. In this case, the more abstract universal of imagery would partially explain the more specific avian and seasonal images. Other universals—literary and nonliterary—in combination with more specific accidental circumstances (e.g., environmental conditions), would yield a fuller explanation of these lower-level universals. For example, the cross-cultural connection between romantic love and bird imagery may derive in part from some universal, metaphorical, nonliterary correlation between "positive" emotions and the direction up.[12]

The more abstract universals may also be explained further. For example, the patterning of images may in turn be an instance of a still broader universal according to which patterning in normal discourse is generalized to all levels of structure in literary art (as I discuss in the following section). At the highest level, the specifically literary universals should indicate what is at the origin of the development of literature, what defines the human urge to make and experience verbal art. Of course, these overarching literary universals are not the end of the story either, for they too should be open to further explanation in terms of even more encompassing universals, such as those of psychology, sociology, history, and so on. (I return to this topic also in the following section.)

Hierarchies of universals are defined not only by the schematization of techniques and by a receding series of explanatory abstractions but also by a series of conditional relations. As a general methodological principle, linguists (like scientists in any other field) seek to redefine universals in such a way as to limit exceptions. Through repeated reformulation, they seek to bring statistical universals closer to absolute universals. Again, this may be done through abstraction, as when the (perhaps) absolute universal of image patterning is derived from merely statistically universal patterns of bird imagery, seasonal imagery, and so forth. However, the goal of absolute universality may be pursued further through the delineation of specific conditions in which statistically universal techniques or correlations occur. In other words, statistical universals of the form "q" may be revised into implicational universals of the form "if p, then q." Ideally, this reformulation would yield an absolute universal (i.e., there would be no cases of p and not q). At least it would limit the number of exceptions, bringing the universal closer to a frequency of one.

Alliteration provides a good example of how universals may be redefined to limit exceptions. It is an obligatory technique in certain forms of poetry in certain societies—as such, it appears more than would be predicted by chance, but there are a great many exceptions. One may abstract from this articulation to some broader principle, such as the no doubt absolute universal that all poetry has some obligatory features relating to sound pattern. However, one may also seek to formulate implicational universal, determining conditions under which alliteration is or is not obligatory. Kiparsky argues that alliteration "seems to be found as an obligatory formal element only in languages where the stress regularly falls on the same syllable in the word, which then must be the alliterating syllable" ("The Role of Linguistics," 9). While this does not fully fix the conditions under which alliteration is obligatory, it does fully fix the conditions under which it is not obligatory (i.e., whenever syllable stress varies in the language). Thus it yields the absolute implicational universal "If syllable stress varies in a given language, then alliteration is not an obligatory feature of poetry in that language." It also yields a second, more complex, absolute implicational universal "If syllable stress does not vary in a language and if alliteration is an obligatory feature of poetry in that language, then the stressed syllable is the alliterating syllable."

Much as unconditional universals may be subsumed into hierarchies of abstraction, implicational universals may be organized into *typologies*.[13] A typology consists in a set of mutually exclusive categories, each of which coordinates a number of implicational universals, forming them into a pattern that is more informative, though less absolute, than any of the implications considered individually. Each type in a typology serves as a partial explanation of any given implication or correlation that it subsumes. In addition, the typology as a whole should come close to defining an absolute, disjunctive universal—that is, all or almost all literatures should fit under one or another type.

The broad distinction between oral and literate composition is a case in point.[14] In effect, it sets up a broad implication of the form "If a culture does not have writing, then its literature will be marked by frequent use of epithets, formulaic phrases, specific sorts of repetition, and so forth," or more generally, "The degree to which a literature is marked by epithets, and so forth, is a function of the degree of literacy of the literary culture in which that literature is produced." As the second formulation indicates, instead of a typology in the narrow sense of a universal grid of discrete types, we may have a continuum of historical change with a universal tendency. Here, more literacy generally yields fewer epithets. We do not simply have two options—oral equaling epithet use and literate equaling no epithet use. On the other hand, such a continuum serves the same organizational and explanatory function as a grid. Thus we may loosely refer to it as "typological." In this particular case, though some writers have disputed the validity of a loose typological distinction between oral and literate composition,[15] it has been convincingly applied to a wide range of literatures: Slavic, Greek, Sanskrit, Tamil, Ainu, Xhosa, and so on.[16] Indeed, this is a particularly interesting universal for our purposes because it refers to historical conditions. Humanists tend to think of historical change and universals as diametrically opposed. In fact, they are not. Marx's isolation of historical/economic laws is an obvious case in which historical change has been understood in relation to universals.[17] Moreover, historical linguists have been no less inclined to isolate universals than have their colleagues in other areas of linguistics.[18] In this case, the proposed typology not only involves historical contingency (the presence or absence of writing); it also involves historical development and thus specificity—though all in the context of a universal principle. Another instance of this type of universal is Arnold Hauser's hypothesis that realism in literature is a function of social structure, the more realistic art being produced in urban, market economies, with feudal or tributary economies fostering stylization (49).

A particularly important related distinction, relevant to historical and cultural variation, is that between *indexical* and *nonindexical* universals. Indexical universals are those that are in part defined by reference to the particulars in which they are instantiated. For example, it appears to be a psychological universal that one's self-conception is structured into a hierarchy of properties; properties such as sex and race are high in the hierarchy, while properties such as ring size are lower. It appears that readers and auditors identify with a character on the basis of shared high-level properties in their self-conception and that they prefer works involving characters with whom they identify.[19] This (likely) literary universal is indexical because those high-level properties necessarily vary from person to person (for example, by sex, race, religion, etc.). Note that, contrary to one common preconception about universals, the existence of such indexical universals not only does not guarantee universal agreement in matters of taste but works strongly against such agreement. Indeed, we have already seen one instance of this type of universal, that articulated by Barreca ("We don't like to laugh at hostile jokes directed at groups of which we are part") and implicitly denied by the sexist joke teller.

Explaining Literary Universals: The Nature of a Research Program

One could draw further, consequential distinctions—for example, between universals bearing on aesthetic experience and those bearing on aesthetic evaluation outside of aesthetic experience (e.g., those concerning canonization and dominant ideology). Obviously, however, it is beyond the scope of this chapter to present a fully developed theory of literary universals. Indeed, an empirically based theory—unlike the speculative theories common in the humanities—cannot arise in a fully developed and final form, ready to be "applied" in explications of individual texts. Rather, an empirically based theory is always and necessarily part of a project, an ongoing, broadly collaborative research program, of the general sort outlined by Imre Lakatos—in this case, a program involving the collaboration of a wide range of scholars in different fields with different areas of literary expertise. For present purposes, the preceding analysis should provide an adequate idea of how a theory of literary universals is likely to be structured and what some parts of that theory might look like.

Of course, any empirically based research program necessarily seeks explanatory as well as descriptive adequacy.[20] Indeed, the two are closely interrelated, and no research program can proceed without both. Obviously, explanation is founded on empirical description. But empirical description is, at the same time, organized and directed by reference to hypothesized explanatory principles. Thus, having treated some broadly structural and descriptive aspects of a theory of literary universals in the preceding section, I consider, in this section, how the explanatory part of a research program in universals might proceed. To do this, I examine two specific cases, one concerning a complex of universal formal techniques and a principle that can be abstracted from those techniques and the other concerning a universal statistical correlation and its likely derivation from cognitive structure. As to the first, consider the list of formal devices that are used in a wide range of genetically distinct traditions—assonance, alliteration, parallelism, and so on. Again, these are best thought of as techniques available to writers in creating (and readers in experiencing) literary works. A first step in an explanatory research program would be to abstract some sort of principle from this list, a principle that indicates what these items share and what pattern they form—ideally, in such a way as to relate this pattern to more general structures and purposes of verbal art. We could call such an abstraction from empirically observable patterns a "secondary principle." Kiparsky has noted this issue, observing broadly that "it appears . . . all literary traditions . . . utilize the same elements of form" ("The Role of Linguistics," 11). Following Roman Jakobson, he goes on to suggest a reason for this continuity: "Language allows certain ways of organizing sounds, and . . . poetic form must draw on this organization" (20). He concludes that the relations "between grammar and poetry account, at least in part, for the universality of poetic form" (22).

The general connection between linguistic sounds and poetic sounds is plausible; however, it seems to fall short of an explanation, even such a minimal explanation as is given in a secondary principle, for it does not say anything about the specific use of the linguistic phenomena in literature. Part of the point of these literary devices is that they are different from the ordinary linguistic phenomena to which Kiparsky reasonably relates them. For example, onsets (the beginnings of syllables) are not used in the same way in ordinary language and in literature. The two are continuous but not identical. We do not seek alliteration (or rhyme or assonance) in ordinary talk, but we do in poetry. To relate the two may be part of an explanatory account but necessarily only part.

What, then, is going on in literature? Literary theorists from different traditions regularly stress the unusual degree of structure and relevance in literature.[21] All speech is patterned. Whenever we speak, we try to make a coherent statement, present a coherent narrative, and so on. We choose words with the right connotations. We try to avoid harsh or comic sequences of sounds, and so forth. However, in the creation of verbal art, we do more of this and we do it more intensively. Perhaps one could say that we seek to maximize this sort of patterning. In other words, we seek to render the causal sequence of the plot more rigorous, reinforcing it with foreshadowing and circularity. We seek to coordinate connotations and ambiguities of the words and phrases—including purely graphic connotations and ambiguities where these occur, as in Chinese.[22] We also seek to pattern the sounds through rhythm, assonance, alliteration, and so forth. One differentia of literature, then, would seem to be a maximization of the relevance or patterning.

But this is only a first approximation. The Jakobson/Kiparsky hypothesis indicates that formal poetic devices are not merely a matter of maximizing relevance but of maximizing a certain sort of relevance—linguistically specified relevance, in their view. As Kiparsky stresses, "Certain patterns of considerable formal simplicity are never utilized in the construction of verse. . . . For example, no one thinks of filling in a stanzaic pattern on the principle that the last words of certain lines must contain the same number of sounds" ("The Role of Linguistics," 12–13). Why not? Kiparsky's answer is that no linguistic rule involves counting sounds in this way and thus no poetic rule will do so. But this formulation is clearly too narrow. It covers the case at hand but does not cover, for example, imagery, foreshadowing, or other nonlinguistic patterns open to maximization. Moreover, it does not seem to provide an adequate explanation of the limitations on maximization even in the case of linguistic phenomena. One is left asking, even in these relevant cases, "Why is there such a linguistic constraint?"

Kiparsky is responding to a genuine problem, but he seems to respond to it too narrowly. One way of trying to resolve this dilemma would be to consider what it is about Kiparsky's account that allows it to solve the linguistic cases and then see if this aspect of the account can be generalized. Consider again Kiparsky's examples. One obvious and crucial difference between, say, onsets (or beginnings) of syllables (used both in language rules and in poetry) and number of speech sounds (used neither in language rules nor in poetry) is that we "hear" the former but have to calculate the latter. More generally, any linguistic feature that is part of a linguistic rule is a feature we "hear"—not in the sense that we are conscious of it (typically we are not) but in the sense that it makes a difference to our experience. For the most part, we do not "hear" features not included in linguistic rules and can at best only calculate them. Indeed, when Kiparsky elaborates his hypothesis, he makes the point himself, arguing that the "faculty of language . . . equips" us with "modes of perceiving" certain features but not others ("On Theory," 191).

Insofar as this notion can be generalized, it would seem to solve the problem we have been considering. And, as it turns out, the idea can be generalized easily. Indeed, it is well known in cognitive science. The linguistic "hearing" or "perceiving" of onsets (but not number of speech sounds) is simply a specific case of a more general cognitive mechanism called "encoding." Encoding, then, appears to be what is crucial in all these cases, both those that fit Kiparsky's model (e.g., alliteration) and those that do not (e.g., foreshadowing). More exactly, when we perceive something, we cannot possibly perceive every aspect and relation of the thing. Rather, we perceive some aspects and store them in memory, while others escape us. The aspects we perceive and store are those that we "encode." Holland et al. give the following example: "Younger children often cannot learn about the rules underlying the behavior of balance beams" simply from observation because they "do not encode the distance of objects from the fulcrum" (55). However, when the distance is pointed out to them, they begin to encode the feature on new observations and are able to induce rules (55). Linguistic rules are just a particular case of cognitive principles that allow for encoding.

Therefore, we must reformulate our earlier principle. Now we would say that a wide variety of formal literary techniques (alliteration, assonance, circularity, foreshadowing, etc.) function to maximize relevance or patterning across *encoded* properties or relations. This new formulation could be thought of as a sort of schema in which the properties or relations in question are values of variables confined to a specified encodable class. Thus when applied to onsets, this schema yields alliteration. When applied to speech rhythm, it yields meter and related forms of patterning. When applied to imagistic analogy (a complex relation, but nonetheless one that is obviously encodable), it yields image patterning. And so on. Note also that encoding can be learned, though there are obviously limits to what can be encoded. This is important because it seems clear that greater experience of and training in literature increases one's sensitivity to certain sorts of pattern, which is only to be expected when the process is understood in terms of the general cognitive process of encoding. It is less obvious that Kiparsky's hypothesis could accommodate this sort of development.

On the other hand, not all of our problems are yet solved. Our revised formulation does not allow for limits on maximization; it treats maximization as a good in and of itself. Literature, however, maximizes patterns only to a certain point.[23] One degree of alliteration is aesthetic, but too extensive alliteration becomes comic. And this too is true cross-culturally. Some traditions may employ more alliteration than others, but, with rare exceptions, they do not equate more alliteration with a better poem (other things being equal), as this formulation would appear to imply. Rather, alliteration, rhyme, and so forth, reach a sort of ceiling, after which they detract from aesthetic effect.

To explain this phenomenon, we merely need to extend our analysis of perception. Again, in perceiving any object, we fail to encode some features at all; other features we do encode. Of those we encode, most never become objects of attentional focus. Typically we scan an object, and in the course of scanning we may intentionally focus our attention on one or another aspect of the object for a moment. However, in some cases, our attention will be drawn to a particular aspect against our will. A well-known example concerns background conversation. Typically we are not paying attention to background conversation when we are engaged in a conversation ourselves. However, if we hear our name mentioned, our attention will suddenly shift to the background conversation, entirely independent of conscious decision and perhaps even against our will.[24] Miller and Johnson-Laird note that "surprising stimuli" have this obtrusive or attention-forcing effect as well (133).

More generally, we might say that any perceptual feature has a certain degree of salience for a particular perceiver in particular circumstances. (Features that are not encoded could be thought of as having a salience of 0.) Various qualities of the feature, the perceiver, and the context determine that degree of salience. As just noted, the unexpectedness of the feature is one such quality. For temporally ordered occurrences, frequency of repetition would be another. Once the degree of salience (resulting from these qualities) exceeds a certain threshold, it automatically draws our attention. We can refer to this as the "threshold of forced attentional focus." Consider the quality of frequency. Suppose I use the phrase "of course" more than other speakers. If I use it once every other paragraph, readers are unlikely to "notice." As frequency increases, however—suppose I use it in every sentence—the usage will become obtrusive, "drawing attention to itself." In other words, it will eventually cross the threshold of forced attentional focus. This threshold probably varies somewhat both culturally and individually; however, it is also no doubt governed by broad cognitive constraints.

A further refinement of our general principle follows from this distinction: a wide variety of formal literary techniques (alliteration, assonance, foreshadowing, circularity, etc.) function to maximize relevance or patterning across encoded properties or relations *within a normative limit, which is defined as the point at which such maximization would surpass the threshold of forced attentional focus.*

There are still exceptions to this formulation, which typically involve an extension of forced attentional focus to the point where use of the feature comes to be seen as humorous or as manifesting a cadenzalike virtuosity on the part of the poet. The precise nature of these exceptions would be further examined in an ongoing research program. However, this discussion should adequately illustrate the abstraction of secondary principles and their refinement in such a program. Therefore, I turn now to another aspect of such a research program, considering a nontechnical correlation in relation to cognitive structure.

As I have already noted, standard line lengths for poetry in a wide range of traditions tend to fall between five and nine words. Standard line length is of course defined not in terms of words but in terms of some acoustic property, but it typically puts the number of words per line in this range. Thus in Chinese, a monosyllabic language, one standard line has only five syllables, which equals five words, while another has seven syllables and thus seven words.[25] The Yirrkalla poems quoted by Berndt in his appendixes, the Dinka songs cited by Deng, the Basotho verses quoted in Kunene, many of the Hawaiian poems in Pukui and Korn, and the Babylonian creation poems discussed by Sandars also fit this pattern reasonably well. As to European literatures, the first twenty lines of *The Canterbury Tiles* contain 144 words, about 7 per line; the first twenty lines of *Paradise Lost* average a bit under 8 words per line; twenty lines taken at random from the *Aeneid* have just under 7 words per line; and twenty from the *Odyssey* have almost exactly 7 words per line. Blake's *Songs of Innocence* have unusually short lines, but the first poem of the sequence, which is in no obvious way formally different from those that follow, has 6 words per line.[26] French lines tend to be unusually long (recall Pope's parody of the alexandrine "that like a wounded Snake, drags its slow length along" [203]), but the first twenty lines of Racine's *Phèdre* include just under 9 words per line and thus still do not exceed the range.

Nonetheless, there are many exceptions. In considering these, we need, first of all, to determine which counterexamples fall within the range of phenomena we are seeking to characterize. Clearly, our concern here is with literature structured around short, fixed, recurrent, nonsyntactic structures, such as iambic pentameter, which makes free verse irrelevant and thus eliminates a large number of possible counterexamples. Moreover, we are, as already noted, speaking about standard line lengths. Anyone can set out to create an odd verse form. Such individual exceptions are irrelevant as well.

Still, there remain a number of recalcitrant cases. One option would be to say that the universal is statistical and limited in application well above chance, certainly, but with many exceptions. This is, of course, possible. But it is an option of last resort. To choose this option is to put an end to one part of a research project.

Another option is to change the predicate of the universal. In every exception of which I am aware, the length of the written line is less than five words and not more than nine. One way of dealing with these exceptions would be to revise the universal to say that all lines are less than nine words. However, the five- to nine-word spread of line lengths fits well with the structure of rehearsal memory.[27] Specifically, rehearsal memory is structured in such a way as to include five to nine chunks of information—and thus, typically, five to nine words—at any given time. There are a number of reasons why this correlation is theoretically appealing. Most importantly, poetry in all traditions demands a sort of plenary attention. As the great tenth-century Indian theorist, Abhinavagupta, put it, we "savor" poetry:

> Aesthetical experience takes place . . . by virtue, as it were, of the squeezing out of the poetical word. Persons aesthetically sensitive, indeed, read and taste many times over the same poem. In contradiction to practical means of perception, that, their task being accomplished, are no more of any use and must then be abandoned, a poem, indeed, does not lose its value after it has been comprehended.
>
> (QUOTED IN GNOLI, xxxii)

Abhinavagupta's view is almost a necessary consequence of the maximization of unobtrusive patterning. As more features become relevant to our experience of a literary work, we are less and less able to appreciate it without "savoring." More features must be encoded in our experience of poetry than in our experience of ordinary speech. And the most obvious way of ensuring this is through rehearsal memory, which does, in effect, allow us to "savor" segments of a poem. It makes a great deal of cognitive sense that the unit of savoring would be the poetic line. Or, rather, given this need for savoring, it makes sense that the recurring unit of poetry would develop in accordance with the structure of rehearsal memory. Moreover, this is true not only receptively but productively. A poet composing a poem is generating short, repeatable, nonsyntactic units. She has to revise and "polish" these units—to satisfy metrical and other constraints and the broader criterion of nonobtrusive maximization of patterning. Given the structure of human cognition, one would expect that any such unit would almost necessarily be structured in accordance with rehearsal memory. This is even more obvious when one takes into account the oral, bardic composition that is at the origin of poetry.[28] Without the aid of writing, the recurring unit of poetic form would almost necessarily be structured by rehearsal memory.

In short, rehearsal memory seems to provide a good explanation of the universal as initially stated. Indeed, it not only accounts for the five to nine words but relates this universal to the maximization of relevance and to other aspects of the experience and creation of poetry. Thus we have broad theoretical reasons not to adopt a formulation of the line length universal that would dissociate it from rehearsal memory. Of course, if lines are only shorter and not longer, then it is still possible to link the poetic line with rehearsal memory. Longer lines simply would not fit into the limited space available for rehearsal memory; shorter lines would fit, even though there would be room left over. And we do sometimes use rehearsal memory in this way. On the other hand, the nature of any link with rehearsal memory is much less clear if we accept the reformulated universal ("less than nine words"). In this case, it would seem that rehearsal memory does not structure the line but merely limits its extent, which would seem to argue against the central aesthetic function just mentioned. In short, if we accept the reformulated universal, the relation to the broader purposes of poetry is attenuated, and the explanatory function of rehearsal memory is reduced considerably.

One option that preserves the straightforward relation to rehearsal memory is to reconsider the notion of the line. Indeed, there seems to be no necessary reason to identify the unit at issue with what is in effect a convention of writing and printing. In many cases, the printed line is indeed the unit we want. In the case of the alexandrine, iambic pentameter, and a wide range of other patterns, the printed line rightly defines the recurring nonsyntactic unit. Other cases, however, are less clear. One of the most obvious exceptions to the universal as initially formulated is the Japanese haiku, a seventeen-syllable poem divided into sections of five, seven, and five syllables. We typically conceive of this as a three-line poem. One way of reconciling the haiku with our universal and with the structure of rehearsal memory would be to conceive of the poem as a single line with a single caesura. Thus it fits perfectly well, yielding roughly six to nine words per unit.[29] (An alternative account that preserves the structural function of rehearsal memory might incorporate silent "beats," akin to musical rests, which would fit with certain aspects of Japanese aesthetic theory. How precisely this might work in rehearsal memory would be a topic for cognitive research.)

On the other hand, a further source of exceptions may be found in such languages as Kuna and Dyirbal, which tend to have between two and four words per verse line[30] and in which the problem does not appear to be one of defining the recurring rhythmic unit. (There is also no obvious motivation for positing silent beats in these cases.) These counterexamples lead us instead to a reconsideration of the nature of rehearsal memory. Both Kuna and Dyirbal are morphologically complex languages. It may be that rehearsal memory is not appropriately measured in terms of words at all, but in terms of, say, morphemes. Even in European languages, it seems odd to count *habeo* as one word but *j'ai* as two, or *et* as one word but enclitic *-que* as none. Perhaps *et virum* takes up two slots in rehearsal memory and *virumque* takes up only one, but it seems counterintuitive.

In any case, at this point, the research project of literary universals abuts the broader research project of cognitive psychology. Before the literary project can proceed, the broader psychological study of rehearsal memory has to proceed further. Moreover, as this example indicates, aspects of this broader study can be inspired by literary study. The problems of Kuna and Dyirbal point to further areas for cognitive research—specifically, to the examination of whether rehearsal memory is best understood in terms of words or morphemes or something else. Should it turn out that it is best understood in terms of words, then the Kuna and Dyirbal data will be difficult to account for and we may have to weaken or modify our hypothesis. Should it turn out that morphemes are the crucial units, the Kuna and Dyirbal problems will be solved. On the other hand, it may render Chinese poetry problematic. Should it turn out to be something else—

syllables, for example—this too will probably produce anomalies. In any event, each possible outcome would point to areas of further research and theorization in an ongoing program. (The possibility of silent beats in Japanese haiku also points to a potentially consequential area for cognitive research, and it too could have significant consequences.)

The maximization of unobtrusive patterning and the relationships among rehearsal memory, line length, and aesthetic experience provide clear illustrations of what will necessarily be two central types of descriptive and explanatory study in a theory of literary universals. However, they are mere starting points for research, hypotheses to be modified, elaborated, and perhaps replaced. Again, the study of literary universals, like the study of linguistic universals, is a project that can progress only through the cooperative efforts of a broad range of researchers engaged in an ongoing process of empirical reevaluation of theories and theoretical reorientation of empirical research. As the final examples in particular illustrate, such a research program could be of great value not only for our understanding of those cognitions and affections that generate and sustain literary art but for our broader understanding of the human mind as well.

Finally, this sort of program is not politically inconsequential. Racial and cultural hierarchies are routinely and necessarily justified by an appeal to putative racial and cultural differences, even if these appeals are sometimes hidden behind universalist rhetoric (much as unequal treatment and double standards are often concealed behind a rhetoric of equality and fairness—and happily, no one takes that to imply that equality and fairness are politically objectionable). A universalist program that succeeds in uncovering genuinely universal principles of human thought and human society, principles that are not relative to race or culture, necessarily runs contrary to racism and ethnocentrism. Of course, we should not decide in favor of universalist hypotheses simply because they appear to be politically beneficial. On the other hand, in the current intellectual climate of the humanities, this seems an unlikely danger. Indeed, one can only hope that, despite the current denigration of universalism, more humanists will follow the lead of Ngũgĩ, Chomsky, Marx, Frantz Fanon, Samir Amin, Kwame Appiah, Aijaz Ahmad, Edward Said, and others, in recognizing both the intellectual and political value of studying universals.[31]

PART TWO

Cognitive Historicism

As the selection of essays in this section demonstrates, cognitive historicism can build on a variety of paradigms from cognitive science, including, but not limited to, studies in modularity (Ellen Spolsky), analogical thinking (Mary Thomas Crane), theory of mind (Lisa Zunshine), cognitive neuroscience (Alan Richardson), and cognitive linguistics and anthropology (Bruce McConachie). Cognitive literary critics have been grappling with the concept of historicity for almost a decade now (see Crane's *Shakespeare's Brain*, Richardson's *British Romanticism and the Science of the Mind*, Richardson and Francis Steen's "Literature and the Cognitive Revolution," Spolsky's *Satisfying Skepticism* and "Cognitive Literary Historicism," Tony Jackson's "Issues and Problems in the Blending of the Cognitive Science, Evolutionary Psychology, and Literary Study," and Zunshine's *Strange Concepts and the Stories They Make Possible*); it is significant that a 1998 MLA forum, convened as a prequel to inaugurating, in 1999, the MLA discussion group on cognitive approaches to literature, was entitled "Historicizing Cognition." Indeed an interest in articulating the meaning of the "weasely" term "historical" in the context of cognitive evolutionary epistemology is quickly becoming a central theoretical commitment of the field of cognitive cultural studies.[1]

In defining cognitive historicism one may consider its practical implementation and its theoretical assumptions. With respect to the former, "cognitive historicism retains the emphasis on specific sociocultural environments" while recruiting and selectively adapting "theories, methods, and findings from the sciences of mind and brain" (Richardson's "Facial Expression Theory" [chap. 2 of this volume]). As to its theoretical assumptions, cognitive historicism views culture as an ongoing interplay—simultaneously a give-and-take and a tug-of-war—between human cognitive architecture and specific historical circumstances. Hence, according to Spolsky,

> The addition of biological, evolutionary, and cognitive hypotheses to the discussion of [cultural] change . . . offers literary historical and cultural studies a way to consider the universals of human cognitive processing as they function in their several contexts. These universals are themselves counted as aspects of the context, and thus, the enormous creative potential of the evolved human mind itself is folded into the investigation of the processes of cultural construction, complicating but also enriching the discussion.
>
> ("COGNITIVE LITERARY HISTORICISM," 168)

In counting human cognitive architecture as a crucial factor contributing to cultural change, cognitive literary critics subscribe cautiously to a view of this architecture as flexible—cautiously, because although the architecture itself does not change (having remained constant across the species for at least the last ten thousand years), the ways in which it expresses itself in specific environments certainly do.[2] To use a well-known example, consider a child born into a culture built around reading. Her brain has to undergo a particular mutually contingent adjustment of several cognitive systems not required of the brain of a child born into a nonreading culture.[3] Moreover, having learned to read will eventually enable her to affect the world around her in a variety of ways—for example, by publishing a poem, starting a new blog, or inventing a new computer game—which will, in turn, create a slightly different cognitive environment for other entering readers.

Indeed, it is this kind of cognitive flexibility—that is, a flexibility that always manifests itself in specific cultural terms—that allows cognitive literary critics to see themselves as equal partners in a dialogue with cognitive scientists. As Jackson puts it,

> For the most part cognitive science uncovers innate mental structures that have been determined by our formative evolution over thousands of generations. But though these structures are innate and arise from our interactions as animals with the world, the structures are still mental and therefore not rigidly constrained like breathing, walking, metabolism, and so on. Cognitive structures can be violated or viti-

ated in ways that biological structures cannot. . . . Because cognitive structures are not determined in a strictly biological sense, specific cultural practices and ideologies will have a strong part to play in the actual manifestation of a given cognitive universal, and the humanities scholar, one way or another, is already the authority on culture and ideology. Thus we have a stronger possibility of a true interdisciplinarity.   ("ISSUES," 176)[4]

CHAPTER TWO

Facial Expression Theory from Romanticism to the Present

ALAN RICHARDSON

The study of facial expression has played a key role both in the development of a cognitive neuroscience of human behavior and in the resurgence of intellectual interest in stable and universal aspects of human nature. Cognitive psychologists and neurobiologists alike see the expressive human face as a particularly salient object for cognition, given the enormous importance of establishing and managing relations with others for our sociable species, from infancy onward. Successful social communication, as one neurobiological researcher puts it, relies on the "correct perception and interpretation of nonverbal cues such as the tone of voice, the emotional expression of a face, and the direction of a gaze that both signifies attention and directs the emotional expression to its target."[1] It is less than surprising, then, that neuroanatomical and brain imaging research points toward dedicated neural systems not only for recognizing faces (as distinct from recognizing objects generally) but for interpreting facial expressions as well. Selective brain injuries can result in prosopagnosia—that is, the inability to recognize human faces while continuing to recognize other objects for perception—and yet at least some prosopagnosiacs can still correctly interpret facial expressions ("he's obviously happy, but I have no idea who he might be"). What's termed our "theory of mind" (see the essays by Alan Palmer and Lisa Zunshine in this volume) would be greatly impoverished if we did not have a reasonably reliable and speedy, and therefore largely unconscious, cognitive mechanism for gauging the emotions and intentions of others through reading their faces. Indeed, this nonverbal form of social communication is too important to be left entirely to acquisition by learning, and those blind from birth manifest (though imperfectly) the basic set of facial expressions—

anger, disgust, fear, happiness, sadness—without ever having seen them.[2] Infants begin to fixate on, and to imitate, facial expressions when still less than a day old.[3]

If the propensity for studying and imitating facial expressions and the basic repertoire of expressions themselves are shaped by innate predispositions well entrenched in the human genome, they should occur independently across geographically distant and culturally distinct human populations. This is precisely what researchers began to find in the late 1960s and early 1970s, against their own expectations and contrary to the then reigning orthodoxy of cultural relativism. Paul Ekman, the leading psychological researcher in this area, describes himself in retrospect as initially an "agnostic about universality," as willing to find experimental evidence against the universality of basic facial expressions as to find evidence for it (Afterword, 317). Ekman's account makes clear, however, that his own experimental findings made a convert of him and, moreover, helped bring about a sea change that contributed to making the older Enlightenment postulate of human universals and of a shared human nature once more a respectable and a legitimate topic for research. Ekman, his colleagues, and rival researchers like Carroll Izard found in a series of influential experiments that people with no exposure to modern industrialized cultures (and modern media) could readily identify (and produce) standard expressions for anger, happiness, and the like. The cognitive anthropologist Donald Brown makes the universal set of human facial expressions one of the key case studies in his 1991 survey, *Human Universals* (23–27), and Ekman's pioneering work (along with its hostile contemporary reception at the hands of leading relativists like Margaret Mead) has become a stock example in popularized accounts of the new science of human nature, such as Stephen Pinker's *The Blank Slate* (107–8).

The psychology and neurobiology of facial expression, then, can productively unsettle the largely unqualified, and by now patently untenable, cultural relativism that continues to prevail within literary studies. Moreover, a theory such as Ekman's does so in a decidedly engaging manner, as it by no means involves the opposite error: an unqualified biological determinism. Although the basic set of human facial expressions make up part of a core and universal human nature, their use in a given social setting will be modified by acquired cultural expectations and norms. Finding that American and Japanese students shared the same basic expressions but modulated them quite differently depending on purely social factors (the Japanese students showed less disgust and more smiles while watching gruesome footage, *if* an authority figure was present), Ekman argued for the importance of culturally instantiated "display rules" guiding the use (including the inhibition) of expressions. Thus, as Brown writes, Ekman arrived at a " 'neuro-cultural' theory of facial expressions. To fully understand or interpret facial expression, we must posit both universals and cultural variants" (25). Or as Ekman himself stresses, "we are biosocial creatures" (Afterword, 393). Elaborating Ernst Mayr's important distinction between "open" and "closed" genetic programs, Ekman notes that for human creatures, with their unusually long period of parental care and extensive opportunities for learning, "there will be a selective advantage" in an open program, although this does not leave us back with the blank slate: there will be constraints, default values, and (quoting Mayr) "certain types of information are more easily incorporated than others" (386–87). This neurocultural perspective (congruent with work such as Patrick Hogan's on literary universals, outlined in his essay in this volume) stands to offer a great deal more to humanist scholars than does the insistence on "hardwired" judgments and behaviors that marks too much recent work in what is termed "evolutionary literary theory."[4]

The history of facial expression theory holds an additional interest for literary humanists in particular. For there has long been something "literary" about the study of facial expressions, and facial expression theory might be said to have been born out of collaboration across the literature and science divide. Tracing out this history makes for an exercise in what Francis Steen and I have termed "cognitive historicism," a term that has been usefully elaborated by Ellen Spolsky and that is beginning to find some currency within literary studies.[5] Cognitive historicism retains the emphasis on specific sociocultural environments, on common discursive strategies linking, say, the poetry of an earlier era with its jurisprudence and its botany, and the acknowledgment of the impossibility of any objective, transcendent historical perspective that marks other "new" literary historicisms. In addition, however, it recruits and selectively adapts theories, methods, and findings from the sciences of mind and brain, partly in the hope that these will provide suggestive (though, it is understood, necessarily imperfect) analogies with past models and partly in the hope that cultural and historical differences will emerge *more* clearly and cleanly when set against what appear to be stable and invariant aspects of human cognition and behavior. If an early interest in what we now call the psychology of facial expression can be found marking both scientific and literary texts of the Romantic era—and indeed there demonstrably can—what might this tell us about the literary and scientific cultures of that era and their zones of convergence? And how might exploring this previously unnoticed feature of Romantic-era writing produce new understandings, not only of early brain scientists like Charles Bell and Matthew Baillie but of literary artists like John Keats and Jane Austen? Before turning to writing from the Romantic era, however, it is necessary to say something about Charles Darwin.

For most psychological and neuroscientific researchers, the history of facial expression theory begins with Darwin's *The Expression of the Emotions in Man and Animals*, first published in 1872. In his brief overview of "natural philosophy before Darwin," for example, the psychologist Lewis Petrinovich finds no relevant work prior to Darwin, apart from some early speculation on evolution generally (224–25). Darwin himself, however, acknowledges the significant precedent of Charles Bell, who "with justice may be said, not only to have laid the foundations of the subject as a science, but to have built up a noble structure" (*Expression*, 7). Bell, the celebrated early neurologist after whom "Bell's palsy" is named, worked out an elaborate account of human facial expressions, one we would have little trouble today describing as "neuroscientific," in his *Anatomy and Philosophy of Human Expression*, first published in 1806 and expanded and revised throughout his career (Darwin drew on the 1844 edition). Ekman, in the introduction to his edition of Darwin's *Expressions*, duly notes Darwin's debt to Bell but minimizes it, making a great deal of Darwin's opposition to Bell's notion of uniquely human facial muscles dedicated to expressions not found among other animals (xxv–xxviii). This notion in turn spoke to Bell's firm conviction in God's special creation of humankind, precisely the sort of creationism that Darwin was arguing against throughout the *Expressions*, which highlights on the contrary the inheritance of certain expressive muscles used by animals but, Darwin argued, of no use to human beings. (How many of us really *can* make our hair stand on end, and why would we want to?) As Darwin remarked in a different work, *The Descent of Man* (1871), it was Bell's insistence that "man is endowed with certain muscles solely for the sake" of expression that motivated his own researches in this area: "As this view is obviously opposed to the belief that man is descended from some other and lower form, it was necessary for me to consider it" (*Darwin*, 202). What then, of the "noble structure" that Darwin nevertheless found in Bell's foundational work? Students of facial expression theory have not thought the question worth pursuing.

This signal neglect of Bell, however, proves rather ironic (to say nothing of the poor scholarship it represents). For, in several important respects, Bell's account of facial expression can be seen as *more* forward looking than that of Darwin; or, put differently, the Romantic-era account resonates in more elaborate and interesting ways with current understandings than does Darwin's Victorian version. As Pinker accurately remarks in relation to the *Expressions*, "Darwin was no Darwinian in one of his most famous books" (*How the Mind Works*, 414). Showing surprisingly little interest here in what he elsewhere terms "beautiful adaptations," Darwin instead relies on Lamarckian notions of acquired characteristics, not randomly produced and then selected for but acquired through repeated experience and then, somehow, passed on to offspring (*Darwin*, 115). Just as surprisingly, Darwin had very little to say about the communicative role of facial expressions, although the importance of the human face for nonverbal social communication makes the cornerstone of Bell's account as well as of more recent theories. Ekman surmises that Darwin may have underplayed the communicative importance of facial expressions precisely out of his opposition to Bell: "Darwin might have thought that if he dealt with communication he would weaken his challenge to the creationists" (introduction, xxxiv). This neglect in turn may have pushed Darwin uncharacteristically into Lamarckian waters, since the communicative value of facial expressions is precisely what would have been (naturally) selected for.

In fact, influential creationist though he was, Bell was remarkably interested in "beautiful adaptations," in the fitting of creatures to their physical and social environments, as well as in the mind's instantiation in and even growth out of the body and its brain—what we would today term the "embodied mind." Although he remained a committed mind-brain (or rather spirit-brain) dualist, Bell reserved the separation of body and mind for the afterlife; in this world, the mind depends all but entirely on the body, so much so that Bell's philosophy of mind can meaningfully be termed "corporeal" if not materialistic. "Since we are dwellers in the material world," he writes in the *Anatomy*, "it is necessary that the spirit should be connected with it by an organised body, without which it could neither feel nor re-act, nor manifest itself in any way. It is a fundamental law of our nature that the mind shall have its powers developed through the influence of the body" (76–77). Emotional experience, for example, would be greatly impoverished if not missing altogether absent the "operation of the instruments of expression" (179), by which Bell means not only the facial muscles that produce expressions but also the neural system (with its crucial connections to the heart and lungs) that subtends and animates them; he may also be thinking of the brain organs that interpret them. That facial expressions begin to appear in early infancy, in advance of any conscious control over them, further underscores their importance for cognitive and affective development: "It may be too much to affirm, that without the cooperation of these organs the mind would remain a blank; but surely the mind must owe something to its connexion with an operation of the features which precedes its own conscious activity, and which is unerring in its exercise from the very commencement" (180).

Bell's entire career featured a presiding interest in the facial expressions and their complex links with the heart and lungs, their role in social communication, their innate (for Bell, divinely endowed) character, and their pervasive contribution to the development of the human mind. The essays that became the *Anatomy* originally grew out of his 1806 lectures to a group of artists, who hired a young and hungry Bell for informal anatomy lessons, and Bell later attributed his discoveries in neuroanatomy to his quest to solve what he initially saw as an aesthetic problem, the painter's ability to capture and the viewer's to interpret emotions through their embodied signs. "I saw that the whole frame is affected sympathetically with expression in the countenance, and it was in trying to explain that sympathy, that I was led to ascertain, that there exists in the body a distinct system of nerves, the office of which is to influence the muscles in Respiration, in Speech, and in Expression" (193). This holistic sense of facial expression as intimately bound up with changes in the circulatory and respiratory systems does much to distinguish Bell's physiological approach to expression from the older physiognomy of Lavater and others: they viewed expressions as fixed and two dimensional, while for Bell they were dynamic and involved internal senses like interoception as well as the external sense of vision. Although lecturing to painters, Bell was inspired by a different aesthetic practice, the multimedia art of theater. I'm not thinking primarily here of the references to Shakespeare scattered throughout Bell's text—and, for that matter, through Darwin's. Darwin's *Expression* is in fact framed by extended quotations from Shakespeare, chief among the poets whom Darwin cites as authorities on human expression, one of the ways in which the science of facial expression has been bound up with literature all along. In addition to citing Shakespeare himself, however, Bell also refers to a specific theatrical performance, Sarah Siddons's celebrated role as Katherine in *Henry VIII*, as capturing the holistic sense of emotional expression that informs his own account. "Has my reader seen Mrs. Siddons in Queen Katherine during that solemn scene where the sad note was played which she named her knell? Who taught the crowd sitting at a play, an audience differing in age, habits, and education, to believe those quivering motions, and that gentle smile, and slight convulsive twitchings, to be true to nature?" (83).

Siddons wordlessly yet eloquently conveys a highly complex emotional state to her audience not through her facial expression—that "gentle smile"—alone but through the quivering produced by an overtaxed heart and respiratory system and the muscular twitchings conveyed along the nerves. Heart, lungs, brain, and the facial muscles, interconnected by an intricate maze of neural pathways, many first traced out by Bell, make expression a dynamic, embodied event unfolding (however rapidly) in time and not a affair of the face alone. "The frame of the body, constituted for the support of the vital functions, becomes the instrument of expression; and an extensive class of passions, by influencing the heart, by affecting that sensibility which governs the muscles of respiration, calls them into co-operation, so that they become an undeviating and sure sign of certain states or conditions of the mind" (88), the nonarbitrary signs of a "natural language" (113). Although Bell (a brilliant draftsman) produced a number of facial portraits as illustrations for his book (anticipating Darwin's use of photographs), for Bell emotional expression is finally less like a two-dimensional portrait than like a dramatic performance—

with the proviso that for Bell such performances, though they may be variously acted out, are always scripted in advance, innately endowed and universally interpretable.

Bell's recourse to a theatrical model in developing his ideas on nonverbal communication was not, I believe, fortuitous. Rather, it attests to how early facial expression theory was being developed in tandem by neurologists and literary artists alike. Key elements of Bell's thinking, in fact, can be found adumbrated in the "Introductory Discourse" to Joanna Baillie's *Plays on the Passions*, published in 1798, less than a decade before Bell first gave his lectures on the anatomy of expression. Although I cannot trace anything like a direct line of influence from Baillie to Bell, there is much to suggest that the resemblance between Bell's theory and that of Baillie is not just a matter of convergent cultural evolution. Both Bell and Baillie had come to London after growing up in Scotland, where both would have been exposed to the "common sense" philosophy of the Scotsman Thomas Reid. (The "common sense" school took special interest in the investigation of human universals, what was "common" to all human subjects, and though like Bell a committed dualist, Reid showed comparable interest in mind-body interaction, innate inclinations, and the "natural language" of facial expressions.) Bell was personally acquainted both with Joanna Baillie (who helped promote his career) and with her brother Matthew, already an established doctor and neurological researcher at the time when Bell began his London career. And Joanna Baillie, drawing on her brother's own neurological speculations, and looking to Shakespeare as a dramatic model, had developed her own account of the emotions (or "passions"), nonverbal social communication, innately driven behaviors, and theatricality in the "Introductory Discourse."

Baillie's interest in facial expression has sometimes been compared to the pseudoscience of physiognomy, but in fact she anticipates Bell's *physiological* approach to issue, which for Darwin marked the beginning of a legitimately scientific approach. As would Bell, Baillie looks not to static emotional displays but to what Bell calls the "*motion* of the features, the expression" (17, emphasis added)—or in Baillie's terms, the "irregular bursts, abrupt transitions, sudden pauses," along with such subtler indications as the "restless eye, the muttering lip, the half-checked exclamation and hasty start" (*Dramatic and Poetical Works*, 3, 8). Like both Reid and Bell, Baillie attributes important universal features of human behavior to a common cognitive developmental process, one requiring extensive inter-action with the social environment to be sure yet impelled nevertheless by drives and guided by templates that are innate or "implanted within us" (2). Baillie begins with that "strong sympathy which most creatures, but the human above all, feels for others of their kind," a sympathetic "curi-osity" that emerges early in life and is found in all normal subjects, that is, all those "not deficient in intellect" (1). "This propensity is universal," Baillie writes. "Children begin to show it very early[.] . . . GOD ALMIGHTY has implanted it within us, as well as our other propensities and passions" (4). Baillie posits a natural, nonverbal "language" of expression that con-veys the passions in a manner that "every age and nation understand" (3). These passions (what would now be called emotions) are themselves innate and universal, the "great original distinctions of nature" (13), and their embodied expression can be readily recognized across cultures. Yet Baillie's facial expression theory manifests an early interest in "biosocial" phenomena as well. Learning to interpret the full range of "native" pas-sions and character traits—especially in spite of attempts to modulate or conceal them—demands "constant" practice beginning in early child-hood, impelled by innate social "curiosity." Much of this cognitive prac-tice takes place beneath conscious awareness—"without [our] being con-scious of it"—and can operate intuitively (2).

For Baillie as for Bell, then, reading human emotions and intentions through their embodied manifestations is an innately driven, experien-tially developed, species-wide human practice. Baillie argues that public executions draw large crowds precisely because of this universal fascina-tion with emotional expression. Few spectators "can get near enough to distinguish the expression of a face, or the minuter parts of a crimi-nal's behavior," under such unusually intense emotional pressure, yet even "from a considerable distance will they remark whether he steps firmly; whether the motions of his body denote agitation or calmness" (2). The-ater, however, the "grand and favorite amusement of every nation into which it has been introduced," could in the right hands and under the right circumstances provide a more intimate look at such nonverbal emo-tional behaviors, including their "finer and more delicate indications" of emotion (232). Baillie's ambitious project for the *Plays on the Passions* was to provide a whole series of such theatrical exhibitions, each dedi-cated to a different emotion, or "passion." In addition, she called for a new, more intimate kind of theatrical venue, one that (unlike the cavernous, "over-sized" auditoriums of the time) would allow for the actors to be "distinctly heard and seen," encouraging a more nuanced—and more natural—performance style (232–33). If a theatrical sense of expression unfolding in time and (implicitly) before spectators lay at the heart of Bell's neuroscientific understanding of facial expression, Baillie's vision of the drama and theater of the future was deeply informed by a view of facial expression very much akin to Bell's.

Baillie's account of facial expression was also fully consonant with the Romantic-era neuroscientific thinking on emotion, expression, and the nervous system that led up to Bell, as I've argued at length elsewhere.[6] Closest to home, of course, was Baillie's brother Matthew—very close, as the siblings shared lodgings at this time. Matthew had studied philosophy with Reid at Edinburgh, before coming to London to work and train with his (and Joanna's) uncles, the great physiologist John Hunter and the gifted surgeon and anatomist William Hunter. Together, the three made up what has been called the "most famous medical family" of the age.[7] Matthew Baillie had sketched out key elements of what would become Bell's theory in his Gulstonian lectures, published in 1794, four years before his sister described her own analogous ideas in her introduction to the *Plays on the Passions*. In the third of his three fascinating lectures on the nervous system, this one addressing the human emotions, Matthew states that the "different emotions of the mind are also conveyed along nerves to different muscles of the body." Thanks to these distinct neural pathways, "each emotion . . . sets in action its appropriate muscles, producing a change in the countenance and attitude, which is expressive of emotion." Emotional expressions arise spontaneously, without "volition," and can be "universally understood" by others. These universal physiological expressions of mental states, of emotion, constitute for Matthew as they do for Joanna—and will for Bell—a "natural language," one "not connected with any arbitrary customs of society," one more innately guided than socially acquired. Human beings are instinctively drawn to studying this "natural language," often unconsciously, and will even unknowingly imitate "singular" gestures or expressions that have "called up the attention of the mind" (*Lectures and Observations*, 145–47).

Whatever the precise lines of influence, the converging interests of Matthew Baillie, Joanna Baillie, and Bell in expression, affect, nonverbal communication, human universals, "natural" signs, and the body as a site for the social performance of emotions represent a larger intellectual tendency of the Romantic era, one shared in common by medical researchers and literary artists. Although this tendency can be found informing literary texts of many kinds, space allows me only to glance here at one poet, John Keats, and one novelist, Jane Austen. In addition to working in different genres and belonging to different genders entailing different rules for the social display of emotions, each stood in a remarkably different relation to contemporary science as well. And yet their works show significant affinities when it comes to the issue of facial expression and the "natural language" of the passions.

Thanks to his medical training at Guy's, then a leading London teaching hospital, Keats had ready access to the neuroscientific ideas of Baillie and Bell. One of his teachers, the noted surgeon, anatomist, and medical lecturer Astley Cooper, was a colleague of Matthew Baillie's and had met Bell in Edinburgh (along with Dugald Stewart, Reid's protégé); Bell put Cooper on the distribution list for his privately printed work of 1811, the *New Anatomy of the Brain*. In addition, Keats's friend Benjamin R. Haydon had been one of the very painters Bell had lectured to while first working out his ideas on facial expression in 1806. Haydon, in fact, later claimed that he had taken the leading role in putting this group together and securing Bell as their anatomy teacher. There is no doubt that Cooper exposed Keats to leading new ideas on brain anatomy and neurophysiology: the evidence survives in Keats's lecture notes.[8]

Keats in his poetry shows a special affinity for the connections Bell posed among the heart, lungs, nerves, emotions, and facial muscles—and by extension, for the further connection between this system, engaged for nonverbal communication, and the system for producing language, which recruits many of the same "organs." This helps explain why the representation of blushing, for example, has been seen as a signature element of Keats's poetry, as noted long ago by Christopher Ricks but only recently connected with the Romantic-era science of mind-body relations and emotive expression. Keats shows a rich appreciation throughout his poetry for what is now termed "hot cognition," thinking that, far from coolly computational, involves the body, the emotions, and the literally hot sensation of blood moving to the face in flushes of anger or sexual excitement, in blushes provoked by embarrassment or erotic self-consciousness.[9] Keats, like Bell, not only posits a tight relation between the psychophysiology of such "hot" facial expressions and the physical production and articulation of language but also shows special interest in how these systems can interfere with one another, in the way involuntary nonverbal expression can trump conscious attempts at articulate speech. Thus Lorenzo, passionately in love with his employers' sister, the title character of *Isabella*, finds his nonverbal signs of love overpowering his initial attempts at a declaration:

> all day
> His heart beat awfully against his side;
> And to his heart he inwardly did pray
> For power to speak; but still the ruddy tide
> Stifled his voice, and puls'd resolve away.
>
> (ll. 41–46)

Fortunately, Isabella proves sufficiently adept at parsing Lorenzo's natural language of sighs and blushes and expressions:

> So once more he had wak'd and anguished
> A dreary night of love and misery,
> If Isabel's quick eye had not been wed
> To every symbol on his forehead high;
> She saw it waxing very pale and dead,
> And straight all flush'd; so, lisped tenderly,
> "Lorenzo!"—here she ceased her timid quest,
> But in her tone and look he read the rest.
>
> (ll. 49–56)

Lorenzo too proves adept at "reading" extrasemantic tones and nonverbal expressions, a universal skill central to Baillie's vision of a more intimate, more natural theater, and to Bell's analysis of how Sarah Siddons could wordlessly convey the complex feelings of Shakespeare's Katherine to the theatrical audiences of the day. Keats departs from Bell, though, in stressing the confusion and sheer "noise" that the human expressive systems can engender; these are, in Spolsky's terms, "good enough" systems, not instances of divine and therefore flawless design as Bell would have it.[10] And yet, in the world of *Isabella*, even communicative short circuits have their value. If it were easier for Lorenzo to declare himself to Isabella, we, and perhaps she, might distrust his smoothness of expression; after all, he's the penniless apprentice, she the wealthy daughter of the house.

As a playwright, Baillie shares Keats's sense of the fragility of human communications systems, despite their considerable (and by no means trivial) successes. As Zunshine has argued in relation to "theory of mind" theories, literary artists may show special interest in the failures of cognitive systems, because such breakdowns can prove instructive, because they ring true to our sense of human fallibility, and, not least, because they can make for more interesting stories.[11] Baillie's tragedy *Count Basil*, which first appeared in 1798 with her "Introductory Discourse," exhibits an entire series of such breakdowns; the hero's consistent misreading of the heroine's emotional expressions, in fact, is what drives the play toward its tragic conclusion. In this way Baillie, who insists on the extensive social practice and observation involved in any successful "reading" of the passions, provides a much more robustly "neurocultural" sense of human emotional expression than does Bell. As a woman writer of her times, Baillie can hardly afford to ignore the display rules involved in the expression of feeling; throughout the conduct literature of the later eighteenth and early nineteenth centuries, women are advised to maintain tight control over their expressions, particularly where these touch on (or might even *seem* to touch on) sexual desire. As Rousseau writes in *Emile*, the "strictness of the relative duties of the sexes is not and cannot be the same"; if her children are to pass as legitimate offspring, a woman must not only be but *appear* to be chaste, to her husband and to "everyone" (369). And yet, at the same time, unmarried women are to appear artlessly inviting, chastely seductive, despite this regimen of self-control and the almost paranoid sense of constant observation that accompanies and demands it. No wonder the system tends to go awry. Victoria, the heroine of *Count Basil*, ends up resorting to all but nonstop simulation of emotion, allowing her genuine feelings to become manifest only obliquely, largely against her conscious wishes, and in the briefest of flashes. Her admirer, the military hero Basil, having spent next to no time around women, remains clueless throughout. As one can readily imagine, this tragedy verges extremely close to comedy.

It was Jane Austen, however, who made nonverbal communication, the bodily revelation of emotion, and the pitfalls involved in "reading" them central features of her wryly comic fiction. Austen, of course, had nothing like Keats's direct exposure to leading medical-scientific ideas—there were no female medical students at the time—nor did her close relations include leading pioneers of modern physiology and neuroscience, as did Baillie's. And yet Austen's relentlessly brilliant comedies of manners, particularly her last two novels, *Emma* and *Persuasion*, show remarkable parallels to the representations of nonverbal communication, and of facial expressions in particular, found in the works of Baillie and Keats and given a theoretical basis in the brain science of her era. These parallels suggest that a keen interest in how the body manifests emotions and intentions—and in how a given human mind attempts to extrapolate from these manifestations the mental dispositions, conscious or not, of others—made for a central rather than peripheral aspect of Romantic-era literary life. In other words, Austen, by keeping up (as she did) with the leading reviews (which covered medical and scientific treatises as well as poetry and fiction), by conversing, and by reading the works of her contemporaries, could draw on the same general intellectual culture as Keats or Baillie without having their special access to the medical sciences. A number of literary writers and scholars today know a fair amount about contemporary neuroscience and cognitive science without ever having studied these areas in school or (at least until very recently) having any special reason to follow them aside from general intellectual curiosity. The intellectual world of Austen's period was much smaller than ours is today and more densely interconnected, and the traditional divide between science and the humanities was a good deal more porous and less firmly entrenched. As a woman writer, Austen shared as well Baillie's acute consciousness of the rules and vagaries of nonverbal social communication; her novels make frequent references to and engage in an ongoing critical dialogue with the very conduct books that sought to define and regularize what Ekman calls "display rules." Few novels better illustrate both the niceties of such display rules and the unconscious revelation of emotion in spite of them than does Austen's *Emma*.

Emma is often read in terms of the linguistic confusion that piles up around the title heroine: despite her ease in solving riddles and other verbal puzzles, Emma chronically misunderstands the men around her, no small difficulty for a woman of marriageable age. Worse, Emma thinks herself singularly adept at social interpretation, setting herself up for a succession of comic reversals. Emma's misfortunes, however, stem just as much from her failures to accurately interpret *non*verbal communication. While the unctuous Mr. Elton is persistently sending signals of erotic attraction Emma's way, for example, Emma, "too busy and eager in her own previous conceptions," just as persistently interprets them as directed toward her protégée, Harriet, failing entirely to "see him with clear vision" (93). Her brother-in-law John Knightley, to the contrary, impartially observes and readily interprets the nonverbal clues broadcast by Elton when Emma offers him a ride in her carriage: "Mr. Elton was to go, and never had his broad face expressed more pleasure than at this moment; never had his smile been stronger; nor his eyes more exulting than when he looked at her" (93). Intoxicated by his own desires, Elton in turn fails to read Emma's increasingly desperate signals once his amorous and unwanted attentions become too direct even for her to miss, and she darts him "such a look as she thought must restore him to his senses" (105). No such luck. When Emma tells him explicitly that his attentions have been directed at Harriet, Elton stubbornly insists that Emma's face-reading abilities can't possibly have failed so spectacularly: "No! I am sure you have *seen* and understood me" (emphasis added). And when Emma proves too shocked to reply, Elton adds, insidiously, "Charming Miss Woodhouse! allow me to interpret this interesting silence. It confesses that you have long understood me" (109–10). Like Baillie's Count Basil, the clergyman Elton simply does not know how to read the women around him.

In contrast to Emma and Elton, several characters in the novel prove quite reliable in reading the natural language of expression. John Knightley shares this ability with his elder brother George, "Mr. Knightley," who emerges by the novel's conclusion as its unlikely hero and Emma's true love. Neither Knightley brother can match, however, the almost unsettling proficiency in this regard of the dashing Frank Churchill, who secretly courts Emma's rival, Jane Fairfax, under cover of erotic interest in Emma herself. Frank's delicate (and duplicitous) situation demands that he constantly dissimulate his own emotions and intentions while closely monitoring the bodily signs of these in others. Perhaps the most striking instance of Frank's prowess, a display that at the same time is his near undoing, takes place during a dinner party that Emma herself considers one extended, tricky exercise in social cognition, "judging" Frank's intentions toward herself from his "manners," especially "towards herself," and deliberating on "what the observations of all those might be" who are seeing her and Frank together in a charged social situation (176). Frank's true love interest, Jane, has recently received the gift of a piano, its anonymous donor soon becoming the talk of the evening, and Frank puts his own theory of facial expressions to use in encouraging Emma to suspect the worst of Mr. Dixon, Jane's alleged admirer though a married man. "Why do you smile?" Emma asks Frank, who responds, "I smile because you smile, and shall probably suspect whatever I find you suspect" (179). His most convincing facial expression—the "conviction seemed real," Emma thinks; "he looked as if he felt it"—accompanies his statement that, seemingly persuaded by Emma's suspicions, he can "see [the piano] in no other light than as an offering of love" (181). Clever Frank: he has secretly given his beloved Jane the piano himself and can recruit a genuine expression of "conviction" to accompany his deceptive remark.

Frank does overreach himself, or nearly. Lovestruck underneath his cool demeanor, he can't stop himself from gazing in Jane's direction at least once, and Emma catches him in the act, asking rather pointedly, "What is the matter?" "I believe I have been very rude," Frank replies, scrambling for time. "But really Miss Fairfax has done her hair in so odd a way—so very odd a way—that I cannot keep my eyes from her. I never saw anything so outrée!" Back in control, Frank claims he will now go and "quiz" (tease) Jane about her hair, adding something about Mr. Dixon to boot, and invites Emma to read Jane's face as he does so: "And you shall see how she takes it;—whether she colours." But when Emma tries to do so, she finds her view of Jane blocked, inconveniently enough, by Frank himself, who "had improvidently placed himself exactly between them, exactly in front of Miss Fairfax, she could distinguish nothing," leaving himself free to exchange rather different looks with his clandestine lover than those advertised (184). Here Frank, or rather Austen, has made the social significance of facial expressions and their interpretation salient precisely by short-circuiting Emma's attempt at gauging her rival's feelings from their bodily signs.

Taking Baillie's neurocultural approach to facial expression a step further, Austen shows throughout *Emma* that expressions are not only subject to display rules but can be hidden, feigned, or willfully misinterpreted. They can be made to bear false witness even when seeming to utter truths that cannot bear verbal expression, as when Frank uses meaningful looks to fan Emma's suspicions regarding Jane and Mr. Dixon: "You may *say* what you chuse," she tells him, as if on cue, "but your countenance testifies that your thoughts on this subject are very much like mine" (179). And yet the natural language of expression retains its value for all that and plays no little part in bringing Emma and Mr. Knightley together toward the end. A blush—the psychophysiological expression par excellence, as significant for Austen as for Keats—triggers one such moment of wordless rapprochement: "Emma's colour was heightened by this unjust praise; and with a smile, and shake of the head, which spoke much, she looked at Mr. Knightley.—It seemed as if there were an instantaneous impression in her favour, as if his eyes received the truth from her's, and all that had passed of good in her feelings were at once caught and honored" (317). Austen's romantic couples are known for their witty and eloquent verbal exchanges; their nonverbal exchanges can be more eloquent still.

Cognitive historicism, with its special interest in representations of minds and of mental behavior in the writings of earlier eras, contributes both to the history of science and to the practice of literary criticism. In demonstrating that Darwin's *Expression of the Emotions* represents not the beginning of facial expression theory but the culmination of a Romantic tradition going back to Bell and the Baillies, I hope to have provided the outlines not only of a more accurate historical account but of a more intriguing one. In particular, we can now see that Darwin both brought new questions, particularly in relation to the origin of specific expressions, to bear in this area and also, in equally crucial ways, *narrowed* the field of expression theory, especially in adopting a largely two-dimensional, painterly view of facial expression in contrast to the more holistic, three-dimensional and theatrical model of his Romantic-era predecessors. In addition, by situating what Darwin himself termed Bell's foundational work in Bell's own cultural environment, we can see how the "noble structure" he bequeathed to Darwin grew as much out of aesthetic as scientific speculation and practice. The literary and theatrical allusions, that is, along with the many references to painting and sculpture, are by no means incidental to Bell's work on expression. They are, rather, integral and testify to how much Bell owed to literature and to the graphic arts and to how his own thinking on facial expression converged with analogous ideas emerging from the literary practice of such writers as the dramatist Baillie, the poet Keats, and the novelist Austen.

Noting this convergence can make us in turn better readers of Romantic-era literary writing by encouraging us to notice and analyze the many moments in the literature of the period that attest to a deep interest in the bodily expression of emotion (such as the blush), in wordless communication (such as what are termed "knowing looks"), and in extrasemantic features of language (such as vocal tones and hitches or tremors in delivery). We can see that these are not isolated effects but rather form part of a culture-wide interest in such phenomena, one that cuts across the arts and sciences divide and that speaks to a much broader sense of social communication than literary critics, with their emphasis on verbal behaviors, generally consider. This is by no means to argue, however, that Baillie, Keats, or Austen were in some way "doing science" in their literary works (any more than the twenty-first-century cognitive historicist is attempting to create a "science of literature" in bringing cognitive and evolutionary interests to bear on the writings of the past). Instead, their very freedom from the rigors of experimental method, which characteristically chops complex behaviors into smaller, more manageable chunks in order to subject them to empirical investigation, allowed Bell's literary contemporaries to create a more complex and holistic picture of social communication than did Bell himself, one that, for example, anticipated the later interest of investigators like Ekman in the rules and the vagaries of the social display of emotion.

Representations of mind and of cognitive and emotional behavior in works of literature may prove most valuable, in other words, in their capacity to remind investigators—literary and scientific alike—of the larger picture of mental life, in all its complex interrelatedness. The field of facial expression, for example, cannot neatly be separated from the larger field of nonverbal social communication generally nor, as Bell insisted, from the seemingly opposed but in fact intimately related field of verbal communication. These areas in turn prove crucial to the study of folk psychology, or "theory of mind," and prove crucially relevant as well to studies of emotional and cognitive development in human infants and children. And behaviors dating back to early childhood—particularly the emergent and emotionally rich social relation between child and its primary caretaker(s)—may in turn provide templates not only for adult social and affective behavior but for that interesting subset of communicative behaviors that we term the "temporal arts" as well.[12] Literature, not least the great works of the past that literary scholars help to preserve, to explicate, and to keep vital, has much to offer the contemporary cognitive or neuroscientific researcher, just as the exciting and provocative work being undertaken in the mind and brain sciences has much to engage literary scholars. Perhaps a more integrated intellectual culture, such as that of the era of Bell, Keats, the Baillies, and Austen, is already beginning to emerge.

CHAPTER THREE

Making "Quite Anew"

Brain Modularity and Creativity

ELLEN SPOLSKY

In 1579 Sir Philip Sidney explained why poets are so exceptionally creative. The astronomer, the grammarian, the lawyer, and the historian all take "the works of nature" for their objects, but "only the poet," he insisted, "distaining to be tied to any such subjection, lifted up with the vigor of his own invention, doth grow in effect another Nature, in making things either better than Nature bringeth forth, or, *quite anew*, forms such as never were in nature" (108, emphasis added). Cultural theorists have not been impressed with this glorification. They return us to an earlier view of artists as craftsmen, like carpenters and jewelers. We are encouraged to understand that cultural products of all kinds—soap operas as well as grand operas—emerge from the interaction of artists with the material circumstances of their specific milieux. Works of art are indeed tied to "nature" they claim; their production owes more to the forms of the local culture than to unique and irrepressible genius.

If, however, we add some of the insights of cognitive science to this view of cultural construction, a more complex and interesting picture emerges, one in which we can see the power of context evoking rather than thwarting individual creativity. We would start by recognizing that culture itself is a product of human minds; people are apparently evolved to live in groups and to build the cultures they need to survive in a hostile world. Fortunately, human cultures are not inert but dynamic; they aren't marble-chambered museums through which intimidated neophytes walk silently, receiving impressions. A culture is more like a force field with no shelter from challenge, no permit for passivity. Like the rest of us, artists have no choice but to be engaged in our shared space. But, also like the rest of us, they have the chance to be active toolmakers. Particularly successful works of art, like other enabling innovations, are engines, not reflections, of culture. The most successful of them have the potential to bring audiences to new understanding.[1]

Recent cognitive studies, from explorations of the individual synapse to the claims of cognitive narratologists for a discursive psychology, endorse a view of human life within the material world as dynamic and relational rather than as static and hierarchical.[2] We are encouraged thereby to consider how works of art, broadly defined, might intervene in and redirect the life around them. Cognitive cultural criticism, then (putting the two together) asks what it is about human cognitive systems—how they have evolved and how they interrelate with the world outside the body including other people—that allows the artist, as Sidney claimed, to make something "quite anew." Since reciprocity is the key concept here, we also want to ask how cognitive and cultural processes allow audiences to recognize and understand something new and then use that new understanding, at least occasionally, to renew the world around them. Seeing stories and paintings as artifacts on a par with arrowheads and antibiotics rather than as messengers from a privileged if useless aesthetic realm prompts us to investigate the hypothesis that the work of artists has work to do. Using Raphael's *Transfiguration* of 1520 as an example, I argue that this great Renaissance artist's innovation was to re-present a situation that was counterintuitive—that a man could simultaneously appear as a god—in a way that made it possible for the specific community in which he worked to understand and accept. Raphael was able to suggest a way of bridging the gap between the categories of humanity and divinity (established as distinct for most people) by changing the mode of presentation from the language of the gospel text to painting. By using some new artistic techniques and reusing some others, by involving additional sense modalities, and by painting a second scene to help interpret the first, he recategorized the problem as something more familiar to his audiences. His novel recategorization, as I describe it here, achieved its goal because different modalities of representation—texts and pictures, in this case—are able to teach different things by recruiting different modalities of sensory understanding.

The description I offer of how Raphael created something new is based on the centrality of categorization processes to human cognition and on the hypothesis that categorization is achieved by the work of a modular brain. I argue here that describing the artistic challenge Raphael faced in terms of these two concepts allows us to retain our conviction that some artists are especially and admirably creative—that they make poems, stories, and pictures "quite anew" for new purposes—even as we understand art as normal work in the sense that it is inextricably enmeshed in, and emerges from, daily material life. I also suggest how audiences can understand the innovation and why they may find it satisfying.

The Modular Mind

In my book, *Gaps in Nature: Literary Interpretation and the Modular Mind,* I recruited for literary service the theory that human cognition is enabled by a collection of specialist sensory intake modules, each of which does a different job, each of which is responsive to a different kind of energy in the world. The sensory modules of vision, hearing, taste, touch, and smell and the proprioceptive system by which we sense the position of our body in space are the channels by which the individual mind in its genetic and historical individuality makes contact with the sun and moon and with the shared cultural world that must be accommodated to the idiosyncratic. They allow the individual to negotiate a dynamic *modus vivendi* with that world, taking large parts of it into memory, storing it as general knowledge (the sun rises in the morning), and integrating it with autobiographical memories (a senior prom sunrise).[3]

These sensory interface systems are called modular because each accomplishes much of its work within its own domain. Any one module is relatively impenetrable (at least at early stages of processing) to information easily received in another: the skin can feel heat, but the ears cannot hear heat. The ears respond to the amplitude and intensity of sound waves, to which the eyes are indifferent.[4] Specific and as yet meaningless initial perceptions such as color contrasts, indications of relative motion, and the pressures of sound waves very soon join pathways with others and with memories of earlier experience to allow the construction of what feels to us like recognition and understanding. The configurations of neural connections produced by the sensory intake modules may be called maps, and the work of the sensory systems (continuing the metaphor) is to keep their maps updated and ready to be used in the production of larger pictures. In order to be useful to us, the different modules need to bring what they have learned separately into alignment, and thus the brain is constantly working, even while we sleep, to calibrate their various maps so that when we wake up we can take into account the weight and heat of a coffee mug as we lift it to our lips. Even after the maps are merged, however, and primary sensory data is joined with input from other sensory systems, some kinds of modular specificity are retained. For example, our understanding that a bird is flying overhead requires the integration of several kinds of visual and aural input, yet the angle at which the light rays first hit the two retinas, and the difference between the time a sound struck one eardrum and then the other must be preserved even after higher level (multimodular or nonmodular) processing so that the directionality of the bird's flight can be known.

Born with a starter set of neural connections, the infant gets right to work making improvements. Food, warmth, touch, and emotional satisfaction become associated, as the brain extends axons (the communicating parts of neurons) from one module or nucleus to neurons at other locations. The hours spent by infants reaching for what they see train their sensory and motor neurons in eye-hand coordination. As they watch people speak, even before they understand the words, they learn to understand how sounds and lip movements work together. Neuroscientists have been able to trace brain pathways shared by neurons that originate in different sensory modules and have also located specific multisensory neurons that do some of the linking work. The brain tests possibilities and grows new connections, organizing and reorganizing itself to be as useful as possible. Use strengthens connections, so that many daily tasks of sensory-motor coordination come to be performed automatically, allowing the brain to direct attention to newly interesting challenges and unexpected dangers. Plasticity and flexibility are important characteristics of healthy brains, because many early-built connections will not serve for a lifetime. Both the world and the body change. As babies' arms grow, the calculations about how they reach out have to be remade, as they learn how to grasp a cup and drink without spilling. Coordination is crucial, but there are many different kinds of connections, and they may be differently useful. Having stepped into the street and hearing loud honking, one needs to be able instantly to connect it to the bus coming into view and to step back up onto the curb. The brain wired to connect the noise only to the children's song about the wheels of the bus going round and round would be in trouble; humming instead of retreating would not be a good response.

Although the brain is always open for business, taking in new information and collating it with old, it isn't clear how or how well we distinguish different kinds of relevance in linking new to old, how memories can be labeled for relevance or survival value (and how they are sometimes mislabeled), or how those values are reset, although it's clear that they sometimes are.[5] Some of the continual readjustment happens slowly, becoming the accumulated wisdom of a lifetime. But my brain also needs to make moment by moment adjustments, keeping my leg muscles in possession of the latest information about the pavement and the curbs, so that I don't trip even while humming. In some instances the brain's achieved coordination is highly focused and, by excluding irrelevancies, produces extraordinary performance, as when a baseball player calculates the arc of a fly ball, runs toward it, arm stretched out with the right tension, and catches it at exactly the right moment. In some cases, achieved calibration is good enough, as when we feel for a cell phone in a pocket and extract it without knowing or needing to know which end of it we are grasping. In other situations, one may never achieve very good calibration, and the failure may not matter a lot, or it may matter quite a lot. Students of literature and art are interested in the unusual connections and also in the failures and mislabeling. If the bus reminds us of the song, it may induce a train of new, perhaps metaphorical, associations.[6]

Probably the most important tool our brains use in deciding which of the myriad stimuli in the environment are currently interesting is an already-in-place set of categories. It would be hard to overemphasize the importance of categorization in all high-level cognitive processes. Categorization is well described as a decision to treat a group of items that are not identical as if they were the same. To do so simplifies and thus speeds up all further cognitive processes of interpretation by predicting relevance: if it looks like a peach, is the size of peach, and smells like a peach, I can assume it also will taste like a peach.[7] From birth, our brains collect and sort stimuli into categories according to features that regularly co-occur in time and space. Is x edible? Is it satisfying? Is y animate, and if so, will it attack me? Will moving toward it satisfy or trouble me? The infant tests out categories (edible, animate, threatening) in as many modularities as possible. Once a set of categories is up and running, they can be refined by experience. A child learns the word "dog" and later to differentiate among collies, poodles, and beagles. Having long ago generalized the advantage of staying out of the way of large moving objects reflexively categorized as dangerous, one doesn't have to deliberate before stepping back onto the curb. It is clear why securely entrenched category boundaries are advantageous when quick response is crucial. These routine categorizations, however, can blind us to new information and can thus also be misleading or dangerous when circumstances change. We need our categorizations to be flexible and our minds able to devise or accept creative recategorizations so that no longer useful ways of understanding can be renovated as necessary.[8]

The Implications

Let me stop for a moment to make clear some of the implications of the description of mind and its development sketched here. Our brains, like the bodies of which they are part, are what biologists call open systems, meaning that they feed on stuff from outside themselves.[9] The brain's separate sensory modules collect information from the world and produce maps that need coordination. Because that outside stuff doesn't stay still for long, the maps our brains make are never finally or completely calibrated, and because categorizations only name approximations of similarity but never identity, they too are also always unstable. Because objects in the world may always be categorized in more than one way, categorization judgments are always relative to the context in which they are used. There are, thus, always discrepancies or gaps, and the brain is always working to catch up with itself. The gaps between sensory maps and the instabilities of categorizations are no more accidental than the brain's achieved connections. The dynamic that allows ongoing realignment is built into the system; it is the logical outcome of evolutionary development. The calibration of the sensory maps can never be complete, because if they could, the modules would lose their valuable distinctiveness. This situation is not a liability. It not only permits but encourages adaptation. Mismatches and gaps need corrective work; they beg interpretation. Artists take advantage of these gaps and instabilities to innovate, and as students of art and literature, it is worth our while to notice the gaps between brain maps before they are patched and to be alert to the potential recategorizations, as well, because it is there that the system's potential for self-renovation is uncovered.

Converging Evidence

The hypothesis that the gaps and miscategorizations within the cognitive system are productive is consistent with hypotheses drawn from the work of paleoarchaeologists on early hominid life. As they see it, the ability of exceptional members of a social group to be inventive and to produce changed interpretations and behaviors when the world outside their bodies became newly threatening was crucial for the survival of the species. According to current thinking, for example, periodic climate change in Africa in the Pleistocene age produced a progressively drier environment and one with greater seasonal change.[10] Those who survived the changes, it is thought, were not those hominids whose bodies could grow thicker fur or store water for longer periods. They were, rather, those whose brains allowed them to reconsider the material affordances of their environment. Those who could imagine controlling fire rather than being threatened by it were recategorizing and restructuring their sensory-motor systems to new work.

The cave paintings of Lascaux in France and the gigantic lamassu figures built at palace gates in Nimrud suggest that they were produced under a similar existential urgency; the galloping bison, painted larger than life, may have instructed and inspired huntsmen, and the Assyrian winged horse with a man's head was intended, as the inscription at its base tells us, to keep malign spirits away.[11] The traditional art historical distinction between "art" as "objects without any apparent mechanical use" and the spears and arrowheads we call tools may not have been one their creators would have made.[12] Our categorization today assumes that statues and wall paintings are less likely than efficient weaponry to bring home meat and keep enemies at bay. But recent reassessments of the power of ideological systems suggest that representations also act in the world by strengthening the confidence of hunters and rulers or by undermining the confidence of potential attackers. If the art didn't always perform as expected, neither did spears. The inconsistent results both produced might have encouraged the belief that both were equally necessary interventions, together responding to pressing problems in the immediate environment.

Further support for the claim that gaps encourage creative filling comes from the evolutionary psychologists Richard Byrne and Andrew Whiten, who have suggested that in the course of evolution, other people presented even greater challenges to human survival than harsh climates and predatory animals. If the enemy is not a force of nature or an animal but another human with a set of complex and partially inscrutable motives and intentions, then the game is no longer a contest of physical strength, and the power of the arrow decreases. The victory might now go to the better mind manipulator—that is, whoever could produce either a remarkably intimidating statue that convincingly threatened aggressors or a narrative that would successfully anticipate what other humans had in mind, especially if those intentions were hostile, and also teach generalizable lessons about anticipating other's intentions.[13]

In these several ways, we can see that an advantage would likely have gone to those who were able to make imaginative leaps over the gaps between what is and what might be. The different kinds of flexibility that have evolved, from automatic physiological change such as sweating to reduce bodily temperature, to conscious habit formation, and to culturally mediated learning from one's own experience and from the experience of others, are all ways of responding to the challenge of being human in the world. Even when the body itself and its gaps are the problem, the body (including the mind) is also the problem solver, itself evolved actively to seek satisfying solutions. An individual's body—both its physiological structures and its history—have together constructed habitual patterns of internal interaction and patterns of interaction between the body and the world. Not only is the body itself capable of self-reconstruction in the face of challenges, but some people, capitalizing on combinations of distinctive individual experience and fortuitous mutations, are able to do even better—surprisingly better—in ways that benefit their larger community. It is the argument of this chapter that redescribing a problem from another point of view, in another mode, or as a revised categorization judgment has often been a good way to begin rethinking a problem. Literature and art are part of the arsenal of tools that can change understanding, and these changes or reinterpretations may then mediate conflicts in ways that make cultural life more tolerable or more satisfying—maybe even more pleasant. These changes, moreover, are culturally heritable: they can and have changed the cultural environment in ways that give later generations a head start. Like the inheritance of money, a cultural inheritance may be an asset to future generations. Kim Sterelny suggests that stories are cultural capital: they are scaffolds we build for our children. He doesn't, however, consider the damage these legacies may do.

Theoretical Support for the Thesis

We may expand the claim that apparent misalignments or gaps and unstable categorizations stimulate change by referring to Chaim Perelman's assertion that what is widely agreed on literally goes without saying (8). We talk, rather, about misalignments, mistakes, misunderstandings, and miscalibrations. They may be threatening, or just interesting, or suggestive of change, but in any case they demand attention. They need to be discussed in words—perhaps narrated or dramatized on a stage—or they may be clarified by means of nonverbal representation, perhaps in painting or sculpture. Mary Louise Pratt describes as an essential feature of literary texts a "display-producing relevance," which she called tellability:

> Assertions whose relevance is tellability must represent a state of
> affairs that are held to be unusual, contrary to expectations, or other-
> wise problematic. . . . In making an assertion whose relevance is tel-
> lability, a speaker is not only reporting but also verbally *displaying* a
> state of affairs, inviting his addressee(s) to join him in contemplating
> it, evaluating it, and responding to it. His point is to produce in his
> hearers not only belief but also an imaginative and affective involve-
> ment in the state of affairs he is representing and an evaluative stance
> toward it. He intends them to share his wonder, amusement, terror, or
> admiration of the event. Ultimately....what he is after is an *interpreta-*
> *tion* of the problematic event, an assignment of meaning and value
> supported by the consensus of himself and his hearers.   (136)

Pratt's assumption is that the tellable is needy. Minimally, it is contrary to expectations, producing a mismatch or gap. It doesn't "go without saying," and it can't be interpreted or reacted to simply by calling up a memory of how the issue was managed in the past. It needs more and new consideration. There is a continuum of tellability, and thus of the need for gap filling. At one end are the implicit beliefs of a community that do not need renegotiation. Further toward the tellable end are problems that may be represented relatively easily and solved by ordinary (but nevertheless new) representation, as when one discusses with children where they must meet the school bus, asking them to imagine why they must stand on the curb until it stops. Some problems at the far end, however, may be so complex that it isn't at all obvious how they are to be represented (described, pictured). These are problems like those faced by European thinkers in the sixteenth century of whether the thousand-year-old religious beliefs and practices of a nation need to be reformed or changed; whether, for example, Christian churches should be adorned with narrative paintings and statues of saints, as they had been for centuries.[14] These problems, according to the cognitive philosopher, Andy Clark, are *representationally hungry*, and they demand feeding with a large amount of representation. Sermons and books then, like charts and newspapers now, functioned to display large amounts of new and difficult information for consideration. These problems are not just complex but also "unruly." Unruly problems, says Clark,

> are cases in which the cognitive system must selectively respond to states of affairs whose physical manifestations are wildly various— states of affairs that are unified at some rather abstract level, but whose physical correlates have little in common. Examples would include the ability to pick out all the valuable items in a room and the ability to reason about all and only the goods belonging to the Pope. . . . The successful agent must learn to treat inputs whose early encodings (at the sensory peripheries) are very different as calling for the same classification, or conversely, to treat inputs whose early encodings are very similar as calling for different classifications. . . . In these representation-hungry cases, the system must, it seems, create some kind of inner pattern, or process whose role is to stand in for the elusive state of affairs. (*BEING THERE,* 167–68)

Note the overlap among the three hypotheses about the sources of cognitive creativity presented so far. My notion of gaps between sensory modules and the instabilities of categorization, Pratt's suggestion that a situation is tellable when, because it is lacking in coherence or regularity, it evokes the cooperative efforts of audiences, and Clark's claim that for unruly issues greater representational resources must be expended all circle around the idea that a new representation arises from a lack. All are claims for a cognitive dynamic, one in which the instability itself actively begs attention. Furthermore, the objects that step forward as new representations are themselves generative. They offer themselves as affordances in complex and problematic situations.[15] The new representation, however, is not guaranteed to solve the problem; it may raise opposition and destabilize things further, as did new machinery in the industrial revolution and some of the more revolutionary works of English modernism, such as the novels of D. H. Lawrence, James Joyce, and Virginia Woolf. The claim cannot be, then, that these new representations are solutions, only that they may be efficacious as deconstructive tools, displaying misalignments and prompting the search for solutions.

How Does a Gappy and Unruly Display Work as a Tool? Raphael's *Transfiguration*

As we have noted, our modular cognitive systems respond to multiple kinds of information, and it is usually assumed that the more information one has the better. That more representation is better is only grossly true, however. In a situation in which calibrations and categorizations are only "good enough" but almost never precise or entirely stable, progress toward a solution of a complex issue may be stymied as small gaps accumulate and may become, for local political and/or ideological reasons, very important. Significant and stubbornly resistant conflicts may emerge, as they did, for example, in early modern Christianity, and then we might observe the work of particularly imaginative artists feeding a community facing a particularly hungry cognitive problem by re-representing the situation in a different modality.[16] A theological problem may be represented as a painting or a social or civic conflict may be dramatized on stage. The re-representation may afford revisionary understanding, although it may expose further problems at the same time. The work of the artist who can rearrange or re-represent a pressing social issue has made a tool out of a display, but, as Raphael's last painting, the *Transfiguration*, suggests, a fully satisfying solution may be elusive.

Highly successful in his own day and known for his influential innovations of style and technique, Raphael is considered by art historians to have solved, in this painting, the problem of how to represent for his audiences a man who was at the same time God and who was, at the very moment depicted, revealing his double nature. Although this mixed categorization (to give incarnation a cognitive name) has long been understood in theology as miraculous and thus highly tellable, miracles are also unruly problems and thus well described as representationally hungry. We know from contemporary sources that Raphael was a competitive innovator, working in Rome during the height of the creative revival of antique styles called the High Renaissance for patrons that included the popes Julius II and Leo X. The *Transfiguration* exemplifies both Raphael's successes and failures.

Both of the scenes depicted in the painting, one above the other, are unruly and tellable.[17] The Gospel according to Matthew 17:1–13 (also Mark 9:1–12 and Luke 9:28–36) relates them as miraculous. The main story is of Jesus's appearance before the Crucifixion, as God, to the disciples Peter, James, and John. The text provides the sensory signs by which the three are meant to understand what they see: (1) "His face did shine as the sun, and his raiment was white as the light"; (2) "There appeared unto them Moses and Elias [Elijah] talking with him"; (3) "While yet he spake, behold, a bright cloud overshadowed them"; and (4) "Behold a voice out of the cloud, which said, This is my beloved Son, in whom I am well pleased; hear ye him."[18] It asks its readers to behold not only the figure of Jesus transfigured and conversing with the prophets but also to imagine a bright cloud and hear the voice coming from it. The story nowhere describes Jesus as levitating, but Raphael's decision to portray him that way flaunts the miraculous, as a serious religious work should. Viewers are forced to recognize the world of the picture as one where normal rules are suspended. Raphael thus begins by increasing the unruliness of the story rather than lessening it. He then moves toward clarification of the categorization problem, which he does by presenting a second story below the first.

He takes advantage, for example, of our normal ways of understanding other peoples' intentions and thoughts by reading the meaning of others peoples' body postures, facial gestures, and hand gestures and analogizing them to our own and to those of others in the community. We do the same with the figure of Jesus, because he looks like a person.

Raphael, *The Transfiguration*, 1520. Pinacoteca, Vatican Museums, Vatican State. Scala/Art Resource, NY

One attaches meaning to Jesus's upturned eyes in the painting, because up is conventionally analogized as good.[19] We also draw on the familiar cultural convention that puts heaven, the dwelling place of God, above. From the combination we infer that the upturned eyes are turned toward the good. That Jesus is rising from the ground then, although it is surely odd, fits with the common categorization of up as good—a categorization that will also inform the audiences' understanding of the relationship of the two halves of the picture, upper and lower.

Note that this cognitive view encompasses rather than displaces the traditional descriptions of Raphael's original solutions to the representationally hungry problem of the gospel text. One art historian notes that the light and seemingly weightless body of Jesus with hands raised and looking up, the surrounding clouds, and the levitation communicate the interpretation that his human visible body is transfigured by the presence within it of the Holy Ghost.[20] Another suggests that his robes look as if they are made out of the sky itself.[21] The motif of levitation was copied through the eighteenth century, evidence that this solution was judged successful.

The painting was intended as an altarpiece, meant to function within the church liturgy as a reenactment of the transfiguration for latter-day Christians. It would, as John Shearman suggests, draw in the spectator to share the space and time of the event depicted, displaying to the priest, for example, the parallel between the miracle on the mountain and the miracle of the transubstantiation in his celebration of the mass, both unnatural category mixes. Raphael's success is due further to his decision to clarify the abstract doctrine of the transfiguration by coloring and positioning the three figures in the center of the upper scene in a relationship to each other that displays a miraculous defiance of gravity and the illusion of movement. The portrayal of the movement of their garments invites us to feel the stirring of the breeze and, together with the dance of the three, even suggests the music of the spheres.

Raphael was also audacious enough to attempt a visual paradox by including another unruly problem within his painting, and that is the story of an exorcism. Directly after the events of the transfiguration, the gospel tells that a young boy, a "lunatick, and sore vexed" (Matthew:17:15) is brought to Jesus, who "rebuked the devil . . . and the child was cured" (17:18). The lower scene includes two groups of figures, the nine unenlightened apostles on the left, all with twisted bodies and/or arms gesticulating, clearly "in the dark," awaiting the intervention of Jesus himself. Earlier artists who had combined the picture of the transfiguration with that of the boy, had always shown Jesus healing the boy. It was Raphael's innovation to show the failure of the apostles and only to imply what is explicit in the text, that Jesus will soon do the work they cannot do because they lack faith.[22] It is also surprising—but consistent with his presentation of the transfiguration as itself a solution to perplexed and needy humanity—that instead of placing the transfiguration in the foreground, Raphael puts it in the background to the scene of the possessed boy below it.

Marcia Hall offers further insights into the formal and thematic contrasts that Raphael exploits. She claims that Raphael learned from the humanists' studies of rhetoric that different subjects should be treated differently and that based on that he developed a practice of symbolic color modes. Here, for example, the painter paints the celestial sphere with lighter colors, in the *unione* mode. Hall describes that mode as "striving to create a flowing unity among the figures, connecting them in a melodious harmony" (6). The terrestrial world below, in contrast, is painted in chiaroscuro with darker colors, suggesting its ignorance and confusion. Having found, in earlier paintings, that these distinctions of modality had an expressive advantage, Hall notes, Raphael decided in this picture to use the two modes together, for this unusually complex task.

What the Cognitive Perspective Adds

In light of the importance of categorization to human understanding, I would suggest that Raphael's decision to show the suffering rather than the healed boy allowed Christians think of transfiguration as a kind of "possession." He presents his audiences with a category analogy that allows them to understand the god-possessed Jesus as the heavenly opposite of something they already understand, namely demonic possession. The contrast is between the light, serene figure above, who is united with the greatest of spirits and looking toward God, and the poor boy possessed by the devil, who tries (he stretches out an arm and raises his head) to see God but cannot even control the direction of his eyes. Jesus's legs dangle comfortably, but the boy's are twisted awkwardly, and he has to be supported. One is clothed in "sky," the other in a garment inadequate even to the task of covering his tortured torso. Jesus's companions look at him admiringly; the people with the boy, on the other hand, look not at him but at the apostles, five of whose faces peer helplessly at the boy. The boy, of course, is not the center of the lower scene, which is tellingly empty.

A cognitive view also lets us see that Raphael does not do so well in re-representing the central problem of the text, namely, how one can understand divinity, mixed or unmixed with humanity, through the merely human resources of the senses. Neither the text nor the painting represents the issue in a fully satisfying way, as is evident from the difficulties of the three apostles who, as the text tells, "fell on their face and were sore afraid" (17:6). They cover their eyes in fear at the exact moment of the revelation they have been brought to witness. By showing two of the apostles shielding their eyes with their hands and the third falling to the ground covering his eyes, Raphael suggests the overwhelming power of the supernatural light signifying the divinity of Jesus. But at the same time he indicates that the revelation is too powerful for mere men, who if they cannot look cannot learn by looking. They are, thus, distinguished from the prophets and even from the two onlookers at the left. The question arises then of why the three apostles on the mount are more privileged than the group below. The text thinks they are, but their double function in the painting, needing both to witness the divinity of Jesus and to learn of it by seeing, confuses rather than clarifies the issue. Those below, unknowing and confused, all have their eyes opened. We must conclude, then, than when a picture illustrates a text, the change of modality mostly helps, yet even Raphael was not able to use human seeing to indicate knowing unambiguously. Though the text assumes the apostles do learn what they are meant to, it also concedes, by adding the voice of God, the difficulty of expecting people to understand on the sole basis of what they see. Painting offers no such voice and so is forced to picture the disciples with their only human senses as failing to see the revelation.

The Evidence of Modularity in the Success and Failure of the Painting

As one sense can't entirely map all that is known by another, so in turning a narrative into a picture, Raphael offered a different kind of knowledge at the cost of what could be said but not depicted. His great success was to home in on the basic cognitive need of his viewers for an understandable categorization. He was able, as we have seen, to re-represent the difficulty of knowing the mixed category of man/god brilliantly and originally by borrowing from other painters, by turning humanist theories of relativity into color and form, and, crucially, by speaking to the powerful human need for categorizing information by painting two scenes in which two contrasting kinds of possession are pictured. Both Raphael's success and failure are not surprising given what we know about human cognitive modalities, namely that they overlap, but not entirely. And it's just as well: we can't easily be fooled into confusing a Grecian urn with a poem about one. We have evolved a powerful capacity for transfiguration ourselves, that is, for closing gaps by, among other things, redescribing categories, but our successive or parallel mappings are never complete translations because they couldn't be. Yet the skills of even the greatest re-representers are not up to all the problems people can imagine—such as the need to understand how divinity and humanity might be combined. If the theological issues of Raphael's day no longer demand resolution, other problems push at the boundaries of our cognitive capabilities. The twenty-first-century version of the problem of how divinity and material humanity are mixed is the problem Descartes struggled with, now called the problem of consciousness: what is it and how does the material body produce it? Now we ask scientists, not priests, poets, or philosophers, to represent and resolve this issue, so far with many words and small success.

Conclusions

Rephrasing the discussion of Raphael's achievement in the cognitive language of modularity and categorization produces a new understanding of the work of the famous painting that adds to rather than contradicts the familiar theological and art-historical interpretations. The painting is itself a revelation of the nature of transfiguration, or of paradox, the figure below explaining the event above by displaying its inverse. His two male figures illustrate the two sides of the mixed categorization: *in bono* and *in malo*. Raphael has emphasized the parallel by clothing them both in similar shades of blue.[23] While Jesus the son of Joseph is possessed by God, the poor boy—just as human—is possessed by the devil. The exorcism of the text that had been read as something that occurs chronologically after the incident on Mt. Tabor is, in the picture, revealed to be its moral inverse. The painting has not, then, quite re-represented the gospel story, but it has managed, because of its medium, to produce an understanding that was not easily available in the sequential narrative. In representing two events as simultaneous, the picture, however, makes the story of the possessed boy not just another example of Jesus's power to work miracles but also a representation of the transfiguration or the mixed categorization understood at an even higher level of generalization. It is, here, a representation of the redemption of all Christians from the possession of the devil.

The grounding cognitive hypothesis is that the primary sensory modules collect and map representations, which then contribute to the construction of higher level understanding. The categories produced by the confluence of sense data allow the brain to make the distinctions needed to get through the day's cognitive work. Because the world doesn't stay still, the result of which is that its categories are permanently unstable, our brains revise categories creatively, that is, in ways "quite anew," when the old ones are no longer satisfying. The research question for cognitive cultural studies is not how one being can be both man and god, and not only how Raphael understood the answer to the question, but rather, how the obsolescent categories in our human minds can be renewed by an artifact—a two-dimensional colored surface. The innovative artist, I conclude, responsive to the environment he shares with his audiences— that force field in which they are mutually engaged—discovers how to take advantage of the way people already know how to know. Cognitive language allows us to offer a novel explanation for the long-recognized success of the painting in the claim that Raphael found a way to help his audiences to new understanding by calling on their visual knowledge and also by appealing to their supersensory need for category stability. He helped them visualize the difficult idea of transfiguration. The idea was difficult because it was a category mix and also because it was an abstraction, meaning that there was no object in the world that could be called up as a visual memory when the word was mentioned. Taking advantage of the way in which knowledge from one module is different from that of the others but can be partially mapped onto others, Raphael made the abstract idea of transfiguration easily visualizable (easy once he showed how to do it) as a contrast between two kinds of possession, possession being something much more familiar to his audiences than transfiguration. I would claim, then, finally, that the preceding cognitive discussion displays Raphael's creativity not as a response to a challenge presented by Neoplatonic theology, the art of painting, or the culture of Renaissance Italy but as a response to a challenge presented by the evolved brain itself, that is, by the human need for multiple and variable ways of understanding within their local cultural envelopes. And so we are returned to historical criticism, needing to investigate how sixteenth-century Europeans misunderstood epilepsy in a way that permitted their understanding of transfiguration.

CHAPTER FOUR

Analogy, Metaphor, and the New Science

Cognitive Science and Early Modern Epistemology

MARY THOMAS CRANE

Some of the most fruitful insights that cognitive science has provided to literary and cultural critics have been those centered on metaphor and analogy. The work of George Lakoff and Mark Johnson, who argue that all thought and language are fundamentally metaphoric, has altered the traditional literary critical view that metaphor is a feature of specialized literary language.[1] Lakoff and Johnson have shown how conceptual metaphors, extended from the basic kinesthetic and spatial experiences of living in the human body and mapped onto abstract concepts, structure our thought and language in fundamental ways. A number of critics have charted the presence of these conceptual metaphors in literary works, and the literature of early modern England has seemed especially suited for such readings: my book *Shakespeare's Brain* is one example.[2] These readings have, for the most part, focused on literary works by Shakespeare and other authors and not on their larger cultural context.

I believe that cognitive studies of metaphor, analogy, and conceptual change can help us shed light on early modern English literary texts and also on the culture in which they were produced, providing new insights into the epistemological changes that accompanied, and made possible, the "scientific revolution" of the seventeenth century. One of the most important historical narratives about the early modern period in England involves the shift from an essentially medieval "world picture" dominant through the sixteenth century to the incipient modernity of the new science that began its ascendance in the seventeenth century. The "New Science" is largely associated with the discoveries of Nicolaus Copernicus (1473–1543), Galileo Galilei (1564–42), Johannes Kepler (1571–1630), Robert Boyle (1627–91), and Sir Isaac Newton (1642–1727). In the second half of the twentieth century, accounts of this epochal change focused on epistemology and intellectual history but have more recently shifted to a preoccupation with the social and political implications of the change.[3] Whatever the emphasis, these accounts share a basic plotline: that by the middle of the seventeenth century, a traditional view of the natural world based on the authority of ancient writers gave way to the rational, empirical, mathematical approach that characterizes modern science. Ideas about astronomy, mechanics, and the composition of matter underwent the most radical transformation, as the old geocentric, deeply hierarchical, and closely interlinked cosmos gave way to a heliocentric and mechanistic one. Analogy (or what E. M. W. Tillyard called "correspondence" and Foucault called, more broadly, "resemblance") plays a large role in this narrative, since historians of ideas have argued that it functioned as the central structuring mechanism of the old epistemological system but was replaced, in the seventeenth century by, variously, "identity," "difference," or "mechanism," depending on who is telling the story (Tillyard, 83–100). "Resemblance," in the words of Michel Foucault, "relinquish[ed] its relation with knowledge" and "disappear[ed], in part at least, from the sphere of cognition" (17).

Contemporary cognitive science offers insights into metaphor, analogy, and human thought that have the potential to radically change our view of the early modern scientific revolution.[4] If, as Lakoff and Johnson have argued, all human thought is built up metaphorically from the basic kinesthetic experiences of living in a body, no scientific system could dispense completely with analogy. Analogy didn't disappear from the realm of cognition in the seventeenth century, as Foucault and others have argued, but became more important, albeit in altered form. An older system of correspondences based on the perception of shared qualities (like heat, cold, and density) gave way to a use of analogy to convey the structural relationships among things that were qualitatively different (like tiny invisible atoms making up what appears to be a solid surface).[5] In addition, cognitive studies of "naïve," or "intuitive," science and of the nature of conceptual change allow us to understand how the transition to the new science drove a wedge between scientists and nonscientists that had never existed before. Cognitive science helps us to grasp the implications of the scientific revolution for ordinary (nonscientific) thought and language in new ways, as everyday experience of the natural world was severed from scientific explanations of it, and ordinary people could no longer trust their experience of the world to reveal the truth about its nature. Finally, a recognition of the difference between qualitative and structural analogies can help us understand the change in poetic language from the sixteenth to the seventeenth centuries, and I'll use a famous example from John Donne—the "stiffe twin compasses"—to illustrate this change.

In characterizing the analogical system of the Middle Ages and earlier Renaissance, critics have always tended to marvel at its strangeness. Ideas like the correspondences or analogies drawn between the microcosm of the human body and macrocosm of the universe, extending to parallels between the four elements and four humors (blood and air, black bile and earth, yellow bile and fire, phlegm and water), seem far fetched today. Tillyard commented that "much of the doctrine cannot but appear remote and ingenuous to the modern mind, which is quite unmoved by the numerical jugglings and the fantastical equivalences that delighted earlier generations" (84). Critics following Foucault have also tended to view the Renaissance system of analogies as having a primarily regulatory function, working to support the system of hierarchies—the "great chain of being"—that structured the universe. As Jonathan Sawday has put it, "Within this world [of resemblance] the body lay entangled within a web of enclosing patterns of repetition" (23)

It's worth beginning, then, by remembering why the Aristotelian theories of the natural world that were still dominant in England through the sixteenth century relied so heavily on their own particular version of analogy.[6] They did so because Aristotelian science was, in the words of E. J. Dijksterhuis, "formed by the things we perceive by the senses; all knowledge we can acquire of them ultimately originates in sense-perceptions." Aristotle "wished to evolve a physical science of qualities, in which material bearers of properties were therefore regarded as explanatory principles" (18). Much ancient science, in other words, read back from observable phenomena to posit the invisible causes of things, constructing an analogical connection between them in which analogy represented a cause or an identity. Aristotelian science constructs its theory of the composition of matter from its sensible qualities and behavior; cold, hot, moist, dry. It constructs its mechanics from observations of the movement of objects in space. It accepts the Ptolemaic universe because the sun and planets appear to revolve around the earth. These sciences, then, explain what they cannot see or feel by analogy with what they can directly experience; however, what we recognize as analogy (one thing resembles another) they assumed to represent a direct material or causal linkage: if matter appeared to be dry, dryness must be its essential property, so it must therefore be largely composed of "earth." This basis of explanation in analogy was then logically extended to construct theories that linked the causes of all observable phenomena with each other: microcosm must mirror macrocosm because both exhibit the same visible qualities, which must therefore have the same material causes.

The Aristotelian system did a good job of explaining the constants in nature, but it could not easily account for change: if substances are defined by their qualities, and the primary quality of a liquid is its watery nature, why does it change into ice or steam, which have completely different qualities?[7] As Stephen Toulmin and June Goodfield put it, "Any theory of the natural world must have two contrasted features: it must *both* give an account of the unchanging ingredients of things *and* explain how those unchanging ingredients can give rise to the changing flux we perceive" (47). Some rival schools of natural philosophy in the ancient world formulated theories of atomism to better account for change. According to this paradigm, the world is composed of tiny, indivisible particles and the interactions of these particles: the distances between them, their collisions and attraction, cause the changing properties of matter. Water is sometimes liquid and sometimes solid because its atoms can arrange themselves differently under different circumstances.[8] Aristotelian theories of matter, however, won out over atomic theories in classical antiquity and were dominant until the late sixteenth century, when some European thinkers turned once again to an atomic theory of matter as a way to explain change.

Aristotle's account of motion was also firmly based in ordinary observed experience and similarly unable to deal with change. As Steven Shapin suggests, Aristotelians conceived of motion in terms of the observed, qualitative nature of objects: "Bodies naturally moved so as to fulfill their natures, to move toward where it was natural for them to be" (29). Solid objects fall because it is their nature to seek the center of things; fire rises because it is in the nature of fire to seek the heavens. Aristotelian mechanics held that the weight of an object is a property of the object itself and determines the rate at which it falls. As Nancy Nersessian has argued, this theory fails to explain "how an object continues in its motion after it has been separated from the source of its motion," making it a "subproblem of the problems concerning the nature of change" that was resolved only after Galileo and Newton came up with "an inertial representation of motion" ("Conceptual Change," 167).

Several researchers have suggested that the "naïve," or "intuitive," theories of motion that people develop based on their ordinary, kinesthetic experience of the world are very similar to Aristotelian and medieval theories of motion and sharply at odds with Newtonian mechanics.[9] John Clement has argued that the "motion implies a force" theory of mechanics that Galileo (as a precursor of Newton) was at pains to discredit is still widely held today and that it is probably "rooted in everyday perceptual-motor experiences like pushing and pulling objects"; as such, he suggests it belongs to our set of "deeply seated mental models in the form of physical intuitions that can be very compelling and resilient" (337). Michael McClosky's research has shown that even students who have completed a college-level physics course can still retain naïve concepts of motion at odds with the Newtonian mechanics taught in both high school and college courses (305–7).[10] Allan Harrison and David Treagust have similarly shown that intuitive theories of matter also make it difficult for students to understand atomic theory. These perceptually grounded mental models are clearly similar to the "conceptual metaphors" that George Lakoff and Mark Johnson see as structuring human thought and language. It isn't surprising, then, that several of Lakoff and Johnson's primary metaphors (through which sensorimotor experience is mapped onto subjective experience) are based in intuitive mechanics: "change is motion," "actions are self-propelled motions," "causes are physical forces" (*Philosophy*, 47, 52–53). To the extent that the new science of the seventeenth-century contradicted basic sensorimotor experience, it opened up a gap between nonscientists and nature that has never been closed.

Historians of science have realized, of course, that "the new philosophy assaulted common sense at a mundane as well as a cosmic level."[11] John Donne's famous lines have long been cited as providing evidence of this disturbance:

And new philosophy calls all in doubt,
The Element of fire is quite put out;
The sun is lost, and th'earth, and no mans wit
Can well direct him where to looke for it.
And freely men confesse that this world's spent,
When in the Planets and the Firmament
They seeke so many new; they see that this
Is crumbled out againe to his Atomies.

("THE FIRST ANNIVERSARY," ll. 205–13)

However, Lakoff and Johnson's insights about the centrality of concrete bodily experience to all human thought raise the stakes: if new theories explaining the structure of the cosmos, matter, and motion were at odds with ordinary embodied experience of these phenomena, then the scientific revolution marked an unprecedented separation between the very bases of cognition and the specialized technologies of scientific thought.[12] There have been many historical explanations for the origins of the feelings of isolation and fragmentation that characterize modernity, but I believe we can add to them this moment when our understanding of the world became counterintuitive.

Recognizing these deep-seated cognitive implications of the scientific revolution can provide insight into literary works from this period that are preoccupied with change, the insubstantiality of the material world, and the ramification of concepts like the void for human understanding of the nature of things: Shakespeare's *King Lear* comes to mind.[13] More generally, the widening gap between everyday observation of the world and scientific explanations of its workings made metaphor and analogy important in new ways, which also impacted literary language. If the causes of natural phenomena are no longer directly linked to their visible or sensible qualities, those causes can only be conceptualized by analogy with phenomena that can be seen or felt.

In some cases, of course, technology allowed scientists to see things that other people couldn't see, thus providing direct empirical evidence for new theories. However, it was not always easy for scientists to convince other people that what was seen through a telescope, for example, was an accurate reflection of reality. Elizabeth Spiller describes Galileo's attempts to persuade resistant observers to trust that his descriptions of what he had observed through a telescope reflected what was actually present in the heavens, even though they couldn't see any of it with the naked eye (101–2). Galileo provided an opportunity for doubters to look through his telescope at distant lettering on the Lateran Palace, so what they saw could be tested against a closer view. However, some of those observers refused to accept that the telescope was just as accurate in its view of the moon as it was of the palace. Galileo was essentially asserting an analogy between the verifiable telescopic view that could be seen on earth and what could be seen (but not verified by the naked eye) in the sky.[14]

The gap between everyday experience and scientific theory was even greater in the case of evolving theories of matter. There were no instruments available in the seventeenth century that could make atoms visible, and, in fact, experimental proof of the existence of atoms that provided information about their actual structure would not become available until the nineteenth century. The particulate theory of matter advocated by Robert Boyle and others sought to explain the observable qualities of matter as produced by the motion, size, and interconnections of the atoms (corpuscles, or particles) that constituted it.[15] Seventeenth-century atomic theory could better account for change than could Aristotelian theories of matter; for instance, the transformation of water into ice or steam made sense when explained as an alteration in the distance and nature of the bonds between atoms. But, as Shapin has suggested, "most practitioners [in seventeenth-century England] accepted that the corpuscular world was, and probably would forever remain, inaccessible to human vision . . . their physical truth could never be *proved* by sensory means" (50). The behavior of atoms could only be conceptualized by analogy with "visible and tangible phenomena" (50).

Nancy Nersessian has argued that the conceptual change from Aristotelian to Newtonian theories of motion similarly produced a greater role for structural analogy. Newtonian mechanics exists "only in mental models. For example, a Newtonian object is a point mass moving in an idealized Euclidean space" and has to be imagined by analogy with actual objects in real space ("Conceptual Change," 178). After Newton, motion was no longer conceived of as a property of objects but rather as a relation. As a result, there was a concomitant shift "from a concrete to an abstract representation" of movement in space (178). Like Dedre Gentner, Nersesssian emphasizes the important role of analogy in facilitating these abstract structural representations.

As many critics have noticed, the seventeenth century saw the increasing prominence of a new analogy for the workings of nature, that of a clockwork mechanism.[16] The mechanistic model of the universe was a necessary component of atomic theory, since the invisible movements and meshings of atoms could be imagined as working like the gears of a tiny machine to produce the visible properties of matter.[17] More importantly, the mechanistic analogy had a heuristic advantage over the previously dominant analogy that linked microcosm and macrocosm through their visible qualities, because the salient features of a mechanism are structural: attention is focused on ways in which the parts fit together and affect each other. A mechanistic atomic theory of matter thus enabled a crucial change in the role of analogy in scientific thought, a change identified by cognitive scientists as basic to conceptual change in modern science.

Qualitative analogy, however, still maintained an important role in the formulation and dissemination of scientific knowledge. Many writers and scientists continued to rely on qualitative analogies well into the seventeenth century, and many used both old and newer forms of analogy almost indiscriminately. Cognitive psychologists like Dedre Gentner and Michael Jeziorski have established the continuing role of what they call structural analogy in contemporary science, in teaching (where electricity, for instance, is explained by analogy with flowing water), and in discovery itself, as in Ernest Rutherford's ability to conceptualize the structure of a hydrogen atom by analogy with the structure of the solar system. In these instances, the analogy does not posit a qualitative or causal relationship (electricity isn't thought to look or feel like water or to be materially the same) but rather maps a system of relationships from a visible domain to an invisible one (the relationship between pressure and rate of flow makes water and electricity behave in similar ways).

Gentner and Jeziorski have argued that the seventeenth century marked a shift in the kind of analogy operative in scientific knowledge. They contrast with modern analogy as it appears in the writings of sixteenth-century alchemists, who took the Aristotelian system of correspondences to an extreme, equating analogy with identity, ascribing causal powers to analogy, and holding that even symbols did not just stand for their referents but were identical to them in essence (467). The alchemical symbol for gold, for example, was a circle, because both the circle and gold were considered to be perfect: the perfection of the symbol was thought to reflect in essence the perfection of its referent.

Writers like Robert Boyle and Johannes Kepler, on the other hand, evince what Gentner and Jeziorski call modern attitudes toward scientific analogy. Boyle, for instance, in his treatise *Of the Great Effects of Even Languid and Unheeded Local Motion* (1590), argued for an atomic theory of matter against "men [who] undervalue the motions of bodies too small to be visible or sensible." Because such small particles cannot be seen, they can only be understood through analogy with what is visible; on the other hand, Boyle breaks with tradition by asserting that the visible surface of matter doesn't directly reveal its composition of particles. He seeks to explain the nature of the particles by analogy with ants moving a large pile of their eggs and with the action of wind in trees. These analogies do not depend on essential similarity (he doesn't argue that the particles actually resemble ants), but, in the words of Gentner and Jeziorski, instead invoke "common relational systems" (462). Boyle can envision the way that invisibly small particles can cause large-scale effects by imagining the ability of ants to move a huge pile of eggs: the analogy reflects the structural relation of an accretion of small, individual actions. Kepler, similarly, advocates use of analogies in geometry, where, again, in the words of Gentner and Jeziorski, "the analogy is useful in virtue of its ability to capture common causal relations" (474) and not an essential identity.

The epistemological shift that accompanied the rise of the new sciences in the seventeenth century, then, did not bring to an end the use of analogy for scientific thought but rather gave rise to a change in the nature and uses of analogy in that context. This change, in turn, sheds light on what has traditionally been called the "metaphysical imagery" used by seventeenth-century writers such as John Donne. Perhaps the most common example of a metaphysical image is that of the "stiffe twin compasses" found in Donne's poem "A Valediction: Forbidding Mourning," where the speaker, attempting to reassure his lover about an impending separation, argues that even though their bodies will be apart, their souls will be connected like the feet of a compass. Critics like Marjorie Hope Nicolson tended to read early seventeenth-century poetic imagery as manifestations of the old analogical system. She reads Donne's famous "twin compasses," perhaps the archetypal metaphysical image, as a manifestation of the old analogy of "the circle of perfection": "More completely than in any other symbol in the universe, the Great Geometer had shown the intricate relationship of the three worlds in the repetition of the Circle of Perfection" (47). W. A. Murray drew a connection between Donne's "gold to airy thinness beat" and the compasses through the alchemical symbol for gold, a circle with a dot in the center, which Gentner and Jeziorski consider to be a prime example of the older version of qualitative analogy. Donne's compasses, in this reading, liken the love between the two to the perfect circles of gold and of the cosmos.

I think the image of the compasses makes more sense as an example of the newer style of structural analogy identified by Gentner and Jeziorski in the writings of seventeenth-century scientists like Boyle. Samuel Johnson famously derided these images consisting of "the most heterogeneous ideas . . . yoked by violence together," and his emphasis on the unlikeness of the two terms of the analogy seems prescient of Gentner's research (218).[18] Its quality of yoking together two unlike things (the souls of lovers and a mathematical instrument) is a function of the fact that it doesn't posit an essential similarity between the two terms but instead indicates only a structural relationship between two joined yet divided poles. The relationship of this image to the concept of circular perfection is therefore more complex than Murray realized.

As various critics have argued in different ways, the poem is in part about the relationship between body and soul, or, to rephrase this, between the sensible and the invisible. The speaker begins by likening his separation from his beloved to the separation of soul from body after death. However, he uses the analogy of the death of a virtuous man to argue that the process of separation is, or should be, itself invisible. He suggests that the process of making the invisible visible through analogy is problematic when he cautions that they should "melt, and make no noise,/No teare-floods, nor sigh-tempests move" (ll. 5–6) that would reflect their unseen inner feelings outwardly, the notion of outwardness here being hyperbolically linked to the larger scale of the macrocosm. The speaker refers to the traditional links between microcosm and macrocosm in a gently humorous way to suggest that the unseen should not always be made visible.

He then offers two different accounts of the relationship between his soul and his lover's, and each is represented by a different analogy. If their souls are united into one, they are like beaten gold. If they possess two separate but connected souls, they are like stiff twin compasses. By choosing two such different analogies, Donne highlights the fact that the analogies are not qualitative (because the gold and the compass are themselves so different) but instead structural (each represents a different relationship between the two souls). The differing materiality of the gold and the compasses is crucial here: although both have traditionally been associated with circular perfection, the emphasis in the poem is on the material process of creating the circle that represents it.

Jess Edwards has shown how early modern mathematics and geometry in particular were situated "in a vacillation *between* the ideal and the material." He traces forward from Neoplatonism a tradition in which mathematical figures such as the circle are merely "analogic props," "worldly analogies for existential primacy" (45). He argues that medieval and early modern mathematical thinkers, as we have seen, began to conflate analogy with reality, and to consider "triangle, circles, and so on . . . not just as metaphors for, or images of, the material inhabited by the ideal, but also as a third realm of being, and a stepping stone between the temporal and the absolute" (46). The mathematician Thomas Harriott, for instance, speculated that geometrical points were identical with the indivisible particles of atomic theory, a hypothesis that proved an obstacle to his progress in geometry. John Dee, in his preface to a 1570 edition of Euclid's *Elements of Geometry*, articulates the view that "thinges Mathematicall" represent a "third being" between the natural and the supernatural because they "are thinges immaterial and neverthelesse, by material thinges hable to be somewhat signified." He contrasts "pure geometrie," which can allow men to be "holpen and conducted to conceive, discourse, and conclude of thinges intellectuall, spirituall, eternall," with practical geometry, which is derived from true geometry and is "the Arte of Measuring Sensible magnitudes . . . by due applying of cumpasse, Rule, Squire, Yarde, Ell, Perch, Pole, Line, Gaging rod, (or such like instrumente)." The instruments of practical geometry are the means by which the invisible and immaterial forms of geometric truth take on visible, material reality. They are, that is, the means of constructing an analogy, which Dee's language reflects when he begins instructions for the practical use of geometry by physicians with "first describe a circle: whose diameter let be an inch."

The fact that Donne focuses on the compasses in the act of describing a circle rather than on the circle itself is thus highly significant. Rather than depicting the invisible circle of perfection, Donne shows the mechanical and imperfect *process* of representing it. John Freccero, in a 1963 essay on this poem, calls attention to a passage from one of Donne's sermons where he contrasts human life with eternal life: "This life is a Circle, made with a Compasse, that passes from point to point; That life is a Circle stamped with a print, endlesse, and perfect Circle as soon as it begins" (339). Freccero argues that Donne's circle in the poem "traces the emblem" of a union of body and soul "that cannot be perfect while it remains disembodied" (339). I would shift emphasis slightly to suggest that Donne's focus is on the process of creating an analogical relationship between visible and invisible, material and immaterial. In a poem about the incommensurability of the visible and invisible, Donne's speaker scorns human lovers whose experience of the insensible consists of analogy with physical qualities—"things which elemented it" (l. 16). In this poem, the speaker wittily applauds the disjunction between experiential reality and an invisible spiritual reality that lies beyond it. The soul cannot be understood as being qualitatively like the body but only as sharing a structural relation with it. The compasses are shown in the act of drawing a circle, and it is this process rather than the circle itself that conveys the structural relation.

Donne, of course, does sometimes rely on the older system of analogy, but I think his most striking "metaphysical" images participate in the new epistemology that I have been describing. Understanding analogy in science and literature from both cognitive and historical perspectives gives us a finer instrument for seeing how those images work. If we replace a dichotomy between resemblance and difference with a subtler understanding of the ways analogy wields both, we can better read the traces of earlier structures of thought wherever we find them.

CHAPTER FIVE

Lying Bodies of the Enlightenment

Theory of Mind and Cultural Historicism

LISA ZUNSHINE

"Creating an interaction" between cognitive psychology and literary criticism, writes Andrew Elfenbein, "requires constant, often skeptical translation across disciplinary boundaries" (484). Such translation becomes particularly challenging when one tries to negotiate between subfields within these disciplines, whose grounding assumptions are expected to be incompatible. For example, there is now a tradition of productive interdisciplinary exchange between discursive psychology and narrative theory, cognitive neuroscience and aesthetics, cognitive neuroscience and cognitive linguistics and cultural historicism, cognitive evolutionary psychology and ecocriticism, and conceptual mapping and postcolonial studies.[1] By contrast, cognitive evolutionary psychology and cultural historicism seem to be destined to remain at odds.[2] On the one hand, this is not surprising given the apparent conceptual gulf between viewing a particular behavior in the context of cognitive adaptations shaped by hundreds of thousands of years of evolution and viewing it as anchored firmly in a specific historical moment. On the other hand, a closer look suggests that there are areas of overlap between the two and that charting out those areas by using the navigation tools from both disciplines might yield distinct interpretive advantages.

I became aware of these advantages as I was trying to make sense of a paradox underlying the representation of liars in eighteenth-century English fiction. While teaching the novels of Defoe, Fielding, Richardson, and Burney, I noticed that these writers treat body language as a pointedly unreliable source of information about the person's true state of mind, and yet they obsessively turn to the body as a privileged source of such information. Moreover, their readers apparently are not expected to view such behavior as strange or illogical; in fact, they may even feel disappointed—as my students often do—when protagonists fail to pay attention to the liars' gestures and facial expressions. In other words, writers and readers seem to tacitly agree that the body is simultaneously a highly valuable and quite unreliable source of information. How does this tacit agreement emerge and why it is culturally sustained in spite of its obvious inconsistency? What did they all "know" so well in the eighteenth century that they didn't even have to discuss and could take for granted in their dual view of the body? And if we still "know" it now, how do we acquire this knowledge?

In trying to answer these questions, I eventually turned to research in cognitive evolutionary psychology dealing with theory of mind (i.e., our propensity to interpret observable behavior in terms of hidden mental states). This proved to be beneficial on several counts. First, it offered me a framework for theorizing the paradoxical double view of the body in novels ranging from Eliza Haywood's *Love in Excess* (1719–20) and Richardson's *Clarissa* (1747–48) to Fielding's *Tom Jones* (1749) and Thomas Holcroft's *Hugh Trevor* (1794). Second, it made me ask questions about contemporary nonfictional texts that I wouldn't have asked otherwise, leading me to trace new connections between different cultural discourses of the long eighteenth century. Third, it turned out to be highly compatible with current research in performance studies. This was particularly important for me because as a cognitive literary critic I think that it is a sign of strength in a cognitive approach when it turns out to be congruent with well-thought-through literary and cultural criticism, and I eagerly seize on instances of such compatibility. Given that the human mind in its numerous complex environments has been an object of study of literary critics for longer than it has been an object of study of cognitive scientists, I would, in fact, be suspicious of any cognitive reading so truly "original" that it could find no support in any of the existing critical paradigms.

The first part of this essay provides a brief overview of theory of mind, drawing on the work of evolutionary psychologists and cognitive neuroscientists. The second part spells out two key assumptions underlying my argument: first, that theory of mind is a "hungry" adaptation that constantly needs to process thoughts, feelings, and intentions, and, second, that the body occupies a perennially ambiguous position in relation to this cognitive hunger, figuring as both the best and the worst source of information about the mind. The third part shows how this ambiguity manifests itself in cultural narratives of *embodied transparency*, in which bodies are temporarily forced to function as direct conduits to mental states.[3] Here I use a selection of eighteenth-century English novels to show how narratives that depicted the body as a site of performance and deceit counterbalanced fictional narratives that portrayed the body as a reliable source of information about a person's mind. The fourth part considers passages from Siddons's *Practical Illustrations of Rhetorical Gesture and Action* (1807) and Austen's *Mansfield Park* (1814) that constructed convincing social contexts for representing different degrees of embodied transparency within the same narrative frame.

Theory of Mind

Theory of mind, also known as "mind reading," is a term used by cognitive psychologists and philosophers of mind to describe our ability to explain behavior in terms of underlying thoughts, feelings, desires, and intentions. We attribute states of mind to ourselves and others all the time. Our attributions are frequently incorrect, but, still, making them is the default way by which we construct and navigate our social environment. When theory of mind is impaired, as it is in varying degrees in the case of autism and schizophrenia, communication breaks down.

Note that the words "theory" in theory of mind and "reading" in mind reading are potentially misleading because they seem to imply that we attribute states of mind intentionally and consciously. In fact, it might be difficult for us to appreciate at this point just how much mind reading takes place on a level inaccessible to our consciousness. For it seems that while our perceptual systems "eagerly" register the information about people's bodies and their facial expressions, they do not necessarily make all that information available to us for our conscious interpretation. Think of the intriguing functioning of the so-called mirror neurons. Studies of imitation in monkeys and humans have discovered a "neural mirror system that demonstrates an internal correlation between the representations of perceptual and motor functionalities."[4] What this means is that "an action is understood when its observation causes the motor system of the observer to 'resonate.'" So when you observe someone else grasping a cup, the "same population of neurons that control the execution of grasping movements becomes active in [your own] motor areas."[5] At least on some level, your brain does not seem to distinguish between you doing something and a person that you observe doing it.

In other words, our neural circuits are powerfully attuned to the presence, behavior, and emotional display of other members of our species. This attunement begins early (since some form of it is already present in newborn infants) and takes numerous nuanced forms as we grow into our environment. We are intensely aware of the body language and facial expressions of other people, even if the full extent and significance of such awareness escape us. As social neuroscientists working with theory of mind speculate,

> [Mirror] neurons provide a neural mechanism that may be a critical component of imitation and our ability to represent the goals and intentions of others. Although the early functional imaging studies have mostly focused on understanding how we represent the *simple actions* of others . . . , recent articles have proposed that similar mechanisms are involved in understanding the *feelings and sensations* of others. . . . The growing interest in the phenomenon of empathy has led to the recent emergence of imaging studies investigating sympathetic or empathetic reactions in response to others making emotional facial expressions or telling sad versus neutral stories.
>
> (SINGER, WOLPERT, AND FIRTH, xv–xvi)[6]

Cognitive scientists have thus begun to enter the territory that has been extensively charted by philosophers and literary critics exploring mimesis (from Aristotle's *Poetics*, David Hume's "Of Tragedy," Erich Auerbach's *Mimesis,* and Walter Kauffmann's *Tragedy and Philosophy* to the recent rethinking of mimesis and performativity in the work of such scholars as Elin Diamond and Michael Taussig), phenomenology (such as George Butte's reintroduction of Maurice Merleau-Ponty into literary and film studies in *I Know That You Know That I Know*), and intentionality (such as Martha Nussbaum's critique of the tradition of correlating "an emotion and a discernible physical state").[7] Although the work on mirror neurons is still in an early stage, one can see exciting possibilities emerging at the intersection of traditionally humanistic research and the inquiry into the neural basis of interpersonal subjectivity. I find it particularly encouraging that the cultural critics who have already taken advantage of the work on mirror neurons and intentionality have done it in the context of a historicist approach.[8]

Two Underlying Assumptions

Let me now spell out two assumptions underlying the present argument. First, I think of our cognitive adaptations for mind reading as promiscuous, voracious, and proactive, their very condition of being a constant stimulation delivered either by direct interactions with other people or by imaginary approximations of such interactions (which include countless forms of representational art and narrative).

To clarify this point, it is useful to compare our adaptations for mind reading with our adaptations for seeing. Because our species evolved to take in so much information about our environment visually, we simply cannot help seeing once we open our eyes in the morning (unless, of course, our visual system is severely damaged), and the range of cultural practices grounded in the particularities of our system of visual adaptations is truly staggering. Similarly, as cognitive evolutionary psychologist Jesse M. Bering observes, after a certain age, people "cannot turn off their mind-reading skills even if they want to. All human actions are forevermore perceived to be the products of unobservable mental states, and every behavior, therefore, is subject to intense sociocognitive scrutiny" ("Existential Theory of Mind," 12). This means that although we are a far way off from grasping the full extent to which our lives are structured by our adaptations for mind reading, we should be prepared for the cultural effect of those adaptations proving to be just as profound and far ranging as that of being able to see.

The second assumption is a paradox. We perceive people's observable behavior as both a highly informative and at the same time quite unreliable source of information about their minds. This double perspective is fundamental and inescapable, and it informs all of our social life and cultural representations.

To begin to appreciate the power of this double perspective, consider the reason we remain suspicious of each other's body language. When I am speaking to you, you count on my registering information conveyed by your face, movements, and appearance. That is, you can't know what particular grin or shrug or tattoo I will notice and consider significant at a given moment (indeed, I don't know either). Our evolutionary past ensures, however, that you will intuitively expect me to "read" your body as indicative of your thoughts, desires, and intentions. Moreover, the same evolutionary past ensures that I intuitively know that you expect me to read your body in this fashion. This means that I have to constantly negotiate between trusting this or that bodily sign of yours more than another. If I put this negotiation in words—which will sound funny because we do *not* consciously articulate it to ourselves in such a fashion—it might go like this: "Did she smile because she liked what I said or because she wanted me to think that she liked what I said, or because she was thinking of how well she handled an argument yesterday, or was she thinking of something altogether unrelated?"

In other words, paradoxical as it may seem, we treat with caution the information about the person's state of mind inferred from our observation of her behavior and body language precisely because we can't help treating them as a highly valuable source of information about her mind—*and we both know it*. Because the body is *the* text that we read throughout our evolution as a social species, we are now stuck, for better or for worse, with cognitive adaptations that forcefully focus our attention on that particular text. (Nor would we want to completely distrust the body—our quick and far-from-perfect reading of each other is what gets us through the day.)

What all this adds up to is that we are in a bind. We have the hungry theory of mind that needs constant input in the form of observable behavior indicative of unobservable mental states. And we have the body that our theory of mind evolved to focus on in order to get that input. And that body—the object of our theory of mind's obsessive attention—is a privileged and, as such, potentially misleading source of information about the person's mental state.

Note how at this point the research on theory of mind complements our own discipline's insight about the body as a site of performance. Because we are drawn to each other's bodies in our quest to figure out each other's thoughts and intentions, we end up *performing* our bodies (not always consciously or successfully) so as to shape other people's perceptions of our mental states. A particular body thus can be viewed only as a time- and place-specific cultural construction—that is, as an attempt to influence others into perceiving it in a certain way.

Cognitive evolutionary research thus lends strong support to theorists in cultural studies who seek to expand the meaning of performativity, such as Joseph Roach, who argues that performance, "though it frequently makes references to theatricality as the most fecund metaphor for the social dimensions of social production, embraces a much wider range of human behaviors. Such behaviors may include what Michel de Certeau calls 'the practice of everyday life,' in which the role of spectator expands into that of participant" (46). Indeed, one point that work on theory of mind brings home forcefully is that our everyday mind reading turns each of us into a performer and a spectator, whether we are aware of it or not.

Mediating between cognitive evolutionary psychology and cultural studies thus has both interpretive and methodological implications. We can now analyze various cultural institutions and social practices as both reflecting our need to attribute intentionality *and* remaining subject to the instabilities inherent to our mind-reading processes. This analysis would amplify the view of Catherine Gallagher and Stephen Greenblatt that the body always "functions as a kind of 'spoiler,' . . . baffling or exceeding the ways in which it is represented" (15), by grounding this view in our evolutionary heritage. Because ours is a mind-reading and hence endlessly performative species, there is no lasting, reliable escape from the double perspective on the body.

But even as the research on theory of mind begins to explain why the body remains both a privileged and an unreliable source of information about the mind, what it cannot explain is why this double view manifests itself differently in different historical circumstances. This is where cultural critics come in with their expertise on specific social milieus, ideologies, aesthetic stakes, and personal histories.

Lying Bodies

Using the cognitive perspective outlined above, I can thus make two predictions about the treatment of the body in the Enlightenment. First, I can say that the desire to revalorize the body as the true source of information about a person's mind must have assumed different forms throughout the century. Second, I can say that these attempts at stabilizing the meaning of the body must have remained relatively short lived, unreliable, and open to subversion.

Note, however, that this dual claim can be applied to *any* period. Hence we need to draw on our knowledge of specific milieus, in my case, eighteenth-century England, to see what unique cultural forms such attempts to tame the body may take. Moreover, these forms do not emerge out of thin air (even if our cognitive heritage makes us particularly susceptible to casting about for sure ways to read the body); they have a concrete cultural history. And reconstructing that history necessarily takes one outside the immediate literary text or genre under consideration. A cultural historicist analysis is thus the logical continuation of an inquiry that has started with, and remains to a significant extent structured by, a cognitive claim.

Consider the "novels of amorous intrigue" of Aphra Behn, Delariviere Manley, and Eliza Haywood that depicted the torrid love affairs of English, French, and Italian aristocrats.[9] From a cognitive point of view, these novels create one specific context in which the body *can* have a reliably recognizable vocabulary. For example, when the protagonists of Haywood's *Love in Excess* fall in love, they can barely control their body language; their sighs, blushes, and confusion (66–67), their tears and ravings (155), and their trembling, panting, and raging (175) offer the reader a pleasurable fantasy in which every state of the amorous mind has its unmistakable bodily expression.

How transparent are those expressions to other characters in the novel? On some occasions they can certainly read these amorous bodies well enough. Thus when Count D'elmont looks into the eyes of his adored Melliora, he discovers there "what most he wished to find," for, as we learn,

> ambition, envy, hate, fear, or anger, every other passion that finds
> entrance in the soul, art and discretion may disguise, but love, tho' it
> may be feigned, can never be concealed; not only the eyes (those true
> and most perfect intelligencers of the heart) but every feature, every
> faculty betrays it! It fills the whole air of the person possest with it; it
> wanders round the mouth! plays in the voice! trembles in the accent!
> and shows it self in a thousand different, nameless ways! Even Mel-

liora's care to hide it, made it more apparent, and the transported D'elmont not considering . . . who might be a witness of his rapture, could not forbear catching her in his arms, and grasping her with an extasie, which *plainly* told her what his thoughts were.

(101; EMPHASIS ADDED)

The novel of amorous intrigue carefully foregrounds such moments, making them seem normative rather than exceptional: In the world of D'elmonts and Mellioras, bodies appear to speak *plainly*.

Still, the narrative repeatedly subverts this strong claim about the transparency of the body in love. *Love in Excess* features numerous situations in which male and female bodies traverse the alphabet of love—from blushing to weeping—but their interlocutors (often the objects of those passions) fail to interpret them correctly. Among such situations, I would like to single out one in which Violetta, another woman in love with the irresistible D'elmont, does the requisite amount of blushing (241) and grows pale, weeps, and faints (245), but because she is disguised as a male page, D'elmont remains oblivious to the meaning of her body language. Violetta's cross-dressing adventure feels both artificial and touching. It draws on the conventions of traditional romance, on Shakespeare's *Twelfth Night* and, to some degree, on the late seventeenth-century fashion of attending the theater masked and on the continuous popularity of masquerades. Still, note how this contrived plot turn is used to bolster the commonsensical intuition of the instability of our mind-reading practices. Ironically, the fancy vocabulary of the genre (disguises are common in the novel of amorous intrigue) is thus used to undercut the attempt to establish the "plain" vocabulary of the body.

What came to be known as the "sentimental" novel during the period between roughly 1740 and 1790 represents yet another endeavor to construct a context in which one can read and trust the body. Here, the emergence of the body as the direct conduit to the mind is accomplished by simultaneously elevating the observer and denigrating the spoken word. Samuel Richardson insisted in a private letter that "Air and Attention will shew Meaning beyond what Words can, to the Observing" (*Selected Letters*, 68). And indeed, in *Pamela* (1740), as John Mullan points out, "mutually affecting looks [awaken] contagious tears," and "attention to the meaning of looks and gestures" binds the members of a social group together. The focus on the body is powerful because it "punctures or interrupts [deceitful] speech" (61).

But no discourse that builds up the body as the portal to perfect mutual knowledge will remain unmolested for long. Richardson's next novel, *Clarissa*, features a heroine supremely attuned to the body language of her admirer but who fares much worse for her trust in these "wordless meanings." Clarissa's friend, Anna Howe, confesses, on getting Clarissa's account of what transpired between herself and Lovelace, that she cannot deduce Lovelace's intentions from his words ("What can the man mean?"), and so she implores her correspondent to be "vigilant" (451). Clarissa's "vigilance" centrally features her ability to interpret her amorous persecutor's gaze. "We are both great watchers of each other's eyes," she observes in reply to Anna (460).

Yet Clarissa pays a heavy price for reading people's hearts in their eyes. Here, for example, is Lovelace, begging "with a very serious air" for Clarissa's moral guidance and claiming that it is his "belief that a life of virtue can afford such pleasures, on reflection, as will be for ever blooming, for ever new!" We as readers may wince or snicker at his attempt to play the stereotypical role of reformed rake. Not so Clarissa. She is "agreeably surprised." She looks "at him . . . as if [she] doubted [her] ears and [her] eyes!—His features and aspect, however, [became] his words" (443). Clarissa gets the bodily testimony and falls for it. Poor dupe.

But what choice does she have, trapped as she is in a cultural discourse both dedicated to reclaiming the body as the portal to the mind and unable to shake off complications inherent to our mind-reading processes? Consider the protagonists of Fielding's *Tom Jones*, who do not share Clarissa's obsession with others' body language, and see if *they* fare any better. Fielding's novel contains a number of scenes in which the sympathetic protagonists fail to register the body language of various liars, the language that as the narrative teasingly implies can reveal those men's secrets, if only properly attended to. Of course, this teasing promise is false, but it gets the readers worked up about the certain lack of observation on the part of favorite characters who really *should* pay more attention to the facial expressions of the lying fiends who converse with them.

Think, for example, of Mr. Allworthy's heartfelt "sermon" about love as "the only foundation of happiness in a married state" (62) and Doctor

Blifil's attempts to refrain from laughing as he listens to the good man whom he and his infernal brother have just imposed on. We are told that it cost the doctor "some pains to preserve now and then a small discomposure of his muscles" (63), and we infer that Allworthy remains oblivious to these half-smothered facial contortions. Of course, one may suggest that Allworthy is smarter than he appears and that, in fact, he is at least partially aware of the doctor's double game, but it seems to me that such a generous take on Allworthy is the direct result of Fielding's manipulation of his audience. We are exasperated by Allworthy's failure to register the doctor's countenance: were he to pause, if only for a second, in the middle of his eloquent speech and take a closer look at the doctor's grimacing mug, surely he would intuit that something is wrong.

As a matter of fact, he wouldn't, for as we have already seen in *Clarissa*, "features and aspect" can be interpreted in a broad variety of ways. Still, note how assiduously the novel cultivates the view of the body as a potential bearer of true information even as it simultaneously undercuts this view.

Here is another, similar scene. During his journey to London, Tom comes across his old Gloucester acquaintance, Mr. Dowling, the lawyer, and the two men sit down to a bottle of wine. When Dowling learns of Tom's poor opinion of Blifil and tells Tom that "it is a pity such a person should inherit the great estate of your uncle Allworthy," Tom's reply makes it clear that he does not know about Bridget's deathbed confession. As Dowling listens to Tom's earnest professions that he has never thought himself entitled to any part of Allworthy's estate and realizes that the young man in front of him has been cheated out of his family and fortune, his body language displays both his shock and his discomfort at the thought of what a heinous crime he has been made an accomplice to. Of course, Dowling endeavors "to hide" his feelings from Jones "by winking, nodding, sneering, and grinning" (576), and, again, readers are made to feel frustrated by Tom's failure to notice the lawyer's strange body language and to ask himself what could have prompted it. The trap that Fielding prepares for his readers—and the one that we are only too ready to tumble into—is the illusion that by registering Dowling's body language Tom might have intuited something about the true state of affairs in his family, which is, of course, the same illusion that Anna Howe and Clarissa Harlowe share when they think that by vigilantly observing Lovelace's body language they will figure out his "real" thoughts and intentions.

We encounter a similar pattern of the body as both profoundly informative and profoundly misleading in Thomas Holcroft's novel *The Adventures of Hugh Trevor*. Holcroft's narrative prominently features the strange relationship between the idealistic young protagonist, Hugh Trevor, and a charming older man known to Trevor as Mr. Belmont and considered by him a good friend and an altogether "delightful companion" (223). In truth, however, Belmont is a fiend who has long lost his credit in the world and has to survive by adapting false identities and swindling trusting strangers. Earlier in the story, Belmont, using his real name, Wakefield, married Trevor's own widowed mother and proceeded to defraud her of all her money. He is now poised to lay claim on the rest of Trevor's inheritance, an endeavor that would leave Trevor completely destitute. Having never met his evil stepfather face-to-face, Trevor has no way of knowing that Belmont and Wakefield are the same person. He thus routinely shares with Belmont all news about Wakefield and discusses with him his plans to thwart the designs of the grasping villain, which, of course, has the effect of putting him even more in Wakefield's power.

During one such scene, "impatient to unburden [his] heart," Trevor hurries Belmont away from the gambling table, takes him to the park, and shows him the letter from his lawyer, which informs Trevor of Wakefield's new plans of defrauding him. As the false Belmont reads the letter, Trevor observes that he is "more than once violently tempted to laugh." As he hands the letter back to Trevor, Belmont is visibly "restraining his titillation," but the effort finally proves too difficult, and, unable to "contain himself" longer, he bursts "into a violent fit of laughter." Understandably astonished "at the mirth so ill placed and offensive," Trevor asks what it means (220–21). Belmont hastily invents an explanation that both misleads his young friend and makes him delighted with Belmont's "flow of spirits and raillery" (223).

Here, then, are questions that I had no way of answering (would you?) had I relied only on traditional theories available to literary critics and ignored the research on theory of mind: Why turn to that lying body again and again? Why pay attention to the language of the eyes? Why register that blushing cheek? Why feel disappointed when characters such as All-worthy or Tom fail to observe the strange facial contortions of Doctor Blifil and Lawyer Dowling? *Let* them ignore those contortions! Let Clarissa ignore Lovelace's "feature and aspect"! Let Hugh Trevor ignore Belmont's visible attempts to restrain his titillation! A protagonist might be better off blind, for registering those half-averted eyes, blushing cheeks, and strangely pursed mouths does not help him to realize that he is dealing with a liar; on the contrary, it makes him more vulnerable to the liar's subsequent crafty explanation of his involuntary "winking, nodding, sneering, and grinning."

The research on theory of mind thus helps me to make sense of the stubborn overprivileging of body language by eighteenth-century fictional protagonists as well as their readers. Their collective cultural experience (which included fictional narratives) no less than their daily social experience must have taught them to remain wary and to distrust appearances, but experience cannot *fully* override our cognitive propensity to "trust" the language of the eyes and of the body; it didn't then and it doesn't now. Nor would we really want experience to override it, given that people's bodies and facial expressions do speak to our minds and bodies in numerous ways, many of which we are not even aware of (as the research on "mirror neurons" demonstrates). Because our evolved cognitive repertoire includes adaptations that attribute mental states based on people's body language, we must constantly negotiate a path between our habitual recourse to that language and the realization that the body often deceives. The tension between our impulse to credit what we perceive and our hard-won skepticism regarding the truth of bodily display remains endlessly productive—a rich source of new representations and cultural renegotiations.[10]

But the story only begins here. True, I have now a provisional answer to my starting question about the paradoxical position of the body in eighteenth-century fiction: fictional narratives built on readers' daily mind-reading anxieties by forcing their protagonists (Clarissa, Tom Jones, Hugh Trevor) to rely on their interpretations of other people's bodies precisely at the moments when these people (Lovelace, Dowling, Belmont) were set to deceive them. Moreover, I can argue now that *Tom Jones, Clarissa,* and *Hugh Trevor* figured as counterpoints to ongoing novelistic attempts to construct the body as the true source of information about the mind. In other words, for every "plainly" speaking body from *Love in Excess, A Sentimental Journey* (1768), *The Man of Feeling* (1771), or *Mysteries of Udolpho* (1794) there is a deceiving body from *Tom Jones, Clarissa, Cecilia* (1782), *Hugh Trevor,* or *Pride and Prejudice* (1813). To adapt Greenblatt's much-quoted phrase, these latter novels reminded their readers that there is a plainly speaking body, no end to such wonderful transparency, only not for them.[11]

But eighteenth-century novels did more than just contrast lying and plainly speaking bodies. They also constructed continuums of embodied transparency, scenes that featured multiple characters *ranging* in their relative readability. And because the example that I consider below (Austen's *Mansfield Park*) evokes the stage in order to construct such a range, we must first see how the double view of the body manifested itself in the period's theatrical discourse.

Acting Bodies

In 1807, Henry Siddons published *Practical Illustrations of Rhetorical Gesture and Action,* a translation from German of Johann Jacob Engel's *Ideen zu einer Mimik* (1785), significantly revised to reflect the conventions of "the English drama." At one point, to illustrate what he calls "the communicative power of gesture" (36), Siddons treats the reader to the following scene:

> When a person sits at the theatre, after having seen a play acted three or four times, his mind naturally becomes vacant and inactive. If among the spectators he chances to recognize a youth, to whom the same is new, this object affords him, and many others, a more entertaining fund of observation than all that is going forward on the stage.
>
> This novice of an auditor, carried away by the illusion, imitates all he sees, even to the actions of the players, though in a mode less decisive. Without knowing what is going to be said, he is serious, or contented, according to the tone which the performers happen to take. His eyes become a mirror, faithfully reflecting the varying gestures of the several personages concerned.
>
> Ill humour, irony, anger, curiosity, contempt, in a word, all the

passions of the author are repeated in the lines of his countenance. This imitative picture is only interrupted whilst his proper sentiments, crossing exterior objects, seek for modes of expressing themselves.

(35–36)

What interests me in this scene is the implicit contrast between the "reality" of emotions as they are portrayed onstage and their mirroring by the unsophisticated observer. For note that nobody in this tableau apparently experiences the real feelings of "ill humour, irony, anger, curiosity [or] contempt." The actors merely put on a show of those emotions. The "youth" unselfconsciously mimics their body language, but does it mean that he is *really* angry or contemptuous at this point? I doubt it. However much I may fear and hate a psychopathic murderer from a movie, those feelings are *nothing* compared to what I would experience were I to encounter such a person in real life. In this respect, the body of Siddons's impressionable "youth" is as unreliable an index to his true feelings as the acting bodies on stage are to theirs.

However, this weak version of ill humor, irony, or anger is not *all* that animates our young man. He feels something else—and very deeply, too—and that something else is plainly written all over his body. *It is his engagement with what he sees on stage.* The smile of contempt that momentarily curls his lips as he watches the actress stare down the double-dealing villain thus expresses not so much any actual contempt on his part but rather his deep involvement with the performance: his complete surrender to the power of the actors.

If we focus on this particular aspect of the young man's feelings, it means that at least for the duration of this episode, his body language reflects his state of mind more accurately than the body language of the performers reflects their state of mind. He is completely taken by what happens on stage, and because he is not faking that state of deep emotional engagement for the benefit of the observer (for he does not know that he is being observed), his unpremeditated show of feelings becomes more engrossing for the theatergoer than the official show of feelings put on by the actors.

To understand what is at stake in the description of the hypothetical spectator attracted by the display of true feelings off the stage, let us take a brief look at the Enlightenment's obsession with the question of whether the actors really feel the emotions they portray. This obsession took different forms throughout the century. First, there were continuous debates about the effect that the regular displays of fear, hatred, treacherousness, or amorous dissipation must have on the moral characters of the actors. Thus the anonymous *The Advantages of Theatrical Entertainment Briefly Considered* (1772) expressed the enduring public suspicion that one cannot *embody* feelings and yet remain unaffected by them: "These gentlemen [actors] arrive at a pitch of virtue, to which few, who are employed in speculation, attain to: they reduce theory to practice. The delusive scenes of love exhibited on the stage are performed by them in real life."[12]

Samuel Johnson begged to differ. As he saw it, "If Garrick really believed himself to be that monster, Richard the Third, he deserved to be hanged every time he performed it." Roger Pickering steered a tentative middle course. While observing that "the Delicacy of Theatrical Expression can never be expected from an Actor that not *feel* his Part," he devoted most of his influential *Reflections upon Theatrical Expression in Tragedy* (1755) to "general instructions on the artificial management of the body and the voice."[13] Feeling the part might have been important but learning how to fake the feeling was a surer way to success.

Hence another aspect of eighteenth-century preoccupation with acting bodies: treatises on acting theory as a science, which compared the oratorical skills of actors and actresses with those of other professional speakers, such as lawyers, clergymen, and politicians. Traditionally grounded in the works of Quintilian (particularly his *Education of an Orator*, ca. 95 CE), publications on elocution and body language expanded throughout the century, coming to feature natural-philosophical discussions of representable passions as well as debates about the "natural" and "national" art of gesture. Siddons included sixty-nine illustrations in his book, ranging from drawings of "Pride" to "Obsequious Attention," to accompany his discussion of postures that presumably captured the essence of each passion, and he was working within a well-established tradition. We can trace this tradition to John Bulwer's *Chirologia; or, The Natural Language of the Hand* (1644), Charles Gildon's *The Life of Mr. Thomas Betterton* (1710), Samuel Foote's *A Treatise on Passions, So Far as They Are Regarded on Stage* (1747), Aaron Hill's *An Essay on the Art of Acting* (1753), Paul Hiffernan's *Dramatic Genius* (1770), Gilbert Austin's *Chironomia; or, A Treatise on Rhetorical Delivery* (1806), and many others.

Thus, if we want to deduce a consensus from the eighteenth-century publications on actors and acting, it would go like this. The gap between the body language of the performer and his or her true feelings can be large (Garrick *never* feels like Richard the Third!), negligible ("these gentlemen" cannot shake off their amorous stage selves even when they step out of their roles), or middling (actors should "feel" their parts, whatever that may mean), but *there is always a gap*. That's where Siddons is coming from, and if we look at his tableau again, we realize that he is additionally emphasizing the "fake" nature of the sentiment portrayed on stage by mentioning casually that this is the third or fourth time that the spectator is seeing the play. Surely, even if we envision an actress working herself up to burning with real "anger, curiosity, or contempt," realizing that she is doing it the fourth night in a row takes away some of our belief in the reality of her feelings.

Moreover, our "novice of an auditor" is not faking anything. There is no gap between his feeling enthralled by the play and his embodying that enthrallment. Note too, his tender age. Youth was sometimes foregrounded in discourses that created contexts in which emotions were transparent.[14] Coming back to the sentimental novel and its valiant attempts to carve a zone of certainty in our daily mind reading, witness the narrator of Rousseau's *Emile* (1762) explaining that parents and preceptors can successfully control young people if they unobtrusively observe their body language: "As long as the young man does not think of dissembling and has not yet learned how to do it, with every object one presents to him one sees in his manner, his eyes, and his gestures the impression it makes on him. One reads in his face all the movements of his soul. By dint of spying them out, one gets to be able to foresee them and finally to direct them" (226).

The voyeuristic pleasure of Siddons's experienced theatergoer is thus grounded in the eighteenth-century cultural discourses that constantly reweighed the relative emotional transparency of variously socially situated bodies. The paradigmatically suspect body on stage (moreover, one that has already been on that stage for quite a while—not the youngest body, perhaps) is contrasted with the young body that one can "spy out" and almost "direct," for the "youth" does not know what new emotion will convulse him in the coming second, while the observer, having seen the play three or four times, knows it quite well.

Siddons succeeds in building a compelling moment of embodied transparency in the least expected setting, the theater. Of course, this setting also ensures that the moment will not last: the "youth" is in thrall now, but the spell will be broken any second. The voyeuristic tableau thus plays with our double view of the body as the best and the worst source of information about the person's mind by teasing us with a vision of a highly readable body in an environment (i.e., the theater) that thrives on cultivating the gap between the body and the mind.

There is more to it, however. The theatrical setting allows Siddons to construct something like a continuum of embodied transparency. First, there is a body on stage, with its deliciously ambiguous discrepancy between actual feelings and their representation. Second, there is a "youth" in the audience whose body delivers direct access to his mind. Third, there is a pleasing (if not necessarily conscious) awareness on the part of the older spectator of his own mind-reading "connoisseurship": he can contemplate the difference between the clearly compelling (for the younger spectator is so taken by it!) portrayal of feelings on stage and the even more compelling portrayal of feelings in the audience. He decides which show of feeling to enjoy at a given moment, while he himself remains impervious to prying eyes. (Which is, of course, an ironic illusion, given that as he sits there savoring his position as an ultimate observer, the reader observes *him*.)

So perhaps it is not a coincidence that when a novel endeavors to construct a continuum of embodied transparency, it turns to theater. In *Mansfield Park*, when Sir Thomas comes back from Antigua in the middle of his children's rehearsals, there is a moment when he steps into the billiard room and finds "himself on the stage of a theatre, and opposed to a ranting young man"—Mr. Yates, who is going over his role. Tom Bertram enters at the same time "at the other end of the room" and just catches the expression of "solemnity and amazement" on his father's face and the "gradual metamorphosis of the impassioned Baron Wildenhaim into the well-bred and easy Mr. Yates," which all adds up to "such an exhibition, such a piece of true acting as [Tom] would not have lost upon any account" (164). Like Siddons's experienced theatergoer, Tom finds himself in the position of an observer who can appreciate the range of performed and real emotions—from Yates's ranting performance of the baron's anxiety followed by the assumption of the properly "easy" air of a gentleman to Sir Thomas's sincere surprise. Also, like Siddons's theater-goer, Tom—an avid and appreciative spectator—is himself observed by the reader.

It is not that Siddons and Austen were the first to discover the discursive territory that lies between the two apparent opposites, the bodies that lie (Lovelace, Dowling, and Belmont) and the bodies that speak "plainly" (Melliora and Emile): that territory had been charted out by treatises on decorum and performed social "sincerity," going back at least as early as *The English Theophrastus* (1702).[15] Their particular achievement was to construct compelling social contexts in which whole spectrums of embodied performativity were present simultaneously, in the same narrative "frame," so to speak.[16]

Staying within traditional disciplinary boundaries, we can consider this achievement either in "cognitive" terms (as particularly titillating to our theory of mind, ever primed to look for a correspondence between body language and state of mind) or in literary-historical terms (as opening a new, rich vein in the representation of fictional subjectivity).[17] However, as I have tried to demonstrate throughout my essay, there is no neat separation between the two: the cognitive, to borrow a phrase from Patrick Colm Hogan, is "instantiated variously, particularized in specific circumstances" ("Literary Universals," [chap. 1 in this volume]); the literary-historical derives its appeal from experimenting with the double view of the body, grounded in our cognitive evolutionary heritage, and constructing plausible contexts in which bodies appear legible or in which the conditions of their illegibility are specified (e.g., Garrick *pretends* to feel like Richard the Third; Yates *assumes* the air of a gentleman as befits his social class and education). But if the separation between the two approaches begins to feel forced, perhaps we should not insist on imposing it. After all, at least at this point, cognitive evolutionary psychology and cultural historicism engage with the same problem. To "translate" from studies in theory of mind "into" cultural studies, both fields want to know why and how bodies perform minds.

CHAPTER SIX

Toward a Cognitive Cultural Hegemony

BRUCE McCONACHIE

Theories of cultural hegemony first made their appearance in the 1920s with the work of Antonio Gramsci, an Italian communist who was trying to figure out why the Italian working class had not risen in revolt against Mussolini's fascism. In the 1970s, British scholar Raymond Williams and others introduced Gramsci's ideas into cultural studies, where they were taken up by many neo-Marxists eager (like Gramsci) to understand how and why working people often embraced ideas and practices that did not serve their interests. Since the 1970s, a variety of intellectual movements—including feminism, psychoanalysis, postcolonial theory, and postmodernism—have put their own spins on Gramsci's ideas to explain several varieties of social-historical domination by consent. This elaboration of hegemony theory has been possible, in part, because Gramsci did not fully explain how hegemony functioned to link cultural practices with ideological oppression.

Several contemporary writers have urged scholars to revisit hegemony theory, in particular its centrality in the work of Raymond Williams, and to reclaim its ongoing importance for the general field of cultural studies. Decrying the fragmentation of cultural materialism into several, often competing, subfields, Andrew Milner argues that it is time to reverse such proliferation and to recover for cultural studies "something at least of its original intellectual purchase and political promise" (132) by focusing on Williams's ideas. John Storey uses the preface of his *Inventing Popular Culture* to remind readers of the many implications of Williams's oft-quoted statement from a 1958 essay that "culture is ordinary" (x). In his intellectual biography of Williams, John Higgins recognizes the shortcomings of some of his subject's work but concludes his study with a quotation about another scholar written by Williams himself that underlines Williams's ongoing significance: "He could be wrong, as anyone can be wrong, in specific cases, but it is the nature and foundation of his thinking which remains relevant" (177). I offer this essay as a part of the necessary revaluation of "the nature and foundation" of Williams's work.

My essay attempts to reconcile Raymond Williams's concept of cultural hegemony with a notion of embodied cognition. This synthesis primarily involves joining Williams's understanding of Gramsci's term to the cognitive linguistic and philosophical ideas of George Lakoff and Mark Johnson. Because an adequate cognitive approach to the historical dynamics of cultural hegemony depends on explaining how external cultural practices get processed and reproduced in the internal workings of the mind/brain, I borrow from the work of cognitive anthropologist Bradd Shore to effect this fusion. Finally, this essay draws on examples from my own work to suggest how a cognitive approach to cultural hegemony can help theater historians understand Broadway theater in the United States during the 1950s.

According to Raymond Williams, Gramsci's ideas about cultural hegemony posit culture as an arena of conflicting ideas and values. Different classes and social groups—Gramsci calls them "historical blocs"—are always contending for legitimacy and power within every historical society. This competition, however, does not occur on a level playing field. Despite what might appear to be consensus among several groups, the ideas and values of the ruling class tend to predominate, primarily because those with more power and wealth effectively manage the cultural conversation. In complex societies, Gramsci argues, the ruling class maintains most of its power through "intellectual and moral leadership" rather than by direct control ("Hegemony," 210). Instead of killing, jailing, censoring, or even conspiring against their political and cultural opponents, the watchdogs of the ruling class mostly constrain the terms of allowable rhetoric within a culture in such a way that truly oppositional ideas and movements rarely gain visibility and traction.

Gramsci calls these cultural watchdogs "organic intellectuals." While all men and women have the capacity for significant intellectual activity, according to Gramsci, some people emerge within every historical bloc to function as class organizers and promoters. These politicians, preachers, lawyers, entertainers, and prominent public figures, along with a few academic intellectuals, give their social group

homogeneity and an awareness of its own function not only in the
economic sphere but also in the social and political fields. The capitalist entrepreneur [for example] creates alongside himself the industrial
technician, the specialist in political economy, the organizers of a new
culture, of a new legal system, etc.   ("HEGEMONY," 212)

Because organic intellectuals function in every historical bloc, Gramsci
recognized that he and other spokespeople for the working class could
help to undermine the cultural hegemony of the capitalists. Williams, the
son of a Welsh coalminer and already a prominent organic intellectual by
the 1960s, embraced Gramscian ideas both for their theoretical vitality
and their political efficacy. In the 1970s and 1980s, this recognition invig-
orated the academic Left in the United States and Britain to challenge the
reigning pieties of Reaganism and Thatcherism. As historian T. J. Jackson
Lears noted in 1985, Gramsci's ideas deepened "at both ends" the question of "who has power":

> The "who" includes parents, preachers, teachers, journalists, literati,
> "experts" of all sorts, as well as advertising executives, entertainment
> promoters, popular musicians, sports figures, and "celebrities"—all
> of whom are involved (albeit often unwittingly) in shaping the values
> and attitudes of a society. The "power" includes cultural as well as
> economic and political power—the power to help define the bound-
> aries of common sense "reality" either by ignoring views outside
> those boundaries or by labeling deviant opinions "tasteless" or
> "irresponsible."   (572)

Contending organic intellectuals from various historical blocs typically
arrive at a "compromise equilibrium," according to Gramsci ("Hegemony," 211). Given the greater cultural power of organic intellectuals supporting the ruling class, this temporary cultural equilibrium usually fa-
vors the status quo, but the rulers may have to bend to accommodate the
values of other groups.

Raymond Williams emphasized that Gramsci's notion of cultural hegemony involved more than ideology. Gramsci, he said,

> introduces the necessary recognition of dominance and subordination
> in what has still, however, to be recognized as a whole process. It is in
> just this recognition of the wholeness of the process that the concept

of "hegemony" goes beyond "ideology." What is decisive is not only the conscious system of ideas and beliefs, but the whole lived social process as practically organized by specific and dominant meanings and values. (*MARXISM AND LITERATURE*, 108–9)

It is organized as well by specific cultural institutions and movements. In his later work, Williams increasingly underlined the importance of institutional practices and artistic movements in perpetuating, challenging, and altering the sequence of temporary compromises that cultural hegemony entails.[1] Williams's "whole process," then, includes both cultural production and reception.

Further, Williams recognized that the constraints of structure and the possibilities of agency operate at both sites of culture. Antihegemonic innovation can occur in production, despite the formulaic nature of most cultural products, but people can nullify challenging cultural communication through their responses if their conventional expectations for reception remain unshaken. Alternatively, audiences can turn even the most reactionary sentiments in a piece of journalism or a film to revolutionary purposes. The uses various groups make of cultural production are not predetermined; in addition, past production and reception are always open to historical investigation. In this, Williams followed Karl Marx's famous statement in *The Eighteenth Brumaire*, published in 1852: "Men [and women] make their own history, but they do not make it just as they please; they do not make it under circumstances chosen by themselves, but under circumstances directly encountered, given, and transmitted from the past" (10). Williams's interpretation of Gramsci folded the ideas of the Italian communist into a complex reading of Marx's musings on agency and structure.

Williams always understood that culture had to work in the mind as well as in society. Regarding the operations of cultural hegemony, he noted:

The processes of education; the processes of a much wider social training within institutions like the family; the practical definitions and organizations of work; the selective tradition at an intellectual and theoretical level; all these forces are involved in a continual making and remaking of an effective dominant culture. If what we learn there were merely an imposed ideology, or if it were only the isolable meanings and practices of the ruling class, or of a section of the ruling class, which gets imposed on others, occupying merely the top of our minds, it would be—and one would be glad—a much easier thing to overthrow. (*PROBLEMS*, 37)

But how does culture get below the "top of our minds," change our cognitions, and shape our subsequent actions? Williams understood that this was an important question, but never arrived at an adequate answer. In the 1950s, he began using the term "structure of feeling" to correlate the form and emotional power of an artistic product with the general psychology of a culture. In the 1970s, adjusting his ideas to the work of Gramsci, Williams modified his concept; he narrowed "structure of feeling" down, using it to refer primarily to the innovative forms and new psychology of emergent cultures of opposition. Williams stopped using the concept in the 1980s, however, and it has not proven theoretically useful to others. According to his biographer and critic John Higgins, "the central notion of a 'structure of feeling' amounts to little more than an ingenious instance of theoretical impressionism, in which a rhetorical figure tries to assume the force of a distinctly articulated theoretical concept" (169). Perhaps Williams sensed the term's weakness, especially in contrast to the apparently robust explanatory force of Lacanian psychoanalysis in the 1980s, and that was the reason he abandoned it. Although Williams opposed the marriage of structuralism and psychoanalysis in Lacan and others, he never took another position on how culture gets internalized in cognition. He continued to believe, however, that certain psychological and cognitive operations must work at levels below the "top of the mind" to enable people to maintain, reproduce, and challenge their culture.

As it happens, Williams's intuition that there must be analogical connections between the artistic products of culture and the workings of the mind/brain put him on a fruitful path. While no single "structure of feeling" can account for these correlations, cognitive anthropologists have investigated similar connections linking external culture to internal minding. In his *Culture in Mind: Cognition, Culture, and the Problem of Meaning*, Bradd Shore advances an argument that can be understood as a cognitive-anthropological elaboration of Williams's "structure of feeling" and its connections to cultural hegemony.

Shore's anthropology emphasizes our species' cognitive dependence on both natural and cultural environments throughout our lives. Regarding culture, the mind/brain is neither "hardwired" for certain cultural responses nor is it a passive recorder that facilitates direct cultural "construction" by individual and social experiences. Rather, what Shore calls "the ecological brain" both enables and constrains perceptions and practices, a process that leads to a range of cultural possibilities (3). For Shore, "cultural models" bridge internal cognition and external cultural practice. Cultural models are cognitive and social, composed of complex mental schemas and elaborated social beliefs and practices. Built from a wide range of cognitive concepts that develop in an infant's mind, these schemas are shaped by local cultural experiences, such as language, ritual, and other events, and memories that occur throughout life. In terms of cognitive science, Shore's approach generally accords with the ecological understanding of James J. Gibson, the evolutionary perspectives of Merlin Donald and Gerald Edelman, and the embodied realism of George Lakoff and Mark Johnson. Shore's insight that culture both enables and constrains human practice also pulls him into broad agreement with Raymond Williams.

In society, cultural models provide the basis for cultural knowledge, but such knowledge is unevenly, though widely, distributed. Not everyone in a culture, for example, will have the same level of knowledge of a frequently performed ritual. Cultural performances such as sports games and political campaigns are especially revealing for Shore; they nicely demonstrate "the complex relations between the external structures of rules and norms and the personal [cognitive] experiences that these make possible" (312). For cultural models to function effectively as a part of a dominant culture, the institutional and experiential sides of such models must be mutually reinforcing. For baseball, for example, to become a model for other practices in their lives, people not only must learn to understand and accept the rules and conventions of the game as a legitimate cultural practice but also must experience the structures and emotions of a certain number of specific games. The first step primarily involves cognitive attention, selection, and memory, and the second, the emotional-cognitive operation of enjoying the game and then projecting the basic mental schemas of baseball onto other cultural domains. In effect, the external structures of the game get internalized at the cognitive level and the emotional-cognitive experience of baseball gets externalized onto other events in the world.

This ongoing give-and-take between internalization and externalization legitimates, maintains, and can alter every cultural model, according to Shore. Although more apparent in cultural performances such as baseball games than in other kinds of cultural models, this dialectic between the institutional and the mental undergirds all the activities of a dominant culture, from reading a book to building a factory.

Shore next asks how the mind/brain facilitates these ongoing processes of internalization and externalization and draws on Lakoff and Johnson's notion of embodied concepts for much of his answer. According to Lakoff and Johnson, mental concepts, the building blocs of schemas, arise fundamentally from the experience of the body in the world. As "neural beings," humans must make meaning within certain "basic-level," "spatial relations," and "bodily action" concepts, plus other concepts resulting from the interplay of experience and constructed patternings in the brain (*Philosophy*, 16–37). Lakoff and Johnson rely on the neuroscientific definition of "concepts;" in contrast to the everyday sense of the word, mental concepts are not ideas stated in words, but networks of neuronal groupings and firings used by the brain to categorize its own activities into elementary units, which are nonrepresentational. Heuristically attaching words to these concepts, they could be said to include such basics as the color "red," the sense of "up," and a notion of "forward." As far as cognitive scientists can tell, these concepts appear to be universal to human development; all individual and cultural cognition rests upon recombinations of the same conceptual primitives. When combined to produce cultural schemas, many of these concepts can create notions of romantic love, social stereotypes, and everything else that we recognize as culture.

Lakoff and Johnson have explored how certain spatial-relation and bodily action concepts take the form of structured cultural experiences, especially language. The cognitive spatial relation of "near-far," for example, helps us to make sense of perspective drawings and the language of history. Regarding bodily action concepts, the "source-path-goal" concept, which humans learn at an early age by crawling from a starting point to an end point, undergirds numerous metaphors that organize certain events in our lives as narratives with a beginning, a middle, and an end. "Balance," another bodily action concept, provides many metaphors for mental health, ethical behavior, and public justice. These primary metaphors are "creative," in the sense that they create an analogy linking two phenomena through similarity rather than by relying on the recognition of an inherent, objective similarity between two phenomena. Because these and numerous other primary metaphors link everyday experience to sensorimotor phenomena, most cultural thinking cannot occur without metaphors.

As the examples above demonstrate, analogical transfer allows people to apply the simplest spatial-relation or bodily action concept to the most complex cultural phenomena. Shore hypothesizes that this same operation facilitates much of the work of internalizing the institutional and externalizing the mental sides of cognitive models. For example, an individual can break down the externalities of a baseball game into several cognitive concepts having to do with salient language, spatial organization, and physical action. Some of these same internal concepts will be brought into consciousness when the individual wants to recall a certain game or decides to project an idea of baseball onto another area of life through metaphor. "He pitched me that sale, but I wasn't swinging" is one example of this analogical transfer. Such transfers often involve some of Lakoff and Johnson's innate spatial and bodily action concepts directly, and they may combine these to create more complex schemas that operate at the level of specific language groups in their societies. Shore notes that his mental model of a baseball park, which builds on several of Lakoff and Johnson's innate spatial relations concepts, helps him to orient himself when he visits any new ballpark. Over time, individuals in a culture built up a large stock of conventional schemas that can be drawn on to understand unfamiliar events.

How might the schemas that make up cultural models and the process of analogical transfer relate to cultural hegemony? Because Shore embraces Lakoff and Johnson's epistemology of embodied realism, which is also broadly congruent with the cultural materialism of Raymond Williams, hegemony theory can be put together with these other theoretical building blocks. All entail commitments to an open-ended methodology, which includes hermeneutics and theory-based probes into realities embedded in empirical evidence. In any investigation, the critic-historian-anthropologist attuned to cognitive realities would recognize that all cultural models, in both their institutional and mental aspects, are embedded in history as well as biology and, consequently, embed those who use them (and who are used by them) in all of the dynamics of tradition, race, gender, class, and the other historical crosscurrents that shape human beings.

No cultural models are historically neutral. American baseball, to continue that example, emerged as a major entertainment primarily for middle-class men and boys at the turn of the last century, a time when color consciousness in the United States demanded the racial segregation of baseball teams. As a cultural performance, baseball evoked strong associations with an idealized agricultural past, but it was also preeminently a city game, dependent for its institutional support on trolley lines, sports investors, and beer merchants. Most spectators at a baseball game a hundred years ago likely carried with them social schemas that folded it into the cultural norms of the time. Just as clearly, though, some of the concepts that made up the schema of baseball in 1906 were not connected to historical constructions of race, gender, and class. The idea of a home run in baseball depends crucially upon Lakoff and Johnson's source-path-goal concept, a bodily action abstraction unrelated to the social construction of the game. Applied to baseball, this abstraction moves a player from home plate (source), around the bases (path), and back to home plate (goal); the race, class, and/or gender of the moving player are irrelevant to the cognitive concept. These and similar concepts helped to ensure that people could gradually reinvent the institution and reimagine their social images of baseball over the next century.

Because cultural models contain historical as well as universal constituents, all cultural models are subject to the vagaries of cultural hegemony. As the example of baseball demonstrates, the constraints of structure operate and the possibilities of agency manifest themselves at the cognitive level as well as at the external level of cultural practice. Despite the dominance of racism and sexism on the social imagination, some baseball managers and spectators could and did play with mental images of all-female and racially integrated teams as well as with images of less homogeneous audiences for the sport. For other managers and spectators, however, the game in their minds would remain male and white, regardless of historical changes and the consequent pressure to adjust their social schemas about baseball. The gap in cultural models between the institutional and the mental levels, though usually bridged by pressure from the dominant culture, also maintains this potential for change. In his closing remarks, Shore emphasizes this capacity: "Because it is always an active construction by an intentional, sentient, and creative mind, analogical schematization introduces a gap, a crucial lifegiving contingency, between the conventional forms of cultural life and their inner representations in consciousness. This gap guarantees the ongoing regeneration of conventions through practice just as it makes possible intersubjective meaning" (372).

As the primitive building blocks of Shore's social schemas, Lakoff and Johnson's universal concepts, most of them always already operative in human beings after infancy, also help ensure that ongoing challenges to dominant cultures are posed. The availability of these concepts and their metaphorical extensions allow for the reframing of socially loaded terms. Organic intellectuals from many oppositional groups have successfully reframed old metaphors in new ways throughout history, with both progressive and reactionary consequences. For many recent U.S. citizens, for example, government "hand outs" have become "entitlements" and "antiabortion advocacy" has become a crusade for a "right to life." Such reframing draws on the enormous capacity of the human mind to challenge a dominant culture by projecting what Lakoff and Johnson describe as universal concepts into historically new fields.

Merging Shore's cultural models, Lakoff and Johnson's cognitive linguistics, and hegemony theory requires some adjustments to Raymond Williams's terminology with regard to the operations of cultural hegemony. Williams distinguished among dominant, residual, and emergent kinds of culture. For Williams, residual culture meant past cultural constellations still current and available for use in the present. Emergent institutions and practices, as the term suggests, put forward cultural innovations. Although both residual and emergent cultures might be deployed to confirm or disrupt conventional dominant forms, Williams generally looked to innovation to challenge the status quo. From a cognitive point of view, however, the well of human experience available in the mind/brain has room for many residual cultures and even includes concepts for building any new cultures that might emerge. Schemas for cultural models are indeed historical, but they are built from universal primitives. Opposition to a present dominant culture can draw on either or both to imagine and effect change. The analogical extension of old metaphors to new targets in history, of course, can also quell progressive reform. Williams's notions of residual and emergent culture remain useful but require some modification.

Perhaps the biggest stumbling block to synthesizing Williams's concept of cultural hegemony with the embodied realism of Lakoff and Johnson is Williams's notion of culture as an organic totality. Like several other Marxists and anthropologists of his era, Williams insisted that culture was a whole way of life, a web of practices, behaviors, and beliefs that was bigger than the sum of its parts. For Williams, as I have already noted, a dominant culture shaped the "whole lived social process" (*Marxism and Literature*, 109). This meant that a change in one part of a culture would necessarily occasion changes in others. In contrast, cognitive anthropologist Roy D'Andrade notes that one of the central features of cognitive anthropology since the 1990s has been the "breaking up of culture into parts . . . cognitively formed units—features, prototypes, schemas, propositions, theories, etc." What this makes possible, says D'Andrade, is "a particulate theory of culture; that is, a theory about the 'pieces' of culture, their compositions and relations to other things" (247). If the cognitive "pieces" of a culture function semi-independently of each other, culture is no longer a whole way of life.

A particulate theory of culture, of course, renders the processes of cultural hegemony more complex and makes cultural-historical explanation more difficult than Williams supposed. If a culture is in cognitive pieces, no single "structure of feeling," or anything like it, could encompass and correlate the forms and emotions produced by a dominant culture with its wider milieu. Domination by consent still occurs, however, even if the cultural schemas inside of people's heads are not all the same. Although the cognitive dynamics maintaining a dominant culture will differ within a population, those with intellectual and moral leadership will still be able to manage significant chunks of those internalization and externalization processes. In effect, the various "historical blocs" that make up a dominant culture can now be understood in cognitive terms; organic intellectuals in each bloc organize and maintain a particular cognitive field and compromise their differences among each other to maintain their authority. A particulate notion of cultural hegemony forces us to modify Williams's notions of structure and agency, but there is no reason to abandon these crucial concepts, especially given the productiveness of the necessary tension between them. A cognitive theory of cultural hegemony must be more flexible than Williams's old model, which will likely make it better attuned to the realities of our increasingly globalized world.

When I wrote *American Theater in the Culture of the Cold War: Producing and Contesting Containment, 1947–1962*, I based my historical framework on the ideas of Raymond Williams and my cognitive theory on the work of Lakoff and Johnson. Because I had not read Shore's *Culture in Mind* at the time, I did not attempt the kind of synthesis of Williams, Lakoff and Johnson, and Shore that I have attempted above. Nor, consequently, did I deploy Shore's notion of cultural models as a bridge between the cognitive and the social. In retrospect, however, I can say that the main argument of my Cold War book rests on a significant element of Shore's position—the assertion that a dominant culture reproduces itself, in part, by analogically transferring concepts and schemas to a network of cultural practices.

In the book, I focused on Lakoff and Johnson's spatial relations concept of "containment" and traced its elaborations throughout the culture, especially in the theater, during the early years of the Cold War. Like all innate concepts, containment functioned with myriad other concepts to structure many schemas in Cold War culture. *American Theater in the Culture of the Cold War*, however, demonstrated that the cognitive logic of containment was at the heart of much of the dominant culture of the United States between 1947 and 1962. From the point of view of a particulate understanding of cultural dynamics, containment culture constituted a large chunk of the dominant culture during this time, and organic intellectuals ranging from generals in the military-industrial complex to Broadway stars facilitated the dominance and maintenance of this cultural field. In Shore's terms, Broadway provided several of the cultural models and schemas that helped this particular field of culture to flourish.

The logic of containment culture can be seen most clearly, perhaps, in the National Security Act of 1947. President Truman had pushed for the act to ensure that the president and secretary of defense would continue to exercise control over the Joint Chiefs of Staff. The 1947 law, however, also created three key agencies that attracted less public attention at the time: the Central Intelligence Agency, whose job was to coordinate spying outside of the United States, the National Security Resources Board, whose task was to link the needs of the armed services with universities and corporations, and the National Security Council, whose function was to advise the president on all matters relating to the security of the nation. Through these agencies, the law empowered the president to mount propaganda campaigns and conduct covert warfare to protect American interests. In effect, the national security apparatus created by this act separated substantial areas of executive authority from the people it was meant to serve and protect. After 1947, the American people and even their representatives in Congress had no legal access to knowledge deemed "top secret" by the security establishment.

A metaphorical reading of the National Security Act from the perspective of Lakoff and Johnson would note that it derives its psychological coherence from cognitive metaphors reliant on containment. The figure of containment involves necessary relations among an inside, an outside, and a boundary between them. In his book *The Body in the Mind*, Mark Johnson summarizes five entailments embedded in this concept:

> (i) The experience of containment typically involves protection from, or resistance to, external forces. When eyeglasses are in a case, they are protected against forceful impacts. (ii) Containment also limits and restricts forces within the container. When I am in a room or in a jacket, I am restrained in my forceful movements. (iii) Because of this restraint of forces, the contained object gets a relative fixity of location. For example, the fish gets located in the fishbowl. The cup is held in the hand. (iv) This relative fixing of location within the container means that the contained object becomes either accessible or inaccessible to the observer. It is either held so that it can be observed or else the container itself blocks or hides the object from view. (v) Finally, we experience transitivity in containment. If B is in A, then whatever is in B is also in A. If I am in my bed and my bed is in my room, then I am also in my room. (22)

From Lakoff and Johnson's point of view, the human proclivity to structure experience through the concept of containment—which is similar to other foundational concepts such as balance, scale, path, and force—is one of several innate functions of the mind that result from genetic inheritance and an infant's interaction with her or his physical and social environment. Different historical cultures, however, privilege some of these structures over others to organize their interactions. Though salient in many of the practices and schemas of American Cold War culture, containment is not likely to be as predominant in most other world cultures and their histories.

The spatial relations concept of containment helped Americans to construct schemas for much of their culture during the Cold War. Using the five entailments of containment outlined by Johnson to analyze the strictures and implications of the 1947 law reveals its significance as a nodal point of the dominant culture in postwar America. Taken as a whole, the act maps the nation-state as a unit of containment; inside the United States is secret knowledge requiring protection. Regarding the first entailment, protection, the act is designed to safeguard contained knowledge from external forces, chiefly the Soviet Union, although theoretically any force in the rest of the world might become an antagonist. In terms of the second, the constrictions caused by containment, the experience of this schema not only limits the ways in which the security establishment will handle these secrets but also puts severe restrictions on the freedoms of all other citizens within the boundaries of fortress America. Next, in relation to the third entailment, the law invites responsible Americans to fixate on people within the United States who have something to do with the secrets being guarded—the president, the security establishment, and potential subversives. With respect to the fourth entailment of the concept, the paradoxes of accessibility, patriotic observers could plainly see some of the guardians and potential thieves of the secrets, but others were hidden in the shadows, protected by the very freedoms that defined the constitutional boundaries of the nation-state. Finally, regarding the fifth, the "transitivity" of containment meant that citizens in all private organizations within the United States must be suspect—a parent in a local PTA was also a citizen in the nation-state and might be an innocent participant in a cell of subversives. McCarthyism was not a later growth of the Cold War; the seeds of paranoiac patriotism had already been planted (and were beginning to sprout) in 1947.

Other containers and their entailments pervaded Cold War culture. Business-class Americans during the 1950s tended to regard not only the nation as a container but the self as well—the self being typically figured as an ego of innocence and vulnerability. Thus popular media analysts like Vance Packard (*The Hidden Persuaders* [1956]) convinced many

Americans to worry that advertising was piercing the mental boundaries of American selves and injecting them with false values. And psychoanalysts, never before (or since) as popular in the United States, probed their patients' dreams to free what had previously been locked within the self. The organic intellectuals leading the news media and Hollywood typically understood the white, suburban family as another container, especially insofar as it exerted sexual restraints on its husbands, wives, and teenagers. Imagining the nation as the chosen people of God encouraged many people to fixate on the presumed qualities of the "American character" during the 1950s. For many in positions of intellectual and moral leadership, the innocent self, the bunkered family, and the chosen people provided a series of transitive Chinese boxes within which American morality could be protected and vindicated as a model for the "free world." Teasing out the entailments of these and other Cold War containers could easily consume several volumes of cultural history. In short, containment was at the hub of a vast network of Cold War schemas that structured much of the dominant culture of the era.

Not surprisingly, containment cognition also shaped many popular theater productions during the 1947–62 period. *American Theater in the Culture of the Cold War* examines several major figures of containment on the Broadway stage. The intertwining of military buildup and popular psychology in postwar America provided a context in which the figure of what I call the "empty boy" exerted fascination for Broadway audiences. Like the persona James Dean played in Hollywood films, the empty boys featured in several plays were searching for an essential "inside" that could overcome the surface distractions and conformities of their "outside" roles. Method acting as taught at the Actors Studio made the pain and compulsiveness of empty boys significant on the stage and legible for American spectators. By teaching actors to discover and present their essential selves in all of their characters, "the Method" propagated containment thinking.

The family circle—sometimes protecting Mom, Dad, and the kids in a bomb shelter, at other times embracing "the family of man" in an empathetic gesture of humanitarian good will—was another significant figure of containment in the early Cold War. Militarization, new female gender roles, the baby boom, and the suburban ideal shaped the figure of the family from 1947 through 1962. The 1951 production of *The King and I* by Rodgers and Hammerstein, for example, expanded the family circle to include nonwhite races even as it legitimated the role of a white, suburban mother as the instigator of the Americanization of nineteenth-century Siam. In several family circle productions, including *The King and I*, the designs of Jo Mielziner underlined the naturalness of the suburban ideal as the appropriate setting for nurturant caregivers and spousal "togetherness." In all of Rodgers and Hammerstein's Asian musicals (including *South Pacific* and *Flower Drum Song*), containment thinking legitimated a postwar American empire that was white and inherently benevolent.

During the 1950s, in the shadow of the atomic bomb, the will of God and the commands of reason provided the best asylum most Americans could imagine for themselves and their loved ones. Contradictory beliefs that positioned mature American males as fragmented heroes, men who were both powerful masters of their fate and impotent in the face of nuclearism, set the stage for the Broadway success of several plays, including Arthur Miller's *Death of a Salesman*. Fragmented heroes had been a contained whole, but forces beyond their control drove them toward fates they could barely comprehend or resist and shattered their identities. Miller crafted Willy Loman's wife, Linda, to serve as a sympathetic witness who could observe her husband's fragmentation, a point of view that legitimated the playwright's liberal, rationalist ethics. Fragmented-hero plays typically branded other female figures—the laughing woman in Boston is an example in *Salesman*—as irrational Others whose voracious sexuality was uncontained.

With oppositional theater relegated to a few productions on the margins of Broadway, professional playwrights trying to make a living at their craft but eager to contest aspects of the dominant culture often had to couch their concerns in traditional forms. Typically, oppositional playwrights in the twentieth century had extended popular cultural metaphors in new directions to challenge the status quo, but the hegemony of Broadway nearly closed down that option in the United States during the 1950s. Consequently, some of the most progressive plays on Broadway in the 1947–62 era returned to the apparently safe mix of realism and romanticism from the residual culture of earlier decades. The romantic realism in *Cat on a Hot Tin Roof* by Tennessee Williams and *A Raisin in the Sun* by Lorraine Hansberry raised significant questions about people relegated to the class of abject Other by containment culture. Because the cognitive logic of containment required an outside Other to delimit an inside Same, abject Others proliferated during the Cold War. The image of the homosexual shadowed the character of the empty boy in *Cat*, and the black family circle stood behind its white counterpart in *Raisin*. Williams strove to defuse the "Are you now or have you ever been a homosexual?" question asked about empty boy Brick Pollit in *Cat*. And Hansberry relativized the category of race to open up questions about class and U.S. imperialism in *Raisin*.

American Theater in the Culture of the Cold War examines the field of containment culture during the postwar era as well as a few of the oppositional voices in the theater that contested it by focusing on both the production and reception of Broadway plays popular with the business class. The study's organizing premise is that one innate cognitive concept, containment, lay near the center of this cultural field, providing a default cognitive mode that helped to organize and maintain a vast array of the dominant culture's mental and institutional schemas. Not all dominant cultures in all historical periods will exhibit a similar organization, but there is copious evidence that the concept of containment provided significant cultural coherence for U.S. citizens in the 1950s.

PART THREE

Cognitive Narratology

According to David Herman, cognitive narratology is "the study of mind-relevant dimensions of storytelling practices wherever—and by whatever means—those practices occur. This definition allows for a capacious concern with narrative across media, but keeps the focus on aspects of narrativity and on how those aspects relate to research on mind, broadly conceived."[1] Herman's emphasis on the "capacious concern with narrative across media" points to a particular development within the parent field of narratology, a development now increasingly reflected in the paths taken by cognitive narratologists. Narratology used to be primarily concerned with novels and short stories, but now, while retaining that concern, it has expanded to include other forms of storytelling, becoming "multimodal" (see Ruth Page's introduction to *New Perspectives on Narrative and Multimodality*) or "transmedial" (see Herman's "Toward a Transmedial Narratology").

Hence a leading program in narrative studies, Project Narrative at Ohio State University—which also features a critical mass of scholars working with cognitive narratology—deals with narrative "in all of its guises, from everyday storytelling in face-to-face interaction, to oral history and autobiography, to films, graphic novels, and narratives associated with digital environments, to the multitude of stories found in the world's narrative literature."[2] Cognitive-narratological studies associated with this inclusive view range from Porter Abbott's *Bad Stories: The Narrative Pursuit of Unnarratable Knowledge* and Suzanne Keen's *Empathy and the Novel* to Frederick Luis Aldama's *Your Brain on Latino Comics: From Gus Arriola to Los Bros Hernandez*. Earlier, foundational, works in cognitive narratology include Monika Fludernik's *Towards a "Natural" Narratology*, Marie-Laure Ryan's *Possible Worlds, Artificial Intel-*

ligence, and Narrative Theory, Alan Palmer's *Fictional Minds*, and David Herman's *Story Logic* and *Narrative Theory and the Cognitive Sciences*.

Cognitive-literary studies of theory of mind (here represented by essays of Palmer, Blakey Vermuele, and Lisa Zunshine) often fall naturally under the broader rubric of cognitive narratology, particularly now that narratology is expanding to include a variety of storytelling forms. Cognitive psychologists and philosophers of mind define theory of mind (also known as mind reading) as our evolved cognitive ability to attribute thoughts, desires, and intentions to other people and to ourselves.[3] Cognitive literary and cultural critics study the ways cultural representations (e.g., fictional narratives, movies, paintings, computer games) and discourses (e.g., philosophical, religious, and political treatises, propaganda, works of criticism) both build on and experiment with our mind-reading capacities. Key readings in this subfield include Palmer's *Social Minds in the Novel*, Per Persson's *Understanding Cinema: A Psychological Theory of Moving Imagery*, and Zunshine's *Why We Read Fiction: Theory of Mind and the Novel*.

Not surprisingly—given the fundamental nature of the relationship between theory of mind and narrative—cognitive and developmental psychologists have begun investigating this relationship from their end. See, for example, the work coming out of the Mind and Development Lab in the Department of Psychology at Yale University: Paul Bloom on the cognitive science of pleasure, Deena Skolnick Weisberg on the creation and comprehension of fictional worlds, Jennifer Lynn Barnes on autism and genre preferences, and Lily Guillot on the relationship between social reasoning abilities and the ability to connect to a narrative.

Although theory of mind is an exponentially growing and influential paradigm in all branches of psychology—most immediately in cognitive, developmental, and clinical psychology but also increasingly in cognitive neuroscience (see the work on mirror neurons) and in social psychology (see John Bargh's *Social Psychology and the Unconscious* and Ran Hassin, James Uleman, and Bargh's *The New Unconscious*)—various aspects of this research remain controversial. See, for example, cognitive philosopher Alvin Goldman's argument about the differences between the "Theory Theory" and the "Simulation Theory" views of theory of mind (*Simulating Minds*) and the cautious response to this argument on the part of cognitive psychologists (Jason Mitchell's "False Dichotomy," Rebecca

Saxe's "Hybrid Vigor," Simone Shamay-Tsoory, Yasmin Tibi-Elhanany, and Judith Aharon-Peretz's "Venteromedial Prefrontal Cortex"). The good news for students of cognitive narratology is that they don't have to take sides in such debates in order to be able to apply research in theory of mind to the study of cultural representations. For instance, the disagreement highlighted by Goldman is meaningful for (some) philosophers, but it's irrelevant for literary scholars, who can simply chose the best of several worlds, picking and combining the aspects of "Simulation Theory" and "Theory Theory" that fit their purposes, as both Zunshine and Vermeule have been doing.

CHAPTER SEVEN

Narrative Theory after the Second Cognitive Revolution

DAVID HERMAN

In parallel with the other contributors' adoption of ideas from cognitive science for the purposes of textual and more broadly cultural analysis, the present chapter uses social-psychological research to outline one strategy for developing "postclassical" approaches to the study of narrative. At issue are frameworks for narrative research that build on the work of classical, structuralist narratologists but supplement that work with concepts and methods that were unavailable to story analysts such as Roland Barthes, Gérard Genette, A. J. Greimas, and Tzvetan Todorov during the heyday of the structuralist revolution.[1] One such framework, or cluster of frameworks, has begun to take shape under the rubric of "cognitive narratology," and my chapter seeks to contribute to this emergent area of narrative inquiry by focusing on the nexus between narrative and mind.[2]

The particular strand of social-psychological research on which I draw in order to explore this nexus is sometimes referred to as "discursive psychology." In Derek Edwards and Jonathan Potter's characterization, a basic contrast can be drawn between, on the one hand, "cognitivist approaches to language, where texts, sentences, and descriptions are taken as depictions of an externally given world, or as realizations of underlying cognitive representations of that world" (8), and, on the other hand, the discursive approach:

> The focus of discursive psychology is the action orientation of talk and writing. . . . We are concerned with the nature of knowledge, cognition and reality: with how events are described and explained, how factual reports are constructed, how cognitive states are attributed. These are defined as discursive topics, things people topicalize

or orientate themselves to, or imply, in their discourse. And rather than seeing such discursive constructions as expressions of speakers' underlying cognitive states, they are examined in the context of their occurrence as situated and occasioned constructions whose precise nature makes sense, to participants and analysts alike, in terms of the social actions those descriptions accomplish. (2)

Theorists working in this tradition, including Molly Andrews, Michael Bamberg, Michael Billig, Jerome Bruner, Derek Edwards, Grant Gillett, Rom Harré, Jonathan Potter, Peter Stearns, and Margaret Wetherell, have collectively sought to make a case for what Harré has termed the "second cognitive revolution."[3] The first cognitive revolution marked a shift away from behaviorism to the study of cognition, postulating that "there are mental processes 'behind' what people say and do, that these processes are to be classified as 'information processing,' and that the best model for the cognitively active human being is the computer when it is running a program."[4] In contrast, although the second cognitive revolution also accepts that there are cognitive processes, it views them as immanent in discourse practices. From this perspective, the mind does not preexist discourse, but is ongoingly accomplished in and through its production and interpretation. Hence the designation *"discursive* psychology."

My chapter uses an illustrative literary narrative—namely, Ernest Hemingway's 1927 story "Hills Like White Elephants"—to test out the productiveness of broadly discursive-psychological research for cognitive cultural studies; one of my goals is to show how ideas geared mainly to the study of intelligent activity in face-to-face interaction can also illuminate analyses of written narrative texts (and vice versa). Sketching a thumbnail history of the developments that have led discursive psychologists to speak of a second cognitive revolution, I outline five key concepts that have emerged from this rethinking of the nature of thinking and use Hemingway's text as a case study to show how those concepts are relevant for narrative inquiry. I also indicate ways in which the study of literary texts like Hemingway's can inform discursive-psychological research—research premised on the idea that minds are always already grounded in discourse. Hemingway's and other authors' representations of discourse practices—their staging of "scenes of talk"—bear importantly on the tradition(s) of research that locate cognitive processes not in the heads of solitary thinkers but rather in sociocommunicative processes unfolding within richly material settings.[5]

"Hills Like White Elephants": Key Aspects

Hemingway's brief story—it has fewer than fifteen hundred words—focuses on a conversation between an unnamed male character and Jig, the woman who has been impregnated by the male character (the reader assumes). The story is set on a hot day at a train station in Spain, in a valley through which the Ebro River flows. As they wait for the train to Madrid, the two characters briefly discuss the appearance of the landscape surrounding them (specifically, Jig mentions that the hills across the valley look like white elephants), then order drinks and engage in a sometimes tense conversational exchange about the possibility of Jig's having an abortion. When the story ends, with the characters expecting the train to arrive momentarily, it remains unclear what course of action they will pursue—although the closing lines perhaps suggest that Jig has acceded to the male character's suggestion that she get the abortion or at least decided that any further discussion of the matter with him would be fruitless. I discuss the story in greater detail below, but some key issues raised by Hemingway's storytelling method can be highlighted at the outset.

Although Hemingway's fiction in general and "Hills Like White Elephants" in particular might be construed as instances of "behaviorist" narrative, presenting only overt, surface behaviors of the characters and omitting narratorial commentary on more or less fugitive internal states (dispositions, thoughts, attitudes, memories, etc.), as the characters' conversation unfolds in the story a rich context of perceptions, inferences, and emotional responses emerges.[6] Here one might cite Hemingway's statement about his own tip-of-the-iceberg method of composition: "I always try to write on the principle of the iceberg. . . . There is seven-eighths of it underwater for every part that shows."[7] In lieu of this surface-and-depth metaphor, however, the story itself suggests the advantages of more "lateralized," or distributed, model. Memory, perception, emotion—in short, the mind—do not reside beneath the surface of the characters' verbal and nonverbal actions but are rather spread out as a distributional flow in what they do and say (as well as what they do not do and do not say), the material setting that constitutes part of their interaction, the method of narratorial mediation used to present the characters' verbal and nonverbal activities, and readers' own engagement with all of these representational structures. One of the chief tasks for postclassical narrative theory is to develop tools for studying the mind relevance of all these dimensions of stories and storytelling. The question is how cognitive processes can be lodged not just in reports about characters' behaviors, utterances, and experiences but also in modes of narration, types of perspective, and details about the spatial and temporal contexts of narrated situations and events. I argue in what follows that ideas from the field of discursive psychology can contribute at least some of the tools needed to explore the mind relevance of these aspects of narrative structure, though story analysts will also need to draw on other, complementary, frameworks that study the interrelations among language, mind, and world.[8]

My next section provides further context for understanding the disciplinary origins and explanatory aims of discursive psychology itself. In other words, to grasp why theorists in this tradition have sought to define mind as discourse, it is necessary to recall part of the recent history of discourse about minds.

Recent Conceptions of Mind: Some Swings of the Post-Cartesian Pendulum

Research concerned with the nature of the mind spans millennia and ranges across multiple fields of inquiry, including neuroscience; cognitive linguistics; the philosophy of mind; cognitive anthropology; artificial intelligence; cognitive, social, and evolutionary psychology; and, as the current volume attests, humanistic scholarship that is increasingly drawing on concepts from these other areas of study to examine cultural processes and artifacts. Although I cannot hope to do justice to this immense body of work here, several recent accounts converge in identifying key junctures in the study of mind since the time of Descartes.[9]

- *Cartesian dualism*: Descartes' account of the mind as immaterial and unextended, and his opposition between the mind and the extended matter constituting the physical world, codified a dualistic conception that can be traced back to Plato (e.g., the *Meno*) and that can be abbreviated with a formula: *the mind in here;*

the world out there. As Anthony Freeman discusses in his overview of theories of consciousness, this dualistic model leads to a
number of paradoxes in the philosophy of mind.[10] Yet Descartes'
bifurcated conception of the mental versus the physical nonetheless set the terms for subsequent debates about the nature of
mental phenomena. Specifically, his dichotomization of the mind
in here and the world out there created two poles, or end points,
of a spectrum between which subsequent theories had to position
themselves, even when those theories were anti-Cartesian in spirit,
as was the case with behaviorism (see below).[11]

- *Introspectionism* (the pendulum swings toward one end of the
  Cartesian spectrum, *the mind in here*): Cartesian dualism licensed
  the introspectionism that characterized philosophical as well as
  psychological discourse in the late nineteenth and early twentieth
  centuries (Franz Brentano, Edmund Husserl, Wilhelm Wundt, William James). If one assumes that the mind is in here, then introspective analysis constitutes a legitimate source of data about the
  mind's nature and workings. The legacy of introspectionism carries over into the first cognitive revolution, that is, the heyday of
  cognitive science after it emerged in the mid-twentieth century as a
  constellation of disciplines that included computer science, cognitive psychology, linguistics, neurophysiology, and so forth (Gardner). As Andy Clark has argued, certain strands of such first-wave
  cognitive science continued to treat "the mind as a privileged and
  insulated inner arena" and "body and world as mere bit-players
  on the cognitive stage" ("Embodied, Situated, and Distributed
  Cognition," 508).

- *Behaviorism* (the pendulum swings to other end of the Cartesian
  spectrum, *the world out there*): As a reaction against introspectionism, early twentieth-century behaviorism (John B. Watson,
  B. F. Skinner) holds that the world out there is the only thing that
  can be studied and known; the mind in here is epiphenomenal or,
  at best, an explanatory fiction postulated on the basis of observable, outward behaviors of material bodies. Chomsky's theory of
  transformational generative grammar, which constitutes one of the
  key developments in the first cognitive revolution, emerged against

the backdrop of what Chomsky viewed as the impoverished conception of language available within a behaviorist framework.[12]

- *The first cognitive revolution* (the pendulum swings back once more to the "mind" end of the spectrum): As a reaction against behaviorism, first-wave cognitive science is sometimes also termed "cognitivism" by its critics.[13] An inherently interdisciplinary enterprise, the first cognitive revolution marks a return to the mind in here, but now the mind is viewed as an information-processing device—the dominant metaphor being, according to Rom Harré and Grant Gillett, the mind as a software program that runs on the "hardware" of the physical brain (17–34).[14]

- *The second cognitive revolution* (the mind is *both* in here *and* out there; so is the world): To reiterate, the basic claim made by discursive psychologists is that cognitive processes exist, but that they are immanent in—that they emerge from—discourse practices. From this vantage point, people acquire the status of psychological beings just by participating in discourse, in normatively accountable ways.[15] Further, for theorists working in this tradition, discourse itself can be defined in broadly Wittgensteinian terms as the rule-based manipulation of symbols in multiperson episodes that unfold within material settings.[16]

But what developments helped precipitate the shift from first-wave, cognitivist models of mind to the second-wave, discursively oriented models? Research contributing to this second revolution in thinking about thinking, which began to unfold in the late 1980s, emanated from several sources. One source was Vygotsky's work on the social roots of human intelligence; his hypothesis that, in the development of individuals, intramental thinking derives from shared, or intermental, thinking has led to a broader interest in socially distributed cognition—as I discuss more fully in my next section.[17] Another source was the approach to discourse analysis (sometimes called "Conversation Analysis") that can be traced back to the ethnomethodological or participant-centered theories of the sociologist Harold Garfinkel. According to this work, participants index their understandings of an ongoing interaction precisely by making particular kinds of contributions to the course of the interaction itself and thereby jointly constructing it as the *kind* of interaction that they understand it to be.[18] Knowing and doing, cognition and discourse, are thus inextricably interlinked. A similar emphasis on the discourse grounding of cognitive processes can be found in a third important source in this context, namely, the philosophy of the later Wittgenstein. Emphasizing the embeddedness of humans' meaning-making practices in larger "forms of life," Wittgenstein characterized meaning as use; in this account, utterances have meanings by virtue of how they are used in particular communicative situations. He also argued that pain and other mental phenomena should be thought of as anchored not in a private, inner language but rather in rule-oriented displays within normative contexts specifying how and when such displays can be produced and interpreted as such.

What links these research initiatives, as diverse as they are, is a shared attempt to nudge the post-Cartesian pendulum away from the "mind in here" pole but without allowing it to swing all the way back to the "world out there" pole at which the behaviorists sought to arrest it. In turn, the discursive-psychological research that builds on these and other analytic frameworks has major implications for the study of the mind-discourse nexus in general and of the cognitive dimensions of narrative discourse in particular. In the next section, I use Hemingway's story to outline specific strategies by which narrative scholars might harness this tradition of inquiry to reconfigure narrative theory after the second cognitive revolution—and to develop ideas that may also be productive for discursive-psychological inquiry.

Hemingway and the Discursive Mind

Putting Hemingway's story into dialogue with discursive-psychological research highlights five key concepts that can productively inform (and be informed by) narrative theory. The first four concepts have emerged directly from the second cognitive revolution; the fifth concept, although it might seem to be orthogonal or even opposed to discursive-psychological research, nonetheless connects up with it in ways that have not been adequately explored, though narrative analysts have begun to sketch some of the links. The five concepts are: (1) positioning; (2) embodiment; (3) the distributed versus localized nature of mind; (4) emotion discourse and "emotionology"; and (5) qualia, or the idea that conscious experiences have ineliminably subjective properties, a distinctive sense or feeling of what it is like for someone or something to experience them.

POSITIONING THEORY

The first key concept is the notion that we make sense of our own and other minds through *positioning*. In Harré and van Langenhove's account, one can position oneself or be positioned in discourse as powerful or powerless, admirable or blameworthy, and so forth. In turn, a position can be specified by characterizing how a speaker's contributions are taken as bearing on these and other "polarities of character" in the context of an overarching storyline—a narrative of self and other(s) being jointly elaborated (or disputed) by participants via self-positioning and other-positioning speech acts. Hence positions are selections made by participants in discourse, who use position-assigning speech acts to build "storylines" in terms of which the assignments make sense. Reciprocally, the storylines provide context in terms of which speech acts can be construed as having a position-assigning force.

In "Hills," positioning is a relevant parameter for analysis on at least two levels: the level of the characters and, given Hemingway's narrative techniques, the level of the reader's engagement with the text.[19] At the first level, the story portrays the unnamed male character and Jig as engaged in both self- and other-positioning acts. At the second level Hemingway's mode of narration—in particular, his use of what F. K. Stanzel would characterize as figural narration (= third-person or heterodiegetic narration in which events are refracted through the vantage point of a particular consciousness or "reflector")—works to position readers.

Consider this early exchange between the characters regarding the appearance of the hills on the other side of the valley:

> "They look like white elephants," she said.
> "I've never seen one," the man drank his beer.
> "No, you wouldn't have."
> "I might have," the man said. "Just because you say I wouldn't have doesn't prove anything."   (211)

Here the male character explicitly rejects the storyline in which Jig seeks to position him. However, given the way the story unfolds and the double entendre embedded in its title, the storyline evoked by Jig's comment does acquire legitimacy. This is a person who doesn't have the ability to contextualize, let alone accept, unwanted gifts—or unwanted children.

Conversely, the male character fails in his own attempt to position Jig within a storyline, one that she questions and exposes as grounded in the male character's self-interest, not in his concern for their shared life and happiness together. The key passage is the following:

> "I'll go with you and I'll stay with you all the time. They just let the air in and then it's all perfectly natural."
> "Then what will we do afterward?"
> "We'll be fine afterward. Just like we were before."
> "What makes you think so?"
> "That's the only thing that bothers us. It's the only thing that's made us unhappy." (212)

Jig's subsequent remarks, including her ironic comment about the happiness of all women who have abortions, work to invalidate the storyline in which the male character tries to position them—a story in which they were a happy couple for whom everything was going well and would go well again, provided the abortion takes place. In other words, the man tries to other-position Jig as part of an "us" to which Jig does not position herself as belonging. She momentarily adopts the male character's language but then repositions herself and other-positions him within a different kind of storyline, one in which things will not necessarily work out in the way that her interlocutor suggests. Similarly, at the very end of the story, the male character tries to emplot their current interaction as one in which Jig, after going through a brief period of feeling "unwell," recovers her equilibrium. Jig rejects this storyline, which is based on an attempt to position her in terms of the polarity feeling worse/feeling better; but she does not necessarily project a storyline of her own vis-à-vis their recent interaction:

> "Do you feel better?" he asked.
> "I feel fine," she said. "There's nothing wrong with me. I feel fine." (214)

Jig thus rejects the presupposition of the male character's question but does not engage in a self-positioning act that might lend a sense of closure to their recent dispute—or to the narrative itself.

At another level Hemingway's mode of narration positions readers vis-à-vis the (inter)action unfolding within the storyworld. Although there are shifts of perspective over the course of the story, the male character functions as the main internal focalizer or reflector figure, whose vantage point provides a window on the action being recounted. Thus, almost all of the nonverbal actions recounted in the story are performed by Jig, confirming that the dominant reflector or perceiver (the one witnessing Jig's actions) is the male character. The use of the male character as the focalizer tends to align the reader with his vantage point: we literally see things through his eyes. Yet, as already discussed, the text ultimately invalidates both the storyline he proposes and his attempt at other-positioning Jig in terms of that storyline. This creates a kind of dissonance in the positioning logic of the story. And whatever Hemingway's conscious stance toward dominant conceptions of gender in the epoch during which he wrote, the technique of positioning readers simultaneously with and against the male character serves to disrupt sexist master narratives in which men are the repositories of authoritative knowledge and sound judgments while women lack these attributes and are therefore unreliable.[20]

Thus the idea of positioning, although originally developed for the purposes of analyzing everyday communicative interactions, can also throw light on processes of self- and other-identification in literary narratives like Hemingway's. At the same time, concepts and methods originating in literary narratology, such as figural narration and internal focalization, can lead to finer-grained analyses of positioning logic itself. Combining the resources of these research traditions allows us to formulate a number of questions that could not have been posed by classical narrative theory: How do the stories we tell about ourselves and others, as well as written literary narratives, position us, our interlocutors, authors, narrators, characters, and readers in networks of presuppositions and norms? Can a person's mind be described as, in part, a byproduct of how he or she is situated at the intersection of multiple storylines? Conversely, how do storylines emerge over the course of sequences of position assignments? Can ideology in general, and gender ideologies in particular, be redefined as entrenched storylines—master narratives that arise through an iterative process of assigning the same position, repeatedly, to the same kind of agent, until the agent and his or her position appear to be indissolubly linked? And if so, how can we best use the formal tools developed by narratologists to show how literary narratives sometimes work to interrupt or even derail this process—to uncouple positions and types of agents and thereby "unwrite" dominant storylines—no matter what the conscious aims of the texts' authors?

EMBODIMENT

The second key concept emerging from the second cognitive revolution and taken up in discursive-psychological research concerns the mind's embodiment. Second-wave cognitive science resists both the cognitivist hierarchicalization of mind over body and the behaviorist prioritization of body over mind. Instead, it holds that the mind is always and inalienably embodied; minds should be viewed as the nexus of brain, body, and environment (or world).[21] By putting mind on the same footing as the world in which we think, act, and communicate, second-wave cognitive science avoids making underlying cognitive processes wholly explanatory of overt verbal as well as nonverbal behaviors. Those behaviors, rather, help constitute the cognitive processes themselves, with which they are related in a feedback loop.

In the field of cognitive linguistics, scholars such as George Lakoff, Mark Johnson, Ronald Langacker, and Leonard Talmy have explored ways the structure of language is grounded in (and constitutes a ground for) embodied human experience.[22] For example, this mind-body-language nexus manifests itself in metaphor systems deriving from the experience of navigating the world in, preferably, an upright position. Thus, in English, "up" is generally valorized as positive and "down" as negative (contrast "Today was a real high point for me" with "I'm feeling really low today"). But it is not just that the structures of language can be *correlated with* the physical embodiment of the mind. What is more, as Hemingway's text suggests, stories help *constitute* characters (and character-narrators) as embodied: the process of narration constructs the experiencing self as inalienably linked to a spatially and temporally oriented body-in-the-world. Thus, in "Hills" the use of internal focalization (that is, the filtering of the action through particularized agents of perception in the storyworld) affords an expressive resource by which the text locates the characters' experiences in space and time. The opening sentence of the story—"The hills across the valley of the Ebro were long and white" (211)—encodes a particular perceptual position: the spatial preposition *across* indicates that the viewers, the man and Jig, are located on one side of the valley and are looking out from the train station across at the other side. The text enacts the situated nature of all perception, both in the passage just quoted and also more globally, given that the role of focalizer shifts from the man to Jig and back to the man again over the course of the story. Not only does "Hills" suggest that what can be seen, what is known about the world, alters with the spatial coordinates of the embodied self that is doing the looking; more than this, it suggests that a self is in part constituted by what it sees and by when and where it sees it—with narrative being one of the principal means for tracing this perceptual flux.

Note, too, that the story also carefully situates the characters in time, using the train schedule to mark off increments of their unfolding interaction. In addition, in disputing the male character's attempt to position her as part of a couple that will regain its equanimity and happiness after the operation, Jig indicates her awareness of time's irreversibility and the constraints such linearity imposes on human decisions and relationships.

MIND AS DISTRIBUTED

In synergy with the concepts of positioning and embodiment, the discursive turn in (social-) psychological research suggests that key properties of mind cannot be grasped without an understanding of the mind as distributed. In other words, minds are spread out among participants in discourse, their speech acts, and the objects in their material environment. From this perspective, cognition should be viewed as a supra- or transindividual activity distributed across groups functioning in specific contexts rather than as a wholly internal process unfolding within the minds of solitary, autonomous, and desituated cognizers. Hence, instead of being abstract, individualistic, and constant across all contexts, thinking in its most basic form is grounded in particular situations, socially distributed, and domain specific.[23]

Although they help organize intelligent behavior in a different way than do stories told in face-to-face interaction, literary narratives like Hemingway's not only represent but also enable the distribution of mind across participants, places, and times. For one thing, the title of the story signals how cognitive processes are constituted through discourse; they are grounded in the characters' relation with one another and with their surrounding social and material environment.[24] Jig's observation that the hills across the valley look like white elephants prompts the exchange in which she positions the man as never having seen a white elephant. This exchange precedes Jig's and the man's conversation about the abortion, but in light of their subsequent remarks Jig's other-positioning utterance can be interpreted as setting into play a chain of metaphorical equations—the hills are like white elephants; white elephants are metaphoric equivalents for unwanted gifts; the baby with which Jig is pregnant is an unwanted gift; hence, the baby is a white elephant—of the sort that the male character has been careful to avoid in the past. In this way, besides *portraying* the distribution of mind across participants, their speech acts, and their larger environment for acting and interacting, the story *vehiculates* distributed cognition of this sort. The communicative and cognitive processes internal to the storyworld function as models for readers, who are cued to use structures of the narrative text as interpretive affordances, just as Jig and the male character use features of the setting to "triangulate" what is going on and how they understand and feel about their situation.[25]

Similarly, when the narrator reports that the male character looks at his and Jig's suitcases and sees "labels on them from all the hotels where they had spent nights" (214), this reference to a feature of the characters' environment suggests how the suitcases do part of the male character's thinking for him, triggering what Erving Goffman would call a lamination of past and present time frames and at the same time supporting readers' inferences concerning the characters' relationship and the causal sequence leading up to their present situation. The same process of lamination, and the same distribution of mind across time, space, and social interactants, at once structures and emerges from the characters' conversational exchange. Thus, in response to the male character's attempt to minimize the likely emotional impact of the abortion, Jig ironically alludes to the life stories of other women who have had the procedure. Her contribution in turn prompts the male character to reposition both

Jig and himself; here the man's use of the discourse marker "Well" signals an effort to manage problems with the reception of his previous utterance and also a shift in his tactics for storyline construction, though his overall strategy remains the same:[26]

> "You don't have to be afraid. I've known lots of people that have done it."
> "So have I," said the girl. "And afterward they were all so happy."
> "Well," the man said, "if you don't want to you don't have to. I wouldn't have you do it if you didn't want to. But I know it's perfectly simple." (213)

The point is that the characters' construal of their situation is jointly (if oppositionally) accomplished and that it recruits from features of their environment as well as from the experiences of others with whom they have engaged in similarly collaborative cognition.

More generally, discursive-psychological research again suggests the need for narrative theorists to expand the scope of what they consider to be mind-relevant dimensions of stories and storytelling. Study of the judgments, inferences, and memories of characters, narrators, and readers can be folded into a broader investigation of the cognitive properties associated with narrative gestalts, that is, with narratively organized systems for making sense of experience. Expressive resources such as deixis ("I," "this," "here," "now"), shifts in point of view, and the embedding of one story inside another allow narratives to represent the distribution of mind across spaces, times, participants, and objects in the environments in which stories are told, a distribution that they represent in the form of storyworlds. Conversely, the process of storytelling facilitates just this sort of distribution. It involves the coordinated interplay of minds whose distinctive profile emerges from the nature and extent of their participation in such interplay.

Emotion Discourse and Emotionology

In research on emotion, as Stearns points out, there is a basic tension between naturalist and constructionist approaches. Naturalists argue for the existence of innate, biologically grounded emotions that are more or less uniform across cultures and subcultures. By contrast, construction-

ists argue that emotions are culturally specific—that "context and function determine emotional life and that these vary" (Stearns, "Emotion,"
41). As Ralph Adolphs notes, however, the naturalist and constructionist
positions can be reconciled if emotions are viewed as (1) shaped by evolutionary processes and implemented in the brain but also (2) situated in a
complex network of stimuli, behavior, and other cognitive states. Because
of (2), the shared stock of emotional responses are mediated by culturally
specific learning processes. In turn, to explore the contribution of cultural
contexts to humans' emotional life, analysts can study "[e]motion discourse [as] an integral feature of talk about events, mental states, mind
and body, personal dispositions, and social relations" (Edwards, *Discourse
and Cognition*, 170).

This approach gave rise to the concept of "emotionology," which was
proposed by Peter Stearns and Carol Stearns as a way of referring to the
collective emotional standards of a culture as opposed to the experience
of emotion itself.[27] The term functions in parallel with recent usages of the
term "ontology" to designate a model of the entities, together with their
properties and relations, that exist within a particular domain. Possessed
by every culture and subculture, emotionologies are systems of emotion
terms and concepts deployed by participants in discourse to ascribe emotions to themselves as well as their cohorts. At issue is a framework for
conceptualizing emotions, their causes, and how participants in discourse
are likely to display them. Further, narratives at once ground themselves
in and help build frameworks of this sort, as when ghost stories and romance novels link particular kinds of emotions to recurrent narrative scenarios. Stories' emotionological profile, like their positioning logic, can
thus be investigated both at the level of the characters' interactions with
one another and at the level of readers' interactions with the text; that is,
stories both represent and are interpreted in light of models of emotion.
It should be noted further that even narratives that background or sup-
press emotion terms necessarily orient themselves to an emotionology.
Emotionological conclusions can be drawn from the absence of emotion
terms and categories in contexts where, in other cultural and communicative settings (and other modes of narration), the terms and categories
would generally be deployed.

Gerald Prince cites Hemingway's "The Killers" as a paradigmatic instance of behaviorist narrative "limited to the conveyance of the char-

acters' behavior (words and actions but not thought or feelings), their appearance, and the setting against which they come to the fore" (10; cf. n. 8). Although "Hills Like White Elephants" might therefore be expected to engage in a similar systematic suppression of the lexicon of emotion, in fact it grounds itself in an emotionology not just lexically but also structurally through the way it sequences the characters' speech acts as well as their silences and nonverbal actions. In other words, Hemingway's story points to the discursive bases of mind by anchoring the characters' emotional responses in what they say and do not say, as well as in the nonverbal actions they perform, at particular junctures over the course of their interaction. Indeed, readers are able to understand the characters' *behaviors* as *actions* in part because of the models of emotion on which they rely to interpret the text. An emotionology specifies that when an event X inducing an emotion Y occurs, an agent is likely to engage in Z sorts of actions, where Z constitutes a fuzzy set of more or less proto-typical responses. For example, police detectives were recently led to conclude that a mother had played a role in her own children's death because of her atypically gleeful behavior at their gravesite. Likewise, a discourse such as Hemingway's acquires coherence, comes across as more than a set of sentences, by virtue of its relationship to a larger emotionological context. The characters' activities can be construed as more than just a series of individual, unrelated doings because of the assumption, licensed by a model of emotions, that those behaviors constitute a coherent *class*. At stake is a class of actions in which one is more or less likely to engage when motivated by anxiety about committing to a relationship or by resentment over another's manipulative attempts to avoid such commit-ment, as the case may be.

At the lexical level, "Hills Like White Elephants" represents the charac-ters drawing on a quite extensive vocabulary of emotion to make sense of one another's minds *as* minds. Early in the story, the characters engage in a verbal exchange that begins with an utterance by the male character:

> "Well, let's try and have a fine time."
> "All right. I was trying. I said the mountains looked like white elephants. Wasn't that bright?"
> "That was bright." (212)

Here Jig overtly thematizes the emotion terms and categories that appear to be holdovers from their previous interactions, thereby drawing attention to how, in the face of the complex issues now facing her and the male character, the terms have become hackneyed, overgeneral descriptors, incapable of helping them make sense of themselves and of what is going on. As the conversation proceeds, Jig continues to press against the limits of the emotionology on which the male character by contrast seems content to fall back, perhaps for cynical, manipulative reasons—namely, so that he can hold the more problematic, self-incriminating aspects of his position at a distance while still trying to convince Jig that he has her interests (and not just his own) at heart. Whereas the male character takes cover in the emotionological status quo, so to speak, Jig tries to find a language with which to express her concerns. At one point she uses a childlike locution that seems designed to strip the situation down to its most basic form, so that she can work toward a clearer understanding of its emotional ramifications: "But if I do it, then it will be nice again if I say things are like white elephants, and you'll like it?" (213). A moment later, referring to the characters' natural surroundings, Jig resorts to strategic vagueness to imply an amorphous, difficult-to-express sense of frustration or defeat: " 'And we could have all this,' she said. 'And we could have everything and every day we make it more impossible' " (213). Toward the end of their conversation, after the male character ignores Jig's request that they stop talking, Jig uses verbal repetition to underscore the emotional urgency of her request: "Would you please please please please please please please stop talking?" (214). As these passages reveal, there is no direct mapping from form to function when it comes to emotionology: depending on context, words that do not designate emotional states can nonetheless perform emotionological functions. Indeed, in contrast with those of the male character, Jig's lexical choices are marked by an attempt to exploit this looseness of fit between form and function, perhaps in an effort to engage in emotionological innovation, to find patterns of usage adequate to the complex dynamics of the characters' current interaction.

Furthermore, and as should already be apparent, emotion discourse goes beyond individual words and includes whole utterances as well as the sequential patterning of multiple utterances. At the most global level, the male character tries unsuccessfully to project a storyline in which the abortion will enable the couple to move from unhappiness to happiness. Jig's noncommittal response to the man's question at the end of the story—"Do you feel better?"—signals her rejection of both that storyline and its emotional premises: "I feel fine. . . . There's nothing wrong with me. I feel fine" (214). At a less global level, subsets of interconnected utterances within the overall conversation, as well as places where speech might be expected to occur but does not, suggest the discursive grounding of emotions. Thus, in the three utterances contained in the following exchange, Jig's speech act (ii) construes the man's speech act (i) as a reflection on his dispositions and attitudes and not just as a report about his past experiences, whereas the man's rejoinder (iii) in turn construes Jig's construal as biased and projects an offended (and defensive) emotional posture:

(i) "I've never seen one [i.e., a white elephant]," the man drank his beer.

(ii) "No, you wouldn't have."

(iii) "I might have," the man said. "Just because you say I wouldn't have doesn't prove anything." (211)

The mind-constructing function of each utterance, in other words, depends on its place in the larger sequence of utterances being co-constructed by the characters in incremental fashion. In turn, readers can understand this series of verbal performances as a conversational sequence by virtue of models of emotion that overlap, more or less extensively, with those used by the characters in the storyworld.

Consider, finally, the passage where the male character first broaches the topic of the abortion:

(i) "It's really an awfully simple operation, Jig," the man said. "It's not really an operation at all."

(ii) The girl looked at the ground the table legs rested on.

(iii) "I know you wouldn't mind it, Jig. It's really not anything. It's just to let the air in."

(iv) The girl did not say anything. (212)

In this case it is the absence of a speech production by Jig in slots (ii) and (iv) and the text's substitution of reports of Jig's act of looking at the ground and of *not* speaking that have implications for emotionology.

These empty slots in the characters' discourse suggest not only that Jig is experiencing an emotional disturbance but also that she may be chafing against the limits of the emotion discourse that she and her interlocutor have used hitherto. A task for postclassical narratology is to explore the degree to which gender asymmetry of the kind we see in Hemingway's story—which portrays Jig as an emotionological innovator and the male character as cynically hiding his self-interest behind established emotion categories—structures other narrative discourse as well, in fictional texts as well as everyday interactions. More generally, narrative analysts can investigate the power of stories to (re)shape emotionology itself. Narrative therapy, for example, involves the construction of stories about the self in which the emotional charge habitually carried by particular actions or routines can be defused or redirected, allowing people to prise apart emotion-action linkages that have become inimical to their psychological well-being.[28] Similarly, by staging the way behaviors are dovetailed with emotions and thereby interpreted as actions, stories like Hemingway's may promote greater reflexivity and self-awareness about emotionologies circulating in the broader culture.

THE PROBLEM OF QUALIA

As Janet Levin notes, "[t]he terms *quale* and *qualia* (pl.) are most commonly used to characterize the qualitative, experiential, or felt properties of mental states" (688). Or, as Daniel Dennett puts it, " 'qualia' is an unfamiliar term for something that could not be more familiar to each of us: *the ways things seem to us*" ("Quining Qualia," 619). In Thomas Nagel's terms, qualia arise from the sense or feeling of *what it is like* to be someone or something having a given experience.[29] In the philosophy of mind, the notion of qualia continues to be debated among scholars who have adopted a range of positions on their status. Physicalists argue for the possibility of reducing qualia to brain states (Dennett). Antireductionists argue that there is an irreducible explanatory gap between accounts of brain physiology and the phenomenology of conscious experience.[30] For their part, functionalists argue that qualia are "multiply physically realizable"—they could in principle be emulated on a computer system, for example, and are therefore not specific to an individual brain.[31] Although the particulars of these philosophical arguments are beyond the scope of the present chapter, the general, underlying issues they tap into are directly relevant to my discussion. The key question is whether the notion of qualia, defined as subjective or "first person" properties of conscious experience, can be reconciled with the conception of mind as constituted in and through discourse.

Here it should be noted that Monika Fludernik has made *experientiality*, or the impact of narrated situations and events on an experiencing consciousness, a core property of narrative itself. Fludernik's account suggests that unless a text or a discourse registers the pressure of events on an embodied human or at least a humanlike consciousness, then that text or discourse will not be construed by interpreters as a full-fledged narrative but rather (at best) as a report or chronicle. On the one hand, this account makes qualia a necessary condition for narrative, suggesting that stories are irreducibly tied to subjective states of mind. Stories are premised on minds. But on the other hand, the approach also grounds qualia in discourse practices, specifically, in the design and interpretation of narratively organized discourse. Minds are an emergent result of stories. Again we encounter important research questions for narrative theory after the second cognitive revolution: Can stories not only encapsulate but also provide access to qualia, pace Nagel? That is, do stories in fact enable us to know "what it is like" to be someone else, and maybe also ourselves? More radically, could we even have a notion of the felt quality of experience without narrative?[32]

In Hemingway's story, qualia enter directly into plot: the conflict at the heart of the narrative concerns what an experience will or would be like for the person who must undergo that experience. In other words, "Hills" portrays an interaction in which one of the participants seeks to manage and minimize the felt experience of events from his interlocutor's vantage point. In the storyline that he seeks to project, the subjectively experienced character of those events is at odds with the character that Jig herself senses they will have; Jig therefore rejects the male character's other-positioning strategies. She is of another mind. Hemingway's text is thus a story about the active, ongoing construction, through the discursive means available to the participants in this scene of talk, of the felt, experienced meaning of events. Rather than preceding their interaction, the experiential profile of events emerges from the participants' use of verbal as well as nonverbal acts, in a richly material setting, to engage in processes of self- and other-positioning in the discursive construction of mind.

Horizons for Cognitive Narratology

Focusing on scenes of talk as a point of convergence for narrative theory and discursive psychology, this chapter has attempted to outline directions for further research—both for cognitive cultural studies in general and for cognitive narratology in particular. But the program for research sketched here constitutes only a beginning. Ideas from discursive psychology will need to be brought to bear on aspects of narrative structure and narrative interpretation besides the ones foregrounded here. In addition, narrative theorists will need to explore the extent to which discursive-psychological concepts can be brought into dialogue with other models for understanding the nexus between narrative and mind. How might discursive psychology contextualize research on the acquisition of narratives by children, for example?[33] By the same token, is it possible to harmonize quantitative methods for narrative study with the mainly qualitative, case-study-based approach of discursive psychology?[34] How can discursive psychology inform the study of narrative across media and be used to illuminate the mind-relevance of storytelling processes in semiotic systems other than those associated with written and spoken language? Finally, how might we work toward a rapprochement between (1) discourse-oriented approaches to the mind as a situated interactional achievement and (2) the work in cognitive grammar and cognitive semantics that likewise promises to throw light on the mind relevance of narrative structures but that focuses on discourse productions by individual speakers?[35] The scope of these questions suggests both the challenges and the opportunities facing narrative theory after the second cognitive revolution.[36]

CHAPTER EIGHT

Storyworlds and Groups

ALAN PALMER

The purpose of this chapter is to show how cognitive approaches to literature can illuminate a particular fictional text. The one that I have chosen is a short passage from the beginning of Evelyn Waugh's novel *Men at Arms*. I use my cognitive approach to reveal what I think are important insights into this passage by approaching it from the following four perspectives: storyworlds, theory of mind, intermental thought, and unconscious thought.

Cognitive Approaches to Literature

As the term "cognitive approaches" means different things to different people, I will explain here what I mean by it. I use the term in a very specific sense. My interest is in the *fictional minds* of characters in novels, and so it makes obvious sense to me that I would want to find out about the various disciplines concerned with the study of *real minds* such as the philosophy of mind; social, cognitive and discursive psychology; cognitive science; and psycholinguistics. My cognitive approach is a very pragmatic, undogmatic, and unideological one: if these real-mind disciplines assist our study of fictional minds, then that is fine; if they do not, then there is no reason to use them. However, it has been my experience that we do, in fact, understand fictional minds much better when we apply to them some of the work done on real minds by psychologists, philosophers, and cognitive scientists, particularly those that are part of the "second cognitive revolution."[1]

I can best explain my particular cognitive approach by asking you to participate in a very simple little thought experiment. Please pick a novel—your favorite novel, one that you read recently and liked, one that you are currently thinking about, one that you are studying, whatever.

Then imagine that you are at a party and that you are describing the plot to someone in the hope of persuading them to read it. I am envisaging the sort of conversation that usually starts along the lines of: "It's about this . . ." Please read on only after you have done so.

Pause.

Finished? Then I will now speculate on the nature of your description of the plot. My guess is that you were describing the *mental functioning* of the characters in your novel, what they were thinking and feeling, their beliefs and desires, and so on. You almost certainly included actions, but the descriptions of these actions would have involved the mental network behind them—the intentions, purposes, motives, and reasons for the actions. Much of your plot summary would have been along the lines of: character A performed action B *because of* her belief C and her desire D. This is a causal network, because action B was caused by the mental events C and D, and it was this causal mental network that enabled you to follow the plot. In fact, these beliefs, desires, and other thought processes *comprised* the plot. To put the point another way, your description was an exercise in attribution. You were attributing a series of mental states and events to the characters. If my guess was right, then it suggests that narrative is, in essence, the description of fictional mental functioning. In my view, readers enter the storyworlds of novels primarily by attempting to follow the workings of the fictional minds contained in them. Specifically, the thought experiment shows, I hope, that we are *all* cognitivists, whether we like it or not. We all think of novels in terms of the mental functioning of characters. In fact, as readers, we *have* to be cognitivists. Otherwise, we would not be able to read at all.

I illustrate my discussion of the four different issues referred to above—storyworlds, theory of mind, intermental thought, and unconscious thought—by applying them to one of the great passages of twentieth-century English literature: the description of Guy Crouchback's departure from Italy at the beginning of Evelyn Waugh's *Men at Arms*, the first volume in the *Sword of Honour* trilogy. Guy Crouchback is leaving his family home outside the Italian village of Santa Dulcina delle Rocce on the eve of the Second World War in order to go to London to enlist in the army. As he is driven away, he thinks about the word "simpatico" (meaning sympathetic in the sense of congenial, compatible, or of similar mind or temperament):

He was not loved, Guy knew, either by his household or in the town. He was accepted and respected but he was not *simpatico*. Gräfin von Gluck, who spoke no word of Italian and lived in undisguised concubinage with her butler, was *simpatica*. Mrs. Garry was *simpatica*, who distributed Protestant tracts, interfered with the fishermen's methods of killing octopuses and filled her house with stray cats.

Guy's uncle, Peregrine, a bore of international repute whose dreaded presence could empty the room in any centre of civilization—Uncle Peregrine was considered *molto simpatico*. The Wilmots were gross vulgarians; they used Santa Dulcina purely as a pleasure resort, subscribed to no local funds, gave rowdy parties and wore indecent clothes, talked of "wops" and often left after the summer with their bills to the tradesmen unpaid; but they had four boisterous and ill-favoured daughters whom the Santa-Dulcinesi had watched grow up. Better than this, they had lost a son bathing from the rocks. The Santa-Dulcinesi participated in these joys and sorrows. They observed with relish their hasty and unobtrusive departures at the end of the holidays. They were *simpatici*. Even Musgrave who had the castelletto before the Wilmots and bequeathed it his name, Musgrave who, it was said, could not go to England or America because of warrants for his arrest, "Musgrave the Monster," as the Crouchbacks used to call him—*he* was *simpatico*. Guy alone, whom they had known from infancy, who spoke their language and conformed to their religion, who was open-handed in all his dealings and scrupulously respectful of all their ways, whose grandfather built their school, whose mother had given a set of vestments embroidered by the Royal School of Needlework for the annual procession of St. Dulcina's bones—Guy alone was a stranger among them. (15–16)

These four issues resolve themselves into the following very simple statements:

- the passage constructs a fictional storyworld that readers have to gain access to in order to understand the narrative;
- readers gain access to this storyworld primarily by trying to follow the workings of the minds of the characters described in it and, in particular, by following how these characters try to follow the workings of each other's minds;

- one of the minds that is active in the passage is the collective or group mind of the inhabitants of the town; and
- some of the thinking that this group mind does is unconscious.

I now turn to explaining the background to each of these statements in turn.

Storyworlds

The concept of possible worlds began its modern resurgence within analytical philosophy. It was developed initially by such philosophers as Saul Kripke and David Lewis in order to deal with various technical issues in modal logic, the branch of logic that is concerned with necessity and possibility. So, for example, necessity can be defined in terms of propositions that are true in all possible worlds; possibility in terms of propositions that are true in at least one possible world; and impossibility in terms of propositions that are not true in any possible world. The idea was then adapted and extended by such narrative theorists as Lubomír Doležel, Thomas Pavel, and Marie-Laure Ryan to refer to the possible worlds that are created in works of literature and that are also known interchangeably as fictional worlds, narrative worlds, text worlds, and storyworlds. These theorists, however, together with others such as Ruth Ronen, are careful to emphasize the differences between the original philosophical model of possible worlds and the new narrative model of storyworlds.[2]

Storyworlds are possible worlds that are constructed by language through a performative force that is granted by cultural convention. When a third-person narrator makes a statement about a storyworld it is, according to speech act theory, a "performative utterance": it creates what it says in the act of saying it. So the question arises: how do readers comprehend fictional texts sufficiently to be able to enter the storyworld that is created by such statements? The work that has been done on this question by possible-worlds theorists builds on the earlier tradition of the reader response theory of Roman Ingarden and Wolfgang Iser. In Doležel's view, from "the viewpoint of the reader, the fictional text can be characterized as a set of instructions according to which the fictional world is to be recovered and reassembled" ("Mimesis and Possible Worlds," 489). Some of these sets of instructions have been well described by traditional, classical approaches, but there are many others (such as theory of mind, intermental thought, and unconscious thought) that are only now becoming visible through the application of cognitive approaches to literature.

We use the idea of the storyworld when we say of novels, as we all do, that they are "true to life" or "realistic," or that they are "inconsistent" or "far fetched" and so on. When we say these things we are positing the existence of a storyworld and then comparing it to our own real world. Let us try the comparison on this beautiful piece of writing. I think it is likely that when we do so the reaction of many readers will be: "How true! It's *so* accurate, *so* true to life. That *is* how people behave! Life *is* unfair!" But what do we mean when we say these things? After all, this is an imaginary town and these are imaginary people. Well, we mean that this imaginary world is like the real world in certain important ways, but what is the relationship that is conveyed by that single, simple word "like"?

The storyworld described in the passage consists in part of physical spaces containing various objects. Let us have a detailed look at this world. It is set in Italy, and the Second World War is about to begin. It contains taxis, households, towns, butlers, fishermen and fishing nets, octopuses, houses, cats, uncles, bores, pleasure resorts, funds, parties, clothes, bills, tradesmen, rocks, holidays, arrest warrants, language, religion, ways of doing things, grandfathers, schools, mothers, vestments, processions, bones, and strangers. I list these elements in such exhaustive and slightly surreal detail in order to illustrate how dense even short descriptions of storyworlds can be. The passage that contains these thirty-odd elements is less than three hundred words long. Even the most apparently simple reading process involves a number of very complex cognitive operations. An obvious point follows, but it is one that is well worth making explicit: in order to understand the passage, in order to reconstruct this storyworld, the reader has to know what taxis, butlers, fishing nets, and so forth are. As the length of the list shows, a good deal of this sort of real-world knowledge is required for narrative comprehension. But, in addition to knowing what these things are, we also have to be capable of making the many inferences contained in the language that describes them if we are to achieve full understanding. For example, when the text says that Uncle Peregrine could empty a room, we have to work out what this really means: everybody knows he is so boring that they leave the room when they see him in it.

Because it is clear that this storyworld is very like the real world in the sense that all of the objects contained in it exist in reality, we are able to apply to it what the narrative theorist Marie-Laure Ryan calls the principle of minimal departure. That is, we assume that any narrative storyworld is like our own until the text provides evidence of such departures from the real world as magical or supernatural entities or events. However, a further comparison between the storyworld and the real world is required. In addition to consisting of physical spaces and objects, storyworlds also consist of the minds of the characters who inhabit those spaces: Guy and the other people who live in the town. Although the sense of place and the existence of objects is important, these fictional minds are far more so. You may have noticed that the reader responses I anticipated above ("How true!") are concerned with fictional minds. Spaces and objects usually only have significance in so far as they affect the mental functioning of the characters in the storyworld. Just as our real minds always operate within a physical and social context, so fictional minds always operate within the specific social and physical context of their storyworld. The fishing nets, the taxis, the cats, and the location of the town are important because they mean something to the fictional minds of the characters who experience those things. Does the principle of minimal departure apply to these fictional minds just as it does to the physical objects? How do the minds described in the text correspond to the knowledge that we have of our own minds and the knowledge that we have of the minds of other people? Do the characters behave like real people? These questions bring us to the next section.

Theory of Mind

Readers have to use their theory of mind in order to try to follow the workings of characters' minds. "Theory of mind" is the term used by philosophers and psychologists to describe our awareness of the existence of other minds, our knowledge of how to interpret other people's thought processes, our mind-reading abilities in the real world. Anyone with a condition such as autism or Asperger's syndrome, and who therefore suffers from what is called "mindblindness," will have difficulty with their theory of mind. (However, it should be borne in mind that there is a very wide range of autistic spectrum disorders and the degree of difficulty with theory of mind will vary greatly between disorders.) Novel-reading is mind reading. Fiction can only be understood in this way.[3]

As I've noted, the physical spaces and objects of the storyworld are experienced by characters. In the same way, readers also interpret the *events* that take place there as the experiences of characters. For example, the Wilmots' flight from the town is not simply an event. It is something that is experienced by the Wilmots because it is an action that they take. They arrive at the belief that they have run out of money; they have the desire to escape the consequences of their lack of money; they come to the decision that it would be in their best interests to take the action of leaving the town. It is also an experience for the town. It watches the departure with relish because it is using its own theory of mind on the Wilmots. It has followed the causal mental network that I have just described and therefore understands why they are leaving. Finally, and more indirectly, it is an experience for Guy. He presumably has also followed the thinking behind the Wilmots' action, and he is also aware of the inexplicably tolerant attitude of the town toward it. The death of the son is another obvious example of an experience for both the family and the town. (By the way, to anticipate the section on intermental thought, for a moment, please note that I am talking quite naturally here about both the Wilmot family and the town as joint or group minds. I bet that you did not even notice this and certainly did not ask yourself, "How can a group of people have a collective mind?")

The storyworld is aspectual. What I mean is that, like the real world, it is different depending on the various aspects under which it is viewed. Its characters can only ever experience it from a particular perceptual and cognitive aspect at any one time. As the philosopher John Searle explains, "whenever we perceive anything or think about anything, we always do it under some aspects and not others" (156–57). The storyworld will therefore appear different to, and be experienced differently by, the various minds of the characters. Guy has knowledge, values, opinions, beliefs, and so on that differ substantially from those of the other people in the passage. For example, the notion of simpatico forms an important part of his mind because he so keenly feels its absence, whereas it appears that it does not form an important part of theirs. Guy obviously knows much more about the town than the Wilmots do, as he has taken the trouble to study it. He is respectful and knowledgeable about it; they flaunt the fact that they are not. He therefore views the storyworld as it relates to the town completely differently from them. In fact, the whole *Men at Arms* storyworld is so aspectual in nature that the Guy storyworld is a substantially different one from the Wilmots' storyworld. His town is a different one from their town.

You may be thinking to yourself by now that I am going too far. We are only talking here about 298 words on the page, and the proper names contained in those words refer only to literary constructs. We should not talk as though they are real people. I would fundamentally disagree. We *do* have to approach fictional characters in quite similar ways to real people; otherwise we will not be able to understand the novels that they appear in. We have to hypothesize, speculate, and theorize in precisely the way that I have been doing in order to make any sense of the 298 words. When we enter a storyworld we have to try to fill the gaps in it. Guy's relationship with the town is a prelude to the rest of the novel, which is concerned with his relationship with his army regiment. If we do not understand the former, we will not understand the latter. The relationship with the army is explored in much greater depth and over a longer period of time, but the initial cognitive frame provided by the passage that I am discussing here helpfully illuminates the problematical nature of his future army career.

At this point I have to introduce two technical terms. As Lisa Zunshine shows elsewhere in this volume, it is revealing to analyze fiction in terms of levels of intentionality. (The term "intentionality" is used in the philosophy of mind to refer to the "aboutness" of mental states. Such states nearly always have some content, are directed at something, are about something.) The other term is "focalization," which is a concept that is used in narrative theory to describe what is more generally known as point of view. Although the whole passage is being narrated by a third-person narrator, it represents Guy's thoughts and is seen from Guy's point of view, and so we say that it is *focalized* through Guy. One implication of this fact is that he may be mistaken about the town's feelings. However, everything that we find out about Guy during the course of the book strongly suggests that he is not wrong about the town.

But although the passage as a whole is focalized through Guy, look again at this sentence: "Better than this, they had lost a son bathing from the rocks." If the sentence is taken in isolation, the phrase "better than this" is extraordinary. What can it mean? It cannot be better for the narrator, or for Guy, the main focalizer, and it is obviously not better for the Wilmots that they have lost their son. The answer is that it is better for the town, in the sense that his death makes the Wilmots more simpatico. In this sentence, the Wilmots are being presented from the town's point of view: the description of the event is focalized through the town. So, although the whole passage is focalized through Guy, this specific focalization is embedded within Guy's focalization. To put the point another way, in this sentence, I have counted six levels of intentionality:

1. The reader understands
2. how the narrator presents
3. how Guy experiences
4. how the town experiences
5. how the Wilmot family experiences
6. the fact that the son experienced a fatal accident.

So, this apparently very simple sentence of only twelve words contains a complex set of different levels of thought. Note in particular, though, that the first, second, third, and sixth levels relate to individual minds and the fourth and fifth levels relate to group minds. This point leads us onto the next section.

Intermental Thought

As storyworlds are profoundly social in nature (even Robinson Crusoe has his Friday), novels contain a good deal of what is called "intermental," or joint, group, shared, or collective thinking, as well as "intramental," or individual thought. Intermental thought is known as socially distributed, situated, or extended cognition, and also, especially in literary studies, as intersubjectivity.[4] Just as in real life, where much of our thinking is done in groups, a good deal of fictional thinking is done by large organizations, small groups, families, couples, friends, and other intermental units. In fact, a large amount of the subject matter of novels is the formation, development, maintenance, and breakdown of these intermental units. Within the real-mind disciplines of psychology and philosophy there is a good deal of interest in distributed or situated cognition: the realization that mental functioning cannot be understood merely by analysing what goes on inside the skull but can only be fully comprehended once it has been seen in its social and physical context. Social psychologists routinely use the terms "mind" and "mental action" not only to refer to individuals but also to describe groups of people working as intermental units. So, it is appropriate to say of groups that they think or that they remember. As the psychologist James Wertsch puts it, a dyad (that is, two people working as a cognitive system) can carry out such functions as problem solving on an intermental plane (27). To illustrate, Wertsch tells the story of how his daughter lost her shoes and he helped her to remember where she had left them. Wertsch asks: who is doing the remembering here? He is not, because he had no prior knowledge of where they were, and she is not, because she had forgotten where they were. It was the intermental unit that remembered.[5]

What is achieved by talking in this way instead of simply referring to individuals pooling their resources and working in cooperation together? The advocates of the concept of distributed cognition such as James Wertsch, Edwin Hutchins (*Cognition in the Wild*), Daniel Dennett (*Kinds of Minds*), Clifford Geertz, Gregory Bateson, and Andy Clark and David Chalmers all stress that the purpose of the concept is increased explanatory power. They argue that the way to delineate a cognitive system is to draw the limiting line so that you do not cut anything out which leave things inexplicable.[6] That was the point of Wertsch's question: who is doing the remembering? If you draw the line narrowly around individuals and maintain that cognition can only be individual, then things remain inexplicable. Neither person remembered. If you draw the line more widely and accept the concept of an intermental cognitive system, then things are explained. The intermental unit remembered.

In the rest of this section, I make some general points about fictional intermental units and then relate these points to the passage. I do not consider the various ways in which these units are *constructed* by fictional discourse (for example, by use of the passive voice).[7] In considering mental functioning in fiction, we need to use both an internalist and an externalist perspective. An internalist perspective stresses those aspects of cognitive functioning that are inner, introspective, solitary, private, individual, and mysterious. By contrast, an externalist perspective stresses those aspects of mental functioning that are outer, active, public, social, behavioral, and evident. It seems to me that an internalist perspective by itself will not tell us much about the mental functioning that is going on in the passage under discussion. It will tell us that the text is describing Guy's individual, private feelings, but after that, it is not much use. Only an externalist perspective will reveal, for example, that the town has an intermental mind, that the cognitive functioning of the individual characters is clearly apparent to the town from their action and behavior, and that Guy's feelings only make sense when understood as a reaction to the feelings of the town. The passage is not just about the intramental functioning of one individual and not just about the intermental functioning of the town: it is about the complex, dialogical relationship between the two.

What do I mean by referring to the *mind* of the town? The claim that I am making regarding the role of the town is a strong one. It should be distinguished from two much weaker arguments. First, I am certainly not simply saying that the town has an important role in providing a social context within which individual characters operate and is thereby a pervasive influence on their intramental thought. Who would disagree with such an anodyne claim? Second, I am not referring to this mind in any metaphorical sense. I am going much further than these two positions in saying that within the storyworld the town actually and literally does have a mind of its own. Look again at the passage and at the range of cognitive functioning of which this group mind is capable. It has known Guy since infancy. It does not love him because it does not find him simpatico, but it does accept and respect him. It finds Guy still a stranger. It does find simpatico the other individuals who are listed in the passage. It can forgive those others their faults. It watches the Wilmot daughters grow up. It participates in the joys and sorrows of the Wilmots. It observes "with relish" their departures. It has its language, its religion, and its ways. How can an entity that is capable of such wide-ranging and sophisticated cognitive functioning *not* be called a mind? You may now be asking yourself: surely, any thinking that a town does must be different from the thinking that an individual does? But of course! It would be silly to disagree. I am not saying that intermental and intramental minds are the same. I am saying that they are similar in some ways, different in others, but they are both still minds. Just different kinds of minds.

Unconscious Thought

I would now like to talk about some of the ideas on unconscious thought that are contained in a brilliant book by the psychologist Timothy Wilson called *Strangers to Ourselves* (2002). A good deal of work has been done by a number of psychologists on unconscious thought, but I am using Wilson because he synthesizes this work in a very clear and approachable way. Although he discusses only individuals, it will be illuminating, I hope, to apply his ideas on the role of the unconscious to the thinking of groups. I argue that because the workings of the town's mind have an important unconscious element the town judges people in the way that the unconscious mind does, that the town's attitudes to individuals are conditioned by "feeling rules," and that, as a result, the town has "dual attitudes" (these two terms are explained below) toward Guy and the other individuals. And, most importantly, these features account for what is most remarkable and distinctive about the passage—its counterintuitive and apparently paradoxical quality.

It is important to stress right from the beginning that the unconscious thought that I discuss consists of much more than just the *Freudian* unconscious of psychoanalytical theory. Here are three examples of this much wider category. First, Wilson quotes a real estate agent as saying that she always listens very carefully to what her clients tell her about the sort of house that they want to buy. She then completely ignores what they have said and simply watches them as they react to the houses that they visit. Often, a very different picture of their *real* wants emerges. The real estate agent finds the evidence of what customers do much more reliable than the evidence of what they say (164). In the second example, students were asked if they would buy a flower as part of a campus charity event and 83 percent said that they would. In fact, only 43 percent did. When they were asked if other people would buy a flower, their prediction (of 56 percent) was more accurate. In a very similar sort of study, people predicted that they would donate an average of $2.44 of their earnings to charity and that other people would donate $1.83. The actual figure was $1.53 (85). The final example is an extraordinary one. Young men were approached by an attractive young woman in a park and asked to take part in an experiment. During the discussion, she gave them her phone number. Some of the men were approached while they were negotiating a flimsy and scary footbridge over a deep gorge and others while they were sitting on a park bench. Sixty-five percent of the men on the footbridge called her and asked for a date while only thirty percent of the men on the bench did so. Why the difference? The researchers predicted that the men on the footbridge would mistake their beating hearts, shortness of breath, and perspiration for physical attraction, and this appears to be exactly what happened (101–2).

Psychologists such as Wilson conclude from this evidence that people are very often simply mistaken about the nature of their mental functioning. They think with their conscious mind that they are going to do one thing, but, because the decisions are in fact taken by their unconscious mind, they end up by doing another. For this reason, we are often much more accurate in predicting other people's behavior than we are in predicting our own. According to Wilson, "There is no direct access to the . . . unconscious, no matter how hard we try. . . . It can thus be fruitless to try to examine the . . . unconscious by looking inward. It is often better to *deduce* the nature of our hidden minds by looking outward at our behaviour and how others react to us and coming up with a good narrative" (16). What Wilson is saying is that our private thought is often not immediately accessible and available to us. *We have to infer what we ourselves are thinking in much the same way as we infer what other people are thinking.* We deduce the nature of the unconscious mind by looking outward at the behavior that results from it. That is what Guy does in arriving at the conclusion that his behavior makes him nonsimpatico even though he tries so hard to be simpatico. So, although thought can be private and inaccessible to others (no one else will know exactly what thoughts Guy is having in the precise form in which he is having them), thought can also be very public and available to others. The workings of the individual minds of Gräfin von Gluck, Mrs. Garry, and the Wilmots are visible to the town and to Guy, and the workings of the town's intermental mind are visible to Guy as well. In particular, he believes from the behavior of the townspeople that they find others simpatico but not him. Remember the externalist perspective that I referred to earlier? This is how it works in practice.

Am I right in saying that the town has unconscious feelings and does not have any direct access to them? Let us speculate. Imagine an inhabitant of the town being asked to make his or her feelings explicit and therefore conscious: "How do you feel about Mr. Crouchback? Do you like Mr. Musgrave more?" I find it quite likely that they would then be conscious of what they are *supposed* to feel and reply that certainly they like Mr. Crouchback as much as Mr. Musgrave, if not more. However, that is the sort of insincere reassurance that people feel that they have to produce in order to be polite. So let us put the hypothetical question to the inhabitants in a different way and ask them, as Wilson suggests, to analyze their behavior. "Do you behave in a less open or more reserved way toward Mr. Crouchback than toward Mr. Musgrave?" It seems quite plausible to me that they would be *genuinely* surprised to hear that this was a possibility and that Mr. Crouchback had noticed any difference. Their conscious minds would find it difficult to recognize the behavior that has resulted from the workings of their unconscious minds.

The unconscious is "a spin doctor that interprets information outside of awareness [and that] does a reasonably accurate job of interpreting other people's behaviour" (31). "One of the most interesting properties of the . . . unconscious is that it uses stereotypes to categorise and evaluate people" (11). In doing so, it is fast, unintentional, uncontrollable, and effortless (41). Specifically, it has a tendency to jump to conclusions and often fails to change its mind in the face of contrary evidence (55–56). This sounds to me like a fairly good description of the cognitive functioning of the town. It certainly categorizes and evaluates people. Precisely how it arrives at its views is a gap in the storyworld, but I would suggest that it is likely to be done in a fast, unintentional, uncontrollable, and effortless way. It is difficult to imagine the townspeople agonizing at length about what they should think about Guy, Gräfin von Gluck, and the others. It also seems that the town has a tendency to jump to conclusions and fails to change its mind in the face of contrary evidence. Guy has been trying for twenty years to get the town to change its mind and has failed. On the other hand, it has done a reasonably accurate job of interpreting or mind reading Guy's mind. (I develop this point below.)

Wilson points out that while forming its views the unconscious can produce feelings and preferences that are not always "rational." That is to say, the workings of the unconscious have their *own* rationality, which is often very different from the rationality of the workings of the conscious mind.[8] He then draws attention to the resulting difficulty in recognizing the feelings and emotions generated by the unconscious mind:

The conscious system is quite sensitive to personal and cultural prescriptions about how one is *supposed* to feel. . . . People might assume that their feelings conform to these prescriptions and fail to notice instances in which they do not. These *"feeling rules"* can make it difficult to perceive how one's . . . unconscious feels about the matter.

(129, EMPHASIS ADDED)

Feeling rules are examples of "emotionology," the concept that David Herman describes in "Narrative Theory after the Second Cognitive Revolution" (chap. 8 in this volume). Wilson refers to the "phenomenon in which people have two feelings toward the same topic, one more conscious than the other," as *"dual attitudes"* (132, emphasis added). To illustrate, he quotes from a short story in which two adult cousins reminisce about their childhoods. One of them, Blake, says that he was about thirty before he realized that he had always hated their childhood pony, Topper. "It wasn't until Blake said it that Kate realized that she, too, had always hated Topper. For years they had been conned into loving him, because children love their pony, and their dog, and their parents, and picnics, and the ocean, and the lovely chocolate cake" (118). This last sentence is a list of feeling rules: children must have positive feelings about their pony, their dog, and so on. As a result, the cousins had a dual attitude toward the pony: the positive feelings that they knew they were supposed to have according to the feeling rules and the negative feelings that they subsequently and consciously discovered they had unconsciously had all along.

The *Men at Arms* passage is a list of feeling rules and also of dual attitudes. It is a list of the reasons why the conscious mind of the town feels it *ought* to find Guy simpatico and *ought* to find the others less so. As with individual minds, collective minds can also experience feeling rules and dual attitudes. These feeling rules are implied in all the details that are given about the individuals and about Guy. Every one of the descriptions of the individuals is a reason for disapproval: not bothering to learn Italian, interfering with the fishing, being boring, being gross vulgarians, being a criminal. Every one of the descriptions of Guy is a reason for approval: he speaks their language and follows their religion; he is open handed and scrupulously respectful of all their ways. Nevertheless, each of these descriptions is balanced by a conclusion that contradicts it: the individuals are simpatico; Guy is not simpatico. The unconscious mind of the town feels the opposite of what it should feel. It is in this way that every sentence in the passage contains a dual attitude toward Guy or toward the others. This conflict gives the passage its characteristic sense of tension and unease, which arises, as I've said, from its apparently paradoxical and counterintuitive nature. The one who seems most likely to be found simpatico is not; all those that seem least likely to be are. So there are deeper, unspecified reasons at work that account for the feelings of the town.

I talked just now about the fact that the apparent irrationality of unconscious thought is simply a different rationality from conscious thought. The narrator exploits this difference by making use of readers' assumptions about what they would think the villagers might find simpatico on the conscious level: this is the list of feeling rules. But in the case of the town of Santa Dulcina delle Rocce, these considerations do not seem to rate very highly. Another apparent irrationality is the disregard for the importance of the theory of mind that I discussed in the third section. The individuals who are simpatico are not aware of the fact that they are. They do not give the impression that they are particularly either self-aware or aware of the feelings of others. Otherwise, they would not behave in such antisocial ways. Guy, on the contrary, tries hard to read the mind of the village and is found to be nonsimpatico. The moral seems to be that the less you care about being simpatico, the more likely it is that you will be. The reader may then be tempted to say that the fictional mind of the town is irrational. But it is clear, I think, that this is not so. It is simply that the town is employing a different rationality. What is this unconscious rationality? In my view, it is simply a love of life. They favor humanity, facing life with gusto, with self-confidence, with self-belief, and, as the passage says, "with relish." They like generosity of spirit. Guy is not simpatico because, for all his timid efforts to be liked, he has a poverty of spirit, a meanness of the soul, a meagerness about him that they recognize. To use a vulgar British expression, he is "tight arsed." His life is sterile. In the words of Deuteronomy (30:19) and also of the opening sequence of the film *Trainspotting*, he should "choose life!" Once this point is realized, the apparent paradoxes dissolve, it is counterintuitive no longer, and the passage makes perfect sense.

Conclusion

This chapter will have succeeded if, having read it, you think to yourself: I have discovered a lot about that piece of writing that I would not have done had a cognitive approach not been applied to it. The chapter will have failed in its purpose if, having read it, you think to yourself: it told me nothing that I would not have thought of by myself.

CHAPTER NINE

Theory of Mind and Experimental Representations of Fictional Consciousness

LISA ZUNSHINE

Let me begin with a seemingly nonsensical question.[1] When Peter Walsh unexpectedly comes to see Clarissa Dalloway "at eleven o'clock on the morning of the day she [is] giving a party" and, "positively trembling," asks her how she is, "taking both her hands," "kissing both her hands," thinking that "she's grown older," and deciding that he "shan't tell her anything about it . . . for she's grown older" (40), how do we know that his "trembling" is to be accounted for by his excitement at seeing his Clarissa again after all these years, and not, for instance, by his progressing Parkinson's disease?

Assuming that you are a particularly good-natured reader of *Mrs. Dalloway*, you might patiently explain to me that if Walsh's trembling were occasioned by an illness, Woolf would tell us so. She wouldn't leave us long under the impression that Walsh's body language betrays his agitation, his joy, and his embarrassment and that the meeting has instantaneously and miraculously brought back the old days when Clarissa and Peter had "this queer power of communicating without words" because, reflecting Walsh's "trembling," Clarissa herself is "so surprised, . . . so glad, so shy, so utterly taken aback to have [him] come to her unexpectedly in the morning!" (40). Too much, you would point out, hinges on our getting the emotional undertones of the scene right for Woolf to withhold from us a crucial piece of information about Walsh's health.

I then would ask you why it is that were Walsh's trembling caused by an illness, Woolf would have to explicitly tell us so, but as it is not, she can simply take for granted that we will interpret it as being caused by his emotions. In other words, what allows Woolf to assume that we will automatically read a character's body language as indicative of his thoughts and feelings?

She assumes this because of our collective past history as readers, you perhaps would say. Writers have been using descriptions of their characters' behaviors to inform us about their feelings since time immemorial, and we expect authors to do so when we open the book. We all learn, whether consciously or not, that the default interpretation of behavior reflects the character's state of mind, and every fictional story that we read reinforces our tendency to make that kind of interpretation first.[2]

Had this imaginary conversation about readers' automatic assumptions taken place twenty years ago, it would have ended here. Or it would have never happened—not even in this hypothetical form—because the answers to my naïve questions would have seemed so obvious. Today, however, this conversation can and must go on because recent research in cognitive psychology and anthropology has shown that not *every* reader can learn that the default meaning of a character's behavior lies with the character's mental state. To understand what enables most of us to constrain the range of possible interpretations, we may have to go beyond the explanation that evokes our personal reading histories and admit some evidence from our evolutionary history.

In what follows, then, I attempt to make a broader case for introducing the recent findings of cognitive scientists into literary studies by showing how their research into our ability to explain behavior in terms of the underlying states of mind—or our *mind-reading* ability—can furnish us with a series of surprising insights into our interaction with literary texts. I begin by discussing the research on autism that alerted cognitive psychologists to the existence of the cognitive capacity that enables us to narrow the range of interpretations of people's behavior down to their mental states and that makes literature, as we know it, possible. I then consider the potentially controversial issue of the "effortlessness" with which we thus read other people's—including literary characters'—minds. To explore one specific aspect of the role played by such mind reading in fictional representations of consciousness, I then return to *Mrs. Dalloway*. Here I describe a series of recent experiments exploring our capacity for imagining serially embedded representations of mental states (that is, "representations of representations of representations" of mental states) and suggest that Woolf's prose pushes this particular capacity beyond its everyday "zone of comfort," a fact that may account partially for the trepidation that Woolf's writing tends to provoke in some of her readers.[3] I conclude by addressing two issues concerning the interdisciplinary potential of the new field of cognitive approaches to literature. First, I discuss the relationship between cognitive analysis and the more traditional literary-historical analysis of Woolf. Second, I suggest that literary critics should take a more proactive stand toward cognitive scientists' increasing tendency to use literature in their study of human cognition.

Theory of Mind and Autism

"Mind reading" is a term used by cognitive psychologists to describe our ability to explain people's behavior in terms of their thoughts, feelings, beliefs, and desires; for example, "Lucy *reached* for the chocolate because she *wanted* something sweet," or "Peter Walsh was *trembling* because he was *excited* to see Clarissa again." They also call this ability our "theory of mind," and I use the two terms interchangeably throughout this chapter.

This proliferation of fancy terminology adds extra urgency to the question of why we need this newfangled concept of mind reading, or theory of mind, to explain what appears so obvious. Our ability to interpret the behavior of real-life people—*and, by extension,* of literary characters—in terms of their underlying states of mind seems to be such an integral part of being human that we could be understandably reluctant to dignify it with a fancy term and elevate it into a separate object of study.[4] Indeed, the main reason that theory of mind has received the sustained attention of cognitive psychologists over the last twenty years is that they discovered people whose ability to "see bodies as animated by minds" (Brook and Ross, 81) was drastically impaired—people with autism. By studying autism and a related constellation of cognitive deficits (such as Asperger's syndrome), cognitive scientists and philosophers of mind began to appreciate our mind-reading ability as a special cognitive endowment, structuring in suggestive ways our everyday communication and cultural representations.

Most scholars working with theory of mind agree that this adaptation must have developed during the "massive neurocognitive evolution" that took place during the Pleistocene, when our brain increased threefold in size. The determining factor behind the increase in brain size was the social nature of our species (which we share with other primates).[5] The emergence of a theory of mind "module" was evolution's answer to the "staggeringly complex" challenge faced by our ancestors, who needed to make sense of the behavior of other people in their group, which could include up to two hundred individuals. In his influential 1995 study, *Mindblindness: An Essay on Autism and a Theory of Mind*, Simon Baron-Cohen points out that "attributing mental states to a complex system (such as a human being) is by far the easiest way of understanding it," that is, of "coming up with an explanation of the complex system's behavior and predicting what it will do next" (21).[6] Thus our tendency to explain observed behavior in terms of underlying mental states seems to be so effortless and automatic because our evolved cognitive architecture "prods" us to learn and practice mind reading daily, from the beginning of awareness. (This is not to say, however, that our actual interpretations of other people's mental states are always correct—far from it!)

Baron-Cohen describes autism as the "most severe of all childhood psychiatric conditions," one that affects between approximately four to fifteen children per ten thousand and that "occurs in every country in which it has been looked for and across social classes" (60). Although "mindreading is not an all-or-none affair [since] . . . [p]eople with autism lack the ability to a greater or lesser degree" (Origgi and Sperber, 163), and although the condition may be somewhat alleviated if the child receives a range of "educational and therapeutic interventions," autism presently remains "a lifelong disorder" (Baron-Cohen, 60). Autism is highly heritable, and its key symptoms, which manifest themselves in the first years of life, include a profound impairment of social and communicative development and a "lack of the usual flexibility, imagination, and pretence" (Baron-Cohen, 60).[7] It is also characterized—crucially for our present discussion—by a lack of interest in fiction and storytelling, differing in degree, though not in kind, across the wide spectrum of autism cases.

In his book *An Anthropologist on Mars*, Oliver Sacks describes one remarkable case of autism, remarkable because the afflicted woman, Temple Grandin, has been able to overcome her handicap to some degree. She has a doctorate in agricultural science, teaches at the University of Arizona, and can speak about her perceptions, thus giving us a unique insight into what it means not to be able to read other people's minds. Sacks reports Grandin's school experience: "Something was going on between the other kids, something swift, subtle, constantly changing—an exchange of meanings, a negotiation, a swiftness of understanding so remarkable that sometimes she wondered if they were all telepathic. She is now aware of the existence of those social signals. She can infer them, she says, but she herself cannot perceive them, cannot participate in this magical communication directly, or conceive of the many-leveled, kaleidoscopic states of mind behind it" (272).

Predictably, Grandin comments on having a difficult time understanding fictional narratives. She remembers being "bewildered by *Romeo and Juliet*: 'I never knew what they were up to' " (259). Fiction presents a challenge to people with autism because in many ways it calls for the same kind of mind reading as is necessary in regular human communication—that is, the inference of the mental state from the behavior.

To compensate for her inability to interpret facial expressions, which at first left her a "target of tricks and exploitation," Grandin has built up over the years something resembling a "library of videotapes, which she could play in her mind and inspect at any time—'videos' of how people behaved in different circumstances. She would play these over and over again, and learn, by degrees, to correlate what she saw, so that she could then predict how people in similar circumstances might act" (259–60). This account of Grandin's "library" suggests that we do not just "learn" how to communicate with people and read their emotions (or how to read the minds of fictional characters based on their behavior)—Grandin, after all, has had as many opportunities to "learn" these things as you and me—but that we also have evolved cognitive architecture that makes this particular kind of learning possible. If this architecture is damaged, as in the case of autism, a wealth of experience will never fully make up for the damage.

Whereas the correlation between the impaired theory of mind and the lack of interest in fiction and storytelling is highly suggestive, the jury is still out on the exact nature of the connection between the two. It could be argued, for example, that the cognitive mechanisms that evolved to process information about human thoughts and feelings are constantly on the alert, checking out their environment for cues that fit their input conditions.[8] On some level, then, works of fiction manage to "cheat" these mechanisms into "believing" that they are in the presence of material that they were "designed" to process, that is, that they are in the presence of agents endowed with a potential for a rich array of intentional stances. Literature pervasively capitalizes on and stimulates theory-of-mind mechanisms that evolved to deal with real people, even as readers remain aware on some level that fictive characters are not real people at all.[9]

Thus one preliminary implication of applying what we know about theory of mind to our study of fiction is that theory of mind makes literature as we know it possible. The very process of making sense of what we read appears to be grounded in our ability to invest the flimsy verbal constructions that we generously call "characters" with a potential for a variety of thoughts, feelings, and desires, and then to look for the "cues" that allow us to guess at their feelings and thus to predict their actions.[10] (The illusion is complete: like Erich Auerbach, we are convinced that "the people whose story the author is telling experience much more than [the author] can ever hope to tell" [549].)

"Effortless" Mind Reading

As we discuss mind reading as an evolved cognitive capacity enabling us both to interact with each other and to make sense of fiction, we have to be aware of the definitional differences between the terminology used by cognitive scientists and literary critics. Cognitive psychologists and philosophers of mind investigating our theory of mind ask such questions as: What is the evolutionary history of this adaptation, that is, in response to what environmental challenges did it evolve? At what age and in what forms does it begin to manifest itself? What are its neurological foundations? They focus on the ways "mind-reading [plays] an essential part in *successful* communication" (Baron-Cohen, 29, emphasis added). When cognitive scientists turn to literary (or, as in the case below, cinematic) examples to illustrate our ability for investing fictional characters with minds of their own and reading those minds, they stress the "effortlessness" with which we do so. As Dennett observes, "watching a film with a highly original and unstereotyped plot, we see the hero smile at the villain and we all swiftly and effortlessly arrive at the same complex theoretical diagnosis: 'Aha!' we conclude (but perhaps not consciously), 'He wants her to think he doesn't know she intends to defraud her brother!' " (48).

Readers outside the cognitive science community may find this emphasis on "effortlessness" and "success" unhelpful. Literary critics, in particular, know that the process of attributing thoughts, beliefs, and desires to other people may lead to *misinterpreting* those thoughts, beliefs, and desires. Thus, they would rightly resist any notion that we could effortlessly—that is, correctly and unambiguously, nearly telepathically—figure out what the person whose behavior we are trying to explain is thinking. It is important to underscore here that cognitive scientists and lay readers (here including literary critics) bring very different frames of reference to measuring the relative "success" of mind reading. For the lay reader, the example of a glaring failure in mind reading and communication might be a person's interpreting her friend's tears of joy as tears of grief and reacting accordingly. For a cognitive psychologist, a glaring failure in mind reading would be a person's not even knowing that the water coursing down her friend's face is supposed to be somehow indicative of his feelings at that moment. If you find the latter possibility absurd, recall that this is how (many) people with autism experience the world, perhaps because of neurological deficits that prevent their cognitive architecture from narrowing the range of interpretive possibilities and restricting them, in this particular case, to the domain of emotions.

Consequently, one of the crucial insights offered by cognitive psychologists is that by thus parsing the world and narrowing the scope of relevant interpretations of a given phenomenon, our cognitive adaptations enable us to contemplate an infinitely rich array of interpretations *within* that scope. As Nancy Easterlin puts it, "Without the inborn tendency to organize information in specific ways, we would not be able to experience choice in our responses" ("Making Knowledge" 137).[11] "Constraints," N. Katherine Hayles observes in a different context, "operate constructively by restricting the sphere of possibilities" ("Desiring Agency," 145).[12] In other words, our theory of mind allows us to connect Peter Walsh's trembling to his emotional state (in the absence of any additional information that could account for his body language in a different way), thus usefully constraining our interpretive domain and enabling us to start considering endlessly nuanced choices *within that domain.* The context of the episode would then constrain our interpretation even further; we could decide, for instance, that it is unlikely that Peter is trembling because of a barely concealed hatred and begin to explore the complicated gamut of his bittersweet feelings. Any additional information that we would bring to bear upon our reading of the passage—biographical, sociohistorical, literary-historical—would alert us to new shades in its meaning and could, in principle, lead us to some startling conjectures about Walsh's state of mind. Note too, that the description of Walsh's "trembling" may connect to something in my personal experience that will induce me to give significantly more weight to one detail of the text and to ignore others, which means that you and I may wind up with wildly different readings of Peter's and Clarissa's emotions "at eleven o'clock on the morning of the day she [is] giving a party." None of this can happen, however, before we have first eliminated a whole range of other explanations, such as those evoking various physical forces (for instance, a disease) acting upon the body, and have come to focus solely on the mind of the character.

This elimination of irrelevant interpretations can happen so fast as to be practically imperceptible. Consider an example from Stanley Fish's famous essay, "How to Recognize a Poem." To demonstrate his point that our mental operations are "limited by institutions in which we are already embedded," Fish reports the following classroom experiment:

> While I was in the course of vigorously making a point, one of my students, William Newlin by name, was just as vigorously waving his hand. When I asked the other members of the class what it was that [he] was doing, they all answered that he was seeking permission to speak. I then asked them how they knew that. The immediate reply was that it was obvious; what else could he be thought of doing? The meaning of his gesture, in other words, was right there on its surface, available for reading by anyone who had the eyes to see. That meaning, however, would not have been available to someone without any knowledge of what was involved in being a student. Such a person might have thought that Mr. Newlin was pointing to the fluorescent lights hanging from the ceiling, or calling our attention to some object that was about to fall ("the sky is falling," "the sky is falling"). And if the someone in question were a child of elementary or middle-school age, Mr. Newlin might well have been seen as seeking permission

not to speak but to go to the bathroom, an interpretation or reading that would never have occurred to a student at Johns Hopkins or any other institution of "higher learning." (110–11)

Fish's point that "it is only by inhabiting . . . the institutions [that] precede us [here, the college setting] that we have access to the public and conventional senses they make [here, the raised hand means the person seeks permission to speak]" (110) is well taken. Yet note that all of his patently "wrong" explanations (e.g., Mr. Newlin thought that the sky was falling; he wanted to go to the bathroom, etc.) are "correct" in the sense that they call on a theory of mind; that is, they explain the student's behavior in terms of his underlying thoughts, beliefs, and desires. As Fish puts it, "what else could he be *thought* of doing?" (emphasis added). Nobody ventured to suggest, for example, that there was a thin, practically invisible string threaded through the loop in the classroom's ceiling, one end of which was attached to Mr. Newlin's sleeve and the other of which was held by a person sitting behind him who could pull the string any time and produce the corresponding movement of Mr. Newlin's hand. Absurd, we should say, especially since nobody could observe any string hovering over Mr. Newlin's head. Is it not equally absurd, however, to explain a behavior in terms of a mental state that is completely unobservable? Yet we do it automatically, and the only reason that no neurotypical (i.e., nonautistic) person would think of a "mechanistic" explanation (such as the string pulling on the sleeve) is that we have cognitive adaptations that prompt us to "see bodies as animated by minds."

But then, by the very logic of Fish's argument, which urges us not to take for granted the complex *institutional* embedment that allows us to make sense of the world, shouldn't we inquire with equal vigor into the *cognitive* embedment that—as I hope I have demonstrated in the example above—profoundly informs the institutional one? Given the suggestively constrained range of the "wrong" interpretations offered by Fish (that is, all his interpretations connect the behavior to a mental state), shouldn't we qualify his assertion that unless we read Mr. Newlin's raised hand in the context of his being a student, "there is nothing *in the form* of [his] gesture that tells his fellow students how to determine its significance" (112)? Surely the *form* of the gesture—staying with the word that Fish himself has emphasized—is quite informative because its very deliberateness seems to delimit the range of possible "wrong" interpretations. That is, had Mr. Newlin unexpectedly jerked his hand instead of "waving" it "vigorously," some mechanical explanation such as a physiological spasm or someone pushing his elbow, perhaps even a wire attached to his sleeve, would seem far less absurd.

To return, then, to the potentially problematic issue of the effortlessness with which we "read" minds, a flagrantly "wrong"—from lay readers' perspective—interpretation, such as taking tears of grief for tears of joy or thinking that Mr. Newlin raises his hand to point out that the sky is falling, is still "effortless" from the point of view of cognitive psychologists because of the ease with which we correlate tears with an emotional state or the raised hand with a certain underlying desire/intention. Mind reading is thus effortless in the sense that we "intuitively" connect people's behavior to their mental states—as in the example involving Walsh's "trembling"—although our subsequent description of their mental states could run a broad gamut of mistaken or disputed meanings. For any description is, as Fish reminds us on a different occasion, "always and already interpretation," a "text," a story reflecting the personal history, biases, and desires of the reader.[13]

Can Cognitive Science Tell Us Why We Are Afraid of *Mrs. Dalloway?*

How much prompting do we need to begin to attribute a mind of her own to a fictional character? Very little, it seems, since any indication that we are dealing with a self-propelled entity (e.g., "Peter Walsh has come back") leads us to assume that this entity possesses thoughts, feelings, and desires, at least some of which we will intuit, interpret, and, frequently, misinterpret. Writers exploit our constant readiness to posit a mind whenever we observe behavior when they experiment with the amount and kind of interpretation of the characters' mental states that they supply. When Woolf shows Clarissa observing Peter's body language (Clarissa notices that he is "positively trembling"), she has an option of providing us with a representation of either Clarissa's mind that would make sense of Peter's physical action (something to the effect of "how excited must he be to see her again!") or of Peter's own mind (as in "so excited was he to see his Clarissa again!"). Instead she tells us, first, that Peter is thinking that Clarissa has grown older and, second, that Clarissa is thinking that Peter looks "exactly the same; . . . the same queer look; the same check suit" (40). Peter's "trembling" still feels like an integral part of this scene, but make no mistake: we, the readers, are called on to supply the missing bit of information (such as "he must be excited to see her again") that makes the narrative emotionally cohesive.

Hemingway famously made it his trademark to underrepresent his protagonists' feelings by forcing the majority of his characters' physical actions to stand in for mental states (for example, as in the ending of *A Farewell to Arms*: "After a while I went out and left the hospital and walked back to the hotel in the rain" [314]). Hemingway could afford such a deliberate, and in its own way highly elaborate, undertelling for the same reason that Woolf could afford to let Peter's trembling "speak for itself": our evolved cognitive tendency to assume that there *must be* a mental stance behind each physical action and the fact that we strive to represent to ourselves that possible mental stance even when the author has left us with the absolute minimum of necessary cues for constructing such a representation.

It is thus when we start to inquire into how writers of fiction *experiment* with our mind-reading ability, and perhaps even push it further, that the insights offered by cognitive scientists become particularly pertinent. Although cognitive scientists' investigation of theory of mind is very much a project in progress, literary scholars have enough carefully documented research already available to them to begin asking such questions as: Is it possible that literary narrative trains our capacity for mind reading and also tests its limits? How do different cultural-historical milieus encourage different literary explorations of this capacity? How do different genres? Speculative and tentative as the answers to these questions are at this point, they mark the possibility of a genuine interaction between cognitive psychology and literary studies, with both fields having much to offer to each other.

This section's tongue-in-cheek title refers to my attempt to apply a series of recent experiments conducted by cognitive psychologists studying theory of mind to *Mrs. Dalloway*. I find the results of such an application both exciting and unnerving. On the one hand, I can argue now with a reasonable degree of confidence that certain aspects of Woolf's prose do place extraordinarily high demands on our mind-reading ability and that this could account, *at least in part*, for the fact that many readers feel challenged by that novel. On the other hand, I have come to be "afraid" of *Mrs. Dalloway*—and, indeed, other novels—in a different fashion, realizing that any initial inquiry into the ways fiction teases our theory of mind immediately raises more questions about theory of mind and fiction than we are currently able to answer. My ambivalence, in other words, stems from the realization that theory of mind underlies our interaction with literary texts in such profound and complex ways that any endeavor to isolate one particular aspect of such an interaction feels like carving the text at joints that are fundamentally, paradigmatically absent.

This proviso should be kept in mind as we turn to the experiments investigating one particular aspect of theory of mind, namely, our ability to navigate multiple levels of intentionality present in a narrative. Although theory of mind is formally defined as a second-order intentionality, as in the statements "I believe that you desire X" or "Peter Walsh thinks that Clarissa 'would think [him] a failure'" (43), the levels of intentionality can "recurse" further back, for example, to the fourth level, as in a statement like "I believe that you think that she believes that he thinks that X." Dennett, who first discussed this recursiveness of the levels of intentionality in 1983, thought it could be, in principle, infinite. A recent series of striking experiments reported by Robin Dunbar and his colleagues have suggested, however, that our cognitive architecture may discourage the proliferation of cultural narratives that involve "infinite" levels of intentionality.

In those experiments, subjects were given two types of stories—one that involved a "simple account of a sequence of events in which 'A gave rise to B, which resulted in C, which in turn caused D, etc.'" and another that introduced "short vignettes on everyday experiences (someone wanting to date another person, someone wanting to persuade her boss to award a pay rise), . . . [all of which] contained between three and five levels of embedded intentionality" (240). Subjects were then asked to complete a "series of questions graded by the levels of intentionality present in the story," into which were also mixed some factual questions "designed to check that any failures on intentionality questions were not simply due to failure to remember the material facts of the story" (240). Subjects were also given "a parallel story that did not involve mind-reading, but was simply an account of a series of events . . . intended to test students' abilities to handle causal embeddedness for purely factual events" (240). The results of the study were revealing: "Subjects had little problem with the factual causal reasoning story: error rates were approximately 5% across six levels of causal sequencing. Error rates on the mind-reading tasks were similar (5–10%) up to and including fourth-level intentionality, but rose dramatically to nearly 60% on fifth-order tasks" (240–41). Cognitive scientists knew that this "failure on the mind-reading tasks [was] not simply a consequence of forgetting what happened, because subjects performed well on the memory-for-facts tasks embedded into the mind-reading questions" (241). The results thus suggest that people have marked difficulties processing stories that involve mind reading above the fourth level.

An important point that should not be lost in the discussion of these experiments is that it is the *content* of the information in question that makes the navigation of multiply embedded data either relatively easy or difficult. Cognitive evolutionary psychologists suggest the reason for the relative ease with which we can process long sequences such as "A gave rise to B, which resulted in C, which in turn caused D, which led to E, which made possible F, which eventually brought about G, etc.," as opposed to similarly long sequences that require attribution of states of mind, such as "A wants B to believe that C thinks that D wanted E to consider F's feelings about G" is that the cognitive adaptations that underwrite the attribution of states of mind likely differ in functionally important ways from the adaptations that underwrite reasoning that does not involve such an attribution, a difference possibly predicated on the respective evolutionary histories of both types of adaptations.[14] A representation of a mind as represented by a mind as represented by yet another mind will thus be supported by cognitive processes distinct (to a degree which remains a subject of debate) from cognitive processes supporting a mental representation, for example, of events related to each other as a series of causes and effects or of a representation of a Russian doll nested within another doll nested within another doll. The cognitive process of representing depends crucially on *what* is being represented.

Consider now a randomly selected passage roughly halfway into Woolf's *Mrs. Dalloway,* in which Richard Dalloway and Hugh Whitbread come to Lady Bruton to write a letter to the *Times* and in which to understand what is going on we have to confront a series of multiply embedded states of mind:

> And Miss Brush went out, came back; laid papers on the table; and Hugh produced his fountain pen; his silver fountain pen, which had done twenty years' service, he said, unscrewing the cap. It was still in perfect order; he had shown it to the makers; there was no reason, they said, why it should ever wear out; which was somehow to Hugh's credit, and to the credit of the sentiments which his pen expressed (so Richard Dalloway felt) as Hugh began carefully writing capital letters with rings round them in the margin, and thus marvelously reduced Lady Bruton's tangles to sense, to grammar such as the editor of the *Times*, Lady Bruton felt, watching the marvelous transformation, must respect. (110)

What is going on in this passage? We are seemingly invited to deduce the excellence of Millicent Bruton's civic ideas—put on paper by Hugh—first from the resilience of the pen that he uses and then from the beauty of his "capital letters with rings around them on the margins." Of course, this reduction of lofty sentiments and superior analytic skills to mere artifacts, such as writing utensils and calligraphy, achieves just the opposite effect. By the end of the paragraph, we are ready to accept Richard Dalloway's view of the resulting epistle as "all stuffing and bunkum"—but a harmless bunkum at that. Its inoffensiveness and futility are underscored by the tongue-in-cheek phallic description of the silver pen (should "silver" bring to our mind "gray"?) that has served Hugh for twenty years but that is still "in perfect order"—or so Hugh thinks—once he's done "unscrewing the cap."

There are several ways to map this passage out in terms of the nested levels of intentionality. I will start by listing the smallest irreducible units of embedded intentionality and gradually move up to those that capture as much of the whole narrative gestalt of the described scene as possible:

1. The makers of the pen *think* that it will never wear out (first level).
2. Hugh *says* that the makers of the pen *think* it will never wear out (second level).

3. Lady Bruton *wants* the editor of the *Times* to *respect* and publish her ideas (second level).

4. Hugh *wants* Lady Bruton and Richard to *believe* that because the makers of the pen *think* that it will never wear out, the editor of the *Times* will *respect* and publish the ideas recorded by this pen (fourth level).

5. Richard *is aware* that Hugh *wants* Lady Bruton and Richard Dalloway to *believe* that because the makers of the pen *think* that it will never wear out, the editor of the *Times* will *respect* and publish the ideas recorded by this pen (fifth level).

6. Richard *suspects* that Lady Bruton indeed *believes* that because, as Hugh *says*, the makers of the pen *think* that it will never wear out, the editor of the *Times* will *respect* and publish the ideas recorded by this pen (fifth level).

7. By inserting a parenthetical observation ("so Richard Dalloway felt"), Woolf *intends us to recognize* that Richard *is aware* that Hugh *wants* Lady Bruton and Richard to *think* that because the makers of the pen *believe* that it will never wear out, the editor of the *Times* will *respect* and publish the ideas recorded by this pen (sixth level).

It could be argued, of course, that in the process of reading we automatically cut through Woolf's stylistic pyrotechnics to come up with a series of more comprehensible, first-, second-, and third-level attributions of states of mind, such as "Richard does not particularly like Hugh"; "Lady Bruton thinks that Hugh is writing a marvelous letter"; "Richard feels that Lady Bruton thinks that Hugh is writing a marvelous letter, but he is skeptical about the whole enterprise"; and so on. Such abbreviated attributions may seem destructive since the effect that they have on Woolf's prose is equivalent to the effect of paraphrasing on poetry, but they do, in fact, convey some general sense of what is going on in the paragraph. However, the fact is we can't just cut through to them. To arrive at such simplified descriptions of Richard's and Lady Bruton's states of mind, we have to grasp the full meaning of this passage, and to do that, we first have to process several sequences that embed at least five levels of intentionality. Moreover, we have to do it on the spot, unaided by pen and paper and without a forewarning that the number of levels of intentionality that we are about to encounter is considered by cognitive scientists to create "a very significant load on most people's cognitive abilities" (Dunbar, 240).

Note that in this particular passage, Woolf not only "demands" that we process a string of fifth- and sixth-level intentionalities but also introduces such embedded intentionalities through descriptions of body language that in some ways approach those of Hemingway in their emotional blandness. No more telling "trembling," as in the earlier scene featuring Peter and Clarissa. Instead, we get Richard watching Lady Bruton watching Hugh producing his pen, unscrewing the cap, and beginning to write. True, Woolf offers us two emotionally colored words ("carefully" and "marvelously"), but what they signal is that Hugh cares a great deal about his writing and that Lady Bruton admires the letter that he produces—two snapshots of the states of mind that only skim the surface of the complex affective undertow of this episode.

Because Woolf has depicted physical actions relatively lacking in immediate emotional content, here, in striking contrast to the scene in Clarissa's drawing room, she hastens to provide an authoritative interpretation of each character's mental state. We are told what Lady Bruton feels as she watches Hugh (she feels that the editor of the *Times* will respect so beautifully written a letter); we are told what Hugh thinks as he unscrews the cap (he thinks that the pen will never wear out and that its longevity contributes to the worth of the sentiments it produces); we are told what Richard feels as he watches Hugh, his capital letters, and Lady Bruton (he is amused both by Hugh's exalted view of himself and by Lady Bruton's readiness to take Hugh's self-importance at its face value). The apparently unswerving linear hierarchy of the scene—Richard can represent the minds of both Hugh and Lady Bruton, but Hugh and Lady Bruton cannot represent Richard's representations of their minds—seems to enforce the impression that each mind is represented fully and correctly.

Of course, Woolf is able to imply that her representations of Hugh's, Lady Bruton's, and Richard's minds are exhaustive and correct because, creatures with a theory of mind that we are, we *just know* that there *must be* mental states behind the emotionally opaque body language of the protagonists. The paucity of textual cues that could allow us to imagine those mental states ourselves leaves us no choice but to accept the representations provided by the author. We have to work hard for them, of course, for sifting through all those levels of embedded intentionality tends to push the boundaries of our mind-reading ability to its furthest limits.

When we try to articulate our perception of the cognitive challenge induced by this task of processing fifth- and sixth-level intentionality, we may say that Woolf's writing is difficult or even refuse to continue reading her novels. The personal aesthetics of individual readers thus could be grounded *at least in part* in the nuances of their individual mind-reading capacities. By saying this I do not mean to imply that if somebody "loves" or "hates" Woolf, it should tell us something about that person's general mind-reading "sophistication"—a cognitive literary analysis does not support such misguided value judgments. The nuances of each person's mind-reading profile are unique to that person, just as, for example, we all have the capacity for developing memories (unless that capacity has been clinically impaired), though each individual's actual memories are unique. My combination of memories serves me, and it would be meaningless to claim that it somehow serves me "better" than my friend's combination of memories serves her. At the same time, I see no particular value in celebrating the person's dislike of Woolf as the manifestation of his or her individual cognitive makeup. My teaching experience has shown that if we alert our students to the fact that Woolf tends to play this particular kind of cognitive "mind game" with her readers, it significantly eases their anxiety about "not getting" her prose and actually helps them to start enjoying her style.[15]

Cognitive Literary Analysis of *Mrs. Dalloway*

It is now time to return to the imaginary conversation that opened my essay. Some versions of that exchange did take place at several scholarly forums where I have presented my research on theory of mind and literature. Once, for instance, after I described the immediate pedagogical payoffs of counting the levels of intentionality in *Mrs. Dalloway* with my undergraduates, I was asked if I could foresee the time when such a cognitive reading would supersede and render redundant the majority of other, more traditional, approaches to Woolf.[16] My immediate answer was, and still remains, an unqualified "no," but since then I have had the opportunity to consider several of the question's implications that are important for those of us wishing cognitive approaches to literature to thrive.

First of all, counting the levels of intentionality in *Mrs. Dalloway* does not constitute *the* cognitive approach to Woolf. It merely begins to explore one particular way—among numerous others—in which Woolf builds on and experiments with our theory of mind and—to cast the net broader— in which fiction builds on and experiments with our cognitive propensities.[17] Many of these propensities, I feel safe saying in spite of remarkable advances in the cognitive sciences during the last two decades, still remain unknown to us.

However, the current state of cognitive literary study already testifies to the spectacular diversity of venues offered by the parent fields of cognitive neuroscience, artificial intelligence, philosophy of mind, cognitive linguistics, evolutionary biology, cognitive psychology, and cognitive anthropology. Literary critics have begun to investigate the ways recent research in these areas opens new avenues in gender studies (F. Elizabeth Hart); feminism (Elizabeth Grosz); cultural materialism (Mary Thomas Crane, Alan Richardson); deconstruction (Ellen Spolsky); literary aesthetics (Elaine Scarry, Gabrielle Starr); history of moral philosophy (Blakey Vermeule); ecocriticism (Nancy Easterlin); and narrative theory (Porter Abbott, David Herman, Alan Palmer). What these scholars' publications show is that far from displacing traditional approaches or rendering them redundant, a cognitive approach ensures their viability as it builds on, strengthens, and develops their insights.

Second, the ongoing dialogue with, for instance, cultural historicism or feminism is not simply a matter of choice for scholars of literature interested in cognitive approaches. There is no such thing as a cognitive ability, such as theory of mind, free floating "out there" in isolation from its human embodiment and its historically and culturally concrete expression. Evolved cognitive predispositions, to borrow Patrick Colm Hogan's characterization of literary universals, "are instantiated variously, particularized in specific circumstances" ("Literary Universals" [chap. 1 in this volume]).[18] *Everything* that we learn about Woolf's life and about the literary, cultural, and sociohistorical contexts of *Mrs. Dalloway* is thus potentially crucial for understanding why this particular woman, at this particular historical juncture, seeing herself as working both within and against a particular set of literary traditions, began to push beyond the boundaries of her readers' cognitive "zone of comfort" (that is, beyond the fourth level of intentionality).

At the same time, to paraphrase David Herman ("Regrounding Narrative"), the particular combination of these personal, literary, and historical contexts, in all their untold complexity, does not suffice for understanding why Woolf wrote the way she did even if it is necessary to that understanding. No matter how much we learn about the writer herself and her multiple environments, and no matter how much we find out about the cognitive endowments of our species that, "particularized in specific circumstances," make fictional narratives possible, we can only go so far in our cause-and-effect analysis. As George Butte puts it, "Accounts of material circumstances can describe changes in gender systems and economic privileges, but they cannot explain why *this* bankrupt merchant wrote *Moll Flanders*, or why *this* genteelly-impoverished clergyman's daughter wrote *Jane Eyre*" (237). There will always remain a gap between our ever-increasing store of knowledge and the phenomenon of Woolf's prose—or, for that matter, Defoe's, Austen's, Brontë's, and Hemingway's prose.

Yet to consider just one example of how crucial our "other" knowledges are for our cognitive inquiry into *Mrs. Dalloway*, let us situate Woolf's experimentation with multiple levels of intentionality within the history of the evolution of the means of textual reproduction. It appears that a written culture is, on the whole, more able than an oral culture to support elaborately nested intentionality simply because a paragraph with six levels of intentional embedment does not yield itself easily to memorization and subsequent oral transmission. It is thus highly unlikely that we would find many (or any) passages that require us to go beyond the fourth level of intentionality in oral epics such as *Gilgamesh* or the *Iliad*. Walter Benjamin captures the broad point of this difference when he observes that the "listener's naïve relationship to the storyteller is controlled by his interest in retaining what he is told. The cardinal point for the unaffected listener is to assure himself of the possibility of reproducing the story" (97). The availability of the means of written transmission, such as print, enables the writer "to carry the incommensurable to extremes in representations of human life" (87) and, by so doing, to explore the hitherto quiescent cognitive spaces.

Of course, for a variety of aesthetic, personal, and financial reasons, not every author writing under the conditions of print will venture into such a cognitive unknown. Even a cursory look at best-selling mainstream fiction, from Belva Plain to Danielle Steel, confirms the continuous broad popular appeal of narratives dwelling under the fourth level of intentional embedment. It is, then, the personal histories of individuals (here, individual writers and their audiences) that ensure that, as Alan Richardson and Francis Steen observe, the history of cognitive structures "is neither identical to nor separate from the culture they make possible" (3).

In the case of Woolf, scholars agree that severing ties with Duckworth—the press that had brought forth her first two novels and was geared toward an audience that was "Victorian, conventional, anti-experimentation" (*Diary*, 1:261)—"liberated [her] experimentalism" (Whitworth, 150). Having her own publishing house, the Hogarth Press, meant that she was "able to do what" she "like[d]—no editors, or publishers, and only people to read who more or less like that sort of thing" (*Letters*, 167). Another factor possibly informing the cognitive extremes of *Mrs. Dalloway* was Woolf's acute awareness of the passing of time: "My theory is that at 40 one either increases the pace or slows down" (*Diary*, 2:259). Woolf wanted to *increase* the pace of her explorations, to be able to "embody, at last," as she would write several years later, "the exact shapes my brain holds" (*Diary*, 4:53). Having struggled in her previous novels with a narrator "choked with observations" (*Jacob's Room*, 67), she discovered in the process of working on *Mrs. Dalloway* how to "dig out beautiful caves behind [her] characters; . . . The idea is that the caves shall connect, and each comes to daylight at the present moment" (*Diary*, 2:263). Embodying the "exact shapes" of Woolf's brain thus meant, among other things, shifting "the focus from the mind of the narrator to the minds of the characters" and "from the external world to the minds of the characters perceiving it" (Dick, 51, 52), a technique that would eventually prompt Auerbach to inquire in exasperation, "Who is speaking in this paragraph?" (531).[19]

Woolf's meditations on her writing remind us of yet another reason that simply counting levels of intentionality in *Mrs. Dalloway* will never supersede other forms of critical inquiry into the novel. The image that emerges when Woolf explains that she wants to construct a "present moment" as a delicate "connection" among the "caves" dug behind each character overlaps suggestively with Dennett's image of the infinitely recursive levels of intentionality. ("Aha," concludes the delighted cognitive literary critic, "Woolf had some sort of prototheory of recursive mind reading!") But with her vivid description of the catacomblike subjectivity of the shared present moment, Woolf also manages to do something else—and that "something else" proceeds to quietly burrow into our (and her) cognitive theorizing.[20]

This brings us to a seemingly counterintuitive but important point underlying cognitive literary analysis. Even as I map the passage featuring Richard Dalloway and Hugh Whitbread at Lady Bruton's as a linear series of embedded intentionalities, I expect that something else present in that passage will complicate that linearity and repose Auerbach's question, albeit with a difference. Will it be the phallic overtones of the description of Hugh's pen? Or the intrusion of the rhetoric of economic exchange—"credit," "makers," "produce," "capital," "margin"? Or the vexed gender contexts of the "ventriloquism" implied by the image of Millicent Bruton spouting political platitudes in Hugh's voice?[21] Or the equally vexed social class contexts of the "seating arrangements" that hierarchize the mind reading that goes on in the passage? (After all, Woolf must have "seated" Lady Bruton's secretary, Miss Brush, too far from the desk to be able to see the shape of Hugh's letters so as not to add yet another level of mental embedment by having Miss Brush watch Richard watching Lady Bruton watching Hugh.) Cognitive *literary* analysis thus continues beyond the line drawn by cognitive scientists—with the reintroduction of something else, a "noise," if you will, that is usually carefully controlled for and excised, whenever possible, from the laboratory settings.[22]

CHAPTER TEN

Machiavellian Narratives

BLAKEY VERMEULE

Ever since Plato, literary theory has sought to explain something apparently puzzling, namely why literary experience feels so rich and vivid. Theorists have tested many different explanations over the centuries. Plato, for one, supposed that poets had a special sophistical power to seduce people away from real knowledge by making them engage with mere representations. In a more positive light, Kant argued in the *Critique of Judgment* that art sponsors a unique harmony of the faculties, a cognitive experience we cannot get from any other source and that completes our other cognitive faculties. Samuel Taylor Coleridge took Kant's ideas in a direction that would prove irresistible to twentieth-century theorists, such as New Critics and deconstructionists. Coleridge sought to isolate moments of especially literary complexity and richness within works of art, a gesture that has sponsored a long engagement with the question of how literary language or experience differs from ordinary language or experience. This essay is roughly in this Coleridgean tradition. My claim is that moments that we consider especially literary, and that have therefore have attracted intense critical scrutiny, tend to reflect a special—and especially intense—kind of reasoning. This kind of reasoning, which I will call Machiavellian, is especially intense because it engages something we care about most—the extremely complicated dynamics of social interactions. In modern literature especially, Machiavellian reasoning reflects the sense that we are at once captive to the swirl of the social and psychologically detached from it.

Why Machiavellian? In the 1970s, researchers began to formulate a loose confederacy of ideas about the origin, meaning, and aims of human intelligence. Humans are primates who have evolved to live in highly complex, socially stratified groups. Depending on material and economic conditions, human groups can either be extremely hierarchical or relatively egalitarian. Humans have evolved mental mechanisms to cope with group living and to help us negotiate the byways of status. These mental mechanisms are especially attuned to calculation, cooperation, and conflict. Indeed one popular theory is that human intelligence evolved to handle the social complexity of living in groups—to outwit our fellow primates, to think several moves ahead of them on a giant social chessboard, and to keep track of our alliances. This view is called the Machiavellian intelligence hypothesis. It posits that social complexity has put even greater adaptive pressure on cognition than many nonsocial activities have and that intelligence evolved in part to meet the rigorous demands of social interactions. The relevant adaptive environment for intellectual evolution, in short, is other people.

The term "Machiavellian," which focuses on the role that cunning plays in helping us form social alliances, may be problematic. "Machiavellian" may turn out to be just as misleading and contentious as Richard Dawkins's "selfish gene," a phrase that got sociobiology off on the wrong foot by stressing the devilish side of our natures rather than our capacity for caring—which is an equally if not more remarkable feature of human nature. Better ways of referring to this view may be the cooperative intelligence hypothesis or the social intelligence hypothesis, although in fact for the purposes of this essay I stick to "Machiavellian."

Machiavellian intelligence is the general rubric under which social reasoning takes place. What are the mechanisms that make it possible? Perhaps the most important mechanism is theory of mind. The clinical psychologist Simon Baron-Cohen has hypothesized that it is in fact a complex modular system that builds on a range of other dedicated structures. These include an intention detector, an eye direction detector, and a shared attention mechanism. The intention detector is the means by which we pick out agents and attribute purpose and motive to them. The eye direction detector is a mechanism for tracking what other people are looking at and indeed for inferring that they are looking at something and that their gaze is intentional. Eyes and eye contact are critically important to theory of mind; another name for the whole system might be "perspective taking." The shared attention mechanism is the ability to call someone else's attention to an external object, to know that they are attending to the object and to know that they know that you are attending to the object. Another term for perspective taking is recursion, or embedded mind reading.

Theory of mind has everything to do with the qualities that, as Kant suggests, make our faculties buzz when we read literary texts. Literary texts almost obsessively deploy techniques that put stress on our theory-of-mind capacities. Lisa Zunshine has analyzed many fruitful examples in her book, *Why We Read Fiction*, showing how authors can use techniques rich in theory of mind to increase the mental pressure that readers experience when we read more difficult or experimental fiction. She also shows how authors can use theory of mind to invent or hone literary techniques that ratchet up the level of our interest in the narrative. In this essay I concentrate on what I see as a long tradition of literary texts engaging our Machiavellian reasoning capacities using techniques that stimulate our theory of mind.

So let me start with set of literary terms that have become canonical in literary history—flat and round characters. As well as being incredibly useful for literary analysis, this distinction is, to me, one of the major techniques that authors use to ratchet up the pressure on our mind-reading abilities. Flat and round characters were described by E. M. Forster in *Aspects of the Novel* (1927), and his definition has been disseminated through scores of literary handbooks and fiction-writing guides:

> In their purest form, they are constructed around a single idea or quality. . . . The really flat character can be expressed in one sentence such as "I never will desert Mr. Micawber" [from Dickens's *David Copperfield*]. There is Mrs. Micawber—she says she won't desert Mr. Micawber, she doesn't, and there she is. . . . The test of a round character is whether it is capable of surprising in a convincing way. If it never surprises, it is flat. If it does not convince, it is a flat pretended to be a round. (48)

Flat characters are allegorical. All of their features come from the idea they represent. They have no capacity to learn from experience. Round characters are open and complex, much more like real human beings in their inconsistency. (I'll admit this distinction is hardly fair to flat characters. I have known one or two real human beings who were so consumed by an idea or a neurosis that they "never surprised.")

Examples of this contrast can be found throughout ancient and modern fiction. For example, Edmund Spenser's parade of the seven deadly sins in the first book of *The Faerie Queene* is a perfect representation of how allegory works. Along comes Lustful Lechery clothed in flowing green garments and bearing in his hand a burning heart "[f]ull of vaine follies, and new fanglenesse." Lechery also rides "Upon a bearded Goat, whose rugged haire,/And whally eyes (the signe of gelosy,)/Was like the person selfe, whom he did beare" (60). The goat is a characteristically witty twist: the very notion of being shot through with a characteristic, Spenser seems to say, is somewhat similar to the relationship between the rider and the animal he rides on. Lechery radiates outward with such force that it creates its own objective correlative, a goat with glassy eyes. If you are a flat character, you have no interiority; instead you ride on an animal who represents the most salient things about you. Spenser thus gives a flat character his own even flatter character as a sidekick.

Here is another, slightly more realistic example of a flat character, one whom even the author on whom she depends for her limited existence holds in contempt. What could be worse than to try to imaginatively inhabit the inner life of Miss Henrietta Stackpole, the lady newspaper interviewer of "decidedly clear cut views," who weaves in and out of Henry James's *Portrait of a Lady* (1881)? James describes Henrietta Stackpole as a "light ficelle," a thread that links all of the incidents in his novel together. But just because she is a thread—and a rather likeable one—does not mean that she is exempt from some memorable humiliations. James denies that either Henrietta Stackpole or Maria Gostrey, another "light ficelle" (from *The Ambassadors* [1903]), is a "true agent"; rather they are mere vehicles for developing the main character, a metaphor that he makes comically literal:

> Each of these persons is but wheels to the coach; neither belongs to the body of that vehicle, or is for a moment accommodated with a seat inside. There the subject alone is ensconced, in the form of its "hero and heroine," and of the privileged high officials, say, who ride with the king and queen. . . . [T]hey may run beside the coach "for all they are worth," they may cling to it till they are out of breath (as

poor Miss Stackpole all so visibly does), but neither, all the while, so much as gets her foot on the step, neither ceases for a moment to tread the dusty road. (53)

Perhaps readers who remember the character of Henrietta Stackpole from James's novel will object that, despite her running and her clinging, she is not exactly a flat character—she cannot easily be sorted into good or bad and hence dismissed; she is hardly static (since motion is her salient quality); she is not in any sense allegorical. But still to be the wheel on a cart, a fishwife jeering the carriage of the royal family as they tumble toward their execution in Paris . . .

The mind-reading payoff comes when flat and round characters interact in what Alex Woloch, in his magisterial study of minor characters, calls the "character-space" of the novel. Flatness and roundness are complex attributes, ever shifting in relation to each other. As they shift, they pick out different textual patterns—a fact that is true both within a single text and over different time frames as well. So consider the fate of Becky Sharp, the heroine of Thackeray's *Vanity Fair* (1848). Becky Sharp, Forster writes, "is round. She, too, is on the make, but she cannot be summed up in a single phrase, and we remember her so easily, because she waxes and wanes and has facets like a human being" (48). And yet Becky Sharp has demonstrably flattened out over time. To Forster in 1927 she lives still in the culture's imagination. Forster is closer to her and sees her many facets; people around him remind him of her; her institutions are his institutions, seventy-five years on. Yet for us at so many more removes, Becky Sharp has become shorthand, a fleeting piece of collective thought if we think of her at all. Indeed Becky Sharp is in danger of becoming that flattest of all flat characters, the "morally compromised Victorian novel heroine," or so she is known—if she is known at all—by writers who need a quick and literate-sounding shorthand.

Forster recognizes that flat and round are necessary twins. He quotes a wonderful passage from a querulous letter by Mr. Norman Douglas to D. H. Lawrence, only to heap gentle scorn on it. Mr. Norman Douglas is shocked by the fact that novelists occasionally reduce their characters to caricatures, an effect he calls "the novelist's touch." The novelist's touch fails "to realize the profundities and complexities of the ordinary human mind; it selects for literary purposes two or three facets of a man or woman, generally the most spectacular and therefore 'useful' ingredients of their character, and disregards all the others. . . . It falsifies life." In reply, Forster observes a deep fact about narrative that will be worked out in much more detail by later narrative theorists, namely that flatness and roundness entail each other: "A novel that is at all complex often requires flat people as well as round, and the outcome of their collision parallels life more accurately than Mr. Douglas implies" (48–49).

Flat characters may not be especially psychologically realistic, but they can be extremely psychologically compelling. When flat characters interact with round characters, they mine a rich vein of theory of mind. In literary narratives from ancient to modern times, some version of the following pattern repeats itself over and over again: a flat or minor character provokes a fit of reflection in a round or major character. The fit of reflection enlarges the scene and the minds of the people in it, who engage in elaborate rituals of shared attention and eye contact. The scene itself becomes soaked in mindfulness, increasing the sense of self-consciousness all around. Let me give an example of what I mean. The example comes from the end of the *Aeneid* and is justly one of the most famous and troubling scenes in Western literature. The Trojan leader Aeneas and his Latin foe Turnus meet in a long-anticipated battle. Turnus, who is proud and stiff necked, challenges Aeneas to single combat but then leads the entire Latin army to bloody defeat at the hands of the Trojans. Turnus realizes his error and offers to fight Aeneas one on one. Turnus falls, and Aeneas pierces him in the thigh with his spear. As Aeneas moves to kill him, Turnus pleads for mercy. His plea causes Aeneas to pause briefly:

> Fierce under arms, Aeneas
> Looked to and fro, and towered, and stayed his hand
> Upon the sword-hilt. Moment by moment
> what Turnus said began to bring him round
> From indecision. Then to his glance appeared
> The accurst swordbelt surmounting Turnus' shoulder,
> Shining with its familiar studs—the strap
> Young Pallas wore when Turnus wounded him
> And left him dead upon the field; now Turnus
> Bore that enemy token on his shoulder—
> Enemy still. For when the sight came home to him,

Aeneas raged at the relic of his anguish
Worn by this man as trophy. Blazing up
And terrible in his anger, he called out:
"You in your plunder, torn from one of mine,
Shall I be robbed of you? This wound will come
From Pallas: Pallas makes this offering
And from your criminal blood exacts his due."
He sank his blade in fury in Turnus' chest.
Then all the body slackened in death's chill,
And with a groan for that indignity
His spirit fled into the gloom below.   (402)

Readers have rightly worried about this ending for two thousand years.[1] Why does Virgil end his epic on such a morally ambiguous note? The epic seemed as though it would end on a note of reconciliation: the Trojans have conquered an indigenous Italian people, yet Juno has won from Jupiter a promise that the Latins will not be annihilated but will mix with their Trojan conquerors to form a new noble race. And when Aeneas visited his father Anchises in the underworld, Anchises had explicitly counseled Aeneas to show clemency to his enemies. Nevertheless the future founder of Rome acts with a brutal lack of pity toward his defeated rival. In the *Iliad*, the wrathful Greek king Achilles, inflamed by memories of his friend Patroclus's death, brutally slew the Trojan prince Hector and dragged his body back and forth in front of the walls of Troy to torment Hector's parents, King Priam and Queen Hecuba. Even though Aeneas was a comrade of Hector's, he behaves just as brutally toward Turnus as Achilles had toward Hector—and the effect is even worse, since at least in the *Odyssey* Achilles had invited Priam into his tent and allowing him to retrieve the body of his son. At the end of the Aeneid, there is no reconciliation, only the shade of Turnus fleeing down to the underworld.

The only apparent bar to describing this ending as unequivocally brutal is the fact that Aeneas hesitates before killing Turnus. Aeneas is described as rolling his eyes (*volvens oculis*) and staying his hand and weighing Turnus's words, which lead to his great hesitation (*magis cunctantem*). Only when his eyes light on the majestic belt of Pallas that Turnus is wearing as a war trophy, does Aeneas fly into a fury and kill him. Michael Putnam has written a long careful exposition of this moment. Drawing on a wealth of linguistic detail, Putnam frames Aeneas's conflict as a philo-sophical one as he struggles between commitment and detachment:

> Aeneas first grapples with the inference of words. The hesitating hero,
> pondering the *clementia* that Turnus proposes, for an instant mulls
> over an abstract principle which, if espoused in statesmanlike fashion,
> would have wide-ranging public repercussions. The belt of Pallas and
> what it represents, tangible reminder of Aeneas' devotion to his pro-
> tégé, which at the same time sports figures bent on a particularly vivid
> example of revenge . . . , drives the hero's fury to its highest pitch.
>
> (162)

Aeneas's "final deed," he concludes, "reminds us of the essential perver-sity of power even in the hands of those who could with some truth lay claim to have established the most orderly society that the world has yet known" (166).

"Perverse" comes from the Latin root *perversus*, turned away from what is right. Even when Aeneas strikes the blow against Turnus he has almost turned away from his commitment to that blow. Commitment entails detachment and vice versa. The perversity of power inevitably re-quires a high degree of Machiavellian intelligence. The friction between dominant Aeneas and the defeated Turnus—the major and the minor characters—leads to an increase in mindfulness all around—or at least in the sort of activity that requires a high level of inference sorting to work out. Turnus—a rather flat character—sponsors Aeneas's enriched and rounded experience. Indeed the interaction between them sponsors the experience of what we think of as literariness—the special buzzing thickness, the strange harmony of the faculties that Kant described when he found himself in the presence of serious art.

Whether or not that experience of literariness closely correlates to a genre (the novel), to a historical period (the nineteenth century), or to a mode (omniscient realism) is a further and interesting question. But the engine itself—the sense of mindfulness that results from round and flat interacting—is remarkably consistent over a wide range of genres and pe-riods. In modern literature, we can extend the idea of flatness and round-ness to literary scenes and indeed to entire literary works themselves. What do I mean by a round literary work? A round novel or work deliv-ers, minimally, the following: a dyadic—or more likely triadic or quadratic—scene of reflection and counterreflection. The scene of reflection is heightened by being set inside an enclosed space or world. Often cleverness is more closely correlated with high status than strength: highly Machiavellian narratives tend to feature a person who sees or thinks he sees farther than anybody else—let us call this person the mastermind. The mastermind, as denizen of comedy or tragedy, stands as the powerful fantasy of someone able to master others through analytical reflection. Such narratives also feature the presence of one or more blocking figures—figures who are especially blind or unresponsive. Furthermore, they also offer several cues in the form of tropes that we are in the presence of high narrative reflexivity. These tropes include chess, tennis, gambling and games of chance, business letters, labyrinths, excessively cruel people, proverbs, gossip, games of "evens and odds," eye contact, and people who "turn a blind eye." This list is not especially internally consistent, but the way high theory-of-mind narratives treat these elements is surprisingly so. Indeed the consistency is puzzling. Texts that are especially rich in theory of mind—from wildly different periods and even national traditions—use these same figures over and over again. When one or several of these tropes of reflection find their way into a narrative, that narrative becomes infinitely more Machiavellian.

The classic Machiavellian narrative is either a comedy of manners or a revenge tragedy—and sometimes both. Let me canvass a famous example, an example that, as it happens, has provoked a storied response, namely Edgar Allen Poe's detective story "The Purloined Letter" (1845). So passionately does it signal that it is a high theory-of-mind text that it can serve as something of a template for others; we can use its own examples to highlight those of other narratives. "The Purloined Letter" is the third story in a trilogy featuring mastermind and reclusive genius C. Auguste Dupin, a forerunner to Sherlock Holmes. Dupin is a person especially high in theory of mind—a fact signaled at the opening of the trilogy's first story, "The Murders in the Rue Morgue" (1841), by a trick of apparent genius he plays on the story's narrator. The narrator (who is never named) lives with Dupin in Paris in a state of funereal claustration. They shroud themselves in darkness during the day and venture out only at night. To the world, they appear to be "madmen." Dupin is cold and analytical, but he can also be a bit boastful, especially about his skills as a mind reader. During one of their night walks, he gloats "that most men, in respect to himself, wore windows in their bosoms," and, the narrator tell us, he "was wont to follow up such assertions by direct and very startling proofs of his intimate knowledge of my own" (5). In the next instant, he offers just such a proof. The two men are strolling along, each apparently lost in thought, until the narrator realizes that Dupin has been secretly tracking his thoughts the whole time:

> Being both, apparently, occupied with thought, neither of us had spoken a syllable for fifteen minutes at least. All at once Dupin broke forth with these words: "He is a very little fellow, that's true, and would do better for the Theatre des Varietes." "There can be no doubt of that," I replied unwittingly, and not at first observing (so much had I been absorbed in reflection) the extraordinary manner in which the speaker had chimed in with my meditations. In an instant afterward I recollected myself, and my astonishment was profound. "Dupin," said I, gravely, "this is beyond my comprehension. I do not hesitate to say that I am amazed, and can scarcely credit my senses. How was it possible you should know I was thinking of ——?"
>
> (5–6)

Dupin plays a rather simple trick: he runs a chain of inferences in just the way his friend would have run them. What appears so mysterious to the narrator is really an exercise in pure rationality. Dupin's trick lies in knowing what inferences his friend will form. Once he figures out the formula, all he needs to do is plug in the first association and the whole chain runs automatically, as an algorithm. But Dupin's mastery has a second element too—Dupin does not merely apply a formula to some inferences; he also runs that chain of inferences in a mode decoupled from his own mental processes and attached to the mental processes of somebody else. The psychological mastermind is often, it turns out, somebody who is able to do just that—think of any charlatan telephone psychic or Henry James and Freud.

The mastermind is the most Machiavellian of characters. He—rarely she—typically occupies a privileged position in a round of reflection and counterreflection. Not only does he reflect on the motivations of others; he also reflects on his own reflections. His gifts are thought to be beyond the realm of ordinary human capacities, but only by one or two degrees and only in ways we might be able to measure. The interest we take in him can become obsessive, but so too can the urge to compete with his powers.

Dupin really comes into his own in "The Purloined Letter," whose epigraph (falsely claimed to be from Seneca) is very fittingly "Nil sapientiae odiosius acumine nimio" (208)—"Nothing is more hateful to wisdom than too much cunning."[2] One night Dupin and the narrator are sitting in their tiny dark room when an old friend of theirs, the prefect of the Paris police, arrives and confesses his despair about an unsolvable case: a royal lady alone in her boudoir was reading a distressing letter from one of her enemies when her important husband suddenly comes in; in her confusion, she drops the letter on the table; soon a Machiavellian Minister D—— enters the room and "with his lynx eye," immediately "fathom[s] her secret" (*Collected Tales*, 210). Casually taking out of his briefcase a letter somewhat like the lady's, he drops it on the table, and after some talk, picks up the lady's letter and leaves the room. The lady sees what he has done but can't stop him; she is in the paradoxical position of the seer who is blind. Her husband, meanwhile, is in the position of the truly blind, whereas the minister stands in the position of greatest insight, insight that is achieved because one person near him is blind, another a blind seer. This schema—the relationship between the three people arranged in what amounts to a triangle of blindness and insight—has played a crucial role in how Poe's story has been interpreted. A rather obvious rule of thumb is that more complex literary works attract more interpretive attention. We can easily translate that into the terms of this essay by noting that highly Machiavellian texts—texts that put extra stress on our mind-reading capacities—have a richer critical history than texts that present a fairly straightforward narrative situation. Certainly this has been true since literary criticism began to develop in the eighteenth century, and literary theory, a specialty of the twentieth century, has been drawn to Machiavellian texts as though they were magnets. "The Purloined Letter" is a case in point: after it was published, the interpretive volcano took about 120 years to blow. When it did, it unleashed a tsunami of interpretation whose force is only now abating. In 1966, Jacques Lacan, the French psychoanalyst, published a now-notorious seminar on Poe's story. Lacan became fascinated by "The Purloined Letter" because he saw in it confirmation of the key tenets of his psychoanalytic system. His seminar then provoked a famous response from another French philosopher, Jacques Derrida. The details of their debate and the controversy it engendered are extremely complex, and I will not rehearse them here, but suffice to say that at the center of it is the question of reflexivity, of who gets to count as a psychological mastermind.[3]

But back to the plot. Now the royal lady has engaged the prefect of the Paris police to retrieve her letter. The prefect sends his men to search every nook of the minister's apartment, even taking apart the furniture to look for secret holes. After several searches, the prefect admits that he is stumped. He confides his difficulties to Dupin. One day to his astonishment, Dupin produces the letter and tells him that it had been hiding in plain sight the whole time. Then he explains how he outwitted the minister. Fitted out in green eyeshades (the blinding agent that heightens his powers of vision by blinding everyone else to what he can see), Dupin soon lights upon the purloined letter—crumpled, kitted up to look like a love letter (with large loopy ladies' handwriting), turned inside out, and hung nonchalantly in a letter holder in plain sight above the fireplace. He returns the next day with a copy of the disguised letter, arranges a commotion in the street to divert the minister, and slips his own copy into its place. Inside the copy he writes "Un dessein si funeste,/S'il n'est digne d'Atree, est digne de Thyeste" (A scheme so infamous, if it is not worthy of Atreus, is worthy of Thyestes) (222). In Greek mythology, Atreus has invited Thyestes to a banquet where he serves up Thyestes' son as the main dish; he thus revenges himself on Thyestes for running off with his wife. As Barbara Johnson paraphrases the lines, "The avenger's plot may not be worthy of him, says Atreus, but his brother Thyestes deserved it" (219). In fact Dupin explains that he steals the letter to avenge himself for "an evil turn" the minister did him once in Vienna, a turn that Dupin promised "good humoredly" to remember: "So, as I knew he would feel some curiosity in regard to the identity of the person who had outwitted him, I thought it a pity not to give him a clew" (222). Dupin gets off scot-free: he gets his revenge and sticks the minister with the responsibility for it too—as if Atreus had handed Thyestes a bill for the dinner he served him. Part of what makes "The Purloined Letter" so thrilling is that the position of the mastermind is so relentlessly unstable, so perverse.

But what is really perverse is the way Dupin reasons. In a pivotal scene, Dupin explains to the narrator how he has managed to deduce the location of the purloined letter by outthinking both the minister and the prefect. The prefect, Dupin says, is perfectly rational in his own way but his thinking is too linear. Dupin explains what it would be like to think in two or more dimensions by telling a story about a schoolboy who plays a game called "evens and odds," in which the one player has to guess how many marbles the other player is holding in his hand. The schoolboy is clever and figures out how to win the guessing game by reasoning what his "arrant simpleton" (215) of an opponent will do on his next turn. When he plays someone slightly cleverer, the schoolboy reasons correctly that his opponent will not simply choose odd if he had chosen even before but will imagine that the schoolboy will think that he has chosen odd and therefore will stick to even. What the schoolboy does, says Dupin, "lies at the bottom of all the spurious profundity which has been attributed to La Bruyere, to Machiavelli, and to Campanella" (216).

Dupin here presents a clinical picture of theory-of-mind reasoning: a young boy reasons his way into a position of social mastery by outfoxing his opponent. He uses a combination of what appears to be foresight—but is really only anticipating the next thought his opponent will have—and imitation. So simple are his methods that they make writers like Machiavelli seem "spuriously profound." We don't even need Machiavelli to tell us how to play the game of social chess since, according to Dupin, all we really need to do is run an algorithm of sorts—call it the evens/odds algorithm. Indeed the Machiavellians might even put us off this algorithm by morally freighting theory of mind—suggesting, as this uninhibited boy does not, that Machiavellian intelligence is something to be ashamed of.

This very algorithm—the evens and odds game—can actually be found throughout the fictional universe, though as far as I know, only Poe calls it that. And when I say algorithm rather than theme or trope, I mean a simple piece of code that runs over and over again and produces some outcome. In this case, evens and odds is an algorithm that produces greater Machiavellian interest and by using it in a fictional text, the author can very precisely signal that he or she is seeking to offer his or her readers a high degree of psychological complexity. Let me turn to one of the greatest sustained examples of cognitive complexity in narrative history, Thomas Mann's magisterial novel *The Magic Mountain* (1924). Mann's achievement is to have created the longest sustained example of irony in all of literature, the kind of irony that, according to Alexander Nehamas, "goes back to the very origins of the concept" (30) and indeed "goes all the way down: it does not reveal the ironist's real state of mind, and it intimates that such a state may not exist at all. It makes a mystery of its author as well as of his characters, and it often turns its readers into fools" (20). Mann's irony may turn us into fools, but we are fools who cannot look away. This is a novel whose meanings lurk almost pathologically between the lines. Scrutinize we can—and must—but to what end? Displacements all the way down.

How funny and telling it is, then, that in a pivotal scene, Thomas Mann throws in a perfect example of Machiavellian reasoning. Hans Castorp, "a very ordinary young man" from Hamburg, has come to the International Sanatorium Berghof to visit his cousin who is dying of tuberculosis. Hans Castorp is a man in a plight, but he does not yet know it. Actually he a man in several plights, but the plights he recognizes come to seem pale and flat compared to the zinging electricity of the plights he has yet to encounter (isn't it always like that?). The plights range from the minor (how to fold a blanket to take the open-air rest cure) to the midrange (how to think about the strange intellectual Herr Settembrini, who seems to be a version of Satan) to the major (how to accept the fact that he is not simply visiting his cousin in the sanatorium but is himself a patient there, that he too has tuberculosis). Love is one of Hans Castorp's plights. He finds himself slowly falling in love with a mysterious, somewhat vulgar, married Russian woman named Clavdia Chauchat. Hans Castorp's awareness of his plight as something he has to face is shot through with memories of a plight he already had to face, although he didn't recognize it as such at the time. When he was a schoolboy, he fell in love with another boy, Pribislav Hippe (and one day borrowed his pencil—that was it). Pribislav had "Kirghiz eyes" (almond-shaped eyes like the residents of the Turkmen plains) of the most stunning Asiatic blue. So, as it happens, does Frau Chauchat. The residents of the International Sanatorium Berghof are each assigned a table—Hans Castorp sits with his cousin and several others; Frau Chauchat sits across the room at the "good Russian table" (there is also a "bad Russian table"). There is little chance for them to interact. Hans Castorp becomes obsessed with the way that Frau Chauchat comes into meals late and lets the heavy glass door slam behind her. This is careless, maybe also willful. Nobody else seems to notice, but

Hans Castorp starts and grows angry every time it happens—at least at first.

> At first he would whip his head around indignantly each time and with angry eyes follow the late-comer to her place at the Good Russian table, even scold her under his breath, rebuking her between his teeth with a cry of outraged protest. But he had given that up, and now he would bend his head farther over his plate, even bite his lips sometimes, or intentionally and elaborately turn to look the other way; because it seemed to him that he no longer had a right to be angry and was not really free to censure her, but that he was an accessory to the offense and answerable for it to the others—in short, he was ashamed. (132)

He was ashamed. Shame, unlike guilt, is a public emotion—it plays to an audience. In this case the audience is not all "the others," as Hans Castorp thinks, but only one—namely the only other person in Hans Castorp's circle who has a similarly obsessive interest in Frau Chauchat. This person is a middle-aged German spinster named Fraulein Englehart who may or may not have feelings for Hans Castorp herself. Fraulein Englehart has discovered Hans Castorp's secret and how best to play the game for her own ends. She provides Hans Castorp with the thing he most craves—information—a commodity that is in desperately short supply at the Berghof sanitorium.

> The only thing that could possibly increase her standing in Hans Castorp's eyes was that she herself was from Konigsberg, a city not all that far from the Russian border, and so could manage a little broken Russian—very meager attributes indeed; all the same, Hans Castorp was prepared to regard them as some kind of extended personal connection to Frau Chauchat. (134)

So now the plight of Hans Castorp has become intertwined with the plight of Fraulein Englehart; is this what he would have chosen? He has provisionally accepted Madame Chauchat as one of his plights, although he still adopts the posture of mental superiority, thinking how soon he'll be back on the flatlands and working at the shipbuilding firm of Tunder and Wilms in Hamburg. But now he finds himself mixed up in another plight. Fraulein Englehart is the conduit for admittedly specious information. Fraulein Englehart is an intrusive player with her own needs and interests. How can a young man accept that his own plight intersects with somebody so irrelevant, charmless, and unpromising?

To Hans Castorp's credit, he takes on the challenge of Fraulein Englehart, engaging with her. Perhaps he doesn't have a choice: being in love makes us all into the most despicable charmers and users of other people. Thus he finds himself playing a strange game:

> That is how he worked it sometimes. With a cunning that was actually foreign to him, he pretended that Fraulein Engelhart's enthusiasm for Frau Chauchat was not in reality what he very well knew it to be, but that her enthusiasm was some neutral, droll fact that he, Hans Castorp, as an uninvolved party standing off at a cool, amused distance, could use to tease the old maid. And since he was certain that his accomplice would accept his audacious distortion and go along with it, it was not a risky tactic at all.
>
> "Good morning," he said. "Did you rest well? You did dream about lovely Minka, your Russian miss, didn't you? No, look at you blush at the mere mention of her. You're terribly infatuated, don't try to deny it."
>
> And the teacher, who had indeed blushed and was now bent deep over her cup, whispered out of the left corner of her mouth, "Shame, shame, Herr Castorp. It isn't at all nice of you to embarrass me with your insinuations. Everyone has already noticed that it's her we're talking about and that you're saying things to make me blush."
>
> What a strange game these two tablemates were playing. Both of them knew that their lies had double and triple twists—that Hans Castorp teased the teacher just so he could talk about Frau Chauchat, but that at the same time he took unwholesome delight in flirting with the old maid; and that for her part, she welcomed all this: first, because it allowed her to play the matchmaker, and second, because she probably had become smitten with Frau Chauchat, if only to please the young man, and finally, because she took some kind of wretched pleasure in being teased and made to blush. They both knew this about themselves and each other, and they also knew that each of them knew this about themselves and one another—and that it was all tangled and squalid. But although Hans Castorp was usually

repelled by tangled and squalid affairs and even felt repelled in this instance as well, he continued to splash about in these murky waters, taking consolation in the certainty that he was here only on a visit and would soon be leaving. (135)

"They both knew this about themselves and each other, and they also knew that each of them knew this about themselves and one another—that it was all tangled and squalid." Hans Castorp "continued to splash about in these murky waters" even though he has created a categorical exemption for himself from his own circumstances by "taking consolation in the certainty that he was here only a visit and would soon be leaving." What kind of reasoning is this? Well, of course it is Machiavellian—but Machiavellian tinged with irony because the point of it is to emphasize Hans Castorp's blindness, not his insight. Or maybe not ironically since the point of it is to produce a classic sort of irony, the sense that a statement really means the opposite of what it says.

Irony, double voicedness, is the hallmark of modern literature. But the perversity of irony is really not much different than the perversity of power. The conflict between Hans Castorp and Fraulein Englehart is obviously much more inward than the conflict between Aeneas and Turnus, but just as much is at stake emotionally—if not more, because emotion is *all* that is at stake. The conflicts may look as though they are opposites—one about physical dominance, the other about emotional dominance—but that is simply the difference between the Ancients and the Moderns. The engine that drives these conflicts is Machiavellian reasoning.

Cognitive Approaches in Dialogue with Other Approaches (Postcolonial Studies, Ecocriticism, Aesthetics, Poststructuralism)

Cognitive postcolonial theory focuses on texts that fall under the rubric of "postcolonial" writing (broadly conceived, since the boundaries of the category "postcolonial" remain contested in cultural studies). The key feature of this subfield is its rethinking of the controversial idea of universalism. Cognitive postcolonial criticism uses the concept of human universalism as reconceived by the recent advances in cognitive science and makes it the ground for a more vigorous cultural-historical analysis.

According to Suzanne Keen, whose *Empathy and the Novel* draws on cognitive psychology, narrative theory, and neuroscience to study strategic uses of empathy by postcolonial writers, although traditional postcolonial theorists "have been ardent in their critique of posited human universals," their criticism often exemplifies what she calls "false empathy criticism"—empathy as an "imposition of supposed 'understanding' on subalterns rather than letting them speak for themselves." In contrast, postcolonial novelists themselves "have assiduously cultivated empathetic responses by employing rhetorical techniques of bounded, ambassadorial, and broadcast strategic empathizing."[1] The term "strategic empathizing" (Keen's play on Gayatri Chakravorty Spivak's "strategic essentializing") denotes a kind of authorial empathy by which authors "attempt to direct an emotional transaction through a fictional work aimed at a particular audience, not necessarily including every reader who happens upon the text" ("Strategic Empathizing," 479).[2] For, as she puts it, "if we experience narrative empathy as readers, we should inquire if we respond because we belong to an in-group, or because narrative empathy calls to us across boundaries of difference" (481). Postcolonial novelists, from Flora Nwapa, Michael Ondaatje, and Opal Palmer Adisa to Mulk Raj Anand and Ngũgĩ wa Thiong'o, "often deliberately employ broadcast strategic empathy in their fiction, provocatively embracing the universality so often rejected by contemporary champions of difference, including many postcolonial theorists, and . . . they do so fully aware of exploiting the tension between universalizing and anti-universalizing positions" (490).

Consonant with Keen's analysis of strategic uses of empathy by postcolonial writers is Frederick Aldama's exploration of "human universals of language and emotion" in authors ranging from Meera Syal, Amitav Ghosh, Hari Kunzru, and Arundhati Roy to Dagoberto Gilb, Luis Rodriguez, and Gilbert and Jaime Hernandez. Aldama's *A User's Guide to Postcolonial and Latino Borderland Fiction* exemplifies both cognitive postcolonial studies' "sensitivity to historical contexts of creation and reception" and its practitioners' conviction that "fiction should not be bent to the purposes of political argument at the cost of interfering with the invitation to intense empathetic response and the unleashing of readers' world-creating imaginations."[3]

Aldama's *A User's Guide to Postcolonial and Latino Borderland Fiction* and Keen's *Empathy and the Novel* (particularly chapter 6, "Contesting Empathy") and "Strategic Empathizing" represent key readings in cognitive postcolonial theory, as do Patrick Colm Hogan's *Empire and Poetic Voice: Cognitive and Cultural Studies of Literary Tradition and Colonialism* and his *Understanding Indian Movies: Indian Culture, the Human Brain, and Cinematic Imagination*. Hogan's essay for the present volume, "On Being Moved: Cognition and Emotion in Literature and Film," focuses on "cross-cultural universals that manifest individual diversity," demonstrating how the "initially puzzling" Hindi film *Yatharth* (*The Truth*) "begins to make sense, both emotionally and thematically" when "placed in the context of a cognitive account of emotion that sets out to understand cultural particularity in a cross-cultural framework."

Hogan's essay builds on ancient studies of emotion developed by non-Western literary theorists that have been reinvigorated by cognitive science. As he puts it, "There have been two main approaches to emotion study in cognitive science. One stresses appraisal processes by which current experiences are related to long-term goals. The other stresses more immediate features of experience along with emotional memories."[4] His own work has taken up both orientations. In his 2003 book *The Mind and Its Stories*, he emphasizes appraisal in relation to narrative structure. However, in *Cognitive Science, Literature, and the Arts* (written after *The Mind and Its Stories*, though published in the same year), he criticizes the appraisal view in favor of a more immediate, neurologically based account. It is probably no accident that he was particularly concerned with the study of film in connection with this change of theoretical orientation. In keeping with Hogan's divided views on emotion and art, theorists stressing literature have tended to take up appraisal theories, while theorists focusing on film have often adopted more "subcortical" accounts.[5]

Cognitive ecocriticism (represented here with an essay by Nancy Easterlin), perhaps the newest subfield of cognitive cultural studies, seeks to integrate a cognitive-evolutionary perspective into ecocriticism. It is still in its formative stages, the multiplicity of potential research topics within its purview underscored by the broad range of issues already engaged by the parent field of ecocriticism. As cognitive ecocritic Glen Love describes it,

> The present state of [the critical] movement, for which the blanket term *ecocriticism* has come to be accepted, is one of ferment and experimentation. What is emerging is a multiplicity of approaches and subjects, including—under the big tent of environmental literature— nature writing, deep ecology, the ecology of the cities, ecofeminism, the literature of toxicity, environmental justice, bioregionalism, the lives of animals, the revaluation of place, interdisciplinarity, eco-theory, the expansion of the canon to include previously unheard voices, and the reinterpretation of canonical works from the past. (5)

Among the issues already broached by cognitive ecocritics are "the intervening nature of mind" (that is, the problematization of a "pure/ naive realist apprehension of nature"), "the importance of evolution, the relationship [between humans and] animals, and the situated nature of humans."[6] Some of the key texts include Easterlin's " 'Loving Ourselves Best of All' " and *What Is Literature For? Biocultural Criticism and Theory*, Glen Love's *Practical Ecocriticism*, and Dana Phillips's *The Truth of Ecology*.[7] Also, studies by philosopher Maxine Sheets-Johnstone (*The*

Roots of Thinking, The Roots of Power, and *The Primacy of Movement*)
and evolutionary anthropologist Ellen Dissanayke (*Art and Intimacy,
Homo Aestheticus,* and *What Is Art For?*), though not self-identified as
cognitive-ecocritical—indeed, they precede the emergence of this subfield by several years—represent useful background readings for this new
area.

The essay by G. Gabrielle Starr represents a subfield of cognitive aesthetics, also referred to sometimes as "cognitive aesthetics of reception."
The latter term was introduced by Alan Richardson in "Studies in Literature and Cognition: A Field Map" to discuss two important investigations
of "mental imaging in literary reading," Ellen J. Esrock's *The Reader's
Eye: Visual Imaging as Reader Response* and Elaine Scarry's *Dreaming
by the Book.* Scholars working in this area bring together "the traditional
concerns of philosophical esthetics . . . with those of literary criticism,
reader response theory, and the relation between sense experience and
image production. [They] draw on cognitive psychology and neuroscience for key terms and models, bringing the study of literary imagination
into a dialogue with research on vision and mental imagery" (17).

In contrast to Esrock and Scarry, however—who work with visual
imagery—Starr's focus is on "cognitive principles governing nonvisual
mental imagery": "olfactory, concerning smell and sometimes taste; haptic, concerning grasp and touch; motor/kinesthetic, concerning movement
and sometimes proprioception (perception of one's own body position);
gustatory, concerning taste." Yet sensory imagery, Starr argues, "goes
further than this: when poems evoke sound inside our heads—the rise and
fall of meter, the symmetry of rhyme—they evoke multisensory imagery,
fundamentally."

Starr introduces yet another important new aspect to the study of mental imagery: the notion of cognitive competition. As she argues in her
other recent essay, "units of our cognitive architecture compete, and this
competition is basic to cognitive function; attention may select for or
against a sight or sound; one image or sound may overwrite or 'mask'
another; and one word may interfere with the ability to recall another"
("Poetic Subjects," 56).[8] Starr's view of the cognitive architecture impli-
cated in the production and reception of poetry is thus compatible with
Ellen Spolsky's modular theory of cognition developed in *Gaps in Nature.*
(See also her "Making 'Quite Anew' " [chap. 3 of this volume].) Broadly

speaking, both are interested in cognitive conflict as a driving force of cultural production. As Spolsky puts it in "Darwin and Derrida," the essay that concludes this volume and is a "key text that seeks to show a deep harmony of core ideas of poststructuralism, the sciences of subjectivity, and Darwin's (non)concept of species,"[9]

> [the] modularity hypothesis explores the implications of our having developed parallel systems of knowledge acquisition. Like other animals, and even some plants, humans learn about an object in more than one way at once, by seeing *and* hearing *and* touching it, for example. While this has on the whole been good for survival, modularity also produces intermodular conflicts. . . .
>
> Assuming, then, that there is always going to be at least a gap if not a conflict between what can be learned from vision and (say) from words or between words and touch, a cultural historian will have to understand the historical/ideological/cultural context in order to gain insight into the question of why any particular intermodular conflict (itself presumably an age-old physiological miscalibration, something *Homo sapiens* had long ago learned to compensate for, ignore, and even profit from), suddenly becomes a cultural crisis.

Concepts of "cognitive competition" and "intermodular conflict" may thus go a long way toward addressing the concern about the "issue of historical change" expressed by Richardson in his original discussion of the work of Scarry and Esrock ("Studies," 18), a concern that is voiced with some regularity by both critics and champions of cognitive approaches to literature and culture.[10] If we get to know and change our world (which some of us do when we write and read poems) by embodying endless ongoing cognitive competitions, and if these cognitive competitions are always historically contingent, then a cognitive analysis of cultural representations necessarily retrains our attention on history. Historicizing is built into the epistemological foundation of cognitive cultural studies.

CHAPTER ELEVEN

On Being Moved

Cognition and Emotion in Literature and Film

PATRICK COLM HOGAN

What Is Cognitive?

In the last two decades, explicitly cognitive accounts of emotion have become quite prominent. While all this work makes reference to cognitive science, particular "cognitive" theories of emotion do not always use the word "cognitive" in the same way. Specifically, there is a commonsense use of the word "cognitive" where it means, roughly, "reasoning." This is, in fact, a precognitivist use of the term. Nonetheless, it persists—even in the work of cognitivists. By this usage, an account of some phenomenon is "cognitive" if it explains the phenomenon by reference to reasoning—thus induction, deduction, means/end inference, even pragmatic calculation that is logically faulty, but always some form of reasoning. By this usage, a cognitive account of emotion is an account in terms of inference, calculation, and so forth. Indeed, one often comes across references to "the cognitive account of emotion." Writers who make such references usually seem to have in mind some version of "appraisal theory," the view that emotion is the result of our evaluation of a situation in relation to goals. Put very simply, in this account, happiness results when we see a situation or event as significantly advancing our achievement of a goal; anger results when we appraise an agent as intentionally inhibiting our advancement toward achieving a goal; envy results when we understand someone else as achieving a goal we wish to achieve but have been unsuccessful in achieving, and so forth. (Obviously, a full appraisal account of any emotion will be more detailed and nuanced. However, this should convey the general idea.)

There is, however, a more technical use of the term "cognitive." In this usage, a cognitive account of a particular phenomenon is any account that makes reference to mental architecture as defined in cognitive science. Once one understands "cognitive" in this sense, there can no longer be any such thing as "the" cognitive account of emotion. This is true for two reasons. First, there is no single cognitive architecture. Second, there is no uniformly accepted account of emotion within a given cognitive architecture.

I return to cognitive architectures below. However, before going on to that, it is important to note that these two uses of "cognitive" are not, in principle, contradictory. The sorts of reasoning I referred to in describing the first use of "cognitive" must be treated in the architectures that fall under the category "cognitive" in the second usage. Moreover, in practice, the two are closely related. Appraisal theories of emotion have been developed explicitly within cognitive architectures, and the main appraisal theorists—for example, psychologists such as Nico Frijda and Keith Oatley—are also prominent cognitive scientists. So the difference in essence between the two uses of the term "cognitive" is one of scope. The first usage is "narrow" in scope, while the second usage is "broad" in scope. The broad scope usage encompasses the narrow scope usage. Thus "the cognitive account of emotion," in the narrow scope sense of "cognitive," is merely one of the (multiple) "cognitive accounts of emotion," in the broad scope sense. Hereafter, I use "cognitive" in the broad and technical sense of "utilizing cognitive architecture." When considering the narrow scope concept, I refer instead to "appraisal" or to some aspect of cognitive architecture that is involved with reasoning in the ordinary language sense.

This, then, leads us to the variety of cognitive architectures.

From Minds to Brains

We may distinguish four levels of cognitive architecture.[1] Each level allows us to isolate patterns that are not apparent at the other levels. Moreover, these four levels are themselves part of a broader sequence of explanatory stratification that runs, roughly, from physics to sociology. Put differently, social analysis isolates patterns that would not be evident at the psychological level. So, too, "classical" cognitivist analyses of mental processes isolate patterns that would not be evident at the level of neurobiology. Moreover, biology isolates patterns that would not be evident at the level of particle physics. This does not mean that there are new or different things that exist independently at "higher" levels of explanation. For example, mentalistic accounts do not require the existence of a soul in addition to biological matter. Consider, by way of illustration, a pointillist painting. The painting comprises nothing but dots of paint. However, when we step back from the painting, we see people seated on a river bank. The people we see are a pattern of dots. Saying that there are human figures there does not mean that anything exists beyond the dots of paint. Recognizing the figures does, however, involve isolating a pattern that is not isolable if we look only at the dots.

More exactly, the four levels of cognitive architecture are represented by four distinct approaches to the human mind, as follows:

1. Intentionalism
2. Representationalism (including "classical" cognitive science)
3. Connectionism
4. Neurobiology

The four levels are not entirely separate. Indeed, they tend to break down into two larger groups—intentional/representationalist and connectionist/neurobiological. Intentionalism encompasses our ordinary talk of goals, beliefs, and so forth. Representationalism systematizes our mentalistic idiom, developing it into a system of structures ("working memory," "episodic memory," and so on), processes ("memory consolidation," "memory retrieval," etc.), and contents (e.g., particular images from one's past experience). Neurobiology is the architecture of the brain, comprising neurons, neuronal circuits, and so forth. (Connectionism may be understood as a simplified version of neurobiological architecture that allows for the mathematical modeling of cognitive processes. It has not figured importantly in cognitive emotion research, except in "hybrid" models where it combines with representationalism or neurobiology. I therefore leave it aside in what follows.)

The two endpoints of intentionalism and neurobiology are the most firmly established. At some point, intentionalism is assumed by every cognitive architecture. For example, neuroscientists will commonly refer to a certain set of brain systems as underlying human motivation and thus the pursuit of goals. Moreover, cognitivists tend to accept that all intentions have a neural substrate, an underlying set of operations in the brain. For example, even the most adamant intentionalist/representationalist agrees that certain sorts of brain damage make it impossible to engage in certain sorts of intentional/representational thought (e.g., certain sorts of brain damage make it impossible to form new memories). These are some of the reasons why I do not view these levels as mutually exclusive. However, there are definite differences among theorists in the degree to which they take one or another level as primary or even definitive of cognitive operation.

Appraisal theorists such as Oatley strongly emphasize a representationalist architecture. Oatley argues that we have various emotion systems that continually monitor the environment and our bodies for signals that our relation to important goals has changed. When a given system is activated, that system may become dominant and initiate actions relevant to the goal. For example, a hunger system monitors our bodies for signals that there has been a change in our goal of being fed. When the system detects a signal of hunger, it shifts our attention from our current task to the pursuit of food. If, when scavenging for food, I suddenly see a bear, my fear system will be engaged. The fear system will appraise the situation as constituting a change in my likelihood of achieving the goal of staying alive. It will therefore usurp attentional focus, initiating the action of flight.

This necessarily simplifies Oatley's subtle account of emotion. However, it does indicate the general orientation of his system. It is no doubt obvious that Oatley's account has an eye on evolution. Cognitivists may or may not treat the evolutionary origins of particular aspects of cognitive architecture. However, their general assumption is that the architecture as a whole is functional. In other words, the architecture as a whole has selective advantages. Specifically, emotion theorists in cognitive science assume that emotions have some sort of reproductive function. Put simply, they assume that emotions are not bursts of irrationality. Emotions are, rather, the product of an evolutionary history and they have been selected because they help us to survive and reproduce. Put in the crudest way possible, imagine a creature that sees a predator and does not react with fear. The creature sits there, only to be eaten by the predator—thus not surviving, mating, and passing on its (unemotional) genes. In contrast, this creature's neighbor feels fear and flees. The second creature is not eaten and thus survives, mates, and passes on its (emotional) genes.

This very positive account of the functionality of emotion underlies even such a highly intentionally oriented version of cognitive emotion theory as that put forth by Martha Nussbaum. Nussbaum sees emotions as appraisals of our current situation in relation to the goal of human flourishing. This account has an ethical component, which leads Nussbaum away from purely evolutionary or biological accounts toward religious belief. Moreover, Nussbaum does find certain emotions problematic. Indeed, for Nussbaum, shame and disgust are almost irredeemably deleterious in their ethical consequences. Nonetheless, she largely accepts the functionalist account of emotion, which is (sometimes tacitly) based on an evolutionary view of the derivation of emotions.

Emphasizing the functionality of emotions is no doubt salutary when one is responding to commonsense views of emotions as merely harmful, as dangerous explosions of irrationality. On the other hand, the exponents of emotional functionality probably overestimate the degree to which antiemotionalism is a central doctrine of contemporary thought and practice. In fact, a romantic trust in emotion, represented in such idioms as "follow your heart," is quite pervasive today. The rhetoric of emotional functionality may thus be excessive. More importantly, this view of emotions represents an overly simple treatment of evolution.

First, it is important to recognize that a great deal of our emotional circuitry is shared with other mammals. Thus it not only evolved in different conditions—it actually evolved for different (ancestral) species. Of course, evolution often "makes use" of ancient systems for new purposes. That is undoubtedly true of emotion systems to some extent. However, evolution only does this when there is mutation that produces competition leading to the replacement of one genetic pattern by another. Note that the production of such mutations is very complex. Suppose that as humans evolve and their conditions change, fear remains adaptive but anger does not. Shouldn't evolution eliminate anger, then? Things are not that easy. Fear and anger are both bound up with the amygdala.[2] To produce a person with fear but without anger, there would have to be a mutation that altered the amygdala in such a way that it retained its fear function but lost the anger function. Moreover, that mutation would have to preserve other aspects of amygdala function and would have to have nondeleterious consequences elsewhere in the body, since a particular gene may be expressed in many regions of the body. There is also the complication that a particular trait may be adaptive only when it pervades a population. For example, it may be that humans would reproduce more if no one experienced anger. However, a nonangry individual in an angry society may have reduced survival and reproductive opportunities.

That is not all. Evolution does not produce functions anyway. Rather, mutations produce mechanisms that have selective advantages because they approximate functions in the current environment (the "environment of evolutionary adaptation"). My fear system does not give rise to flight or avoidance behavior in cases where there is danger per se. Rather, it (mechanically) gives rise to flight or avoidance behavior in particular sorts of cases where there is usually though not necessarily always danger. Thus our fear system tends to make us respond with fear to snakes, whether they are poisonous or not. While fear mechanisms regularly produce adaptive results, they can err significantly in two directions. First, they can lead us to be overly fearful of objects or situations that are not dangerous, even in nonpathological cases. For example, our fear system may lead us to feel fear of nonpoisonous snakes that is roughly the same as our fear of poisonous ones. That would constitute excessive fear. We could feel this excessive fear without having a snake phobia. Second, fear mechanisms can lead us to be trusting of objects or situations that are dangerous. For example, one is much more likely to be injured in a car than on an airplane. However, people are generally fearful of airplanes but not cars. In part, this is a matter of habituation, since most of us are in cars far more frequently than we are in airplanes. But it also seems to result from a series of other factors—our fear sensitivity to heights, our fear sensitivity to enclosed spaces without an exit, our anxiety at the sensation of being unsupported and related feelings of uncontrolled bodily movement, and so on. Note that we experience the sensation of being unsupported and of undergoing uncontrolled bodily movement most strongly when the airplane changes altitude, thus at takeoffs, landings, and during turbulence—the moments when flyers are most likely to experience anxiety. When precisely we first began to ride in cars and when we first began to fly in airplanes may also be a factor. I do not have any particular anxiety about airplanes. Perhaps this is because I first flew in airplanes when I was only a few years old.

In any case, the very circumscribed functionality of emotion is important for the development of a cognitive account of emotion. Among other things, at least prima facie, the limited nature of emotional functionality does not appear to be consistent with appraisal theory. One would expect an appraisal account to predict that we will feel greater fear when there is actually greater danger to our flourishing. Thus, it would seem that we should have greater fear of automobiles than of airplanes, at least those of us who know the statistics. But this is not the case.

The idea that emotions are evolved—but not always continuously adaptive/functional—mechanisms leads us to an alternative account of emotion. This account does not stress representational and intentional architecture but neurobiological architecture. The basic principle of this account is that there are concrete, experiential triggers for emotion. In the first place, these concrete triggers may be sensory (either external or internal to the body) or imaginative (thus imitating sensory experience). Thus I will experience anxiety if I see certain sorts of object, feel certain internal changes in my body, or imagine certain situations. (Clearly, the precise nature of imagination needs to be clarified here. However, the crucial point is simply that our brains respond in roughly the same manner when we imagine something and when we perceive it.[3] While the intensity of emotional response is likely to be less in the case of imagination, the general process of how emotion is triggered is the same in the two cases.)

But where do these triggers come from? One set of triggers is directly innate. As Antonio Damasio puts it, "We are wired to respond with an emotion, in a preorganized fashion, when certain features of stimuli in the world or in our bodies are perceived, alone or in combination. Examples of such features include size (as in large animals); large span (as in flying eagles); type of motion (as in reptiles); certain sounds (such as growling)" (*Descartes' Error*, 131). On the other hand, it may be that Damasio accepts too much as being innate here. Elsewhere, he explains that "the monkey's innate fear of snakes requires an exposure not just to a snake but to the mother's expression of fear of the snake. Once is enough for the behavior to kick into gear, but without that 'once' the 'innate' behavior is not engaged" (*Looking for Spinoza*, 47). There is clearly room for debate on just how much is innate. I suspect that a set of sensitivities to other people's emotion expressions is innate—a sensitivity to facial expressions, tones of voice, postures, and so forth. I would add to this certain propensities toward bonding. Finally, there are certainly some innate sensitivities relating to bodily experience (e.g., hunger) and tacit expectations of perceptual and motor continuity. To say that these are directly innate is not to say that they are all present at birth or that they do not have anything to do with environmental conditions. However, it is to say that they do not require special environmental conditions to result from ordinary genetic development.

A second set of triggers is also genetically organized. However, they are not fully specified. These are often differentiated by particular experiences in critical periods. The famous (nonemotional) case of this general sort is language. In Chomsky's "principles and parameters" framework, we are all born with the same set of principles. However, these principles have parameters that will be set in different ways in different environments during the critical period of language acquisition. In particular cases, aspects of one's emotional orientation may be understood as parametric in this sense. However, there may also be wider or more various differentiation of emotion during development—all within the general framework provided by genetic programs. While these developmental triggers recur across cultures, they do not have the same universal uniformity or near uniformity of the directly innate triggers.

Finally, a third set of triggers comes from emotional memories. These are "implicit" memories that affect our emotional response to current situations, even when we are unaware of their content. These may seem to be entirely idiosyncratic. However, they have patterns within a culture, and other patterns are cross-cultural.

Here we might return briefly to the case of the airplane. This view of emotion gives, I believe, a reasonable account of our greater propensity to experience fear in planes than in cars. Many of the emotional sensitivities that foster anxiety in planes are good candidates for innate emotion triggers—emotional sensitivity to heights, enclosed spaces with no exit, sensations of involuntary movement, and so forth. Of course, some of these occur in automobiles but with less intensity. For example, we are in an enclosed space, but we can in principle open the windows or have the driver stop so that we can get out—a possibility that we can readily imagine, even if we do not act on it. (If we cannot in principle open the window or ask the driver to stop—as in, say, a carjacking—our response to the enclosed space of the car is probably rather different.) Moreover, there are aspects of the difference that seem open to an explanation in terms of something like critical-period exposure. Most of us ride in cars at a much younger age than we fly in airplanes. Finally, emotional memories are no doubt involved as well. Some of these emotional memories are shared or collective. An obvious instance of this sort may be found in the increased anxiety Americans had about flying after the September 11, 2001, hijackings.

I should note that the "neurobiological sensitivity" account of emotion does not entirely reject appraisal theory. This account allows that emotions may be—indeed, often are—triggered by appraisal processes. However, it is different from appraisal accounts even here. Specifically, in the neurobiological sensitivity account, appraisal processes do not produce emotions through their evaluative conclusions, their estimations of outcomes or of changes in the likelihood of outcomes. In short, they do not produce emotions through probability estimates or any other calculation of the relation between one's current conditions and one's flourishing. Rather, appraisal processes produce emotions through the concrete imagery they recruit and the emotional memories they trigger.[4]

Literary Feeling

Up to this point, I have been speaking of emotion generally, without specific reference to literature or the arts. This is because there is no special emotion system for literature. Thus, to understand literary emotion, we need to understand emotion generally. Indeed, this continuity itself poses a problem. In particular, there is a recurring issue in aesthetics as to why we respond emotionally to literature. For example, why do we cry at the depiction of suffering? We are not suffering ourselves. Moreover, we know perfectly well that the characters are not real. Thus they are not suffering either. Appraisal theorists, such as Oatley, suggest that we respond emotionally to literature because we mentally simulate the experiences of a character from his or her point of view.[5] As his or her situation changes, we calculate the likely outcomes and the changes in the likelihood of those outcomes. As goal achievement becomes more likely, we become happy. When goal achievement—particularly goal achievement bearing on attachment—seems impossible, we become sorrowful. But this does not really explain fiction. It explains why we might cry when we hear a true story of someone's suffering. But it does not explain why we cry when we hear a story that is clearly fictional. One might get around this by arguing that we assume things like this happen all the time. Romeo and Juliet are not real, but there are real lovers who are separated like that. So perhaps we are weeping for them. But that seems odd. I know right now that real lovers are often separated, and I know it just as well as I know it at the end of *Romeo and Juliet*. Why is my response to that fact so different in those two situations? After all, it would seem that my appraisal of the situation of some abstract lovers being separated is the same now as at the end of Shakespeare's play.

Obviously, the neurobiological sensitivity account of emotion does not have this problem. That account may easily treat all the preceding facts. In the case of a live performance or film, we directly experience the actor's and actress's facial expressions, their gestures, tone of voice, gait, posture, and so forth—all important emotion triggers. More significantly for our present purposes our emotional response is bound up with our simulation of a character's experiences, as Oatley indicates. However, our emotional response is not a matter of the probability calculations that go along with that simulation. Rather, it is a matter of the concrete images we experience when engaging in that simulation. It is also a matter of the emotional memories that are activated during simulation—in the case of *Romeo and Juliet*, memories of romantic love, separation, and the death of loved ones.

Indeed, in a neurobiological sensitivity model, the fictionality of the work is irrelevant. Moreover, this is not a case of a discrepancy between mechanism and function. It is directly a case of a functional property. One function of emotion for humans, and one important reason for the involvement of the prefrontal cortex in emotion circuits, is to guide our selection of future behaviors. Take a simple case. Suppose I am thinking of going out alone to hunt in a dangerous part of the jungle. In the course of imagining this, I envision encountering a lion. This scenario is wholly fictional. However, if I do not feel some inkling of fear when imagining that scenario, I am much less likely to avoid going to that dangerous area in order to hunt. The emotion is a crucial part of the function of imagination. Thus this account leads us to expect emotional responses to fiction.

Finally, this model indicates that we should respond more forcefully to more detailed and more concrete images and less forcefully to abstract likelihoods or related evaluations. This is, of course, precisely what occurs. Writers such as Elaine Scarry have discussed the exquisite sensory vivacity that great writers are able to create in our minds. That vivacity is just what we would expect in emotionally compelling works, for it is concrete experience that triggers emotional response.

On the other hand, a problem remains here. The neurobiological sensitivity view of emotion predicts that we will have strong emotional responses to some fictions. But at the same time it raises the question of why our emotional responses in some ways so inhibited. Consider film, where the issue can be put very concretely. If a lion jumps out on the screen, why do we not run from the theater or at least hide under our seats? One way of accounting for this is by reference to habituation.[6] I believe that this is, in fact, a significant part of the explanation. However, it fails to fully connect our limited response to fiction with our limited response to imagination. Most components of an emotion play an important role in our imagination of actions. These most obviously include eliciting conditions (what gives rise to the emotion; in this case, the content of the imagination), phenomenological tone (what it feels like to have the emotion), and attentional focus. In extreme cases, they include expressive outcomes as well (such as crying or laughing), if typically in a muted form. What they do not include are the partially stereotyped actional outcomes that commonly result from emotions. Obviously, an emotion-eliciting imagination may lead us to act. But it leads to planned action, not to the spontaneous response of emotion. For example, if I imagine lions roaming in a certain part of the savanna, I avoid going there to hunt. However, I do not immediately start running, for fear of the imagined lions. The situation seems fundamentally the same as that in our experience of literature.

In the case of imagination, the fact that I don't act in response to imagined dangers is clearly not a matter of habituation. Thus it seems likely that the fact that I don't do so in the case of fiction is also not a matter of habituation. Norman Holland has suggested that our involvement with literature and film is bound up with our physical immobility and our location of objects in space.[7] Though I would not follow Holland's specific analyses here, I believe that he is onto something in drawing our attention to action, inaction, and space. The facts of imagination indicate that it is possible for us to inhibit the actional-response component of an emotional episode completely or almost completely without affecting the other emotion components. I suspect that this is connected with our location of events in space.

Standard neurocognitive architecture includes two sorts of spatial organization. One sort is objective and based in the hippocampus. This maps the relations of objects to one another, independent of one's own location. The other is egocentric and is connected most importantly with the superior parietal lobule.[8] This keeps track of one's spatial relation to the rest of the world. In other words, this maps out not just the spatial relations of things on my desk but where they are in relation to me right now. The ventral intraparietal area, which borders the superior parietal lobule, includes neurons "responsive to visual targets representing spatial reference frames (maps)." Among the "multiple reference frames" are, for example, neurons that "react to stimuli within reaching distance."[9] My conjecture is that there is a critical proximity range that is calculated by the superior and inferior parietal lobule and that bears on our position in the world and our activity within that position. The likelihood of actional outcomes for a given emotion is sharply increased by the location of triggering conditions within that critical range, currently or by anticipation. Take a simple example. I am up on a cliff. I see a lion below me on the plain. I feel fear. But I do not run. Indeed, I have no need to run. I probably do feel some tenseness in my muscles, resulting from the more general orienting response. But there is no actional outcome of the fear. Imagination, in my view, is basically the same sort of thing. In imagination, we typically do not integrate the emotional object (e.g., the lion) into that egocentric space of direct action, even in anticipation.

Yet this is not a full answer either. Sometimes we do integrate the emotional object in this way. Indeed, one could distinguish planning from fantasy largely on these grounds. In planning, we bring the object into the space of direct actional engagement in imagination. The point is even clearer in connection with literature, and it returns us to Oatley. Again, simulation involves imagining from the point of view of the character. That imagination must involve not only objective, hippocampal organization of space but egocentric, parietal situatedness as well. Of course, this does not always happen in literature. But when it does occur, why do we not respond with actional outcomes?

In fact, it may be that we do respond, only under limited conditions and in a limited way. The most obvious case is the startle reflex. When something very surprising happens on screen in a movie, I may jerk back in my seat. I may even jump up or push my feet into the ground, giving the start of a push away for flight. The same point holds in life. Imagine again that you are on a cliff overlooking a field. A lion appears. You see a fawn and, even without realizing it, adopt the spatial perspective of the fawn in imagination. The lion leaps toward the fawn. Your whole body pushes back as if to avoid the lion.

It seems likely that the limited conditions under which we respond and the limited scope of the response are a function of the speed of the reaction and the degree to which it can be inhibited. The startle reflex operates very quickly and is notoriously difficult to inhibit. Fleeing in fear allows some room for decision, thus inhibition. In the case of imagination, the issue does not typically arise as the default response is to end the imagination, which eliminates the eliciting conditions for the actional response. A similar point applies to reading a book. Typically, one has to put down the book before one runs. But putting down the book puts an end to the imagination and thus the eliciting conditions. Moreover, it is difficult (perhaps impossible) to produce very swiftly operating, inhibition-resistant responses, such as the startle reflex, through literature.

This reference to putting down the book suggests precisely what it is that inhibits our actional response to fictionally or imaginatively produced emotions. It is our direct engagement with critically proximate egocentric space. Even when initiated, our actional outcomes do not proceed to unfold precisely, because they rely at every moment on recalibrations in relation to subjectively fixed space. When I see danger and run away, I do not run in precisely the same way no matter what the conditions are. I swerve to avoid running into things; I jump over obstacles in my path. Our actional outcomes are partially stereotyped. But they are necessarily in part variable as well, open to continuing modification. In the case of flight, for example, one component of that modification is stopping when one reaches safety. Safety is defined, in part, by reference to some critical area of egocentric space. That is precisely what we experience at the first moments of actional response to a fiction when we press against the back of the chair in the theater or set the novel down on the table.

How, then, does this inhibition occur? It may be the result of cingulate cortical operation. Consider the case of fear. Again, the amygdala is crucial to the operation of fear. But the amygdala is, so to speak, "what" oriented. As Clark, Boutros, and Mendez explain, the "sensory information that reaches the amygdala provides details that help identify the object rather than determine its location" (228). Both the amygdala and the parietal cortex project to the cingulate cortex, which plays "central role . . . in mediating our emotion and cognitive function on the one hand and motor response on the other" (213). It is perhaps worth noting, as Clark, Boutros, and Mendez point out, that the parietal and amygdalar projections do not overlap and that the amygdalar projections terminate in the frontal pole of the cingulate cortex, which also includes the region functionally involved with vocalization (204). The latter fact may suggest why we are apparently more likely to engage in vocalizations than full-fledged actions during, say, films.

The Place of Culture

The preceding discussion of emotion is universalist. This is, I believe, as it should be. Emotion and literature both show remarkable universal patterns. To some extent, these patterns form "complete universals" or "nearly complete universals," which is to say, they are common to all are nearly all individuals. More often, they are cross-cultural universals that manifest individual diversity. For example, there is certainly individual variation in emotion. Principles of emotion are cross-culturally universal if their diversity is limited and that diversity reappears in different social groups. An obvious example comes from attachment theory in the tradition of John Bowlby. This theory posits several distinct attachment styles.[10] The styles result primarily from different sorts of experiences in a critical period in early childhood. The fact that there are distinct attachment styles entails that there is no complete universal of attachment style. However, it does not follow from this that there is broad cultural, historical, or other difference in attachment. If indeed Bowlby and his followers have isolated genuine types of human emotional development, then we should expect these types to recur across all societies and periods. (This is the sort of universality stressed by, for example, David Buller.)

This is not to say that there are no cultural differences. However, this analysis does suggest that cultural difference may be much more limited than is commonly thought. To understand this limitation, we need to draw two distinctions. The first concerns the degree to which and the way in which traits may vary culturally. There probably are no traits that can vary without limit. However, there are traits that vary with such latitude that we may in practice think of them as being unlimited in their variation. For example, it seems that there are very few constraints on what sounds we can pair with what meanings—though there are constraints on what sorts of sound we can make and thus on what sorts of sound will form part of a language. Other traits may be much more tightly constrained with respect to variation. For example, it seems that a wide range of structural aspects of language do not vary greatly from language to language. In some cases, these variations may be parameterized, organized into a limited number of distinct possibilities. Emotion almost certainly falls into the second category, that of more tightly constrained traits.

The second distinction concerns traits that are (relatively) uniform within a society and traits that are not uniform. One significant problem with much discussion of cultural difference is that it tends to assume a high degree of uniformity within cultures, particularly within foreign cultures. Everyone recognizes that their own in-group is diverse. However, we tend to see out-groups as "less complex, less variable, and less individuated" than in-groups.[11] Great uniformity does prevail in certain areas. In language, for example, fluent speakers of a given language are uniform in head directionality, placing heads first or last.[12] However, it is again probably the case that all styles of Bowlbyan attachment turn up in every culture.

Where, then, do cultural differences enter? In consequential areas, such as emotion, they will be largely a matter of variations within parametric or other constraints. These variations derive from accidents of history, group dynamics, physical environment, and related factors. For example, even short-term differences of historical accident and circumstance may lead one society toward liberal social democracy at one point and toward fascism at another. With respect to attachment, historical accidents may lead to different proportions of parenting styles appearing in different groups. These different proportions of parenting styles will lead to different proportions of attachment styles. These differences, along with distinct patterns in emotional memories, may lead to palpable differences in broad social behavior. As this indicates, social and cultural distinctions are clearly significant. However, despite their sometimes overwhelming cumulative consequences, the scope of differences in emotion—as well as in literature, language, and other areas—seems to be quite limited.

Disgust, Untouchability, and Desire

In order to illustrate the preceding points and at least gesture toward their interpretive consequences, I conclude by briefly considering some aspects of a recent Hindi film, *Yatharth* (*The Truth*), and the surrounding culture depicted in the film. The story concerns a family of untouchables in a small village in India. Their hereditary occupation is cremating the dead and, as such, they are the object of a series of strict taboos, prominently taboos on physical contact with nonuntouchable Hindus.

The story begins with Budhai marrying. The couple has a child, Bijuria, but the mother dies almost immediately. The girl grows up suffering constant hunger. From childhood, she begins to dance whenever she hears the chant of an approaching funeral, "Ram nam satya hai" (roughly, "The name Rama [or God] is truth"; the truth referred to in the title of the film is death, as suggested by this chant). There is some indication that she dances in this context for appraisal-based reasons, since she knows that there will be food following the funeral. However, her response is entirely automatic and dissociated from any actual consideration of benefits. For example, as an adolescent, she goes to see her first movie. There is a funeral in the film and she begins her dance there, although it is clear that this funeral will not further her goal of getting food. In keeping with the preceding analysis, this seems to be a spontaneous response that has not undergone habituation through exposure to cinema. When Bijuria reaches puberty, the villagers begin to object to her highly inappropriate response to the grief of the mourners. (Contrary to some peculiar Western cultural commonplaces, joy is not the standard Asian response to death.) Eventually several prominent men in the village begin to notice Bijuria's physical attractiveness. One tries to buy her from her father. Another three try to abduct and rape her. Eventually, she is married to the man who saves her from the three rapists. Her final dance is performed when he dies and she is faced with his motionless corpse. This dance leads to her own death.

Before going on to make a few interpretive comments on the story, we need to consider some aspects of the cultural and cognitive/affective context. Cross-culturally, people tend to respond to corpses with disgust. There are different possible explanations for this. Perhaps we have an innate disgust response to corpses. Alternatively, the case may be parallel with that of monkeys and snakes. Thus disgust responses to corpses would be acquired through critical-period experiences. This would be a case of "cultural construction" but cultural construction that is convergent across societies (i.e., different societies would converge toward viewing corpses as disgusting). There are several reasons why this is likely. For example, we may have innate disgust responses to the smell of decaying flesh. When corpses begin to decay, this will provoke a disgust response. Adults may repeat this disgust response with even new corpses owing to the activation of emotional memories. A child's disgust response to corpses would be fixed when an adult expressed such a response before a child in the critical period. We would also expect cultures to converge on inferences to connections between corpses and disease, inferences that recruit disgust-provoking imaginations and emotional memories.

Suppose that disgust at corpses is not innate but rather the result of critical-period experiences. If this is the case, we would expect several things. First, we would expect that children will not acquire that disgust if they are raised in contexts where caregivers do not exhibit disgust at corpses. Second, we would expect that cultures might vary in the boundary conditions for disgust. For example, some cultures might cultivate disgust toward corpses only after a certain period of decay, minimizing the disgust response. Other cultures might extend the disgust beyond the corpse to those who could have suffered contamination. On this spectrum, ancient Hindu culture falls into the latter extreme.

These are points of cultural difference. However, there are, so to speak, hidden cross-cultural patterns here as well. Specifically, there are two other things we might expect. First, we might expect culturally unusual expansions of the disgust response to be less stable than the more minimal disgust responses. For example, we would expect them to be less strongly inhibitory of conflicting emotion systems. Hunger (or, more properly, the desire to taste) and sexual desire are the emotion systems that conflict most directly with disgust. We might expect disgust to have a stronger force in inhibiting these systems to the extent that it bears on innate triggers or critical-period experiences that are closer to innate triggers.[13] As cultures expand disgust responses beyond this "core," we would expect the targets to be less resistant to contradictory emotion systems.

Second, when the disgust response is extended to living people, we might expect it to be recruited for social hierarchization. We would expect this for general reasons of group dynamics. We form in-groups and out-groups very easily, as soon as any group property becomes salient.[14] A disgust response makes its objects highly salient. When extended to living people, it seems very likely that this will be taken up to enforce social hierarchies.

We are now in a position to understand at least part of the movie. The filmmakers in effect portray Bijuria's emotional development as a matter of critical-period experiences. An early scene shows Budhai holding the infant as he tends to a cremation. Assuming that the disgust response to corpses is not innate but critical-period determined, we would expect Bijuria to have no disgust response to corpses at all. This allows for her subsequent, positive association of corpses with food. Had she developed the usual disgust response to corpses, the association should have at least partially inhibited her desire to eat as well. More importantly, this prepares for her subsequent, joyous response to death. Desperate to feed his hungry daughter, Budhai learns of an imminent death in the village. His delight at the prospect leads him to go and dance with his tiny daughter. This shared delight, presumably repeated on more than one occasion, is the key critical-period experience for her response to death as an eliciting condition for joy.

Subsequent developments show the relative instability of extended disgust, as our account predicts. Most of the villagers evidence repulsion at the possibility of contact with Budhai. However, this disgust proves weak when faced with the competing emotion system of sexual desire. Indeed, the film strongly suggests that this cultural extension of disgust from corpses to untouchables is fragile. In this way, the system should be easy to change. However, it is not easy to change because the disgust serves as an emotional justification for financial, physical, and political power within the village setting.

The conclusion of the film takes us to emotional memories. Viewers from different cultures will recognize the bitter contrast between Bijuria's initial, uncontrollable response of joy on hearing "Ram nam satya hai" and her terrible grief at finding her husband's motionless, unresponding corpse, a grief stressed by flashbacks representing emotional memories. However, only some viewers will come to understand what the dance itself signifies at this point. Clearly, a dance is too complicated a motor routine to be invariably triggered by eliciting conditions for joy—particularly since this is an expressive outcome, not (technically) an actional outcome. Why, then, do the filmmakers represent the expressive outcome in this way? The dance is there to suggest something beyond the realism of the rest of the film—the dance of the goddess Kali on the cremation grounds. The iconography is deeply moving for anyone who has built up a store of emotional memories relating to stories of Kali and her spouse, Siva. In keeping with the preceding account, this part of the work is the most culturally distinctive, because it relies on emotional memories rather than innate propensities or critical-period responses.

When placed in the context of a cognitive account of emotion that sets out to understand cultural particularity in a cross-cultural framework, this initially puzzling film begins to make sense, both emotionally and thematically.

Conclusion

I have argued that emotion is, first, the response of dedicated neurobiological systems to concrete experiences, not a function of the evaluation of changing situations relative to goals. These concrete experiences may be perceptual or imaginative. In evolutionary terms, it is important that they operate through imagination. However, it is also important that the imaginative versions are capable of being disengaged from (parietally based) egocentric space, thus discouraging the activation of actional outcomes, except in very limited ways. The triggers for emotion systems may be innate or they may result from experience. Relevant experiences are of two sorts. The first sort involves primarily critical-period experiences. Experiences of this type may have limited structural effects on the relevant emotion system. The second sort comprises emotional memories. This account predicts that there will be some traits shared by everyone or almost everyone. But it also predicts that there will be different sorts of diversity. One sort of diversity will carry across cultures (i.e., individuals will vary in roughly the same ways in different cultures). Another sort of diversity will involve differences between cultures. Such differences will most often be a matter of limited statistical variations in the proportions of emotional subtypes. (This limitation in variation results not only from genotypic commonality but from commonalities in the physical environment, developmental experience, and principles of group dynamics.) Finally, this account has consequences for a range of literary issues, from general theoretical topics, such as why we respond to literature emotionally but without significant actional outcomes, to concerns of practical criticism, such as the nature of a particular character's emotion or the reasons for audience response to a particular work. Moreover, it allows for the incorporation of cultural variation into these literary analyses.

CHAPTER TWELVE

Cognitive Ecocriticism

Human Wayfinding, Sociality, and Literary Interpretation

NANCY EASTERLIN

Like many schools of theory that have emerged since the late sixties, eco-criticism developed out of political and ethical commitments, whereas cognitive criticism emerged from an interest in the developing sciences of mind and takes as its starting point human mental processes. The prospect of a cognitive ecocriticism, then, might seem to be an unwarranted conjunction of fields motivated by different principles and focused on quite distinct phenomena. But in fact, cognitive science and evolutionary psychology are relevant to all areas of literary studies. Because human minds stand behind all human activity, including literary activity, knowledge of the mind is relevant to any literary account of the environment. Indeed, that environment and its representations cannot be apprehended via any mechanism other than the mind.

"Environment" itself denotes a distinctly human concept, not a stable, concrete entity, and its meaning is context dependent, relative to individuals or groups of observers, perhaps located in or journeying through physical space, perhaps, like ecocritics, engaged in a shared intellectual or political pursuit. My perceived environment, as I sit and write in my air-conditioned study, is this quiet and enclosed space; but if I go down the steps and out my front door, I'd define "environment" quite differently; now it would include the magnolia tree in my front yard rather than simply providing a view of it. But let's take a leap forward in time: the sentences just preceding this one were written sometime in July 2005, along with the rest of the first draft of this essay, and things in New Orleans have changed considerably in the intervening period. As I revise, my immediate physical surroundings, by some miraculous good fortune, are basically unaltered (though the magnolia is not in bloom). But in truth, no thinking person would now apply the word "environment" to the intact spaces (30 percent of the city, at best) in New Orleans, a sign of how consciousness alone can so readily transform concepts and words. Even more to the point, it would not even occur to me to define my study as my "environment," a conceptual shift reflective, I gather, of a heightened awareness of the frangible boundaries between proximate places.

Evolutionarily, this ability to observe distinct entities within larger wholes and to break down processes aids analysis and facilitates decision and action. It is more important to perceive the threatening other that is pursuing you as *shark* and punch him in the nose than it is to experience oneness with the totality of nonhuman nature. Philosophically, the recognition that our identification and naming of entities has primarily instrumental value is an inheritance of classical pragmatism; moreover, the modernization of scientific thought was itself a fundamental influence on pragmatic philosophy.[1] For instance, as naturalists and geologists became increasingly aware of the dynamic rather than fixed nature of natural phenomena, theory followed suit, resulting in the hypothesis of evolution by natural selection and in probability theory.

The pragmatists, unlike other thinkers of their day, were influenced by a correct understanding of natural selection and its implications for human knowledge. Species not only change but are identified as new species at points in the evolutionary process marked as substantively different by human perception.[2] Likewise, all species, including humans and everything they create, are part of the organic order, but we need to separate species from the larger whole to analyze their behavior and evolutionary success, and the term "environment" enables us to do just this. Yet when the term invites us to conceptualize "nature" or "environment" as fixed and bounded entities excluding humanity, it is disabling. It is one of the ironies not infrequently found in human history that the processes of modernization—expansion of the cities with the growth of factories; mass migration to these new industrial centers; and the creation of policies and infrastructure aimed to maintain a rapidly growing population—encouraged, psychologically, the perceived division of culture and nature, even though theory and research stemming from the Enlightenment and developing up through the nineteenth century was pointing toward the continuity of the whole, toward what Dewey called the unity of knowledge.

The popular concept of the ecosystem to which ecocritics have gravitated employs the language of process, but the evident teleological vision on which it is based does not correspond very well to the operation of chance, incredible variety, and frequently conflicting interests normal science continues to discover in nature.[3] This notion of the ecosystem is attractive because it asserts the benign compatibility of all elements of the natural order—and it is in this figuration most certainly an *order*—but in positing such an order practitioners must ignore some less-than-encouraging perceived natural facts (e.g., sharks kill). Because the operant system model characterizes the interaction of individual organisms and *environment* as benignly symbiotic, and because such a picture does not correspond to perceived reality, a culprit (the human species) must be subtracted from the natural domain and vilified as an independent entity. The abstract model, incompatible with biological facts and species behavior, cannot account for the place of humans in nature and cannot escape the rationalistic, compartmentalized thinking it accuses, with much justice, of facilitating environmental degradation.[4]

By contrast, the theory of evolution by natural selection is compatible with all research in biology for the past 150 years. Human beings—including modern human beings who write literary works—are in and of nature, and their way of perceiving organic features external to the human organism or group is guided by distinctly species-typical modes of cognition that enabled responses conducive to survival in the major period of species evolution.[5] Nonhuman nature, the environment, or whatever we wish to call it, can never be known in an other-than-human sense. To acquire knowledge of human cognitive predispositions, so far as we can, will help us identify species biases. From the point of view of environmentalism, such knowledge is useful in analysis of the productive and destructive dimensions of human activities. From the point of view of ecocriticism, such knowledge is valuable in a potentially wide variety of ways, since it may well illuminate the relationships between modes and forms and their depiction of places, between minds and nonhuman nature, and between urban and natural environments, to give only a few examples.

"Landscape is personal and tribal history made visible," says geographer Yi-Fu Tuan (157). I believe a more comprehensive, related claim can be made for all the arts: prototypically human modes of thinking and feeling about the physical surround and about social groups (together constituting the environment) as well as the individual character and experience of the artist are evident in the final product. And although landscape painting, poetry, drama, and other arts differ from everyday perception in the manner of their human inflections, species-typical perception nevertheless governs all.

The orientation of any organism toward its surround will depend on its physical needs and the patterns of behavior that serve those needs. Evolutionary theory surmises that higher intelligence must be useful to have emerged and that, therefore, survival in an extensive physical domain containing a wide range of organisms is promoted by relatively high intelligence as well as cognitive flexibility. For our human ancestors one to two million years ago as well as for our earlier evolutionary kin, the negotiation of the surround, which changed considerably as they traveled through it, was a complex task. A far-ranging but home-based species, humans evolved the higher intelligence required to successfully negotiate the varied, extensive environment required to serve their needs.[6]

Like other species, humans exhibit a range of instrumental biases, all of which enhance their ability to identify attractive resources, to avoid predators, to negotiate physical space, and to engage in sexual-procreative activities. Since wayfinding entails travel in time and through space without getting lost, the evolution of intelligence, memory, causal thinking, environmental attunement, time consciousness and goal orientation are all integral to it. As Stephen Kaplan points out, wayfinding biases do not have the same direct and immediate payoff as other evolved predispositions, like an attack response in the presence of a predator, and thus, with respect to wayfinding abilities, the knowledge produced can be enormous and the uses to which that knowledge can be put are many. The advantage of extensive environmental knowledge most surely precipitates the evolution of memory, necessary to sustain vast knowledge. Though modern humans are assisted by maps and written directions, we travel—via automobile, airplane, boat, spaceship, and so forth—far greater distances than our hunter-gatherer ancestors. We would not be able to make maps, give directions, or ride a bike round-trip to the store without our wayfinding disposition. By the same token, these wayfinding abilities depend on an emotional connection to the environment, for it is such a connection that promotes interest. Walking itself is pleasurable, and the need and desire to move precipitates the actions and perceptions that result in knowledge. In our evolutionary past, what was seen and heard provided our ancestors with valuable information about resources, predators, and the like; moreover, the affective charges connected to specific environmental features still resonate with humans today, whether or not we have any conscious knowledge of the evolved basis of our predilections (for mountains, for instance, from which visual advantage could be secured) or aversions. In turn, aesthetic representations of natural phenomena—paintings, descriptions, dramatic presentations, and so on—are always related to our evolved preferences, not least when those preferences are turned on their proverbial heads.[7]

Although an understanding of humans as wayfinders suggests a complex and dynamic interest on the part of humans in the environment, the surround itself is complex and dynamic and is frequently in a state of change as the individual or group moves through it—that is, *no* surround comes to us whole. For a wayfinder, a memorable disposition of elements, a perspective that suggests a way forward while providing opportunities for cover and for visual advantage, and evidence of resources along the way and/or memory of them at the endpoint all excite interest. Hence, the wayfinding mind is stimulated by complexity and mystery, yet the emotional tenor of a complex or mysterious aspect of the environment varies considerably depending on the specific elements and their disposition. If a phenomenon suggesting mystery (a clump of trees, for instance, or the mouth of a cave) is foregrounded in a painting, and thus perceptually close to the viewer, it will evoke a sense of foreboding; at a distance, it is more apt to stimulate curiosity. Although humans may well be predisposed to prefer savanna-type vistas and representations, such a preference is mediated by other predispositions and by cultural experience, because plasticity of response proved essential to species faced with complex and shifting environmental challenges. Teenagers familiar with the hardwood forests of the eastern United States enjoy images of them equally with those of rolling hills. This is consistent with the survival needs of a wayfaring species that must map its way and evaluate habitat, a judgment it often makes based on indirect features of the environment. The evaluation of habitat entails several stages, each of which includes automatic, unconscious responses that impinge on the cognitive decision to explore the domain further, to move on, or to stay. Dramatic changes in sound and light trigger reflexive responses, during which the processing of stimuli and bodily preparation for further response inhibit all ongoing activity. Cloud patterns are a strong emotional trigger; elevations, which provide visual access, are preferred to low-lying areas; and large mammals, potential sources of food or threat, are intrinsically interesting.[8]

One other feature of evolved human psychology, very apparent in recorded human history and certainly central to species survival, dramatically colors human perspectives on given environments: strong social relationships. Humans are a markedly social species; the development of strong emotional attachments from infancy onward encourages them to seek a physical proximity to others, promoting individual and group bonds and behavior that were crucial to our hunter-gatherer ancestors. The positive emotions associated with the social group are similar to positive feelings members have for the environment and also significantly affect group members' attitudes toward the environment with which that group is associated. Originally, positive affective response to the areas in which early humans were raised was probably tied to the identification of viable habitat. On the other hand, *no* environment looks good to a primitive person who is accidentally separated from his or her group or who unexpectedly finds himself fending off a predator single handed. The tendency to overlay the positive or negative quality of human emotions on the perception of physical place may now be even stronger than it was for our ancestors, since modern life entails engagement with a greater number of persons and places than did hunter-gatherer life. Contemporary research suggests that humans typically adjust to radically new environments when they have established strong ties in those environments, especially love relationships and families.[9] In sum, an environment not only is perceived and known through categories themselves emotionally charged for selective advantage but is affectively colored by the viability, dysfunction, or lack of human social relationships experienced within it.

Human cognitive predispositions support our wayfinding, knowledge-seeking, and highly social nature, having evolved to solve environmental challenges in our evolutionary past. The tendency to create dichotomies, for instance, is a product of the need to simplify input, especially in severing the *self* from the *other*. This consolidation of the self enhances the sense of agency and thus promotes the ability to act quickly. *Narrativity*, or narrative thinking, arises from the perception of chronologically related causes and effects. The basic observation that beings and objects impinge on and change one another through actions carried out in time facilitates inferences about future effects and likewise enables the formation of plans and goals. Thus binding the individual to the social group and to the physical environment through a causal sequence of events, narrative thinking and its organized, communal manifestation in the language of sequential action plans and stories impose order on the group's past, providing information, meaning, and identity amid the contingencies of existence.[10] Although cognitive and evolutionary psychology assume that these ways of thinking enhanced inclusive fitness in the ancestral past, they do not assert that such predispositions accede to the same degree of functional utility in our much different contemporary environment.

To summarize: (1) the adaptive pressures in our evolutionary past resulted in an intelligent, social, wayfinding, knowledge-seeking, and, ultimately, culture-producing species; (2) human affective ties to places and persons are interrelated, because the combination of a protective group and a fitness-promoting habitat are essential to species survival; (3) knowledge of the world, for us, is *always* specifically human knowledge; (4) our dominant ways of knowing, which bias our procedures for gathering, synthesizing, analyzing, reproducing, and transforming information, undergird our artistic modes and patterns.

How can this revised perspective on the human species inform ecocritical practice? First, the inclusion of human life and thought within natural processes cancels the nature-culture dichotomy, for all cultural innovations develop out of our adaptive strategies and propensities. Human modes of thinking and being are enmeshed in the selective advantages accruing to our ancestors, which arose in the effort to survive in a varied physical surround. And the implication that our epistemology is embedded in our functional response to environmental pressures has direct bearing on literary artifacts. Art is, in effect, a way of knowing and coping with the world, one that initially, perhaps, served to strengthen human groups. While its function has mutated somewhat in modern culture, art still serves as a way of coping and knowing—of exercising problem-solving skills, of imagining alternatives, of simply taking a break from the strains of daily living. Ecocriticism has a history of participating in "the 'gotcha' manner of [the] eco-policeman, dragging past writers to the dock for today's sense of environmental incorrectness," but a cognitive and evolutionary view, because it is based in a reasonably objective account of species psychology, can help us avoid that accusatory style.[11] Literature *is*: it exists, in all its great variety, yet nevertheless is a product of the adapted human mind. Realism in this perspective is neither good nor bad; it is one mode of response, and not necessarily one that will establish an affective connection between the reader and the nonhuman natural world; it is in any case a human fashioning of perceived actuality, since an evolutionary perspective renders obsolete the infatuation with grasping the thing-in-itself.[12]

Recently, ecocritics have begun to address a greater variety of environments and have gleaned the central significance of human relationships to place attachment. An evolutionary and cognitive approach to the area provides the theoretical basis for this expansion and suggests new dimensions to the study of literature and the environment. Depending on how ecocritics define the goals of their subdiscipline, especially depending on whether they wish to limit themselves to the analysis of representations of places or whether they also wish to explore the human dimension to the environment, they will define variously what projects lie inside or outside the subdiscipline's purview. Below, I make some suggestions about directions ecocritics might wish to take, directions based on the evolutionary phenomenology and cognitive tendencies of our wayfinding, knowledge-seeking species. Not intended to be comprehensive, these suggestions are even less to be thought of as obligatory avenues for future ecocritical study. However, perhaps in the spirit of going against the grain that has informed so much contemporary scholarship, I focus on selected modes of literature and subject matters that would have been considered irrelevant to the ecocritical project ten years ago. In keeping with this and with the philosophy that species-typical characteristics are mutually dependent features of long-term human survival and not, in the larger sense, usefully segmented and divorced from the integrated and dynamic explanations of evolution, the thematic literary categories below flow into one another, since wayfinding, supported by the twin attractions of travel and rooted-ness, underscores all and explains their logical interrelatedness.

Human wayfinders are richly aware of and responsive to *environment*, meaning both physical places and living beings, often at a level below consciousness. Lawrence Buell has presented a similar, though untheo-rized, concept of environmental attunement, the "environmental uncon-scious" (23). Recognition that the "environmental unconscious" is part of our evolved nature informs the longstanding appeal of certain types of writing—indeed, informs all writing in one way or another, an assertion following logically from the simple view that there is no being, much less any writing, if there is no environment.

Nature Writing

The very existence of traditions in poetry and prose devoted to meditation on and description of nonhuman nature attests to our special sensitivity to the environment, and this body of literature is in a sense remarkable. Our eagerness to lavish so much attention on physical places and things should not be taken for granted, for it is, in effect, testimony to the value of the physical world for humans. Paradoxically, though, nature writing also bears witness to the conceptualization of nature as *other*—that is, to the perceived separation of the human self from nonhuman nature. Often the narrative frame of nature writing, whether stated or implied, takes the shape of the journey away from civilization and toward and into the world of nonhuman nature. Thus, after his twenty-six-month sojourn at Walden Pond, Thoreau characterizes himself as "a sojourner in civi-lized life again" (1). The desire to escape the rat race of modern life—to lose oneself in, reflect on, and express one's observations of nonhuman nature—is itself a symptom of the dichotomization of nature and culture and the attendant objectification of nature that has been facilitated by industrialization. From an evolutionary perspective, the beginnings of this perceived split between nature and culture are of relatively recent origin, dating back only about ten thousand years. According to Steven Mithen, archaeological evidence suggests that the first sedentary human establish-ments were among the Natufians between 12,3000–10,800 BCE, but that then the Natufians were forced by climactic change to resort to a nomadic life (29–55). It is likely that these people and our Neolithic ancestors who developed the settlement at Jericho about 9,600 BCE when the summer droughts ended mark the starting point of the view that *nature* is an entity other and apart from human culture.

Placing nature writing within the context of human prehistory promises to broaden the framework of ecocritical interpretation, enabling, among other things, a twofold analysis of what it means to pursue nonhuman nature for its own sake on one hand and what has been lost in rendering it as an object of consciousness on the other.[13] This is the larger narrative that stands behind all cultural activity; more locally, all lyric moments, as Patrick Hogan astutely observes, imply background narratives, and these would include all short reflections on natural beauty within the lyric tradition.[14] What are the background narratives, both large and local, that render forays into bucolic settings personally and environmentally sanative? What personal and cultural knowledge do we stand to gain from a sympathetic and naturalistically informed consideration of the occasions on which humans perhaps ask too much of the world of insensate nature? Literature is rife with renderings of diverse reflections on nonhuman nature, and it is more productive to consider how all nature poems— including, for instance, Ann Finch's dichotomized depiction of nature and civilization, Wordsworth's difficult assertion that nature is nurse and guardian of his being, Gary Snyder's disciplined observations—reveal the dimensions of our modern conceptualization of nature than to suggest that some of these works are morally acceptable, others not. Of course, this claim rests on my conviction that the way to sustain life of all kinds on this planet depends on understanding all forms of human action and response rather than delivering judgments that encourage us to shut the door on troublesome knowledge.

Narrative and Journey

Many forms of writing—travel literature, the picaresque, the bildungsroman, the long poem—involve journeys. Whether these journeys define the basic narrative frame or are incorporated into another, larger, structure, travel in these works is rarely incidental but instead central to the overall purpose and meaning of the work. This coheres with the basic phenomenology and epistemology of wayfinders, since movement and travel presuppose engagement with new environments and thus always entail expanded knowledge. Travel means discovery: Ulysses fights mythical monsters, Han Solo et al. escape from the mouth of a snakelike creature inhabiting an asteroid, and Barbara Gowdy transposes the quest motif into the life of elephants, but no matter how fanciful a narrative is, the basic pattern of such stories attests to a fundamentally wayfinding disposition, because it conjoins a knowledge-seeking orientation with movement in time through space and with the negotiation of relationships among diverse creatures and places. Different as such stories are in their content and specific goals from, for example, Annie Dillard's *Pilgrim at Tinker Creek*, many of the general cognitive and emotional motivations underlying them are the same.

Traveling alone for our social species represents a challenge, and it is particularly a challenge when the individual travels over long distances, and even more so when that person is a woman or girl. Sometimes it is easy for us as modern humans to think abstractly about the security of groups, but in our evolutionary past, there was nothing metaphorical about safety in numbers, the group being a condition of survival. While survival no longer depends so strictly on sticking close to the pack, the complicated emotions related to solitary travel and the still-existing vulnerabilities of the isolated traveler drive the writing of and readerly interest in literary journeys. This is especially so, perhaps, when there is no solid home base. Jane Eyre cannot grow and learn without leaving Gateshead, but the atmosphere of every one of her "homes" is slightly oppressive, even threatening, though each one she moves to is less so than the one before, and her time on the road alone is pervaded by a sense of vulnerability and danger. In the less censored nineteenth-century French novel, especially those of Zola, the dangers to women are more explicitly depicted in the routine occurrence of rape. The emotional and psychological register of such stories generally matches that of our default states as human beings. The incorporation of buddies or sidekicks into the picaresque transforms the emotional register of that subgenre and makes possible a greater range of incidents, especially comic ones, which seem to require a baseline of social support to establish the acceptable ground of comedy.

Understanding that a wayfinding nature underwrites the basic patterns of our stories provides us with the tools for analyzing cultural change and difference in the human relationship to the environment. For instance, if in spite of the risks entailed, travel is basically exciting to human beings because the thrill of movement and of new environments served the adaptive advantage of our ancestors, modern modes of transportation heighten this excitement but may also heighten feelings of uncertainty and anxiety. Modern transportation likely increases opposed feelings of freedom and constraint, of adventure and fear, for although one can travel faster on a boat or in a coach, train, car, or airplane, one is confined within a limited space with strange persons and can't suddenly disembark. This combination of elements defines a situation that is charged with conflicting emotions and therefore potentially volatile, and it has presented special opportunities to writers since the nineteenth century. In Katherine Mansfield's story "The Little Governess," for example, the young woman who must travel alone to her new job has been sternly warned about the dangers of her journey by the woman at the Governess Bureau: "You had better take an evening boat and then if you get in the compartment for 'Ladies Only' in the train you will be far safer than sleeping in a foreign hotel. Don't go out of the carriage; don't walk down the corridors and *be sure* to lock the lavatory door if you go there. The train arrives at Munich at eight o'clock, and Frau Arnholdt says that the Hotel Grunewald is only one minute away. A porter can take you there" (51). Her spirit of adventure thus effectively extinguished and her sense of vulnerability and danger raised to a subdued hysteria, it is ironic but certainly no surprise that the little governess turns to the first kindly, elderly gentleman she meets for comfort and protection. When he requests a kiss after a day of sightseeing in Munich, her horrified reaction is both comic and poignant. In Alice Munro's disturbing version of this story, "Wild Swans," Rose is informed in advance by her stepmother about how kindly older women in cahoots with ruthless men kidnap pubescent girls, luring them from trains and forcing them into a life of prostitution: "Flo said to watch for White Slavers. . . . They kept you a prisoner in the White Slave place (to which you had been transported drugged and bound so you wouldn't even know where you were), until such time as you were thoroughly degraded and in despair, your insides torn up by drunken men and invested with vile disease, your mind destroyed by drugs, your hair and teeth fallen out. It took about three years, for you to get to this state" (57). Flo's sensational depiction of female exploitation is easy for the knowing Rose to dismiss and leaves her unprepared for the more mundane act of molestation, yet it contains more than its element of truth ("Watch out, Flo said, as well, for people dressed as ministers. They were the worst").

Although both stories suggest that modern travel, with its vast possibilities, requires that young women be indoctrinated into a psychology of fear as a means of protecting their virginity, both also suggest that this indoctrination must of necessity fail. Mansfield's young woman, traveling alone in an era when doing so renders her automatically liable to suspicion and reproach, cannot be psychologically encaged while simultaneously experiencing the environmental richness afforded by modern travel. These are, after all, her last moments of independence before she will have to devote herself entirely to the needs and demands of her employer and charges. Journeying at night like a thief, she is counseled to transport herself from boat to train to hotel in a way that suggests she is more like a stolen object. But the disconnection from persons and places is dizzying for one so advised of the lurking dangers, and thus she seeks to ground herself, even if just temporarily, through a new person to a new place, in spite of knowing all along that doing so is not entirely respectable. Munro's Rose, traveling not quite so far (only from West Hanratty to Toronto) later in the twentieth century and, besides, sure that she is smarter than her stepmother Flo, learns of the ultimate impersonality of sex and of the conjunction between degradation and physical pleasure. The possibilities presented by the movement out of the small Ontario town, by the romantic specter of predatory White Slavers, rapidly contract in the wake of an experience that might have happened at home.

These narratives surely represent, in some respects at least, the antithesis of the healing and stabilizing nonhuman natural world celebrated by Finch, Wordsworth, Emerson, Whitman, Thoreau, Snyder, Oliver, Dillard, and others. Yet these stories of young women traveling alone are a part of the total picture of our environment that includes the nature writer's reflections on place. What can ecocritical—and, in light of my examples, specifically ecofeminist—scholars illuminate about the literary depictions of human wayfinders in a democratized, industrialized world? Considering the whole picture of journeys into and meditation on nature and through modern civilization via modern modes of travel, what can ecocriticism reveal to us about our literary output and about its ability to illuminate the coherence and sustainability of our lives and of the planet?

Confinement

If an understanding of the wayfinding sensibility helps explain our love of journeys and movement and our attentiveness to diverse surroundings and thus to the literature representing these, it likewise raises interesting questions about confinement and its literary representations. I suggested above that the combination of confinement and rapid movement draw on a diverse mix of central emotions, but the theme or representation of confinement alone is quite another matter. Charlotte Perkins Gilman's story "The Yellow Wallpaper" and John Fowles's early novel *The Collector*, narratives in which the characters are literally confined against their wills, exploit our extraordinary feelings of anxiety about being trapped. It would be interesting to see a comprehensive list and analysis of works of literature depicting entrapment as a continuous state, particularly those represented wholly or in part from the point of view of the imprisoned character and particularly those where the central character is entirely confined to his/her cell.

In other works, such as the novels and stories of Henry James, the theme of confinement is less literal but nevertheless frequently employed to illustrate the conjunction of physical confinement and social control, both of which are to varying degrees related to informational or social deficits. Daisy Miller, frequently described as "natural," resists physical confinement and social control, and her resistance is repeatedly (though not exclusively) manifested in outdoor excursions: to the Chateau de Chillon, to the Pincio, to the Coliseum. Yet the result of this determined freedom is an informational deficit regarding, specifically, the consequences of her actions. While on the one hand Daisy resists this knowledge, on the other she is intentionally deprived of information—by Mrs. Costello, Mrs. Walker, and, most importantly, Winterbourne—for refusing to accede to confinement. James hereby suggests that social conventions respecting the behavior of eligible young ladies complicate the relationship between wayfinding and knowledge. He does this also in the late story "In the Cage," where the actual physical confinement of the young woman in the telegraphist's cage stands in contrast to her vast knowledge of the fast and glamorous social set whose telegrams she dictates. Yet out in the world, her fund of information proves deficient, because she fails to make inferences about character based on knowledge of behavior. Her physical confinement thus serves as a metaphor for both her social confinement and, ultimately and even surprisingly, in one with such an active imagination, her imaginative confinement to an idealized view of the upper classes. But these are at the same time the ground of her moral freedom, and to the reader who gathers information with her from within the cage and who makes the inferences about character and events that she does not quite make, the rich and privileged appear trapped in their own immorality and decadence.

James may seem like an odd, even the oddest, writer to bring into an essay on ecocriticism, yet his concentration on the overrefinements of late nineteenth-century culture emphasizes the self-delusions and cruelties it perpetuates, and its environments are confining and claustrophobic, corrupting and impoverishing, to the interior and physical lives of human characters. Not himself a product of the American aristocracies of Boston and New York, James spent his life on the periphery of various aristocratic worlds, observing the human mind at work in those milieux. What is the impact on the adapted human organism, which delights in physical movement and discovery; sensory and sexual stimulation; affectional bonds to other humans, animals, and nonhuman nature; preparation and consumption of food; and the creative elaboration—of this mode of living? If Wordsworth praises the mind that grows well in nature, then what has the wayfinding mind become under the conditions James explores? Knowledge of such works forms a central part of the web of understanding that includes those who write specifically about nonhuman nature and "her" life-giving and restorative power.

In a similar manner and in the same era, works like *A Doll's House* suggest the dubious consequence of turning *home*, which originates evolutionarily as a protective place, into a prison. Indeed, the drama itself might seem to present a special challenge to ecocriticism, generically limited in its ability to represent nonhuman nature or the patterns of wayfinding. Yet theater is among the earliest forms of representation, and in its origins indistinguishable from rituals that were a central part of the ecology of our human ancestors. Furthermore, as the ecocritic Theresa May points out, play production is interactive and physical and thus offers opportunities not provided by other genres. In addition, because theatrical performance particularly weights our interest toward the actions of human characters on stage in an artificially limited space, it may, ironically, have distinct advantages in presenting environmental themes directly.

Place Attachment

Since humans are a home-based, wayfinding species, this chapter cannot be complete without a brief discussion of place attachment and its relevance to literature, a subject I have covered elsewhere.[15]

Developmental, cognitive, evolutionary, and social psychology; behavioral ecology; anthropology; and contemporary geography offer a rich explanation for our emotional connections to places, and analyses of literary representations of the love of or aversion to specific places are crucial to an expanded awareness of the dynamic between human social relationships and physical places. When, in book 2 of *The Prelude*, he attributes the core of his poetic gifts to an early affectional bond with his mother that gradually extends outward to the adjacent rivers, trees, and mountains, Wordsworth depicts a process in remarkable accord with contemporary psychology. Because emotional ties motivate people to stay close together, and because physical proximity of the primary caregiver to the infant is essential for humans, our attachments, in comparison to other species, are especially strong. Likewise, attachment to specific geographical places originates in the need to identify viable habitats. Just as our initial attachments to places are mediated by human relationships, so, too our adult feelings about place often reflect our social relationships and bonds.

By the same token, literary works that represent the relationship between social disarray and attitudes toward physical place can dramatically deepen our understanding of our species' distrust and abuse of the material world. Because of the instabilities of the social worlds they represent, postcolonial works frequently depict stunted relationships to urban and natural environments that mirror alienation from and distrust of other humans. J. M. Coetzee opens *Disgrace* with a sentence emblematic of David Lurie's generalized, cultivated detachment from other people: "For a man of his age, fifty-two, divorced, he has, to his mind, solved the problem of sex rather well" (1). This ironic view of sexual need as a problem and of intercourse as a function somehow detached from the physical and emotional arousal on which it depends is at the outset doomed by its very self-contradiction, but this does not prevent David Lurie from using his intelligence to retreat into irony and disillusionment. These, in turn, facilitate his objectification and abuse of the student he desires and further ensure a social disconnection that parallels humanly and physically uncongenial environments. His presumed ironic detachment from his ex-wife, his colleagues, his students, and his daughter governs as well his attitude toward physical places and spaces, and he cannot fathom his daughter's willing submission to her former laborer as the price she must pay to stay on her farm.

Coetzee's David Lurie, like Jean Rhys's Antoinette (Bertha) Cosway Mason and Peter Carey's Jack Maggs, lacks a productive relationship to physical place, for place attachment inheres in an emotional and psychic ecology that also includes stable human connections and personal identity. The chaos governing postcolonial life is one source of placelessness and homelessness, of an alien and alienating environment that renders nonhuman nature, cities, cultures, and people all less than they can be.

Homescript

Because I am by inclination a pragmatic thinker, I evaluate ideas in light of the quality of research and argument supporting them and in light of the complementary ideas in related disciplines but against my own experience and my perceptions about the experiences of others as well. When I read the literature in behavioral ecology and developmental psychology about twelve years ago, for instance, it was consistent with my observations of the behavior of small children, and it also helped me understand my profound attachment to that part of Pennsylvania where I grew up. It had, as we say, the ring of truth to me.

My evacuation to California after Hurricane Katrina, my four-month separation from my husband, and my return to a ruined place I still call "home" only further convinces me of the validity of these analyses. Those who have visited New Orleans since 29 August 2005 (my twenty-fourth wedding anniversary) have gleaned the enormity of the recent disaster, the damage to land, trees, animals, people, houses, schools, businesses.

Why have people returned, in the midst of all this destruction? Because, as the word "oecology" reminds us, it is home, a place greatly cared about but, as has been made so woefully apparent, not cared for enough. The land, animals, people, and culture together constitute this home, the ecology of this place, and because all three are connected in the affectional system of New Orleanians, none can be eliminated if the home place is to survive.

CHAPTER THIRTEEN

Multisensory Imagery

G. GABRIELLE STARR

Elizabeth Bishop's "At the Fishhouses" opens at the limits of the visual:

> Although it is a cold evening,
> down by one of the fishhouses
> an old man sits netting,
> his net, in the gloaming almost invisible.
>
> (ll. 1–4)

Sensory images seem to compete, and smell almost wipes out sight: "The air smells so strong of codfish/it makes one's nose run and one's eyes water" (ll. 7–8). As the sky grows dark, the scene takes on almost dazzling reflections, where herring scales appear like "creamy iridescent coats of mail," and "the sparse bright sprinkle of grass" flashes next to "long bleached handles." Sight is on the edge of failure as darkness falls in the far north, and at the heart of the poem are images that evoke other senses and other modes: not just images of smell but images of movement, touch, sound, and taste. Bishop sketches a seal listening to hymns, while the singer sits at the edge of an ocean "[c]old, dark, deep, and absolutely clear":

> If you should dip your hand in,
> your wrist would ache immediately,
> your bones would begin to ache and your hand would burn
> as if the water were a transmutation of fire
> that feeds on stones and burns with a dark gray flame.
> If you tasted it, it would first taste bitter,
> then briny, then surely burn your tongue.   (ll. 73–79)

There are several kinds of nonvisual imagery here: olfactory, concerning smell and sometimes taste; haptic, concerning grasp and touch; motor/

kinesthetic, concerning movement and sometimes proprioception (perception of one's own body position); gustatory, concerning taste. But sensory imagery goes further than this: when poems evoke sound inside our heads—the rise and fall of meter, the symmetry of rhyme—they evoke multisensory imagery, fundamentally. Aural imagery emerges as we see words on the page: the "voice" in our mind that "says," as we take in the first lines of Hopkins's "Pied Beauty," "Glory be to God for dappled things,/For skies of couple-color as a brinded cow" and the "ear" in our mind that "hears" smooth assonance and the beat of sprung rhythm. However, the imagined aurality of reading a poem is not just about imagined sound. Horace recommends that writer and reader use "fingers and ear . . . [to] catch the lawful rhythm" (473) of poetry; recent investigations have shown that as we read metrical writing, we may imagine our throats, tongues, breath, even hands, moving to evoke the stress, make the words, or keep the beat.[1] Meter produces motor imagery, and poetry, from the moments our minds "hear" or "speak" what our eyes see, is multisensory.

In the terms of ancient aesthetics, art blends two practices: *poeisis*, making, and *mimesis*, the imitation of nature and matter. But the minds that remake the world are inextricably part of the world: the world of matter makes us, too. It is thus that the architecture of the mind, given and (developmentally or culturally) made, has much to say about the architecture of art. As I. A. Richards argues, understanding how literature affects us requires that we better understand "the hierarchies, the modes of systematization, in that unimaginable organization, the mind" (47). This chapter engages part of that organization, detailing the cognitive principles governing nonvisual mental imagery. These principles help structure our encounters, as individual readers or viewers, with the world of art, but they also, as Susan Stewart might point out, give our imagined perceptions a structure that enables us to share them: the structure of cognition helps make art possible as social endeavor and social experience. Art is able to move us because of the structures of thought.

Imagery and Cognitive Neuroscience: Preliminaries

The phenomena of mental images occur when we have the subjective experience of sensation without corresponding sensory input: closing your eyes and imagining your mother's face or constantly rehearsing a musical phrase you can't get out of your head. Just as with most research on perception, most research on mental imagery in cognitive neuroscience has focused on the visual, for reasons that go beyond the Western privilege given to sight. The human visual system takes up a proportionally larger part of the brain than other perceptual systems and responds well to tools of investigation that have been dominant in the last eighty or so years. Visual imagery, like visual activity, plays perhaps the largest sensory role in our imaginative economies and is often experienced as having the greatest vivacity; so it has had, similarly, the most prominent position in imagery research. With the advent of brain-imaging tools like functional magnetic resonance imaging (fMRI), this is changing, and an increasing amount of research addresses imagery from the other senses.[2]

Mental images share a few key features. They are as reliant on the mechanics of memory as they are on propositions about the world or patterns for engaging with it. Some imagery can be prompted by instruction, and some is spontaneous. Images also vary in vividity.[3] Some forms of imagery can be so strong that one confuses image with sensation; and most of us experience almost all of the forms of imagery, in varying degrees, in dreams.[4] However, the strength of mental images, as well as their ability to be controlled and manipulated by the person experiencing them, varies from person to person, from time to time, and by sensory mode. Visual images for most people are more strong and controllable than any other kind; auditory and motor images can be strong as well as controllable; and images of smell and taste are generally neither strong nor particularly subject to individual control (think of Proust and his Madeleine). Such variations—across modes but also across individuals and cultures—are of structural importance. What is essential about mental imagery is at once its variability and predictability. What happens when a poet seems inclined toward one mode of imagery and ignores or subordinates others, especially when that mode seems counterintuitive (taste over sight, e.g.)? Most of us are aware of our own imaginative limits; how do we as readers, poets, dancers, viewers, negotiate those boundaries? How do the varying power and limitations of the modes of imaginative experience shape the pleasures of art and of imagination?

Auditory Imagery

Auditory imagery has proven to be, after visual, the mode of imagery most readily investigable in experimental settings. There are at least four categories of auditory images: those of music, speech, metrical speech, and general images of sound (some more semantically clear—dogs barking, trucks passing; some less—thuds or bangs). The processes involved in these categories differ in significant ways physiologically, and physiological differences may translate phenomenologically and artistically: for example, listening to music involves areas of the brain that listening to other sounds does not, perhaps because of the demands of musical pitch (pitch, with curious artistic effects, can be separated out from other musical features, as with some avant-garde music).[5] Auditory imagery may behave differently if it carries semantic information (words, certainly, but dogs don't just sound, they signify, and they signify differently to different people). Differences also emerge if the image combines categories (imagining music with lyrics involves different parts of the brain than does imagining music without words).

Generally speaking, however, auditory images involve many of the same areas of the brain as actual audition, and many of the same principles of organization. Auditory images are organized temporally (as opposed to visual and haptic images, which tend to be organized to reflect spatial detail and relations), but the time of imagined sound can be compressed; it can be shorter than that of actual tunes and tones.[6] In addition, though one may rarely notice it, images of sound only occasionally employ features indispensable for actual sound, for example, a quality as basic as loudness. The ambiguity of volume for imagined sounds is central to Keats's "The Eve of St. Agnes": "The music, yearning like a god in pain,/She scarcely heard . . . //. . . she sighs/Amid the timbrels" (ll. 56–57; 66–67). Madeline is so absorbed in her inner world that she sees and hears almost nothing, but *our* "seeing" and "hearing" are different: these lines are able to make "sense" because of sonoral characteristics of mental imagery that generally escape our notice. Keats manipulates imaginative levels of sound and silence to lay a ground of uncertainty that promotes the centrality of Madeline's consciousness, even when she is sleeping. Porphyro seduces her by manipulating sound as he steals into her room:

> he took her hollow lute,—
> Tumultuous,—and, in chords that tenderest be,
> He play'd an ancient ditty, long since mute,
>
> . . . .
>
> Close to her ear touching the melody;—
> Wherewith disturb'd, she utter'd a soft moan:
> He ceased—she panted quick—and suddenly
> Her blue affrayed eyes wide open shone.
>
> (ll. 289–95)

The modulations of imagined sound, from lute to breath, mark out the phenomenal borders of Madeline's inner world—where sound is equally modulated by imagination—and give us access to the blurred boundaries where dream and reality intertwine.

One of the most common forms of auditory imagery is musical. Many people, with minimal prompting, can hum, say, the theme of *Star Wars*; we also can imagine it, and it may, seemingly endlessly, repeat. There is a neural correlate to—a set of underlying brain processes that corresponds with—"hearing" imagined music and sound.[7] Many such images are involuntary; experiments have shown that a small blank space inserted into a recording of a well-known song may trigger auditory imagery, so that subjects replace lost notes and lyrics without conscious effort.[8] Intensity may also vary. For a song with lyrics, we might simply repeat the words, without the tune. Brain-imaging studies show that this phenomenon does not recruit primary auditory cortex, the neural center of hearing; however, when we imagine instrumental music, primary auditory cortex is strongly active: in one interpretation, we "hear" the music more fully than we might "hear" the lyrics alone. It is reasonable to propose that some kinds of imagery may be more difficult to control than others because of such processing differences.

Musical images may offer one place to pursue enquiry into the aesthetic dimensions of imagery. Simple pleasure and displeasure—hedonic tone—are key for musical images, especially for songs one can't seem to let go. Seemingly endless loops are often annoying, but they may be pleasurable as well—when a phrase from a melody, suddenly and surprisingly, comes fully to mind in the midst of daily life. More complex emotions—those of beauty, for example—ought matter as well. I return to some of the aesthetic dimensions of imagery below, as I speculate that the aesthetic pleasures of auditory images may be "moving" in more ways than one.

Auditory imagery may recruit areas of the brain that encode motion. When we experience musical imagery, we may participate in "subvocal singing or humming" so that part of experiencing imagined music may involve remembering movements.[9] More broadly, perception of timing in auditory experience may be coordinated through areas of the brain that involve motor activity.[10] Indeed, the temporal organization fundamental to auditory imagery may rely on the cerebellum. The cerebellum coordinates perceptual and motor input and requires temporal coordination: we need to know not just what we are doing but when we're doing it in order to run without falling or catch a cup as it falls. The cerebellum is important not just for coordinating our actions in the outside world but also for something so seemingly "internal" as understanding metrical writing that is read silently: what enables the timing of action also enables us to understand and produce metrical speech.[11]

As parts of the brain's architecture that coordinate motion are also recruited by metrical writing, it makes all the more sense that poems may make us wish to keep time, to move and imagine motion. In Hopkins's "The Woodlark," the bird's motion is an effect not just of mental vision but of motor imagery accompanying meter:

> The blue wheat-acre is underneath
> And the corn is corded and shoulders its sheath,
> The ear in milk, lush the sash,
> And crush-silk poppies aflash,
> The blood-gush blade-gash
> Flame-rash rudred
> Bud shelling or broad-shed
> Tatter-tangled and dingle-a-dangled
> Dandy-hung dainty head.   (ll. 26–34)

Visual images are fractured; our attention is drawn progressively and ultimately away from color, toward a graphical, alliterative index of words and toward indices of sound. The motion of poppy heads, swaying in a field, is subject to auditory texture, and this may mean that with reading breath and pulse quicken. In fact, the way that motor imagery may accompany meter and music may indeed physically matter: heart rates and breathing increase when we imagine lifting heavy loads or performing complicated physical tasks.[12]

Many of us already know how much sound may physically "move" us, and we rediscover this every time we listen to music or read poems we love: rhythmic sound is powerful in motor terms, and such motion seems linked to pleasure.[13] The metaphor of "moving" words certainly implies a question of aesthetic evaluation; as we have seen, Horace conceived that the felt beat of poetry was both an index of pleasure and a tool of evaluation: "finger and ear" catch the "lawful" music of poetry, and neither motion nor sound should be ignored. In the case of Hopkins, pulse and fingers may quicken not just with the swiftness of imagined flight but with the swiftness and elegance of meter; equally, Madeline's sudden panting as she rouses from sleep in "Eve of St. Agnes" is not just the result of her half-conscious recognition of her lover's voice but of rhythm blending artfully with consciousness.

Motor Imagery

Much research on perceptual imagery associates imaginative experience with localized neurological activity; many of the areas in which this activity occurs are also involved with external perception. The pattern holds for images of motion.[14] Not everyone agrees how best to interpret this: that is, while we have strong evidence that when we experience imagery of sound or motion, there is corresponding brain activity in auditory or motor cortical areas, it is not necessarily the case (though it is presumptively the case, and TMS may give us more insight) that such activity *causes* or is *inseparable from* imagery.[15] Cognitive neuroscience proposes that neural activity in particular areas, the sequence of these activities, and the connections between areas are key to mental experience. Such a proposition about imaginative activity may sound familiar to humanists: associationist Enlightenment theories argued that imagination functions by establishing connections of similarity, contiguity, and cause and effect in ideas and events.[16] In *Tristram Shandy*, for example, Mrs. Shandy cannot help thinking of winding the hallway grandfather clock while having sex with her husband, because he has made it his practice to take care of all household maintenance—including conjugal activity—on the first

Sunday of every month. What works at the level of idea or emotion may work in part because of the physical proximity of and physical connections between portions of our cognitive architecture.[17] For example, parts of the brain governing motion are active in looking at images of motion, and adjacent areas are active in reading words that describe motion.[18] Motor imagery, whether invoked by vision or words, is thus physically, semantically, and temporally linked closely to the experience of motion.[19] Such physical proximity corresponds to a continuum of motor imagery, from the abstract to the concrete; different kinds of representations—verbal, visual, kinetic—evoke imagery along this scale in varying degrees.[20]

Motor images are involved in many kinds of imagery that appear primarily to belong to other senses; equally, imagining motion often involves multiple kinds of imagery. Generally, motion is imagined along with sight—bodily motion is, for sighted persons, both visual and kinetic. Significantly, however, when we imagine other people moving, we usually, and preferentially, employ visual images: imagine, for example, your mother walking across a room. By contrast, when we imagine ourselves moving—clapping our hands, reaching for the stars, sticking out our tongues—we may use visual images, but we usually also imagine the sensations of proprioception and movement for ourselves—what it would be like *if we actually were to do what we are thinking*. Instead of using solely or primarily parts of the brain corresponding to vision and imagined vision, we also use areas normally employed in planning our own movements.[21] This parallels the way human beings learn to move: we watch others and then slowly come to imitate their motions by associating our own planned movements with our actual ones.[22] Such a process may involve "mirror neurons": specialized cells that become active not just when we are in motion but also when we perceive others moving.[23] Some scholars argue mirror neurons point toward the involvement of imagined action not just in mimesis but in empathy.[24] This means that motor imagery may play a significant role in producing literary effects of sympathetic identification, as John Sitter argues.[25] Such work is suggestive; it is certainly the case that motor effects have powerful potential for helping us think about imagination and embodiment: imagery of motion is not "just in your head" but can cause changes in muscles throughout the body as well.[26]

Dryden's "Alexander's Feast" exploits links between meter, music, motion, and vision differently. The second stanza starts with Timotheus's physical movement as he plays his lyre:

> Timotheus, plac'd on high
>> Amid the tuneful choir,
>>> With flying fingers touch'd the lyre:
>> The trembling notes ascend the sky,
>>> And heavenly joys inspire.
>>>>> (ll. 20–25)

The physical motions that produce music translate back to imagined movement, first as Jove reaches for Olympia and "stamps" his impression by engendering a child. Dryden blends visual and motor imagery:

> The song began from Jove,
> Who left his blissful seats above,
>
> . . . .
>
> A dragon's fiery form belied the god:
> Sublime on radiant spires he rode,
>> When he to fair Olympia press'd;
>
> . . . .
>
> Then, round her slender waist he curl'd,
> And stamp'd an image of himself, a sov'reign of the world.
> The list'ning crowd admire the lofty sound,
> "A present deity," they shout around:
> "A present deity," the vaulted roofs rebound.
>>> With ravish'd ears
>>> The monarch hears,
>>> Assumes the god,
>>> Affects to nod,
>> And seems to shake the spheres.   (ll. 25–41)

Musical motion, for Dryden, ends in an imagined, mimetic space: the king "seems" to cause celestial trepidation, and he only "affects" to nod. Dryden is intrigued by poetic mimicry of music; he wants our attention on imagination and its effects. The poem explores a mythical subordination of instrumental music—that of Timotheus—to music of the human voice—that of St. Cecelia. The superiority of voice is also the superiority of words, and for Dryden, poet laureate, the ultimate superiority of poetry. The poem makes its claim to exceptional imaginative vivacity because imagined motion is what it offers its readers: Dryden's chosen image of the poetic imagination, after all, is of motion, a spaniel springing after its quarry.[27]

The importance of imagery of motion appears not just with music and poetry, where sound may provoke us to move or imagine movement, but also with arts of motion. Watching dance involves both the perception of motion and the engagement of mirror neurons and the evocation of sympathetic movement.[28] Both experts and novices "feel" the movement of dance by way of motor images.[29] Ivar Hagendoorn advances several hypotheses about how dance affects its viewers, arguing saliently that as one watches a dancer, one imagines a trajectory for her movement: we "see" the end of a jeté, knowing where the dancer's foot will fall. Such imagery contributes to two sources of pleasure: one, the heightened expectation of motion and two, a euphoria that follows the completion and success of the motion, when the image matches the movement. Motor imagery may here be integral, again, to aesthetic pleasure.

Olfactory and Gustatory Imagery

Smell and taste are closely related; indeed, much of what seemingly involves only taste also involves smell.[30] Those who study the imagery of smell and taste have great difficulty separating the two as well.[31] Most people find images of smell the least vivid and the most difficult to evoke or control. In part, the small degree of voluntary control over images of smell comes because there are weak connections for most people between the *words* for a smell or for an object with a distinctive odor and the *sensation* of the smell: the word "potato" does not usually lead one to imagine, first, a starchy, green, scent.[32] Keats's "Eve of St. Agnes" offers one way of negotiating the general ineffability or difficulty surrounding olfactory imagery: "Into her dream he melted, as the rose / Blendeth its odour with the violet,—/ Solution sweet" (ll. 321–22). Keats may be evoking well-known scents, like that of a common English posy or contemporary eau de toilette.[33] However, he also makes odor fugitive; one scent blends into another so that the resolution is primarily semantic: sweet mixture. Indeed, there is considerable debate as to whether olfactory imagery is primarily semantic or perceptual: do we imaginatively "perceive" a smell, or do we rather operate based on meaning and association? The fact that most people have problems evoking olfactory imagery on command makes it probable that people use a variety of strategies for making "sense" of imagined olfaction, including focusing on associations or categories like "sweet" or "foul."[34] Work in brain imaging has also indicated that semantic information is particularly important to taste.[35] Significantly, part of the semantic weight of imagery of smell or taste may be hedonic. Strong images, especially hallucinatory ones, generally involve evaluations of pleasure and displeasure; they are rarely neutral, something which may differentiate olfactory and gustatory from other forms of imagery.[36]

When it comes to the semantic and propositional content of mental imagery, there is a debate reaching beyond smell and taste. Some people report very little in the way of images that mime perceptual experience, and some investigators argue that much of what we attribute to "images" could be ascribed to propositions denoting "greenness" or "roundness," say, rather than to any phenomenon of "seeing" a green ball in the mind's eye.[37] It is significant, then, that experiments suggest that even imagined olfaction and taste, despite the difficulties of evocation, may produce effects that are more likely with images than with propositions and that seem to exclude the possibility of at least explicit propositional knowledge. Most of us are familiar with the experience of expecting a drink to be one thing (say, cola or red wine) and then picking up the glass without looking, only to be confronted with the taste of water. Not only are we surprised at the fact that we are drinking water but also at the fact that the water actually seems to taste strange or bad, unlike water. Expectation and anticipation may trigger strong imagery with perceptual effects. Something similar has been demonstrated with imagined odors, which may interfere with or alter our perception of actually present tastes.[38] Investigations have also shown that the experience of imagined taste and odor combinations corresponds better to actual experience than to subjects' beliefs about these combinations.[39]

If taste and smell are difficult to evoke linguistically, it makes sense to think about what help one may be given in making these evocations. Specific tastes may be difficult to imagine, but textures may not be so awkward. While I am unaware of any research on imagined taste that pursues texture, there is data about the way perceptions of taste work with texture and temperature. A variety of sensations from the tongue become part of a "multimodal representation . . . very early" in cognitive processing, and there is considerable overlap in the neurological activity underlying taste and other lingual sensations.[40] Based on the generally close relation between sensory processing and imagery, it is reasonable to assume that texture or temperature contribute fundamentally to imagery of taste. Imagined temperature and texture may promote more difficult gustatory images, as with Keats's "jellies soother than the creamy curd" in "Eve of St. Agnes" (l. 266). Keats's poem is instructive about other ways of using more vivid modes of imagery to aid the mental palate, as when visual aspects of delicacies are key—"lucent syrops, tinct with cinnamon" (l. 267)—or when gentle sensations of touch and strong odors supplement underdescribed tastes—"spiced dainties, every one,/From silken Samarcand to cedar'd Lebanon" (ll. 269–70).

Imagery of Touch, Grasping and Feeling

Work in neuroscience may allow us to understand the priority of certain kinds of tactile imagery. Wilder Penfield and Herbert Jaspers identified a functional map of the body in the human brain in 1954. Neuroanatomical areas are specialized to keep track of sensory and motor information; there are two homunculi in the brain (in somatosensory cortex, to be specific, in a strip that sits right about where the band of old-fashioned headphones would lie), with sections dedicated to representing sensations from and movement of each body part: hands, tongue, wrists, and so on. The somatosensory homunculus is adjacent to the motor homunculus, and they have similar scales. They are not exactly homeomorphic with our bodies—some body parts have more cortical space given to them than do others, and the face is separate from the rest of the body. Proportionally, the face, lips, mouth, thumb and hands get the greatest cortical area, while the lower body, arms, head, and neck get less.[41]

The greater the area assigned to a part of the body, the more detailed the sensations and finer the motor control. Because tactile images recruit many of the same areas of the brain involved in actual sensation, it is probable that similar rules of organization and detail apply to them as to real touch.[42] This gives us some sense of why the gesture and image of touching hand to face are so powerful—they evoke or enact extremely detailed sensations. Whatever semantic weight (of love, tenderness, care) the gesture may carry is well matched by its sensory richness.

Imagery of touch is more important for some genres than others—satire, for example, as Stewart points out, often relies on images of touch as well as of smell and taste. Erotic literature is probably one of those genres most keenly interested in the tactile and in promoting hedonic evaluations of tactile imagery (30–32). Throughout *Fanny Hill*, John Cleland places priority on imagined experience in the heroine's backward glance at amorous adventure. In seeking to isolate touch from the other senses, Cleland often draws on images of texture and temperature to describe what is "tender" and "warm." Sensations of touch may also be evoked via images of motion: "Curling round him like the tendril of a vine, as if I feared any part of him should be untouched or unpressed by me, I returned his strenuous embraces and kisses with a fervour and gust only known by true love" (70). Strong imagery of touch may be evoked, as here, without making a human body the metaphorical/perceptual agent of touch at all.

Imagery of touch is often multisensory. For Cleland, "sight must be feasted as well as . . . touch" (50); often the two types of imagery work in consort, as with the careful aesthetic of vision, texture, and grasping Cleland uses to describe genitalia.[43] Multisensory images having to do with the hands may be understood in terms of the sensory-motor homunculi and their relation to other systems. Haptic activity is almost essential to human survival: the networks enabling it are complex, recruiting sensations of touch, motor processes, and visual systems to enable robust and detailed imagery.[44] Vision and touch are closely related for most people; imagined reaching and grasping or the sensations of texture involve both visual and haptic representations. Some investigators argue we have common forms of representation, which are used for imagining objects visually as well as in terms of touch and the motions of grasping.[45]

Synaesthesia

For neuroscientists, synaesthesia involves the involuntary and persistent coupling of different sensory modalities: an individual with synaesthesia will *always* see the number seven as yellow, or hear high C as green.[46] The experience is automatic. The most prominent explanations for these phenomena involve neural development. Sensory data are aggregate early in the development of the human brain and in perception itself; dissociation and differentiation (color from sound, say) are the result of developmental processes. This differentiation either occurs abnormally or fails to occur at all in individuals with synaesthesia.[47] Synaesthetes can experience this blending in imaginative conditions as well: a woman who on seeing the number seven always sees the color yellow, for example, also sees yellow when thinking "five plus two" or "three plus four."[48] Synaesthetes include Vladimir Nabokov, David Hockney, and Jimi Hendrix, and around one in twenty-five thousand of the general population. Synaesthetic imagery in language is less rare—in Keats, certainly ("I cannot see . . . what soft incense hangs upon the boughs" ["Ode to a Nightingale," ll. 41–42]), but also in everyday usage: "sour" expressions, "loud" colors, "smooth" voices. In lived synaesthesia, some couplings predominate—audio-visual and typographic-color—while others are exceedingly rare—synaesthesia involving taste or smell.[49] In suggestive research, Sean Day proposes that the most common form of synaesthetic imagery in English-language literature—blends of touch and sound—are not those most common in lived synaesthesia—there, blends of sound and sight predominate. There is clearly a mismatch: neurological concepts of synaesthesia and what individuals with synaesthesia experience differ greatly from the blending of sensory imagery in metaphor and art. The more fruitful cognitive approach to blended forms of imagery may thus be through exploring multisensory images.

Multisensory Imagery

Many instances of sensory imagery, as I have shown, do not rely on only one sensory modality; even perceptual experience primarily identified with one sensory modality can be substantially cross-modal: in a noisy room, for example, we may think we are primarily *listening* to the person across the dinner table, but our understanding depends a great deal on being able to see her as she speaks, too.[50] Multisensory imagery may also be centrally important to aesthetic pleasures, as with Hopkins, Dryden, and Keats. This may be in part because multisensory imagery gives access not to something like the "real" complexity of experience but to aspects of the ways our minds *internally represent* experiences and objects.

Work on memory has demonstrated some key features of multisensory representations. People tend to remember a tone and image presented together much better than either alone; more than this, when data from one sense is presented, the entire multisensory image is triggered. The connections that multisensory imagery can form are rapid and strong.[51] A cognitive approach to multisensory imagery may give us a window on aesthetics as the study not just of sensation (*aesthesis*) but also of imagined sensation. In the preceding discussion, aesthetic and hedonic characteristics of imagery have played a persistent role. I believe that motor imagery, in part because it is peculiarly multisensory, may have the most powerful potential for evoking and structuring aesthetic pleasures.

Colin Martindale argues (in a way that owes some debt to Kant) that much of our experience of beauty comes from the ways our brains represent the world to us. His working hypothesis is that hedonic pleasures and displeasures, including those of aesthetic contemplation, correspond to the degree to which parts of our cognitive architecture are stimulated. Some representations will promote these pleasures better than others, because of the way they are constructed:

> Cognitive units are connected in several ways. [Some] connections
> are excitatory. . . . [C]ognitive units are [also] hypothetically con-
> nected in [an] . . . inhibitory fashion [neurons are certainly thus
> connected]. Units inhibit neighboring units in proportion to their dis-
> tance. . . . The more similar two units are, the more they will inhibit
> one another. There are also indirect excitatory . . . connections. While
> the units coding the concepts CAT and DOG should laterally inhibit
> each other because of similarity, there are also mediated . . . excit-
> atory connections between units on the same level (e.g., DOG-chases-
> CAT). (60)

This means, for instance, a key element of the classical concept of beauty, uniformity amid variety, is pleasing because uniformity (similarity and proximity) excites cognitive and neurological connections—speeds them up, reinforces them—while variety (distance between elements, physical and representational) ensures that inhibition—slowing down, contradiction, counterbalancing—will be minimal (Martindale, 67–68). Overall, the interplay of excitation and inhibition leads to a powerfully pleasing experience. If Martindale is correct, it would thus be possible to understand aesthetic pleasures, what Joseph Addison calls the pleasures of the imagination, in terms of underlying structures of perception, theorized by cognitive science.

Martindale's model provides a basis for understanding how multi-sensory images and the interconnections they produce enable strongly pleasurable representations: such imagery may allow sometimes surprising connections between ostensibly disparate sensory effects, so that not only does the strength of the image produce pleasures but we experience pleasures of surprise as well. Such effects are not about descriptive realism, as we see if we return to our starting point, Bishop's "At the Fishhouses." The final lines recombine the varying modes of sensory imagery that the poem has evoked. The poem approaches the time when no more sense can come, when everything is "flown." The insights of cognitive neuroscience help us trace Bishop's effects as she reorganizes images of the sensory world. She forges new connections between the senses, which push beyond mimesis of the natural world.

The ocean, twice "cold, dark, deep, and absolutely clear," evolves in the final lines:

It is like what we imagine knowledge to be:
dark, salt, clear, moving, utterly free,
drawn from the cold hard mouth
of the world, derived from the rocky breasts
forever, flowing and drawn, and since
our knowledge is historical, flowing, and flown.

(ll. 78–83)

The sense-strewn landscape melds onto a world of words. That thing which we "imagine knowledge to be" is counter, original, spare, strange (to borrow terms from Hopkins's "Pied Beauty"); but the poem's doublings and returns—back through the layers of sensory imagery—matter. Bishop recalls to us, in new combinations, the sensory images we have been given; but she surprises by intensifying the proximity between these images, so that the (oxymoronic) dark clarity becomes anew a briny burn, in a mouth other than ours. The quick shifts through sensory modalities offer challenges to realizing any of them fully and brightly; the "image" of knowledge is on one level fractured and distanced from realistic perception. But the sensory combinations we have seen before leave traces:

briny-burn layers with salt dark. Ultimately, vision, taste, touch, all blend into the imagery of motion, which, "drawn . . . forever, flowing and drawn, . . . flowing and flown," unites the sensory modes together, from audition to vision, taste, and touch. Motion emerges not just as denoted or described but as felt—making the lawful rhythm of the poem in mind, or hands, or tongue. The fragmented, yet curiously whole, beauty that is knowledge—invisible, flowing, cold as it passes us—is revealed as the architecture of the imagery of the senses.

CHAPTER FOURTEEN

Darwin and Derrida

Cognitive Literary Theory as a Species of Post-structuralism

ELLEN SPOLSKY

Situated within and enriching the insights of post-structuralist theory, cognitive literary theory confirms and clarifies issues previously dealt with by philosophical, psychoanalytical, and cultural theorists and is beginning to produce the kind of sophisticated literary scholarship that is rightly valued within our profession. Were I to locate the source of my optimism in a single moment of epiphany, I would refer to my having been convinced that Darwin's theory of evolution is significantly homologous to the post-structuralist critique of representation. A helpful text here is Daniel Dennett's reading of Darwin as a natural theory of permanently unstable ontological categories. Drawing on Darwin's observation that evolved mechanisms might be reused for new purposes in new environments, Dennett extends this natural argument against biological essentialism to a performative theory of natural (and perpetual) meaning (*Darwin's Dangerous Idea*, 404–11). In this theory, language meaning is fundamentally contingent, or as Derrida described it in his deconstruction of Austin's speech act theory, compromised by the unsaturability of context ("Signature," 174). This confirms, for me, J. Hillis Miller's claim that there is no escaping the "performative or positional power of language as inscription." The deconstructionist project has made it impossible to ignore "how the rhetorical or tropological dimension of language" undermines our confidence in the possibility of stable, iterable, meaning ("Triumph," 291).

My understanding of the usefulness of the cognitive way of talking about the cultural production of human minds and brains is, thus, based on an analogy between some elementary facts about the human evolved brain and the post-structuralist view of the situatedness of meaning and of its consequent vulnerability to the displacements and reversals deconstructionist criticism reveals.

My neurons, it seems, are like me. They spend their time collecting messages from different (often differently reliable and often conflicting) sources and weighing them. The complicated "decisions" they make about whether or not to continue the transmission (to fire) seem not unlike mine on a normal day of watching, thinking, making connections with other information, and finally acting, often on less than the best evidence. My decisions, that is, are often, like my brain's, preference judgments.[1] Although an evolved brain cannot be said to have been built for all that I use it for, it has adapted, and for now at least, its functioning is good enough to get me through the day. (Mostly.)

The philosophical parallel to the brain's not-after-all-so-oddly human way of working is to be found in the critique of metaphysical idealism as expounded, for example, in the work of Stanley Cavell. Cavell's rereading of Wittgenstein in *The Claim of Reason* moves philosophical discussion toward a neurologically authentic plane by struggling to find a way to display, express, and understand how ordinary everyday truths are indeed working for us well enough most of the time. Cavell's work enlightens and also lightens the problems of miscommunication, arriving again and again at the claim that it is possible to live an intelligent, satisfying, and even a moral life with the mental equipment that is the human inheritance. It is possible to recover, in his words, from the tragically debilitating skepticism that rejects "good enough" knowledge in a vain struggle for an impossible ideal.

But this is to jump too quickly to the happy ending. We need neither neurology nor philosophy to tell us that human beings are hardly perfect knowers. Sometimes we get it, but often we just get confused. People are often rather pathetic misunderstanders, not to mention megaforgetters, chronic confusers, malaproposers. We laugh at the human comedy of television sitcoms and cry at the high cultural texts that display the tragic limits of our understanding. Homer Simpson stumbles through, but Oedipus, Hamlet, and King David—leaders of men, philosophers, poets—using their senses and all the intuition they can muster, fail to know enough when it matters most.

From an evolutionary perspective, then, Aristotle's opening assertion in his *Metaphysics* is incomplete. "All men, by nature," he says, "desire to know." Forfeiting his gnomic elegance, the sentence might be rewritten thus: "It's a good guess that the survival of the human species depended and probably still depends on an ability to collect and collate reasonably reliable information about the environment and apply it to the projection of possibilities (including counterfactual possibilities) and to decision making processes. If this assumption is true, then it's probably true that all people, by nature, desire to know and that those who did not innately desire to know and who did not develop reasonably accurate (but not necessarily perfect) ways of assessing their relationships to the world around them have long since died off."

One general answer to the question of how the capacity to know has developed with the requisite flexibility is suggested by a modular theory of cognition. In short, the modularity hypothesis explores the implications of our having developed parallel systems of knowledge acquisition. Like other animals, and even some plants, humans learn about an object in more than one way at once, by seeing *and* hearing *and* touching it, for example. While this has on the whole been good for survival, modularity also produces intermodular conflicts.

The advantages first: one advantage of modularity is that by having a set of different receptor/processors (ears *and* eyes, etc.) instead of having a single all-purpose one, we are equipped to respond variously to the various kinds of energy in the world (to sound waves *and* to light waves, to words *and* to smiles). Another positive consequence of modularity is that if one system fails, all is not lost. The various modules are sufficiently independent to defer and perhaps avoid general shut down, often allowing the individual to survive, even if compromised.

There is, however, a price paid for the relative insularity of modules, and that is that translation systems are needed to integrate the knowledge received and produced in the separate modules.[2] And here we can make use of another evolutionary postulate: if the translation systems between modules were perfect—if knowledge from one module was so well translated into knowledge from another that the two were entirely the same (that is, seemed the same to consciousness and functioned in the same way)—then we would lose the advantage of being made aware of the differences. If you know that there is a stream nearby *both* by noticing the relative richness of vegetation in a linear pattern *and* by hearing it, you can find it, day or night. The modular system of knowing makes good use of a set of less than ideal receptors by combining them to produce redundancy, that is, confirmation, even at the cost of producing conflict now and then. The gaps or miscalibrations between the information from the different modules may be filled by analogy with memories of past experience or by inference and deduction. This story of modularity was originally told by Jerry Fodor in *The Modularity of Mind*, but the version offered here includes revisions by Ray Jackendoff, who in *Semantics and Cognition* first pointed out the gaps between structures of information. In *Gaps in Nature: Literary Criticism and the Modular Mind* I adduced a further advantage of modularity: the creative potential of the gaps. Since a gap must be filled by an inference based on individual experience and memory, different people will make different inferences even when they are in similar situations. The evidence of cultural diversity (indeed the difficulty of locating and describing cultural universals) strongly suggests that the genetic inheritance does *not* predict how it will be used, nor does it control the outcome of its processes. Assuming, then, that there is always going to be at least a gap if not a conflict between what can be learned from vision and (say) from words or between words and touch, a cultural historian will have to understand the historical/ideo-logical/cultural context in order to gain insight into the question of why any particular intermodular conflict (itself presumably an age-old physi-ological miscalibration, something *Homo sapiens* had long ago learned to compensate for, ignore, and even profit from), suddenly becomes a cultural crisis.[3]

Let me pause for a minute to punctuate. I have begun to suggest that cognitive and evolutionary hypotheses produce new questions about his-tory and culture, questions that require further historical study. Because the human genetic inheritance is so complex, providing so many possi-bilities, differently actualized in different circumstances and by different people, it will not be possible to answer the new and interesting ques-tions about literature and culture without consulting the historical con-text of the questions. The evolutionary perspective will not relieve us of our responsibility to understand how conflicts produced by our inherited human brains are modulated and managed within their cultural contexts.

If one is to take this responsibility seriously then, it must be argued that the two kinds of study—cognitive and cultural—are noncontradictory before their complementarity can be considered.

I argue, then, that the assumptions that emerge from the study of evolved human brains in their successive contexts, far from being inconsistent with post-structuralist thought, actually extend and enrich it. My questions and my mode of response arise, of course, from my own intellectual econiche, specifically from the barrage of skeptical challenges to the human ability to know that have been raised in the last forty years. The historical situation itself, in a cognitive evolutionary literary theory, provides a way to see into the larger question of how people make or produce knowledge from the combined resources of body (including the mind/brain), and culture. How does the cognitive equipment allow people to learn from the world around them? What role does culture (or do various cultures) play in that process, and how does any specific historically situated culture negotiate its claims with the innate and grown claims of the human body and brain? What kind of knowledge can be had, and how is it acquired? How do I presume to get a piece of it and share it with you?

The claim that the ultimate goal of literary theory is to tell a story about the human mind can be traced back to Aristotle and in modern criticism to Northrop Frye. In his *Anatomy of Criticism,* Frye claimed that the generic forms of literary works have a psychological reality that is separable from what he dismissed as "the history of taste." Literature, he assumed, displays the structure of the mind, the same claim Claude Lévi-Strauss was making for the material culture of Brazilian peoples in *Tristes tropiques* and Chomsky in *Syntactic Structures* was making for syntax. Whatever empirical data is studied, syntax or poems, face painting or pottery, the goal is ideologically humanist: the proper study of humankind is the human mind.

Although the details of Frye's proposals linking the seasons to the genres of literature have not weathered well, many cultural historians and literary scholars are still pursuing the same goal, still seeking to find the theory that will describe the interconnections between being human and living in a culture. To what extent is artistic work predicted or projected from a culture, and how does artistic production work to produce that culture? The paradigm I believe this kind of study fits into is most accurately called post-structuralist (the hyphen has deliberately been preserved for reasons that will become clear). The oversimplification of the phenomenon of post-structuralism I am about to produce here is motivated by my intention of displaying as sharply as possible the multiphase emergence of the paradigm over the course of the twentieth century. Any more complex exposition would quickly lose sight of the forest for the trees, the undergrowth, the mossy rocks, the rolling stones, the nonbiodegradable postpicnic rubbish . . .

The first breakthrough was the discovery of structure. Although there are good reasons to trace this to Saussure's linguistics, it was actually a discovery made simultaneously in several branches of the human and the physical and biological sciences as well.[4] The structuralists directed our attention to connections between phenomena that had previously seemed unconnected, denigrating, in the process, the "merely" empirical. Methodologically, it moved social science away from an interest in description and taxonomy of particulars and toward the description of the underlying dynamic or structure—the self-sustaining and self-modifying system that describes the function of the empirical data. Scholarly work in many fields was now fundamentally revised; the task was not just to collect and record but to posit or discover relational hierarchies and syntax, that is, grammars. The meaning of the structures, as Saussure argued for language, lay in the relationships, not in the words (or data or artifacts) themselves.

As the structuralist perspective in language study became familiar, even routine, and was generalized throughout the humanities and social sciences (one might credit Umberto Eco's interpretive work on semiotics here), it became possible to understand several great pre-Saussurean thinkers as protostructuralists. Among these were Darwin, Marx, and Freud. All of them had described substructures and superstructures—the former "governing" the latter—such that hitherto unexplainable or unintegrated phenomena could be seen as systematic. The substructures were understood by both the structuralists and the protostructuralists as the equivalent of the forces of gravity that keep the planets in their orbits. They not only borrowed the language of science but also the assumption that these forces were stable and eternal.[5] "Human nature" was understood to be the equivalent in the human world of the laws of physics.

A later phase in the articulation of the paradigm was a critique of structuralism, now widely called deconstruction. Its roots were in philosophy rather than in the social sciences. It also has founders and protodeconstructors. Aspects of human life and culture (motherhood, poverty) that had been understood to be as permanent as Platonic ideals and that had, after the Romantics, been demoted to "human" but still stable aspects of nature were now redescribed as indeed changeable *because* historically determined. Nietzsche was noticed to have called attention to this in his critique of the historical scholarship of his day.[6] The "historicizing" of philosophical and historical categories of knowledge had already been adumbrated in theoretical physics as the recognition of the dependence of knowledge on the spatial location of the observer.[7]

The deconstruction of language, indeed, of representation in general, which Derrida popularized in the late sixties and seventies was well underway in the work of Husserl, Heidegger, and later Wittgenstein. Husserl, for example, challenged both concepts ("the concept of man") and distinctions that had been assumed to be axiomatic in metaphysical philosophy. It was now possible to appreciate the power of the conventional to make itself felt as natural and thence to surmise that the hierarchies of the binary oppositions and their weightings, which had been thought to be as natural as the orbit of the sun, were in fact sustained in their current configuration by dynamic tension—not to say war—by and within specific cultural settings.[8] Most important to literary studies—both theory and practice—was the deconstruction of language, or of logocentricity as it was called in the new vocabulary, a deconstruction itself begun by Saussure. The relationship between a word and its referent had been assumed to have a transparent bond and natural directionality: there was a solid "real" world of objects and a secondary representational system that was assumed to mirror, define, or describe it. On this view, a word (every word) has a primary, a "real," a literal meaning, though it may also serve other uses. Although Saussure's revolutionary insight into the arbitrary nature of the sign and the conventional nature of its functioning provided the crucial wedge by which objects and words could be pried apart and reinvented as signified and signifier, he seems not to have fully recognized the price that would have to be paid for the disconnection when the stabilizing power of convention itself could be (and was) deconstructed.

However, in spite of that logical possibility, human discourse has not returned entropically to chaos, and, as Malcolm Bradbury reassured us, "just for the moment the instructions on a jar of instant coffee remain more or less usable" (7). While human communication surely depends on the relative stability of word meaning—its iterability across contexts—the maintenance of the rich cultural life of human societies probably depends as fully on our ability to trope, or to distort, the probable or conventional meaning of a word and to be understood when we do so. This *catechresis*, or misuse of language, has long been recognized; its varieties were cataloged by the early rhetoricians as a set of "devices." But the effect of the work of the deconstructionists in describing phenomena such as metaphor and irony has been to make clear the implications of these figures, exposing the weakness of the traditional distinctions between literary and ordinary language, or figural and literal meaning. The result of several decades of post-structuralist argument has been to allow the emergence of a very important insight: the functioning of human language depends on both its iterability *and* its instability. The combination is more than just a paradox of simultaneous transcendence and limitation. It allows a glimpse of how words that are vulnerable in their instability are also usable for the propagation of new meanings.

Saussure's original observation, namely that meaning was in the relationship between words and not in the words themselves, was slowly understood to have destabilizing implications for the study of just about everything. Since it (the study of just about everything) is conducted in words, these inherent instabilities or ambiguities, previously described as "literary" phenomena parasitic on "normal" language, were now understood as a general condition of language use, including language used to conduct scholarly debate.[9] And if words are only unreliably anchored to referents, their meaning determined by the context of other words and cultural artifacts, how can scholarship proceed?

The effect on the activity of literary criticism, both Anglo-Saxon and French, of this simultaneous skepticism and liberation is well known. If we previously had to be right, declared Stanley Fish in *Is There a Text in This Class?*, we have now only to be interesting. We have a new freedom—freedom to play, as Derrida's punning language exemplified, and to eschew concluding. As long as the context can change as easily as the weather, the life span of a scholarly conclusion is not much longer than that of a cloud. The observation that the center cannot hold briefly produced a comic vision for those who were, sociologically speaking, in the right places during the right years.

The arguments however, continued, and the skepticism became too deep to be borne lightly by many scholars. It is important to see how it was that the deconstructionist critics and their exciting and flagrantly boundary-breaking essays had backed themselves into a corner over the issue of representation. The entirely defensible assertion that language representation is not stable was transformed by a kind of rhetorical hyperbole into the indefensible assertion that language can't ever provide any access to truth (even if there were any). Surely because that assertion is so counterintuitive, it provoked an eruption of professional hysteria eventually somewhat calmed by the concession that self-referentiality (meaning within a closed system), since that's all we have, works almost as well as what we thought we had: referentiality or representation.

Stanley Fish, for example, soon regretted his dismissal of "being right" and recast the situation in a way that returned some of his (and our) lost scholarly dignity. Being right hasn't disappeared, as a standard, he argued, there still are standards—but their ontological position has moved over a notch. Since we are always somewhere, always within a context, there is always a literal meaning and a right interpretation (well, maybe a few). And there are always some wrong ones.[10] For now. Fish's clear responses to the lightheadedness induced by French rhetorical interpretation of German antimetaphysics produced a certain degree of containment, although it took the Paul de Man scandal finally to subdue the American literary academy's enthusiasm for the unbounded transformational activity of deconstructive criticism.[11]

What has taken some time to establish, then, isn't the error of the claim that representational systems such as language provide no access to a "real world" but only the absoluteness of that claim and, further, the interpretation of that claim as ultimately comic or tragic. If human representational systems indeed provide no access to unmediated reality, our rejection of the entire Darwinian program of evolution and adaptation is entailed. Here's why: if it were the case that human beings (or any species, for that matter) could not get some relatively reliable information about the world external to their body, they couldn't survive for long, couldn't reproduce, and so forth. Note that this doesn't mean that the representational systems on which we depend are entirely or ideally reliable, it just means that they are reliable enough to have insured the survival of the species thus far.

The evolutionary argument thus compromises the absoluteness of the deconstructive claim but also, crucially, affirms the gradience of the claim: precisely because the human species and its ways of knowing are evolved by the accumulation of random mutations, in interactions with changing environments, rather than genetically engineered for the task of knowing, it is not at all surprising that they are unstable. They were not purpose designed and are always vulnerable to further environmental change. It is just this instability, however, that provides the possibility for advantageous flexibility. People, then, and their ways of knowing, and their languages, are responsive (a word that doesn't have the negative connotation of unreliable or unstable), that is, adaptable within a changing environment. The only "goal" we can speak of with reference to adaptation is species survival, and the only thing required for that is the survival of a certain number of individuals long enough to breed and rear offspring to the age when those offspring can breed. This does not mean that everyone has to understand everything or that understanding is a logically watertight, foolproof system. All it has to be is *good enough*.

This argument produces two inferences: first that there has been, over the course of human evolution, a curve of adaptational improvement toward a good enough representational system and second that the curve will eventually flatten out, that is, stop producing an ever-more reliable system, since once it is *good enough* for the survival of the species, improvements due to random mutations would cease to be selected for. (Or to put it the other way, once a *good enough* level is attained, the good enough and the more successful representers can both survive.) This hypothesis in itself supports the claim that the representational system is indeed unstable but not the argument that it is always paradoxical or always misleading. Furthermore, there is counterpressure against the tendency for the representational system to become increasingly more rigid: the flexibility of the system has its own advantages. The evolutionary success of the species would be compromised by an entirely rigid or dependable representational system. As I argued in *Gaps in Nature*, the gap between the signifier and the signified is no tragedy; it builds in the flexibility to allow the system to meet the challenge of new contexts and use old words in new combinations and with new meanings. It is true that deviations from conventional or expected uses are risky. Attempts to communicate might fail or might not succeed unless buttressed with other communications—facial or hand gestures, pictures, paraphrases, and wordy explanations. And even then they might fail. But the prospect of never being able to adapt the representational system to new contexts is worse, from the point of view of species survival. Thus one could hypothesize that the human representational system evolved in response to a tension between two needs: the need for good enough (reliable enough) representation and the need for a flexible representational system. Evolution in that area would slow down when the lines of the two curves intersected, and thus we live with a system that is a gradient version of the deconstructive hypotheses: the system is not entirely stable—it is always open to *catechresis*, that is, to deliberate rhetorical hijacking or troping. And that vulnerability is just what allows creative innovation, keeping the species going at the two jobs that never get done: survival and adaptation.

In sum, both the deconstructionist debates of the last thirty years and the evolutionary argument collude in stripping us of our innocence. We are no longer able to continue as if words simply mean what they say, as if we didn't know that words cannot be entirely reliably identified with the things they normally, habitually represent (even though they often do just that) or know that language can be "misread," since we now understand that it is its nature, its cultural function, to be available for misreading. A misreading, in this sense, is a judgment about the suitability of a reading in a context, not about any absolute or objective meaning.[12] Since words can't always be identified with what they "normally" represent (a matter of numerical probability in a context), then in principle the system is entirely destabilized. However, it works fine a lot of the time, although it is always at risk. For better or for worse, familiar language structures may be spoken in new contexts, may be slanted, troped, or otherwise betrayed—forced, as Humpty Dumpty insisted, to mean what their masters want them to. Literary texts, not to mention diplomatic documents, historical records, diaries and many other genres in fact, depend on this margin for their creativity. The system is good enough for most of us to get through the day with no more than the accustomed undertow of misunderstanding. And often, it's just what is needed.

We might have been back where we started, as, indeed, those who declared that theory changed nothing argued.[13] But we aren't, and that is because there is another stage of post-structuralism to be reckoned with— one different and very difficult to resist. This disturbance arises from the recognition of the possibility, exposed in the powerful rhetoric of Michel Foucault, that if the representational center is indeed moveable, as it is now understood to be, then it is probably manipulable. It doesn't just change; it is changed by someone or some group.[14] In this phase of the post-structuralist debate, then, it was repeatedly argued that theoretical hypotheses of structures are not only "out there" somewhere in the contexts of the scholarly world (though they are that) but are also, and in chartable ways, determined by the interests and contexts of their proposers and supporters. The subject of subjectivity becomes central. Lévi-Strauss never asked why the unnaturalness of infanticide should be manifest by asymmetrical face painting among the Caduveo women of eastern Brazil. It seemed to him self-explanatory on the grounds of analogy (or reduction): both were "unnatural" behavior (killing one's children and painting one's face without regard for its natural features). He still relied, as Derrida pointed out, on an untenable opposition between nature and culture.[15] Once, however, the question of agency and subjectivity was raised, it was immediately seen to have two aspects. Who decided that infanticide is "unnatural?" Would the Caduveo women agree with the French anthropologist? Who produces and/or polices the cultural structures that determine human self-definition and freedom of movement within the inherited structures? And, inevitably, can I, or how can I, seize that power of structuration for myself or my group? This challenge to the assumption of structural essentialism now meant that suspicious reading was inescapable, as the reader is challenged to locate the prime mover, so recently banished by the dynamic of structuration itself. And furthermore, if one agrees that someone is pushing the buttons within one's own society, it begins to seem that it may be within one's power to direct change.

Suspicious reading itself isn't a Derridean or Foucauldian invention. Few could have been more suspicious than Freud about the discrepancies between what was said and what was meant, between what was said and where it came from and how and why it was distorted. But for Freud, the god-in-the-machine was a set of dark instincts that might be unmaskable and understandable but were probably unappeasable. Heidegger also, it would seem, considered individuals to be helpless: caught in a hermeneutic circle, with nowhere to stand from which to survey all the possibilities and with no way to control the levers that move them. For some prominent post-structuralists, Paul de Man, for example, the source of this dark, even classically tragic, situation in which the possibility of honest representation is warped by forces greater than any individual is itself a mystery. It might well be objected, however, that the history of Europe in the twentieth century, in which the promise of scientific progress was mocked by the violent uses to which science was put, backlights painfully and not so mysteriously Foucault's recognition that someone's interests are served by the definition and manipulation of the material and cultural substructure. One of Foucault's early arguments was that the use of language and grammar as a metaphor for human structuration—a metaphor the early structural linguists had claimed was no metaphor but "truth"— had concealed as much as it had revealed. War, he proposed, was the more instructive metaphor. It would not conceal that someone or some class of people always benefits from an established structure and, furthermore, does so specifically by insisting on its naturalness and permanence. If mystification or mythification are insufficient to maintain the status quo, then force can be used to do so, revealing, to a suspicious reader, that the structure isn't, after all, entirely natural.

In today's usage, post-structuralism (or, more generally, postmodernism) is the cover-all term for the generalized suspiciousness of interpretation. In spite of its rhetoric, however, post-structuralism does not replace structuralism: post-structuralists still understand the phenomena of human bodies, minds, cultures, and theories to be structured. They may not be structured entirely "naturally" and are certainly not structured entirely permanently, as was at one time assumed. They are, it is now said, constructed (and variously so) by the interface of our genetic inheritance with the environment into which we are born, that is, by the constantly changing interaction of individual needs, hegemonic cultures, and an unstable class of culturally empowered arbiters.[16] The flexibility of the cultural system as a whole doesn't mean that it doesn't exhibit fairly reliably repeated sequences of events. It isn't necessary to adopt the view that the world is a Borgesian encyclopedia, even though postmodernist art and literature produce both tragic and comic views of a world freed from many of the specific structures so long assumed to be inevitable. But if I remain a structuralist, I am also a post-structuralist, because I believe both that structures are describable simultaneously in more than one way and that they are permanently open to revision. I am thus a skeptic in the sense that I do not believe in the singleness of truth and in that I am a suspicious reader.[17] I feel unsettled until I can determine the assumptions of the current context and who institutes and enforces its prevailing rules. This suspiciousness of the contexts others have established—"agendas" that they have declared or not declared—combined with the distrust of rational argument on the grounds that it is just one of many possibilities, has made it attractive to simply declare one's own agenda more loudly or, in our discipline, more widely and more interestingly (Stanley Fish again). But the sword cuts two ways; it must be acknowledged that others may find their own concerns more compelling.

Yet if the ground for truth is no longer what it was, and if there is no other, then an oddly Buddhist resignation is produced from a supposedly radical critique. Foucault, it seems to many, saves the day, producing a neo-Marxism usable for literary studies. Whatever is, he urges, might be otherwise. And so Foucault provides the rationale for readers and interpreters who want to see their scholarship as *praxis*, as effecting their world. After Foucault, it is become difficult to pretend one doesn't know that social structures produce gains and losses—and not randomly. It seems to me that it would be difficult to justify *not* asking how the structures we investigate as literary or cultural historians are constructed and valued. Many feel that traditional scholarship is newly energized by the possibility that the mechanics of social structures, that is, their politics, might be understood and that individuals or groups might be in a position to discover tools with which to challenge them. The possibility that "discourse"—for example, literature—might be one of those tools has understandably been found exhilarating to scholars in a field long patronized as decorative.

My defense of the cognitive study of literature, then, having located it within the post-structuralist paradigm, needs now to make clearer what has already been broadly suggested, and that is how Charles Darwin also fits there. Just as Freud and Marx provided literary scholars with productive questions about their texts and their interpretive procedures, so Darwin's texts, through the readings of them by scholars in anthropology, biology, neurology, philosophy, psychology, and literature have opened new ways of talking about our subject. This perspective is an important new tool for the literary scholar because it asks new questions about the relationship between the biological and the cultural, between the living human body and its environment.

The general shape of my claim is that nothing could be more adaptationist, more Darwinian, than deconstruction and post-structuralism since both understand structuration—the production of structures (and this is the same thing as the production of theories of structures, ad infinitum)—as an activity that happens within and in response to a specific environment. Structures are always already designed for cultural use but also always ready to be reused or redesigned as needed. It is important, however, to emphasize here that this is not a panglossian vision in which satisfaction is always available. In fact, the opposite is more likely true: since the cultural/biological nexus is always in motion, the structure never exactly fits. It is always on a journey between novelty and obsolescence. The motto of this world is certainly not "whatever is, is right" but more accurately "whatever fits well enough will do for now." The categories of the world, and the structures of categories, remain the same or revise themselves depending on their interrelation with other categories in their environment, but only slowly. There are no absolute unchanging categories or structures. Like the reciprocal mutations between parasites and hosts, recategorization is constantly in process.[18] The variations and revisions, for both Darwin and for post-structuralists, are not divinely and benignly directed. Here Darwin and Foucault must part company. Darwin would no more have attributed change to a malignant intention, as Foucault always seemed to, than to an angelic.

Darwinism is appealing as a theory of mind and meaning because it is a theory of survival that depends on adaptation (troping, reinterpretation, rerepresentation) by recategorization. To put it another way, it is a theory that justifies the centrality of potential recategorization by describing it as a mechanism for survival. It is a theory of how living organisms survive in an unreliable environment by dynamic metamorphosis. In its extensions into the realms of culture it suggests how metamorphoses spread throughout populations and become entrenched.[19] Water-dwelling creatures became amphibious as the swamps dried up, Syrinx was changed into a reed to escape Pan.

The comparison with Ovid is not as far fetched as it may at first seem because although the word "adaptation" sounds good-naturedly cooperative, in fact, Darwinism is also a theory of unpredictable death and catastrophic variation and recategorization, or as Tennyson put it, it is a theory that understands nature to be "red in tooth and claw." The grotesqueries with which Ovid's stories often end bear comparison with the random variation and sudden loss that are necessary conditions of evolution under conditions of natural selection. Ovid was frequently circumspect about the causes of the metamorphoses he describes, which are mostly overdetermined. If they are punishments, it may not be clear who is the punisher. Did Syrinx decide she'd rather be a reed than a victim of Pan's lust? Or was someone punishing her by her recategorizing her? Darwin, similarly, never credited the individual mutant animal or plant with solving a problem of environmental change by deciding to develop lungs or chlorophyll.

Indeed, I see the value of Darwin's theory as a description and not as an explanation of change and adaptation. What Darwinism explains best is not change but speciation or recategorization. On these grounds, it is attractive to literary theory because the processes it hypothesizes for the natural world of plants and animals (i.e., spontaneous change/variation, followed by survival and loss and temporarily stable subspeciation) is consistent with many of the most interesting theories of mind, knowledge, meaning, and interpretation. Insofar as it can be argued that an evolutionary theory of how living creatures in the natural world adapt and survive is also a theory of mind, that is, is a theory of the way the human mind/brain adapts and learns (I am assuming these are not two different things), then both theories would be strengthened.

Theorists working in several fields of the human sciences have indeed described the activities of minds in ways that seem parallel to Darwin's description of natural evolutionary processes. The case has been explicitly argued, of course, for connectionist or parallel processing models of mind, but Darwinism is implicit as well in the Chomskian hypothesis of an innate language module that is modified in interaction with the environment to produce knowledge of a specific language.[20] Wittgenstein's model of language games as conventions similarly suggests the simultaneous systematicity and plasticity that allow both meaning and meaning change. Stephen Greenblatt's view of the circulation of social energy in a dynamic of challenge and containment, my discussion of genre change in

Gaps, and Lorraine Code's feminist, relational epistemology also describe models characterized by change and interactive adaptation and self-regulation. Susan Oyama makes clear the importance of what she calls "constructivist interactionism" as a replacement for the misleading distinction between a presumably unchangeable nature and flexible culture.

All of these theories are Darwinian, I would claim, for at least this reason: they all manage to account for systematicity—that is, for stability and predictability—while allowing for the possibility of adaptive change. Crucially, they do so without the notion of an unchanging anchoring center, a set of Platonic universals, or literal meanings. The givens of these systems are only as mysterious as the architecture of the mind/brain itself (although that is still pretty mysterious). The "well-defined species" of Darwinian theory is like the literal meaning of a word. Both are, at least for now, the most probable meanings of the word in a given community. Both are liable, even likely, to change eventually, because they are embedded within unstable semantic and ecological systems. On Dennett's description of Darwin's account of the origin of species, the process begins and ends with well-defined species, the differences at any stage among members of a species being small. If the habitat changes, however, some of those differences may turn out to offer a reproductive advantage. This sounds a lot like the kind of differences that poets can risk in making use of words for new purposes—on the assumption that they want to be both original and understood. Experienced readers of poetry (or any unconventional text) have learned a set of cognitive procedures whereby they can make sense of novelty.[21] Eventually what was novel (metaphorical—say, using the word "broadcast" for radio transmission instead of for sowing seed) may become probable or literal meaning, and a mutant may come to be recognized as a well-formed species. Darwin, according to Dennett, "declines to play the traditional game of declaring what the 'essential' difference is" (*Darwin's Dangerous Idea*, 44).[22] Remember here Wittgenstein's example of games: there is no single condition that all members of the category must have. As Dennett notes:

> "Well-defined" species certainly do exist—it is the purpose of Darwin's book to explain their origin—but he discourages us from trying to find a "principled" definition of the concept of a species. Varieties, Darwin keeps insisting, are just "incipient species," and what nor-

mally turns two varieties into two species is not the *presence* of something (a new essence for each group, for instance) but the *absence* of something: the intermediate cases, which used to be there—which were necessary stepping-stones, you might say—but have eventually gone extinct, leaving two groups that are *in fact* reproductively isolated as well as different in their characteristics. (45)

So if the well-defined species is the literal meaning, it is as fuzzy a category as literal meaning ever was and as unstable, measurable only by its difference from other species. There can be no natural category that will never change, any more than there can be a permanently literal meaning. The potential for change is all that is permanent, and the direction of the change is not predetermined. Just as the algorithmic process of evolutionary change contributes to the survival of life on earth in changing circumstances, the systematic flexibility of language keeps it able to serve changing communicative needs. Neither system changes without lurches and loss; both are self-stabilizing over time, but neither is rigid. If the systems were rigid, neither could serve its purpose.

The analogy between Darwin's stable categories and literal meaning can be extended further. In both, there is a difference between the material situation of continuous change, disappearance, and survival, clearly a gradient process, and the description of the resulting state of affairs. Naming and categorizing, like the rest of language, have an inevitable ad hocity to them, yet once they become entrenched, they aren't easily changed. At any given moment, the set of names and categories that any individual has available for use is only a near approximation of the set of material phenomena that might need describing. Speakers are bound to use words and language in a rough way in order to remain within a communicative community. For a small child, "doggie" will do fine for all varieties of dogs, while "cat" at the same age will certainly not encompass "lion" and "tiger" but may include a toy cat. Biologists will of course try to come closer to "cutting the world at its joints" with their terminology, but they also recognize that new empirical evidence (the so-called missing links) may someday prompt recategorization. Poets, similarly, try to get it right—to use the full range of language resources to make the description fit the speaker's singular perception as closely as possible, although by the community's conventional standards, the utterance may sound odd or unusual—deviant, as structuralists called it, since, and to the extent that the result is less than conventional, it will be less easily understood. This flexibility in categorization, even with its limitations, is extremely fortunate: it allows innovation. We can invent words when the need arises (gridlock) and make sense of someone else's neologisms (pied beauty). We can also influence our niche—that is, effect a change: a speaker can comfort his beloved before a separation by making a comparison between them and a pair of compasses, and an essayist can stimulate the political will of her peers by inventing the word "phallocracy."

The project of cognitive literary studies is only just beginning. The discipline will, I hope, continue to explore the new questions that emerge from a consideration of literary issues in the light of various kinds of cognitive evidence and to reconsider old issues with new evidence. Elaine Scarry, for example, proposes several ways in which literary texts take advantage of the brain's ability to reproduce and understand what writers want us to envision. My studies of early modern texts and pictures chart some of the ways creative works may provide satisfaction in a violently changing social world.[23] Mary Crane's study of Shakespeare argues for the importance of a consideration of embodied brain processing to an understanding of the author function in a literary text, and Alan Richardson's exploration of the growth of Romantic-era brain science extends and deepens the ways post-structuralist cultural studies can be enriched by a cognitive perspective. My assumption is that, taking due precaution and always taking care not to confuse the analogical or metaphoric use of data from cognitive science with its analytic use, cognitive literary study is uniquely positioned to carry forward the advances in understanding made by the post-structuralist critique of representation; to understand, that is, the simultaneous good enoughness and instability of meaning.[24] And it will do this, I believe, without the high unseriousness of post-structuralism.

NOTES

Introduction: What Is Cognitive Cultural Studies?

1. See Robert D. Hume's *Reconstructing Contexts*.

2. Zunshine, *Why We Read Fiction*, 5. See also a useful broader argument made recently by Steven Johnson in *Everything Bad Is Good for You*: "There's quite a bit in the structuralist and poststructuralist tradition that dovetails with new developments in the sciences. To give just a few examples: The underlying premise of deconstruction—that our systems of thought are fundamentally shaped and limited by the structure of language—resonates with many chapters of a book like Steven Pinker's *The Language Instinct*, despite the fact that Pinker himself has launched a number of attacks on recent cultural theory. The postmodern assumption of a 'constructed reality' goes nicely with the idea of consciousness as a kind of artificial theater and not a direct apprehension of things in themselves. Semiotics and structuralism both have roots in Lévi-Strauss's research into universal mythology, which obviously has deep connections to the project of evolutionary psychology. And [Manuel] De Landa has amply demonstrated the fundamental alliance between Deleuzian philosophy and complexity theory, an alliance that goes back to Deleuze's interest in the work of Nobel Laureate (and founding complexity theorist) Ilya Prigogine" (208).

3. Leitch and Lewis, n.p.

4. Leitch and Lewis, n.p.; Nelson, 31.

5. Compare to Dick Hebdige's argument that subcultures "manifest culture in the broader sense, as systems of communication, forms of expression and representation" (129).

6. Compare to Williams's argument in *Communications* that "society is a form of communication, through which experience is described, shared, modified, and preserved" (18).

7. See also Williams, *Communications*, 18–20, 120, 134–35.

8. See also Williams, *Communications*, 106.

9. Compare to Hayles's argument that reality "does not exist in any of the usual conceptual terms we might construct (such as reality, the universe, the world, etc.) until it is processed by an observer. It interacts with and comes into

consciousness through self-organizing, transformative processes that include sensory and cognitive components" ("Constrained Constructivism," 29–30).

10. This quote comes from the abstract of "Literary Universals" as published in *Poetics Today*.

11. I am grateful to graduate students in my spring 2007 ENG 660 seminar, "Modern Critical Theory: Cognitive Literary Studies," at the University of Kentucky: Krista Callahan, Alan Church, Scott Engholm, Jeffrey Gross, Sarah Landenwich, Katherine Osborne, Gregory Ruppert, and Geraldine Show.

12. For a related discussion of species-specific cognition, see Hayles, "Constrained Constructivism," 27–30, and Hart, "Epistemology," 322–24.

13. Spolsky, "Purposes Mistook" and "Narrative as Nourishment." See also Keen for the intriguing observation that "empathy with situations tends to zero in on episodes, circumstances, or states of relationship at points of irresolution. That is, empathy with plot situation gravitates toward middles of plots, when problems and enigmas have not yet been solved or brought to closure" (*Empathy and the Novel*, 79). It seems then that breakdowns in communication, which drive many a plot, have a particular power for drawing readers in.

14. Engholm provides a useful discussion.

Chapter One: Literary Universals

1. Bernheimer et al., 5–6.

2. See Ngũgĩ wa Thiong'o, 26.

3. Davidson, 183; see also Brown, 151–52.

4. See, for example, Comrie, 11–12, 19–22.

5. Assonance: Bownas, lii; Sandars, 17. On the related phenomenon of rhyme, see Kiparsky, "The Role of Linguistics," 10. Alliteration: Miller, introduction, 12; Bownas, lii; Philippi, 29. Verbal parallelism: Firth with McLean, 41; Egudu and Nwoga; Kunene, 68; Sherzer, 105; Cooper, 92; Liu, *The Literary Mind*, chap. 35; Sandars, 17.

6. On these and other possibly universal organizational devices see Hogan, "Beauty."

7. For a discussion of this issue, see the final section of Hogan, "Toward a Cognitive Science of Poetics."

8. As the Middle East is often said to have had no precolonial theater, it is perhaps worth referring the interested reader to Moreh; Martinovitch; and Badawi, chap. 1.

9. See Woolner and Sarup; Brandon, *Manohra*; and Liu, *Chien-nu* and *Chang*.

10. See Lal; Liu, *Chien-nu* and *Chang*; Dolby, 155–56; "Sinbad " and "Aladdin" (on dating see Dawood, 8–9); Waley; and Brandon, *Love Letter*.

11. See Hogan, "Shakespeare"; Kunene, chap. 7; Firth with McLean, 36–39; Berndt, 73–76.

12. See Lakoff and Johnson, *Metaphors*, chap. 5.

13. On this and other aspects of universals linguistic study, see Comrie and Croft.

14. On this distinction, see Ong.

15. See, for example, Sherzer and Woodbury, 9–10.

16. See Lord 1960; Kailasapathy; Hart, *Poem*; Philippi, introduction; and Opland, chap. 6.

17. Marx, *Capital*, 8.

18. See, for example, Comrie, chap. 10, and Croft, chaps. 8 and 9.

19. See Klemenz-Belgardt, 367–68.

20. See Chomsky, *Aspects*, 24–26.

21. See, for example, the valuable discussion in Bateson, *Structural Continuity*, esp. 14.

22. See Cooper, 68–72.

23. Bateson, *Structural Continuity*, 18.

24. See Johnson-Laird, 148.

25. See Cooper, 63.

26. Kazin, 83.

27. See Garman, 322; for a fuller discussion see Gathercole and Baddeley.

28. On the nature of oral poetic composition, see Lord and also Ong.

29. See, for example, the haiku in Keene, *Anthology*, 361–69.

30. See Sherzer, 107–10, and the poems in Dixon and Duwell.

31. Marx, *Economic and Philosophic Manuscripts*, 114; Fanon, 10; Amin, esp. the preface and final chap.; Appiah, 58, 152; Ahmad, 316; Said, 6.

Part Two: Cognitive Historicism

1. "Weasely" is Spolsky's term ("Cognitive Literary Historicism," 162). Significantly, the lack of interest in such an articulation characterizes the field of Literary Darwinism, which has unreflexively imported "scientific methods" into the study of literature and has thus emerged as antithetical to cognitive literary studies. For a discussion, see Richardson, "Studies," and Spolsky, "Frozen in Time?"

2. See Cosmides and Tooby, "Psychological Foundations."

3. See Pugh et al.

4. In a forthcoming study, James A. Berger suggests that the research in cognitive sciences that shows that neurologically we have not evolved for the last hundred thousand years makes a very strong argument for the importance of historicist studies of culture. As he puts it: "Human physical evolution, after all,

including the evolution of the brain, was complete at least a hundred thousand years before any narrative of human culture or history came be started. To the neuroscientist, the brains that executed the paintings at Lascaux, or the brains that first began to use symbols, are the same as the brains that composed *Gilgamesh*, the *Divine Comedy*, and *Finnegans Wake*. Brains work in certain ways to manipulate symbols, to perceive human agency and imitate it in language, to organize events in time, to imagine situations as different from what they are, to lie, or to empathize, to give backrubs, to gossip, to sing, to coo to infants. Physically, neurologically, we have not evolved further. Our societies and social lives and subjectivities and cultural products and technologies and genres and ideologies, however, *have* changed. To say that all our cultural products are made possible by particularities of brain anatomy is to say at the same time everything and nothing. Obviously this is the case. But to say anything meaningful about cultural products, we must focus attention on the histories and social contexts of those products, since brain anatomy has remained the same" ("The Dys/Dis-Articulate").

Chapter Two: Facial Expression Theory from Romanticism to the Present

1. McCarthy, 403. McCarthy reviews the studies on face recognition, prosopagnosia, and neuroanatomy that I allude to here.

2. See Galati, Scherer, and Ricci-Bitti.

3. Gopnik, Meltzoff, and Kuhl, 27–30.

4. For a discussion of the problems with evolutionary literary theory, see Richardson, "Rethinking Romantic Incest."

5. See Richardson and Steen; Spolsky, "Cognitive Literary Historicism"; and Moschovakis.

6. See Richardson, "A Neural Theater."

7. McMillan, 70.

8. See the chapter on Keats in Richardson, *British Romanticism*, 114–50.

9. I borrow the phrase "hot cognition" from Van Peer (219).

10. See Spolsky, "Darwin and Derrida" (chap. 14 of this volume).

11. See Zunshine, "Theory of Mind" (chap. 9 of this volume).

12. See Dissanayake, *Art and Intimacy*, 165.

Chapter Three: Making "Quite Anew"

1. Margaret Boden describes creativity in detail and notes that for something novel to be considered creative it has to have a point. That point, in this discussion, is an advantageous cultural change.

2. On discursive psychology, see Herman, "Narrative Theory" (chap. 7 in this volume).

3. Jerry Fodor's original proposal produced useful controversy and has been modified. Brain localization studies are beginning to reveal how the input from the sensory modules is integrated. See Uttal for a subtle discussion of the interactivity of brain nuclei and the neurological work of Stein and Meredith and Calvert, Spence, and Stein that has begun to describe what multisensory neurons do.

4. There are some obvious exceptions, such as the fact that people can feel bass notes and sounds.

5. For the arguments that the brain is always foraging for nourishment, see Freeman, chap. 4, and Changeux, 32.

6. See Modell for a discussion of the hypothesis that cross-modal associations are the basis of metaphor. See Feldman for a later and fuller argument that reframes Lakoff and Johnson's understanding of the origins of metaphor in terms of connectionist neurobiology.

7. See Mervis and Rosch, 89–115.

8. On categorization, see Jackendoff, *Semantics and Cognition*. For a discussion of genre categorization in literature, see my *Gaps in Nature*. Note that categories are maps in that they also represent the relationships among a set of percepts or conditions. The terms are distinguished here to highlight the differences between a map produced within a single sensory module—a map that needs to be coordinated with other maps—and a category that is produced (at the level that concerns us here) by more than one sensory map.

9. Rosen, 7–24.

10. Klein, 579.

11. To see the bisons and the Assyrian lamassu, go to http://images.google .com and search for Lascaux and (separately) lamassu.

12. Piper, 12.

13. See Zunshine, "Lying Bodies" (chap. 5 in this volume), and "Theory of Mind" (chap. 9 in this volume).

14. See my *Word vs. Image* on the cognitive problems brought on by the Protestant Reformation in England.

15. The idea of affordances comes from James J. Gibson.

16. In Spolsky, *Satisfying Skepticism*, and Spolsky, *Word vs. Image*.

17. You can see the picture in color at www.christusrex.org/www1/stanzas/ Rb-Transfig.jpg or find it via a Google image search.

18. The text is from the King James Bible of 1611.

19. Lakoff and Johnson, *Metaphors*, 5.

20. Schiller, 152.

21. Oberhuber, 16.

22. Oberhuber, 12.

23. Thanks to Orley Marron for calling this to my attention.

Chapter Four: Analogy, Metaphor, and the New Science

1. Lakoff and Johnson, *Metaphors*; Lakoff, *Women*; Lakoff and Johnson, *Philosophy*.

2. See essays by Crane, Sweetser, Freeman, Turner, Bradshaw, and Brandt in Bradshaw, Bishop, and Turner. See also Freeman, "Catch[ing] the Nearest Way"; Freeman, " 'According to My Bond' "; Freeman, " 'The Rack Dislimns' "; and Hogan and Pandit, introduction. For a critique of cognitive approaches to metaphor, see Anderson.

3. Historians of science call these traditions "intellectualist" and "contextualist." Work on this transition has been undertaken both by historians of science and by literary and cultural critics. See Shapin's useful bibliographic essay in *Scientific Revolution* for an account of central work in the history of science. For the purposes of this essay, the most useful historical works in the epistemological tradition have been Koyré, Dijksterhuis, Kuhn, *Structure,* and Toulmin and Goodfield. The most important work taking a social approach is Shapin and Schaeffer. Work on the history of ideas by literary and cultural critics includes Tillyard and Nicholson. For literary/cultural studies focused on the social implications of the new science, see Sawday and Paster. Recent work like that of Turner, *English Renaissance Stage*, and Spiller consider both epistemological and social aspects of the transition.

4. On metaphor, see Lakoff and Johnson, *Metaphors*, and especially Lakoff, *Women*, and Lakoff and Johnson, *Philosophy*. For a cognitive analysis of the role of analogy in scientific thought, see Gentner and Gentner; Gentner and Jeziorski; Nersessian, "Conceptual Change"; and Thagard and Toombs.

5. See Gentner and Jeziorski, who characterize the change as a shift from "metaphor" to "analogy."

6. By "Aristotelian," I mean the theories of nature based in the writings of Aristotle and his medieval commentators, which represented "an intellectual synthesis of several traditions—scientific ideas drawn from Aristotle, medical ideas from Galen, and theological doctrines handed down from the Christian fathers" (Toulmin and Goodfield, 139). Platonic ideas were sometimes included in this mix to the extent that they could be reconciled with the basically Aristotelian system.

7. Aristotle explained these transmutations as a product of "forms" or "modifiable, rather than . . . enduring[,] characteristics of base matter." However, this

theory of forms was "occult," or hidden, and therefore not very satisfactory as an explanation. See Kuhn, "Robert Boyle," 223.

8. Thagard and Toombs, 247, note that according to the ancient atomic theories of Leucippus, Democritus, Epicurus, and Lucretius, "atoms are in constant motion and come in a great variety of shapes, which account for the different characteristics of different compound bodies. . . . Things that are hard and firm, such as diamonds and iron, are composed of atoms that are more hooked together than the atoms of soft substances like liquids."

9. See Champagne, Klopfer, and Anderson for the similarities between intuitive physics and Aristotelian theory. See also McCloskey, 318, who argues that naïve theories are medieval and not specifically Aristotelian, and Clement, 325–29, for "qualitative arguments" used by Galileo to counter the deeply entrenched theories of medieval mechanics.

10. This research was based on a study of thirteen students at the Johns Hopkins University.

11. Shapin, 28.

12. There were, of course, philosophical and religious traditions preceding this historical moment that helped people accept the fact that the ultimate nature of reality is not directly perceivable and the ultimate causes of experience in the world are not directly perceivable either. Platonic philosophy, for instance, offers the theory that worldly experience is just an imperfect reflection of a truer reality. Various traditions of skepticism suggest that our inability to achieve certainty about the causes of natural phenomena should not be a cause for anxiety or concern. Various traditions of religious mysticism emphasize the mysterious and unknowable nature of God. My argument here is that in early modern Europe, the Aristotelian tradition was the accepted means of understanding natural phenomena, and that when its basis in direct perception of the world was questioned, a rupture resulted that, for some thinkers, could not be resolved by existing philosophical or religious explanations. They sought a materialist set of explanations, and that impulse led to the new science of the seventeenth century.

13. See Crane, "Physics."

14. Latour, 78–79, similarly argues that the relationship between the evidence produced in a laboratory and the "real world" of nature is representational: "We have taken science for a realist painting, imagining that made an exact copy of the world. The sciences do something else entirely—paintings too, for that matter. Through successive stages they link us to an aligned, transformed, constructed world."

15. Shapin, 49.

16. See Dijksterhuis.

17. Nersessian, "Kuhn," 178–211, discusses possible connections between Kuhn's theories about paradigm shifts and cognitive work on conceptual change.

18. Johnson's sense that these images involve "a combination of dissimilar images, or discovery of occult resemblances in things apparently unlike," allies him with Nicholson, however, on whose account far-fetched resemblances is a property of the old world picture, which posited "occult" forces to explain changes it could not otherwise account for.

Chapter Five: Lying Bodies of the Enlightenment

1. See Herman, "Narrative Theory" (chap. 7 of this volume); Scarry, *Dreaming by the Book*; Starr, "Multisensory Imagery" (chap. 13 of this volume); Crane, *Shakespeare's Brain* and "'Fair Is Foul'"; Hart, "Embodied Literature"; Easterlin, "Cognitive Ecocriticism"; Hogan, *Empire and Poetic Voice*; and Aldama, "Race."

2. For a discussion, see Alan Richardson, "Studies," 12–14.

3. For a detailed discussion, see Zunshine, "Theory of Mind and Fictions of Embodied Transparency."

4. Borenstein and Ruppin, 229.

5. Rizzolatti, Fogassi, and Gallese, 662.

6. See also Goldman for a detailed discussion of relationship between mirror neurons and theory of mind, and Ramachandran, *Brief Tour*, for a discussion of anosognosia (38) and autism (119) as possibly associated with damage in the system of mirror neurons.

7. Nussbaum, 96.

8. See Spolsky, *Word vs. Image*, and Stafford, "Romantic Systematics."

9. Warner, xii.

10. Bear in mind, too, that, as Gabrielle Starr observes, "even if we, as savvy readers and critics are on guard against fallacies of sincerity, we do well to note that being taken in—or at least along—by expectation and illusion is part of the pleasure of art, and the strategy of artists" (*Lyric Generations*, 219n14).

11. "There is subversion, no end of subversion, only not for us" (65).

12. Quoted in West, 13.

13. Quoted in Wasserman, 265.

14. As Porter Abbott suggests, the eighteenth-century cultural discourse on youth as a state of transparency was complemented by the discourse of "innocence"—frequently associated with but not limited to youthful protagonists. We can trace, he maintains, "the cultural need to maintain the idea of innocence as by definition incapable of distrusting appearances. Such innocence is meant to be part of Squire Allworthy's nature, and Tom's, and consequently keeps them from

sensing deception. It's such an important eighteenth-century issue that *Pamela* was written in part to address the problem—to make a convincing case for 'conscious innocence'" (reader's report on "Introduction to Cognitive Cultural Studies" for the Johns Hopkins University Press, March 2009).

15. As *The English Theophrastus* puts it, "Sincerity is the disclosing and opening of one's Heart: This is hardly to be found in anybody; and what we commonly look upon to be so, is only a more cunning and shrewd sort of Dissimulation, to insinuate our selves into the Confidence of other People. . . . Half-witted People can never be sincere" (334).

16. For a discussion of narrative "frames" within a cognitive perspective, see Emmott, 158.

17. For a discussion of Austen's use of theater to introduce "the subjectivity of private experience into the novel," see Marshall, 198, 237, and Cohn, 115. See also Tanner for a related analysis of "acting" and "role-playing" (162) in *Mansfield Park* and Gay for an analysis of Julia Bertram's "fine dramatic entry" (98).

Chapter Six: Toward a Cognitive Cultural Hegemony

1. See especially *Culture*.

Part Three: Cognitive Narratology

1. David Herman, e-mail, 15 September 2008. For further discussion, see Herman, "Cognitive Narratology."

2. http://projectnarrative.osu.edu/aboutUs/default.cfm. Accessed 28 October 2008. Other international programs in narratology include Center for Narratological Study at the University of Southern Denmark, Centre for Narrative Research at the University of Wuppertal, Centre for Narrative Research at the University of East London, and Interdisciplinary Centre for Narratology at the University of Hamburg (Page, introduction).

3. This ability also allows us to attribute mental states not only to imaginary entities, such as literary, film, and cartoon characters and people depicted in paintings but also—casting the net as broad as possible—to inanimate objects (see the long tradition of research, from Heider and Simmer to Johnson, Slaughter, and Carey and Scholl and Tremoulet), to groups of people (see the work of Knobe and Prinz), and to historical events (see the work of Bering on existential theory of mind: "The Folk Psychology of Souls" and *Under God's Skin*).

Chapter Seven: Narrative Theory after the Second Cognitive Revolution

1. For a fuller account of classical versus postclassical approaches to narrative theory, see Herman, Introduction. For accounts of the structuralist revolution and of the way it shaped structuralist theories of narrative in particular, see, Herman, "Histories"; and Dosse.

2. See Jahn for a synoptic account of developments in cognitive narratology; see also Herman, *Narrative Theory*.

3. See Harré, "Introduction," and also the website maintained by Andrew Lock at Massey University in New Zealand: www.massey.ac.nz/~alock/virtual/welcome.htm

4. Harré, "Introduction," 5; cf. Harré and Gillett, 1–17.

5. See also Herman, "Dialogue."

6. On problems with the very notion of zero-degree "behaviorist narrative"— that is, a mode of narration utterly devoid of clues about characters' dispositions, inferences, attitudes, and so forth—see Palmer, *Fictional Minds*, 205–39.

7. Quoted by Johnston, 31.

8. See Herman, "Cognitive Narratology."

9. Sources consulted in this context include Agre; Bechtel and Graham; Block, Flanagan, and Güzeldere; Clark, *Being There*; Damasio, *Descartes' Error*; Edwards, *Discourse and Cognition*; Freeman; Gardner; Harré, "The Discursive Turn"; and Harré and Gillett.

10. See, for example, chaps. 5 and 12.

11. For a comic account of Cartesian dualism and its implications for attempts to understand the nature of the mind, see Samuel Beckett's *Murphy*, chap. 6.

12. See Chomsky, rev. of *Verbal Behavior*.

13. Cf. Edwards, *Discourse and Cognition*.

14. See Gardner for a rich account of the historical and intellectual contexts from which first-wave cognitive science emerged as well as for a description of the overall program for research that defined the first cognitive revolution.

15. See Edwards, *Discourse and Cognition*, and "Discursive Psychology"; and Harré and Gillett.

16. See Harré, "Discursive Turn"; Wittgenstein.

17. Research on distributed cognition that was inspired by Vygotsky includes Agre; Herman, "Genette"; Hutchins, *Cognition*; Lave and Wenger; and Rogoff.

18. For foundational work in this tradition, see Drew and Heritage; Garfinkel; Sacks, *Lectures*; and Schegloff.

19. Cf. Bamberg.

20. For feminist (and other) critiques of Hemingway, see contributions to the volumes assembled by Benson and by Wagner-Martin.

21. See Clark, *Being There*, and "Embodied, Situated, and Distributed Cognition."

22. For an overview of this work, see Croft and Cruse. For a critique of some aspects of cognitive-linguistic research from a discursive-psychological perspective, see Edwards, "Categories," and *Discourse and Cognition*, 202–62.

23. See Vygotsky and the items listed in n. 17. For more discussion of distributed cognition and also of the systems of emotion concepts or "emotionologies" that I examine in my next section, see Alan Palmer's "Storyworlds and Groups" (chap. 8 of this volume).

24. For more on the role of "setting" in Hemingway's text, see Johnston, 125–34. My analysis, however, questions the traditional division of narrative representations into character and setting, because features of Jig's and the man's material environment factor into the sense-making activities represented in the story.

25. Cf. Herman, "Genette."

26. On discourse markers, see Schiffrin, 102–27.

27. See, in addition to Stearns and Stearns; Kotchemidova; Edwards, *Discourse and Cognition*, 170–201; Harré and Gillett, 144–61; Lee, " 'Feelings of the Mind' "; and Stearns, "Emotion." For an account of emotion that derives from the tradition of narrative semiotics, see Greimas and Fontanille.

28. See Mills.

29. See Nagel for a classic study.

30. See Frank Jackson and also Levine.

31. See Tye, sec. 4.

32. Significantly, many of the arguments about qualia in the philosophy of mind are couched in the form of stories or storylike thought experiments. Thus Jackson's "knowledge argument" centers around Mary, the neuroscientist, who encounters a qualitative difference between what she knows through her study of the physiology of brains experiencing color, on the one hand, and the subjective, phenomenological knowledge of color that she herself acquires when she is finally let out of her windowless, colorless laboratory, on the other hand. In a similar vein, Chalmers uses an imagined race of zombies (humanoid beings exactly like us except that they have no conscious experiences) to argue against both strict physicalist and functionalist critiques of the concept of qualia (cf. Kirk).

33. See Berman and Slobin.

34. For a discussion of quantitative techniques, see Herman, "Quantitative Methods."

35. See Langacker; Talmy; and Taylor.

36. A different version of material included in this chapter was incorporated into Herman, *Basic Elements*.

Chapter Eight: Storyworlds and Groups

1. See Herman, "Narrative Theory" (chap. 8 of this volume).

2. See also Werth for a more linguistics-based perspective.

3. For an excellent discussion of how readers use their theory of mind, see Zunshine's "Theory of Mind" (chap. 9 in this volume). For fuller treatments, see Zunshine, *Why We Read Fiction*; and Palmer, *Fictional Minds*.

4. David Herman discusses both socially and physically distributed cognition in "Narrative Theory" (chap. 8 of this volume).

5. Sperber and Hirschfeld, cxxiv.

6. Bateson, 465.

7. For more specifically on the construction of intermental minds in the novel, see Palmer, "The Middlemarch Mind."

8. See Wilson, chap. 8.

Chapter Nine: Theory of Mind and Experimental Representations of Fictional Consciousness

1. I am grateful to James Phelan for his thoughtful suggestions and comments, many of which I have eagerly seized on and quoted verbatim in my essay. Parts of the present argument, particularly those dealing with theory of mind and autism and "effortless" mind reading, overlap with the argument I make in my essay "Richardson's Clarissa," in Spolsky and Richardson's collection *The Work of Fiction*, and I am grateful to Alan and Ellen for their patient and generous engagement with my "theory of mind and fiction" argument.

2. Like Hermione Lee, we could ground it in Woolf's position as a "pioneer of reader-response theory." Woolf, she writes, "was extremely interested in the two-way dialogue between readers and writers. Books change their readers; they teach you how to read them. But readers also change books. 'Undoubtedly,' Woolf herself had written, 'all writers are immensely influenced by the people who read them'" ("Virginia Woolf's Essays," 91).

3. For a related analysis of "representations of representations" or "meta-representations," see Zunshine, "Eighteenth-Century Print Culture."

4. An important tenet of a cognitive approach to literature is that, as Paul Hernadi puts it, "there is no clear division between literary and nonliterary signification.... Literary experience is not triggered in a cognitive or emotive vacuum: modern readers, listeners, and spectators mentally process the virtual comings and goings of imagined characters as if they were analogous to remembered actual events" (60, 62). For a related discussion, see Turner, *The Literary Mind*.

5. On the social intelligence of nonhuman primates, see Byrne and Whiten,

Machiavellian Intelligence, and "The Emergence of Metarepresentation"; Gomez; and Premack and Dasser.

6. For a discussion of alternatives to the theory-of-mind approach, see Dennett, *The Intentional Stance*.

7. Leo Kanner first described autism in 1943. For more than twenty years after that, autism was "mistakenly thought to be caused by a cold family environment." In 1977, however, "a landmark twin study showed that the incidence of autism is strongly influenced by genetic factors," and, since then, "numerous other investigations have since confirmed that autism is a highly heritable disorder" (Hughes and Plomin, 48). For the "prehistory" of the term "autism," particularly as introduced by Eugen Bleuler in 1911 and developed by Piaget in 1923, see Harris, 3.

8. By using the word "mechanism," I am not trying to smuggle the outdated "body as a machine" metaphor into literary studies. Tainted as this word is by its previous history, it can still function as a convenient shorthand designation for extremely complex cognitive processes.

9. For a discussion, see Leslie, 120–25; Carruthers, 262–63; Hernadi, 58; and Spolsky, "Why and How."

10. The scale of such investment emerges as truly staggering if we attempt to spell out the host of unspoken assumptions that make it possible (for a discussion, see Zunshine, "Richardson's *Clarissa*"). This realization lends new support to what theorists of narrative view as the essential underdetermination or "undertelling" of fiction, its "interior nonrepresentation" (Sternberg, 119).

11. For a qualification of the term "inborn" in relation to the processing of incoming data, see Spolsky, *Satisfying Skepticism*, 164.

12. For an important recent discussion of "constraints," see Spolsky, "Cognitive Literary Historicism."

13. For a discussion, see Fish, *Is There a Text in this Class?*

14. See Carey and Spelke and Cosmides and Tooby on domain specificity. For a recent application of the theory of domain specificity to the study of literature, see Zunshine, "Rhetoric, Cognition, and Ideology."

15. Thus, bringing the findings of cognitive scientists to bear on the literary text does not diminish its aesthetic value. As Scarry has argued in response to the fear that science would "unweave the rainbow" of artistic creation, "the fact of the matter is that when we actually look at the nature of artistic creation and composition, understanding it does not mean doing it less well. To become a dancer, for example, one must do the small steps again and again and understand them, if one is to achieve virtuosity. Right now we need virtuosity, not only within each discipline, but across the disciplines as well" ("Panel Discussion," 253).

16. For a discussion, see Easterlin, "Voyages."

17. As Blakey Vermeule observes, "literature-fiction-writing is so powerful

because it eats theories for breakfast, including cognitive/evolutionary approaches" (personal communication, 20 November 2002).

18. For a discussion of embodied cognition, see also Hart, "Embodied Literature."

19. Strictly speaking, Auerbach's question refers to *To the Lighthouse*, but it is equally pertinent for our discussion of *Mrs. Dalloway*.

20. George Butte's study *I Know That You Know That I Know: Narrating Subjects from Moll Flanders to Marnie* offers a fascinating perspective on a writer's interest in constructing a "present moment" as a delicate "connection" among the characters' subjectivities. Applying Maurice Merleau-Ponty's analysis of interlocking consciousnesses (*Phenomenology of Perception*) to a broad selection of eighteenth- and nineteenth-century novels, as well as to the films of Hitchcock, Hawks, and Woody Allen, Butte argues compellingly that something had changed in the narrative representation of consciousness by the time of Jane Austen: writers had developed the ability to represent the "deep intersubjectivity" of their characters, portraying them as aware of each other's perceptions of themselves and as responding to such perceptions with body language observable by their interlocutors, which generated a further series of mutual perceptions and reactions. Although Butte does not refer in his work to cognitive science or the theory of mind, his argument is in many respects compatible with the literary criticism that does.

21. On Woolf's definition of narrative ventriloquism, see DiBattista, 132.

22. The final section of the essay as it appeared in *Narrative* has been deleted in reprinting it here.

Chapter Ten: Machiavellian Narratives

1. I am grateful to Sue Curry, who in a presentation at Indiana University, Bloomington, in September 2005 brought the passage from the *Aeneid* and Michael Putnam's book to my attention.

2. The translation can be found in Muller and Richardson, 24.

3. See Muller and Richardson for the Lacanian and Derridean responses.

Part Four: Cognitive Approaches in Dialogue with Other Approaches (Postcolonial Studies, Ecocriticism, Aesthetics, Poststructuralism)

1. Keen, e-mail, 16 April 2009.

2. As Keen explains, like strategic essentializing, strategic empathizing occurs when an author employs empathy in the crafting of fictional texts, in the service

of, quoting Gayatri Spivak, "a scrupulously visible political interest" ("Strategic Empathizing," 121).

3. Keen, blurb, Frederick Luis Aldama's *A User's Guide to Postcolonial and Latino Borderland Fiction*.

4. Hogan, e-mail, 15 September 2008.

5. According to Hogan, "Among appraisal theorists, the most prominent is Keith Oatley, whose *Best Laid Schemes: The Psychology of Emotions* is a classic in the field. (See also his essay 'Simulation of Substance and Shadow: Inner Emotions and Outer Behavior in Shakespeare's Psychology of Character.') Other appraisal-based approaches to literary study may be found in the writings of literary critics, such as Lalita Pandit ('Emotion, Perception, and *Anagnorisis*'). In contrast, a number of film theorists have stressed more 'bodily' approaches to emotion and the arts. (See, for example, Greg Smith's *Film Structure and the Emotion System*.) On the other hand, this division is far from absolute—as suggested by Ed Tan's work on film ('Emotion, Art, and the Humanities') and Donald Wehrs's work on literature ('Moral Physiology, Ethical Prototypes')" (e-mail, 15 September 2008).

6. Easterlin, e-mail, 30 October, 2008.

7. See Easterlin's review of Love's and Phillips's books.

8. Compare Zunshine's use of Dan Sperber's notion of modular competition in *Strange Concepts* (168–70).

9. Abbott, reader's report on "Introduction to Cognitive Cultural Studies" for the Johns Hopkins University Press, March 2009.

10. In fact, cognitive aesthetics is sometimes thought of as a form of close reading, and to the extent that it is, it answers the charge of reductionism leveled by its critics. See, for example, Starr's argument that "tools from cognitive psychology can be used in conjunction with close reading to engage persistent questions about imagery and pleasure, and about how images shape the ways we encounter poems as reading, feeling, and indeed poetically engaged subjects" ("Poetic Subjects," 49).

Chapter Eleven: On Being Moved

1. See chapter 8 of my *Cognitive Science*.

2. See Damasio, *Looking for Spinoza*, 60.

3. See Kosslyn, 295, 301, 325; and Rubin, 41–46, 57–59.

4. On the integration of memories into appraisal, see Smith and Kirby.

5. See Oatley, *Best Laid Schemes*, 107–8.

6. See chapter 7 of my *Cognitive Science*.

7. See Holland, "Willing Suspension," and "Where Is a Text?"

8. See Clark, Boutros, and Mendez, 43.

9. Clark, Boutros, and Mendez, 46.

10. See Cassidy and also Schore.

11. Duckitt, 81.

12. When a word is added to a phrase, resulting in a larger phrase, the added word is the "head" of the larger phrase. For example, joining "to" with "the park" yields "to the park." "To" is the head of this (prepositional) phrase. Languages either place heads before the phrases with which they join (as in English) or after those phrases (as in Japanese). For a discussion of this phenomenon, see Baker, 68–75.

13. These triggers include some innate, nonemotional perceptual sensitivities. For example, we may have innate sensitivities to direction of gaze and intentional movement. Such sensitivities guide our attention, particularly when we encounter expectancy violations, as with corpses. Through attentional orientation, these sensitivities facilitate the isolation of eliciting conditions (e.g., a corpse) in critical-period calibrations of emotion systems.

14. See Smith and Mackie, 429.

Chapter Twelve: Cognitive Ecocriticism

1. For a thorough historical account of the emergence of philosophical pragmatism, see Menand, *Metaphysical Club.*

2. See Darwin, *Origin.* In chapter 11, "Variation under Nature," for example, he stresses the relative utility of the categories "species" and "variety" (108).

3. For an excellent discussion of the history of ecology as a concept and of the gap between the popular and scientific notions of ecosystem, see Phillips, chap. 2.

4. See, for example, Howarth and also Manes.

5. For the first significant account of the relevance of evolutionary psychology to the study of culture, see Cosmides and Tooby, "Psychological Foundations." For a longer account of the relevance of evolutionary and cognitive psychology and philosophy of science to literary theory, see my essay "Making Knowledge."

6. Kaplan's "Environmental Preference in a Knowledge-Seeking, Knowledge-Using Organism" emphasizes the relationship between wayfinding and knowledge acquisition and has particularly aided my efforts to think dynamically about human relationships to physical places.

7. For analyses of visual art informed by evolutionary psychology, see Appleton, *Experience of Landscape* and *Symbolism of Habitat.* For a critique of simplistic applications of theories of evolved preference to aesthetic matters, see Dissanayake, "Komar and Melamid."

8. For theoretical discussions of environmental preference, see Kaplan and Orians and Heerwagen. For application of the theory to landscape art, see Appleton, *Experience of Landscape*.

9. See Hammerstein.

10. For a longer discussion of these predispositions, see my essay "Making Knowledge." The psychological literature on narrativity and on its application to fictional stories is now extensive, but good starting points for research in this area are Bruner and also Schank.

11. Love, 11.

12. See Phillips, chaps. 4 and 5, for incisive analyses of the problem of ecocriticism's morally generated literary desiderata, including realism and nature writing.

13. Among the first ecocritics to include anthropology as well as Appleton's environmental aesthetics in her analysis is Westling, *The Green Breast of the World*.

14. Hogan defines lyrics as "elaborations of junctural moments in narratives" (*Mind and Its Stories*, 153).

15. For an analysis of the development of place attachment in Wordsworth's *Prelude* in the context of developmental psychology, see my "Psychoanalysis"; for a discussion of the connotations of the word "home" in *The Prelude*, see my "Voyages"; for a general theoretical overview of the development of place attachment, see my " 'Loving Ourselves Best of All.' "

Chapter Thirteen: Multisensory Imagery

1. On the perception of metrical stress involves motor imagery, see Aleman and Van't Wout.

2. fMRI, positron-emission tomography (PET), transcranial magnetic stimulation (TMS), electroencephalography (EEG), and magnetoencephalography (MEG) enable localization of neurological activity in experimental conditions in response to specific stimuli. fMRI and PET measure changes in a subject's cerebral blood flow (PET employs radioactive tagging, fMRI does not), which correspond to increased firing rates in neurons and thus to increased activity in a specific region of the brain. Both are *indirect* measures of brain function and produce a probabilistic map of neural activity: they do not pinpoint the location of increased blood glucose and increased activation but show the region or regions that correspond to areas in the brain where, with highest probability, a measured increase originated. EEG measures changes in electrical activity, while MEG traces changes in the magnetic fields around neurons (recall that you can make a magnet by running a current through a wire): both measure brain activity directly. The

magnetic fields used in TMS may be employed to temporarily disrupt brain activity in a given area, allowing investigation of what happens when areas suspected to be involved in particular brain processes are unable to function properly. Since the advent of these techniques, scientists have come much closer to being able to study events that had previously seemed too subjective to be available to experimental investigation. On the history of brain imaging, see Kevles.

3. Several tests for vividness and controllability, primarily visual, exist: the Vividness of Visual Imagery Questionnaire (Marks), the Betts Questionnaire Upon Mental Imagery, the Gordon Test of Visual Imagery Control, the Verbalizer-Visualizer Questionnaire (Richardson), and the Vividness of Movement Imagery Questionnaire (Isaac et al.). See Isaac et al.; Marks; Richardson, *Mental Imagery*; and Sheehan.

4. See Okada, Matsuoka, and Hatakeyama, who show that imagery of taste, smell, and cutaneous sensation are the least common forms of mental imagery during dreaming. About 25% of their subjects experienced taste and smell in dreams occasionally or more often, while around 60% experienced cutaneous sensation occasionally to always (109).

5. Most music study involves Western musical forms. See Peretz and Zatorre.

6. See Halpern, 435, on the difference between auditory and visual and haptic images. Compression of imagined sound is not just a matter of consciously speeding up playback but has to do with how we encode the image (see Yabe et al.). To me, this suggests why we need to be careful about taking visual images as analogues or patterns for other kinds of imagery. Visual imagery seems to have similar spatial characteristics to actual sight—imagined objects often seem to maintain the same spatial relations as real ones. The limits on visual images often have to do with size and detail. However, most of us can preserve a tone or series of tones in a song with some accuracy. It may seem useful to read visual and auditory imagery as analogues, with space being the key dimension for one and time for the other, but that analogy would lead us to imagine that "errors" in each form of imagery or differences between imagined and real encounters should be similar. They are not.

7. Halpern and Zatorre.

8. Kraemer et al.

9. Halpern and Zatorre, 703. Halpern et al. argue that much more work needs to be done to ascertain whether we really are doing something like humming along or whether parts of our brains usually used for motor activity "may be involved in some more general aspect of auditory imagery, such as image generation of preparation, regardless of any potential subvocal contribution to the image" (1291). I am unconvinced that the subthreshold SMA (supplementary motor area) activation they find with imagined timbre is significant. They argue

that because timbre is not vocalizable, any motor activity in imagined timbre should not come from imagined vocalization, and the SMA activation should come from something else. However, they note that "although subvocalizing the timbre of an instrument is difficult, the timbre was accompanied by pitch, which itself is easily vocalizable" (1291).

10. See Peretz and Zatorre, 95. They summarize the evidence showing links between music and motion developed through musical training (102ff.).

11. Ackermann, Mathiak, and Ivry.

12. Decety et al., "Central Activation."

13. Here we may suspect that cultural and historical differences play a role. If such movements are seen as vulgar, for example, are they still indices of pleasure? Frances Burney gives us a glimpse into the problem. Mme. Duval, the novel's epitome of vulgarity, responds vividly to some inferior music: she "was in extacies; and the Captain flung himself into so many ridiculous distortions, by way of mimicking her, that he engaged the attention of all the company; . . . while Mme. Duval was affecting to beat time, and uttering many expressions of delight, he called suddenly for salts. . . . [He] protested he had . . . concluded, from her raptures, that she was going into hysterics" (78–79). However, the elevated taste of the heroine is also subject to ridicule by the vulgar, and physical response seems crucial to enjoyment: "This song, while slow and pathetic, caught all my attention, and I lean'd my head forward . . . ; but upon turning round, when the song was over, I found that I was the object of general diversion . . . ; for the Miss Branghtons were tittering, and the two gentlemen making signs and faces at me, implying their contempt of my affectation. This discovery determined me to appear as inattentive as themselves; but I was very much provoked at being thus prevented enjoying the only pleasure, which, in such a party, was within my power" (94).

14. Most cognitive neuroscientists argue for varying degrees of functional specialization in the brain—motion, color, pitch, sensations from the hand or face, for example, are, they suggest, each processed in a separate area of the brain. On motor imagery and neural correlates, see de Lange, Hagoort, and Toni; Fox et al.; Grafton et al.; and Porro et al.

15. This debate is too nuanced to be recapped either in this chapter or in an endnote: it is bound up in problems of understanding consciousness and the relation of conscious experience to the material world. My position is that mental experience as we know it is inseparable from physical processes; we are slowly defining and discovering those processes.

16. The classic work on Enlightenment ideas of the imagination remains James Engell's *Creative Imagination*.

17. For example, practice can improve your performance of motor imagery:

"Imagining making movements might not only exercise the relevant brain areas, but also build associations among processes implemented in different areas, which in turn facilitate complex performance" (Kosslyn et al., 639).

18. Kable et al.

19. Perceptions are stored in a distributed fashion—emotional components of a frightening moment, for example, may be stored separately from information about the face that caused the fear, even though the two are reunited in the phenomenal remembrance of the experience. On distributed representation of objects, see, for example, Lehmann and Murray, 331.

20. Kable et al.

21. See Stevens. Much research into imagery uses interference to determine functional exclusivity: for instance, experience that relies on visual imagery or vision can be altered or inhibited by other visual activity. It is hard both to concentrate on the details of a picture in front of you and to concentrate on the imagined details of an imagined image at the same time. However, we can concentrate on the detail of a piece of music while also looking intently at a painting or imagining one. We cannot do both as easily together as we can separately, but we can do them together. We can measure the degree of difficulty or challenge involved in such potentially interfering activities by measuring the amount of time it takes to do them together as opposed to separately. Stevens shows that imagining someone else moving can be inhibited more significantly by visual interference than by motor interference. Imagining ourselves moving, however, shows greater interference from motor activity than visual. In general, "visual and motor imagery [are] cooperative processes" but not always. Similar results to Stevens's—concerning the difference between imagining yourself moving something and imagining someone else doing so—may be found in Kosslyn et al.

22. Stevens, 345.

23. For an overview, see Rizzolatti and Craighero. On learning and mirror neurons, see also Stefan et al.

24. Jean Decety has been doing some very interesting work on the multiple processes involved in empathy. Motor imitation may play a role (though not the only role); see Decety and Jackson.

25. Sitter contends that as readers of Swift's "A Beautiful Young Nymph Going to Bed" focus on sensations of touch and the painful movements that the prostitute makes as she prepares for sleep without rest, they move from disgust to identification with her frail body.

26. Rossini et al.

27. "Imagination in the writer" is "like a nimble spaniel, [which] beats over and ranges through the field of memory, till it springs the quarry it hunted after" (Dedicatory epistle, 26).

28. Stevens and McKechnie.

29. "Action observation in humans involves an internal motor simulation of the observed movement" (Calvo-Merino et al., 1246).

30. A review of these interconnections can be found in Cerf-Ducastel et al.

31. Stevenson and Case, "Olfactory Imagery."

32. Stevenson and Case find that people whose dreams often involve smell are better at volitional olfactory imagery and at discriminating smells, suggesting that in these individuals the connections between memories of smell and semantic memories are stronger than average ("Olfactory Dreams").

33. Thanks to John C. Harpole for this reminder.

34. Stevenson and Case, "Olfactory Imagery."

35. This was shown with salt solutions (Cerf-Ducastel et al.).

36. Compared to visual perception, olfactory perception involves hedonic and emotive evaluation more frequently, and the emotions may be stronger (Stevenson and Case, "Olfactory Imagery," 245–46).

37. The most vocal critic of the analogic view of images (images as mimetic of actual sensation) is Zenon Pylyshyn. See, for example, his "Is the Imagery Debate Over?"

38. Certain smells, like that of strawberry, make it easier for us to taste sugar. The imagined smell of strawberry does the same (Djordjevic, Zatorre, and Jones-Gottman, "Effects"). Visual imagery has no such effect (Djordjevic, Zatorre, and Jones-Gottman, "Mind's Nose").

39. Stevenson and Case give a critical overview of this work in "Olfactory Imagery," 251–52. They caution that more needs to be done to differentiate between phenomenal imagery and performance on experimental tasks that might stem from other causes. One important problem with some work on taste imagery is that the behavior used to verify the effects of imagery is salivation. It is unclear in these circumstances whether we are dealing with an effect mediated by an image or simply the effect of a conditioned stimulus (in the manner of Pavlov), where imagery is not necessarily involved.

40. Cerf-Ducastel et al.

41. The topographical organization of sensation explains phantom limbs, where amputees still "feel" the presence of lost limbs. After amputation, the somatosensory cortex is reorganized, so that areas previously assigned to hands, for example, would receive stimulus from an adjacent area in the cortex, like that for the face. Facial stimulation then becomes interpreted as coming from the phantom hand. See Flor et al.; and Ramachandran, "Behavioral and Magnetoencephalographic Correlates."

42. Yoo et al.

43. "I . . . could not help feeling what I could not grasp, a column of the

whitest ivory, beautifully streaked with blue veins, and carrying . . . a head of the liveliest vermillion: no horn could be harder or stiffer; yet no velvet more smooth or delicious to the touch" (83).

44. On the relation of grasping to visual "what" and "where" pathways, see Prather, Votow, and Sathian. On motor imagery, vision, and grasping, see Buxbaum, Johnson-Frey, and Bartlett-Williams.

45. See Sathian; and Zhang et al.

46. Cytowic lays out the basics. Synaesthesia is inherited, and more women than men and more left-handed than right-handed individuals are synaesthetes. Cytowic's discussion of the emotional components of synaesthesia should be viewed with some skepticism owing to his reliance on somewhat outdated models of emotional processing.

47. See Ramachandran and Hubbard. Their discussion of language is speculative, and I am skeptical of it. For follow-up discussion, see Hubbard and Ramachandran; and Pribram.

48. Dixon et al. For an unusual case, see Beeli and Jancke. This kind of blending with arithmetical functions is not always the case. I am grateful to the anonymous reader of this chapter (also a synaesthete) for pointing this out.

49. See Cytowic.

50. Grant et al.

51. Murray et al.

Chapter Fourteen: Darwin and Derrida

1. Preference models were first described in Jackendoff's *Semantics and Cognition* as a way to display word meaning without fatal rigidity. Schauber and I demonstrated how the model describes literary genres in *The Bounds of Interpretation*.

2. See Jackendoff, *Consciousness and the Computational Mind*.

3. I have explored some examples of these miscalibrations in *Satisfying Skepticism, Word vs. Image*, and "Elaborated Knowledge." See also my "Why and How," where I explore in depth the variety of creative productions whose raison d'être is to display and order the anxiety that results from these gaps within the specific historical context of early modern Europe.

4. See Piaget's *Le structuralisme* for a survey of early structuralism.

5. This may be an instance of what Paul de Man called the blindness that comes with insight. While such blindness is probably inevitable, as he thought, it is not necessarily paradoxical, as he asserted—it may be just wrong and misleading.

6. A key text is Nietzsche's *On the Advantage*. These links are summarized by Spivak, xxi.

7. In Einstein's general theory of relativity in 1916 and as Heisenberg's uncertainty principle in 1927.

8. Culler's *On Deconstruction* contains a clear explanation of how these reversals are argued.

9. See Austin's *How to Do Things with Words* for an account of how "literary" language is parasitic on "normal" language.

10. Fish, *Is There a Text in This Class?*, 174.

11. Probably the most poignant evidence that the hyperbolic promotion of the recognition that words are unstable was indeed an unsustainable claim was the inability of de Man's good friends and colleagues to entirely erase, reread, or reinscribe the dram of anti-Semitic fascism in his early essays. When these boa-deconstructers, as Geoffrey Hartman had called them (in Bloom's *Deconstruction*), couldn't entirely or satisfactorily deconstruct some texts that they very much wanted to deconstruct, then maybe the power of trope had found its limit. More analysis is still needed, not of de Man's juvenilia but of the apologetics produced in their wake.

12. There is an instructive parallel here with Austin's felicity conditions outlined in *How To Do Things with Words*. Appropriateness rather than truth is the standard by which the success of the utterance is judged. Note also the parallel with the Darwinian idea of fitness.

13. For the argument that theory changes nothing, see Fish, *Is There a Text in This Class?* 370; Fish, *Doing What Comes Naturally*, 315–41; and Knapp and Michaels "Against Theory."

14. Rabinow, 51–75.

15. A sustained critique of a Lévi-Strauss text is Derrida's "La structure, le signe et le jeu dans le discours de sciences humaines" delivered as a talk in 1966 to the "The Languages of Criticism and the Sciences of Man" symposium at the Johns Hopkins University and subsequently translated as "Structure, Sign, and Play in the Discourse of the Human Sciences."

16. See Oyama.

17. The argument for this conclusion from the scientific point of view is made nicely by Arbib and Hesse in *The Construction of Reality*.

18. See Dawkins, *The Extended Phenotype*; and Dennett, *Darwin's Dangerous Idea*.

19. See Dawkins, *The Selfish Gene*; and Sperber.

20. Dennett discusses Chomsky's denial of this in *Darwin's Dangerous Idea* (384). Deacon in *The Symbolic Species* describes how the language module might have evolved not before human language developed but within a context in which it developed.

21. See Culler, *Structuralist Poetics*; and Schauber and Spolsky.

22. Dennett notes that there is a "standard" (*Darwin's Dangerous Idea*, 44) way of marking species differentiation, the existence of interbreeding, but then goes on to provide examples of exceptions to this rule. It is, thus, not a necessary rule.

23. See Spolsky, "Elaborated Knowledge" and "Why and How."

24. Literary scholars can inoculate themselves against the naïve overestimation of what social science or evolutionary biology can offer by remembering to ask themselves: what is the probability that *their* field (as compared with mine) is *not* riven by competitive hypotheses? That while I struggle to deal with apparently irreconcilable complexities, *they* know exactly what they're doing, so that I may borrow their theories and empirical data as unimpeachable evidence to resolve my controversies? Indeed the field of evolutionary biology is the throes of several different controversies, which literary scholars are not professionally trained to evaluate.

WORKS CITED

Abbott, H. Porter. "Humanists, Scientists and Cultural Surplus." *SubStance* 30.1/2 (2001): 203–17.

Ackermann, Hermann, Klaus Mathiak, and Richard B. Ivry. "Temporal Organization of 'Internal Speech' as a Basis for Cerebellar Modulation of Cognitive Functions." *Behavioral and Cognitive Neuroscience Reviews* 3 (2004): 14–22.

Adolphs, Ralph. "Could a Robot Have Emotions? Theoretical Perspectives from Social Cognitive Neuroscience." *Who Needs Emotions: The Brain Meets the Robot.* Ed. Michael Arbib and Jean-Marc Fellous. Oxford: Oxford University Press, 2005. 9–28.

Agre, Philip E. *Computation and Human Experience.* Cambridge: Cambridge University Press, 1997.

Ahmad, Aijaz. *In Theory: Classes, Nations, Literatures.* New York: Verso, 1992.

"Aladdin and the Enchanted Lamp." Trans. N. J. Dawood. *Tales from the Thousand and One Nights.* New York: Penguin, 1955. 165–236.

Aldama, Frederick Luis. "Race, Cognition, and Emotion: Shakespeare on Film." *College Literature* 33.1 (2006): 197–213.

———. *A User's Guide to Postcolonial and Latino Borderland Fiction.* Austin: University of Texas Press, 2009.

———, ed. *Toward a Theory of Narrative Acts.* Austin: University of Texas Press, 2010.

Aleman, Andre, and Mascha Van't Wout. "Subvocalization in Auditory-Verbal Imagery: Just a Form of Motor Imagery?" *Cognitive Processing* 5 (2004): 228–31.

Amin, Samir. *Eurocentrism.* Trans. Russell Moore. New York: Monthly Review Press, 1989.

Anderson, Judith. *Translating Investments: Metaphor and the Dynamics of Cultural Change in Tudor-Stuart England.* New York: Fordham University Press, 2005.

Appiah, Kwame Anthony. *In My Father's House: Africa in the Philosophy of Culture.* New York: Oxford University Press, 1992.

Appleton, Jay. *The Experience of Landscape.* London: John Wiley, 1975.

————. *The Symbolism of Habitat: An Interpretation of Landscape in the Arts*. Seattle: University of Washington Press, 1990.

Arbib, Michael A., and Mary B. Hesse. *The Construction of Reality*. Cambridge: Cambridge University Press, 1986.

Armstrong, Nancy. *How Novels Think: The Limits of British Individualism from 1719–1900*. New York: Columbia University Press, 2005.

Ashcroft, Bill, Gareth Griffiths, and Helen Tiffin. *The Empire Writes Back: Theory and Practice in Post-Colonial Literatures*. New York: Routledge, 1989.

Auerbach, Erich. *Mimesis: The Representation of Reality in Western Literature*. Princeton: Princeton University Press, 1991.

Austen, Jane. *Emma*. 1815. Ed. Fiona Stafford. Harmondsworth, UK: Penguin, 1996.

————. *Mansfield Park*. 1814. Oxford: Oxford University Press, 1990.

Austin, John L. *How to Do Things with Words*. Oxford: Oxford University Press, 1962.

Badawi, M. M. *Early Arabic Drama*. Cambridge: Cambridge University Press, 1988.

Baillie, Joanna. *The Dramatic and Poetical Works of Joanna Baillie*. 2nd ed. London, 1853.

Baillie, Matthew. *Lectures and Observations on Medicine*. London, 1825.

Baker, Mark C. *The Atoms of Language: The Mind's Hidden Rules of Grammar*. New York: Basic Books, 2001.

Bamberg, Michael. "Positioning." Herman, Jahn, and Ryan 445–46.

Bargh, John A., ed. *Social Psychology and the Unconscious: The Automaticity of Higher Mental Processes*. Philadelphia: Psychology Press, 2007.

Barkow, Jerome, Leda Cosmides, and John Tooby, eds. *The Adapted Mind: Evolutionary Psychology and the Generation of Culture*. New York: Oxford University Press, 1992.

Barnes, Jennifer Lynn, and Simon Baron-Cohen. "Language and Autism: Pragmatics and Theory of Mind." *The Handbook of Psycholinguistics and Cognitive Processing: Perspectives in Communication Disorders*. Ed. Mandy J. Williams, Jackie Guendouzi, and Filip Loncke. New York: Taylor and Francis, forthcoming.

Baron-Cohen, Simon. "The Eye Direction Detector (Edd) and the Shared Attention Mechanism (Sam): Two Cases for Evolutionary Psychology." *Joint Attention: Its Origins and Role in Development*. Ed. Chris Moore, Philip J. Dunham, et al. Hillsdale, NJ: Lawrence Erlbaum, 1995. 41–59.

————. *Mindblindness: An Essay on Autism and Theory of Mind*. Cambridge, MA: MIT Press, 1995.

Barreca, Regina. *They Used to Call Me Snow White . . . but I Drifted: Women's Strategic Use of Humor.* New York: Viking, 1991.

Bateson, Gregory. *Steps to an Ecology of Mind: A Revolutionary Approach to Man's Understanding of Himself.* New York: Ballantine, 1972.

Bateson, Mary Catherine. *Structural Continuity in Poetry: A Linguistic Study of Five Pre-Islamic Arabic Odes.* The Hague: Mouton, 1970.

Bechtel, William, and George Graham, eds. *A Companion to Cognitive Science.* Oxford, UK: Blackwell, 1998.

Beeli, Michaela Esslen, and Lutz Jancke. "Synaesthesia: When Coloured Sounds Taste Sweet." *Nature* 434 (2005): 38.

Bell, Charles. *The Anatomy and Philosophy of Expression as Connected with the Fine Arts.* 7th ed. London, 1877.

Benjamin, Walter. *Illuminations.* New York: Harcourt, Brace and World, 1955.

Benson, Jackson J., ed. *New Critical Approaches to the Short Stories of Ernest Hemingway.* Durham: Duke University Press, 1990.

Bering, Jesse M. "The Existential Theory of Mind." *Review of General Psychology* 6.1 (2002): 3–24.

———. "The Folk Psychology of Souls." *Behavioral and Brain Sciences* 29 (2006): 453–98.

———. *Under God's Skin.* New York: Norton, forthcoming.

Berman, Ruth A., and Dan I. Slobin, eds. *Relating Events in Narrative: A Crosslinguistic Developmental Study.* Mahwah, NJ: Lawrence Erlbaum, 1994.

Berndt, Ronald M. *Love Songs of Arnhem Land.* Chicago: University of Chicago Press, 1993.

Bernheimer, Charles, et al. "A Statement of Purpose: Comparative Literature at the Turn of the Century." Report, October 1993, American Comparative Literature Association.

Bharatamuni. *The Natya Sastra.* Delhi: Sri Satguru, n.d.

Bishop, Elizabeth. "At the Fishhouses." *The Complete Poems, 1929–1979.* New York: Noonday, 1983. 64–66.

Block, Ned, Owen Flanagan, and Güven Güzeldere, eds. *The Nature of Consciousness: Philosophical Debates.* Cambridge, MA: MIT Press, 1997.

Bloom, Harold, Paul de Man, Geoffrey H. Hartman, and J. Hillis Miller. *Deconstruction and Criticism.* New York: Continuum, 1979.

Bloom, Paul. *How Pleasure Works: The New Science of Why We Like What We Like.* New York: Norton, 2010.

Boden, Margaret A. *The Creative Mind: Myths and Mechanisms.* 2nd ed. London: Routledge, 2004.

Borenstein, Elhanan, and Eytan Ruppin. "The Evolution of Imitation and Mirror Neurons in Adaptive Agents." *Cognitive Systems Research* 6.3 (2005): 229–42.

Bownas, Jeoffrey. Introduction. *The Penguin Book of Japanese Verse*. Ed. Geoffrey Bownas and Anthony Thwaite. New York: Penguin, 1964. xxxvii–lxxiii.

Boyer, Abel. *The English Theophrastus; or, The Manners of the Age, Being the Modern Characters of the Court, the Town, and the City*. London, 1702.

Bradbury, Malcolm. *My Strange Quest for Mensonge: Structuralism's Hidden Hero*. London: Arena, 1989.

Bradshaw, Graham, Tom Bishop, and Mark Turner, eds. *The Shakespearean International Yearbook 4: Shakespeare Studies Today*. Aldershot, UK: Ashgate, 2004.

Brandon, James R., ed. *Love Letter from the Licensed Quarter. Kabuki: Five Classic Plays*. Honolulu: University of Hawaii Press, 1992. 220–24.

———, ed. *Manohra. Traditional Asian Plays*. New York: Hill and Wang, 1972. 121–72.

Brook, Andrew, and Don Ross. *Daniel Dennett*. Cambridge: Cambridge University Press, 2002.

Brown, Donald E. *Human Universals*. New York: McGraw-Hill, 1991.

Bruner, Jerome. *Acts of Meaning*. Cambridge, MA: Harvard University Press, 1990.

Bryson, J. Scott. "The Ambivalent Discourse: Words, Language, and the Human-Nature Connection." *Literary Ecocriticism*. Ed. Ian Marshall. Spec. issue of *Interdisciplinary Literary Studies* 3.1 (2001): 41–52.

Buell, Lawrence. *Writing for the Endangered World: Literature, Culture, and Environment in the U.S. and Beyond*. Cambridge, MA: Harvard University Press, 2001.

Buller, David J. *Adapting Minds: Evolutionary Psychology and the Persistent Quest for Human Nature*. Cambridge, MA: MIT Press, 2005.

Burney, Frances. *Evelina*. 1778. New York: Oxford University Press, 2002.

Butte, George. *I Know That You Know That I Know: Narrating Subjects from "Moll Flanders" to "Marnie."* Columbus: Ohio State University Press, 2004.

Buxbaum, Laurel J., Scott H. Johnson-Frey, and Megan Bartlett-Williams. "Deficient Internal Models for Planning Hand-Object Interactions in Apraxia." *Neuropsychologia* 43 (2005): 917–29.

Byrne, Richard, and Andrew Whiten. "The Emergence of Metarepresentation in Human Ontogeny and Primate Phylogeny." Whiten 267–82.

———. *Machiavellian Intelligence: Social Expertise and the Evolution of Intellect in Monkeys, Apes, and Humans*. New York: Oxford University Press, 1988.

Calvert, Gemma A., Charles Spence, and Barry E. Stein, eds. *The Handbook of Multisensory Processes*. Cambridge, MA: MIT Press, 2004.

Calvo-Merino Beatriz, et al. "Action Observation and Acquired Motor Skills: An fMRI Study with Expert Dancers." *Cerebral Cortex* 15 (2005): 1243–49.

Carey, Susan, and Elizabeth Spelke. "Domain-Specific Knowledge and Conceptual Change." Hirschfeld and Gelman 169–200.

Carruthers, Peter. "Autism as Mind-Blindness: An Elaboration and Partial Defense." *Theories of Theories of Mind*. Ed. Peter Carruthers and Peter K. Smith. Cambridge University Press, 1996. 257–73.

Carruthers, Peter, and Andrew Chamberlain, eds. *Evolution and the Human Mind: Modularity, Language, and Meta-Cognition*. Cambridge: Cambridge University Press, 2000.

Cassidy, Jude. "Truth, Lies, and Intimacy: An Attachment Perspective." *Attachment and Human Development* 3.2 (2001): 121–55.

Cavell, Stanley. *The Claim of Reason: Wittgenstein, Skepticism, Morality, and Tragedy*. Oxford: Oxford University Press, 1979.

Cerf-Ducastel, Barbara, et al. "Interaction of Gustatory and Lingual Somatosensory Perceptions at the Cortical Level in the Human: A Functional Magnetic Resonance Imaging Study." *Chemical Senses* 26 (2001): 371–83.

Chalmers, David J. *The Conscious Mind: In Search of a Fundamental Theory*. New York: Oxford University Press, 1996.

Champagne, Audrey B., Leopold E. Klopfer, and John H. Anderson. "Factors Influencing the Learning of Classical Mechanics." *American Journal of Physics* 48 (1980): 1074–79.

Changeux, Jean-Pierre. *The Physiology of Truth: Neuroscience and Human Knowledge*. Cambridge, MA: Harvard University Press, 2002.

Chariton. *Chaereas and Callirhoe*. Trans. B. P. Reardon. *Collected Ancient Greek Novels*. Ed. B. P. Reardon. Berkeley: University of California Press, 1989.

Chomsky, Noam. *Aspects of the Theory of Syntax*. Cambridge, MA: MIT Press, 1965.

———. *Language and Mind*. New York: Harcourt Brace Jovanovich, 1972.

———. Rev. of *Verbal Behavior* by B. F. Skinner. *Language* 35 (1959): 26–58.

———. *Syntactic Structures*. The Hague: Mouton, 1957.

Clark, Andy. *Being There: Putting Brain, Body, and World Together Again*. Cambridge, MA: MIT Press, 1997.

———. "Embodied, Situated, and Distributed Cognition." *A Companion to Cognitive Science*. Ed. William Bechtel and George Graham. Oxford, UK: Blackwell, 1998. 506–17.

Clark, Andy, and David J. Chalmers. "The Extended Mind." *Analysis* 58 (1998): 7–19.

Clark, David L., Nashaat N. Boutros, and Mario F. Mendez. *The Brain and Behavior: An Introduction to Behavioral Neuroanatomy.* 2nd ed. Cambridge: Cambridge University Press, 2005.

Cleland, John. *Fanny Hill; or, Memoirs of a Woman of Pleasure.* 1748. New York: Penguin, 1985.

Clement, John. "A Conceptual Model Discussed by Galileo and Used Intuitively by Physics Students." Gentner and Stevens 325–39.

Code, Lorraine. *What Can She Know: Feminist Theory and the Construction of Knowledge.* Ithaca: Cornell University Press, 1991.

Coetzee, J. M. *Disgrace.* New York: Penguin Books, 1999.

Cohn, Dorrit. *Transparent Minds: Narrative Modes for Presenting Consciousness in Fiction.* Princeton: Princeton University Press, 1978.

Comrie, Bernard. *Language Universals and Linguistic Typology: Syntax and Morphology.* Chicago: University of Chicago Press, 1981.

Cooper, Arthur. Introduction. *Li Po and Tu Fu.* New York: Penguin, 1973. 15–101.

Cosmides, Leda, and John Tooby. "Origins of Domain Specificity: The Evolution of Functional Organization." Hirschfeld and Gelman 85–116.

———. "The Psychological Foundations of Culture." Barkow, Cosmides, and Tooby 19–130.

Crane, Mary Thomas. "'Fair is Foul': *Macbeth* and Binary Logic. Richardson and Spolsky 107–26.

———. "The Physics of *King Lear*: Cognition in a Void." *The Shakespearean International Yearbook 4: Shakespeare Studies Today.* Ed. Graham Bradshaw, Tom Bishop, and Mark Turner. Aldershot, UK: Ashgate, 2004. 3–23.

———. *Shakespeare's Brain: Reading with Cognitive Theory.* Princeton: Princeton University Press, 2001.

Croft, William. *Typology and Universals.* Cambridge: Cambridge University Press, 1990.

Croft, William, and D. Alan Cruse. *Cognitive Linguistics.* Cambridge: Cambridge University Press, 2004.

Culler, Jonathan. *On Deconstruction.* Ithaca: Cornell University Press, 1982.

———. *Structuralist Poetics: Structuralism, Linguistics, and the Study of Literature.* Ithaca: Cornell University Press, 1975.

Cytowic, Richard E. "Synesthesia: Phenomenology and Neuropsychology. A Review of Current Knowledge." *Psyche* 2 (1995): n.p.

Damasio, Antonio R. *Descartes' Error: Emotion, Reason, and the Human Brain.* New York: G. P. Putnam, 1994.

———. *The Feeling of What Happens: Body and Emotion in the Making of Consciousness.* New York: Harcourt Brace, 1999.

——. *Looking for Spinoza: Joy, Sorrow, and the Feeling Brain*. New York: Basic Books, 2003.

D'Andrade, Roy. *The Development of Cognitive Anthropology*. Cambridge: Cambridge University Press, 1995.

Darwin, Charles. *Darwin*. Ed. Philip Appleman. New York: Norton, 1970.

——. *The Expression of the Emotions in Man and Animals*. 1872. 3rd ed. Ed. Paul Ekman. New York: Oxford University Press, 1998.

——. *The Origin of Species by Means of Natural Selection*. 1859. Ed. J. W. Burrow. New York: Penguin Books, 1982.

Davidson, Donald. "On the Very Idea of a Conceptual Scheme." *Inquires into Truth and Interpretation*. Oxford, UK: Clarendon, 1984. 183–98.

Dawkins, Richard. *The Extended Phenotype: The Long Reach of the Gene*. Oxford: Oxford University Press, 1982.

——. *The Selfish Gene*. Oxford: Oxford University Press, 1976.

Dawood, N. J. Introduction. *Tales from the Thousand and One Nights*. Trans. N. J. Dawood. New York: Penguin, 1955. 7–12.

Day, Sean. "Synaesthesia and Synaesthetic Metaphors." *Psyche* 2 (1996): n.p.

Deacon, Terrence W. *The Symbolic Species: The Coevolution of Language and the Brain*. New York: Norton, 1997.

Decety, Jean, and Philip L. Jackson. "The Functional Architecture of Human Empathy." *Behavioral and Cognitive Neuroscience Reviews* 3 (2004): 71–100.

Decety, Jean, et al. "Central Activation of Autonomic Effectors during Mental Simulation of Motor Actions in Man." *Journal of Physiology* 462 (1993): 549–63.

Dee, John. "Mathematicall Preface." Euclid, *Euclides Elementes of Geometrie: The First VI Books*. London, 1650.

de Lange, Floris P., Peter Hagoort, and Ivan Toni. "Neural Topography and Content of Movement Representations." *Journal of Cognitive Neuroscience* 17 (2005): 97–112.

de Man, Paul. *Blindness and Insight: Essays in the Rhetoric of Contemporary Criticism*. New York: Oxford University Press, 1971.

Deng, Frances Mading. *The Dinka and Their Songs*. Oxford, UK: Clarendon, 1973.

Dennett Daniel. *Consciousness Explained*. Boston: Little Brown, 1991.

——. *Darwin's Dangerous Idea*. New York: Simon and Schuster, 1995.

——. *The Intentional Stance*. Cambridge, MA: MIT Press, 1987.

——. *Kinds of Minds: Towards an Understanding of Consciousness*. London: Weidenfeld and Nicholson, 1996.

——. "Quining Qualia." *The Nature of Consciousness: Philosophical Debates*.

Ed. Ned Block, Owen Flanagan, and Güven Güzeldere. Cambridge, MA: MIT Press, 1997. 619–42.

Derrida Jacques. *Of Grammatology.* Trans. Gayatri Chakravorty Spivak. Baltimore: Johns Hopkins University Press, 1976.

———. "Signature Event Context." *Glyph* 1 (1977): 172–97.

———. "Structure, Sign, and Play in the Discourse of the Human Sciences." *The Structuralist Controversy: The Languages of Criticism and the Sciences of Man.* Ed. Richard Macksey and Eugenio Donato. Baltimore: Johns Hopkins University Press, 1972. 247–72.

DiBattista, Maria. "Virginia Woolf and the Language of Authorship." Roe and Sellers 127–45.

Dick, Susan. "Literary Realism in *Mrs. Dalloway, To the Lighthouse, Orlando* and *The Waves.*" Roe and Sellers 50–71.

Dijksterhuis, E. J. *The Mechanization of the World Picture.* Oxford, UK: Clarendon, 1961.

Dissanayake, Ellen. *Art and Intimacy: How the Arts Began.* Seattle: University of Washington Press, 2000.

———. *Homo Aestheticus: Where Art Comes from and Why.* New York: Free Press, 1992.

———. "Komar and Melamid Discover Pleistocene Taste." *Philosophy and Literature* 22.2 (1998): 486–96.

———. *What Is Art For?* Seattle: University of Washington Press, 1988.

Dixon, Mike J., et al. "Five Plus Two Equals Yellow." *Nature* 406 (2000): 365.

Dixon, Robert M. W., and Martin Duwell, eds. *The Honey Ant Men's Love Song and Other Aboriginal Song Poems.* Melbourne: University of Queensland Press, 1990.

Djordjevic, Jelena, Robert J. Zatorre, and Marilyn Jones-Gotman. "Effects of Perceived and Imagined Odors on Taste Detection." *Chemical Senses* 29 (2004): 199–208.

———. "The Mind's Nose: Effects of Odor and Visual Imagery on Odor Detection." *Psychological Science* 15 (2004): 143–48.

Dolby, William, ed. and trans. *Eight Chinese Plays from the Thirteenth Century to the Present.* New York: Columbia University Press, 1978.

Doležel, Lubomír. *Heterocosmica: Fiction and Possible Worlds.* Baltimore: Johns Hopkins University Press, 1998.

———. "Mimesis and Possible Worlds." *Poetics Today* 9.3 (1988): 475–96.

Donald, Merlin. *A Mind So Rare: The Evolution of Human Consciousness.* New York: Norton, 2001.

Donne, John. "The First Anniversary." *The Poems of John Donne.* Ed. Herbert J. C. Grierson. 1912. Oxford: Oxford University Press, 1968. 231–45.

Dosse, François. *History of Structuralism*. 2 vols. Trans. Deborah Glassman. Minneapolis: University of Minnesota Press, 1997.

Drew, Paul, and John Heritage, eds. *Talk at Work*. Cambridge: Cambridge University Press, 1992.

Dryden, John. "Alexander's Feast." *The Major Works*. Ed. Keith Walker. New York: Oxford University Press, 1987. 545–50.

———. Dedicatory epistle to *Annus Mirabilis*. *The Major Works*. Ed. Keith Walker. New York: Oxford University Press, 1987. 23–30.

Duckitt, J. H. *The Social Psychology of Prejudice*. New York: Praeger, 1992.

Dunbar, Robin. "On the Origin of the Human Mind." Carruthers and Chamberlain 238–53.

Easterlin, Nancy. " 'Loving Ourselves Best of All': Ecocriticism and the Adapted Mind." *Mosaic* 37.3 (2004): 1–18.

———. "Making Knowledge: Bioepistemology and the Foundations of Literary Theory." *Mosaic* 32.1 (1999): 131–47.

———. "Psychoanalysis and 'The Discipline of Love.' " *Philosophy and Literature* 24.2 (2000): 261–79.

———. Rev. of *Practical Ecocriticism* by Glen A. Love and *The Truth of Ecology: Nature, Culture, and Literature in America* by Dana Phillips. *Interdisciplinary Literary Studies* 8.1 (2006): 118–29.

———. "Voyages in the Verbal Universe: The Role of Speculation in Darwinian Literary Criticism." *Interdisciplinary Literary Studies* 2.2 (2001): 59–73.

———. *What Is Literature For?* Baltimore: Johns Hopkins University Press, forthcoming.

Edelman, Gerald. *The Remembered Present: A Biological Theory of Consciousness*. New York: Basic Books, 1989.

Edwards, Derek. "Categories Are for Talking: On the Cognitive and Discursive Bases of Categorization." *Theory and Psychology* 1.4 (1991): 515–42.

———. *Discourse and Cognition*. London: Sage, 1997.

———. "Discursive Psychology." *Handbook of Language and Social Interaction*. Ed. Kristine L. Fitch and Robert E. Sanders. Mahwah, NJ: Lawrence Erlbaum, 2005. 257–73.

Edwards, Derek, and Jonathan Potter. *Discursive Psychology*. London: Sage, 1992.

Edwards, Jess. "Points Mean Prizes: How Early-Modern Mathematics Hedged Its Bets between Idealism and the World." *The Arts of Seventeenth-Century Science: Representations of the Natural World in European and North American Culture*. Ed. Claire Jowitt and Diane Watt. Aldershot, UK: Ashgate, 2002. 43–57.

Egudu, Romanus, and Donatus Nwoga. *Igbo Traditional Verse*. London: Heinemann, 1973.

Ekman, Paul. Afterword. Darwin, *Expression* 363–93.

———. Introduction. Darwin, *Expression* xi–xxvi.

Elfenbein, Andrew. "Cognitive Science and the History of Reading." *PMLA* 121.2 (2006): 484–500.

Emmott, Catherine. "Frames of Reference: Contextual Monitoring and the Interpretation of the Narrative Discourse." *Advances in Written Text Analysis*. Ed. Malcolm Coulthard. London: Routledge, 1994. 157–66.

Engell, James. *The Creative Imagination*. Cambridge, MA: Harvard University Press, 1981.

Engholm, Scott. "The Brain of Stephen Dedalus." Unpublished ms. University of Kentucky, Lexington, spring 2007.

Esrock, Ellen J. *The Reader's Eye: Visual Imaging as Reader Response*. Baltimore: Johns Hopkins University Press, 1994.

Evola, Vito. "Cognitive Semiotics and On-Line Reading of Religious Texts." *Journal of Consciousness, Literature and the Arts* 6.2 (2005): http://blackboard .lincoln.ac.uk/bbcswebdav/users/dmeyerdinkgrafe/index.htm.

Fanon, Frantz. *Black Skin, White Masks*. Trans. Constance Farrington. New York: Grove, 1963.

Feldman, Jerome A. *From Molecule to Metaphor: A Neural Theory of Language*. Cambridge, MA: MIT Press, 2006.

Fielding, Henry. *Tom Jones*. 1749. Ed. John Bender and Simon Stern. Oxford: Oxford University Press, 1996.

Firth, Raymond, with Mervyn McLean. *Tikopia Songs: Poetic and Musical Art of a Polynesian People of the Solomon Islands*. Cambridge: Cambridge University Press, 1990.

Fish, Stanley. *Doing What Comes Naturally: Change, Rhetoric, and the Practice of Theory in Literary and Legal Studies*. Durham: Duke University Press, 1989.

———. "How to Recognize a Poem When You See One." *American Criticism in the Poststructuralist Age*. Ed. Ira Konigsberg. Ann Arbor: University of Michigan, 1981. 102–15.

———. *Is There a Text in This Class? The Authority of Interpretive Communities*. Cambridge, MA: Harvard University Press, 1980.

Flor, Herta, et al. "Phantom-Limb Pain as a Perceptual Correlate of Cortical Reorganization Following Arm Amputation." *Nature* 375 (1995): 482–84.

Fludernik, Monika. *Towards a "Natural" Narratology*. London: Routledge, 1996.

Fodor, Jerry. *The Modularity of Mind: An Essay on Faculty Psychology*. Cambridge, MA: MIT Press, 1986.

Forster, E. M. *Aspects of the Novel*. New York: Harcourt, Brace, 1927.

Foucault, Michel. *The Order of Things: An Archaeology of the Human Sciences*. New York: Vintage, 1973.

Fox, Peter T., et al. "Supplementary Motor and Premotor Responses to Actual and Imagined Hand Movements with PET." *Neuroscience Abstracts* (1987): 1433.

Frawley, William. *Vygotsky and Cognitive Science: Language and the Unification of the Social and Computational Mind*. Cambridge, MA: Harvard University Press, 1997.

Freccero, John. "Donne's 'Valediction: Forbidding Mourning.'" *ELH* 30 (1963): 335–76.

Freeman, Anthony. *Consciousness: A Guide to the Debates*. Santa Barbara: ABC-CLIO, 2003.

Freeman, Donald. "'According to My Bond': *King Lear* and Re-Cognition." *Language and Literature* 2 (1993): 1–18.

———. "Catch[ing] the Nearest Way: *Macbeth* and Cognitive Metaphor." *Journal of Pragmatics* 24 (1995): 689–708.

———. "'The Rack Dislimns': Schemata and Metaphorical Pattern in *Antony and Cleopatra*." *Poetics Today* 20.3 (1999): 443–60.

Freeman, Walter J. *Societies of Brains: A Study in the Neuroscience of Love and Hate*. Hillsdale, NJ: Lawrence Erlbaum, 1995.

Fromm, Harold. *The Nature of Being Human: From Environmentalism to Consciousness*. Baltimore: Johns Hopkins University Press, 2009.

Frye, Northrop. *Anatomy of Criticism: Four Essays*. Princeton: Princeton University Press, 1957.

Galati, Dario, Klaus R. Scherer, and Pio E. Ricci-Bitti. "Voluntary Facial Expression of Emotion: Comparing Congenitally Blind to Normal Sighted Encoders." *Journal of Personality and Social Psychology* 73 (1997): 1363–79.

Gallagher, Catherine, and Stephen Greenblatt. *Practicing New Historicism*. Chicago: University of Chicago Press, 2000.

Gallese, Vittorio, and Thomas Metzinger. "Motor Ontology: The Representational Reality of Goals, Actions, and Selves." *Philosophical Psychology* 16.3 (2003): 365–88.

Gardner, Howard. *The Mind's New Science: A History of the Cognitive Revolution*. New York: Basic Books, 1985.

Garfinkel, Harold. *Studies in Ethnomethodology*. Englewood Cliffs, NJ: Prentice-Hall, 1967.

Garman, Michael. *Psycholinguistics*. Cambridge: Cambridge University Press, 1990.

Gathercole, Susan, and Alan Baddeley. *Working Memory and Language*. Hillsdale, NJ: Lawrence Erlbaum, 1993.

Gay, Penny. *Jane Austen and the Theatre*. Cambridge: Cambridge University Press, 2002.

Gaylin, Ann. *Eavesdropping in the Novel from Austen to Proust*. Cambridge: Cambridge University Press, 2002.

Geertz, Clifford. *The Interpretation of Cultures: Selected Essays*. London: Fontana, 1993.

Gentner, Dedre, and Donald R. Gentner. "Flowing Waters or Teeming Crowds: Mental Models of Electricity." Gentner and Stevens 99–129.

Gentner, Dedre, and Michael Jeziorski, "The Shift from Metaphor to Analogy in Western Science." *Metaphor and Thought*. 2nd ed. Ed. Andrew Ortony. Cambridge: Cambridge University Press, 1993. 447–80.

Gentner, Dedre, and Albert L. Stevens, eds. *Mental Models*. Hillsdale, NJ: Lawrence Erlbaum, 1983.

Gibson, James J. *The Ecological Approach to Visual Perception*. Boston: Houghton Mifflin, 1979.

———. "The Theory of Affordances." *Perceiving, Acting, and Knowing: Toward an Ecological Psychology*. Ed. Robert Shaw and John D. Bransford. Hillsdale, NJ: Lawrence Erlbaum, 1977. 67–88.

Glotfelty, Cheryll, and Harold Fromm, eds. *The Ecocriticism Reader: Landmarks in Literary Ecology*. Athens: University of Georgia Press, 1996.

Gnoli, Raniero, ed. *The Aesthetic Experience according to Abhinavagupta*. Varanasi: Chowkhamba Sanskrit Series Office, 1968.

Goffman, Erving. *Frame Analysis: An Essay on the Organization of Experience*. New York: Harper, 1974.

Goldman, Alvin I. *Simulating Minds: The Philosophy, Psychology, and Neuroscience of Mindreading*. New York: Oxford University Press, 2006.

Gomez, Juan C. "Visual Behavior as a Window for Reading the Mind of Others in Primates." Whiten 195–208.

Gopnik, Alison, Andrew N. Meltzoff, and Patricia K. Kuhl. *The Scientist in the Crib: Minds, Brains, and How Children Learn*. New York: Morrow, 1999.

Grafton, Scott T., et al. "Localization of Grasp Representation in Humans by PET 2: Observation Compared with Imagination." *Experimental Brain Research* 112 (1996): 103–11.

Gramsci, Antonio. "Hegemony, Intellectuals and the State." *Cultural Theory and Popular Culture: A Reader*. 2nd ed. Ed. John Storey. London: Prentice Hall, 1998. 210–16.

———. *Selections from Prison Notebooks*. Ed. and trans. Quintin Hoare and Geoffrey Nowell Smith. London: Lawrence and Wishart, 1971.

Grant, Ken W., Virginie van Wassenhove, and David Poeppel. "Detection of Auditory (Cross-Spectral) and Auditory-Visual (Cross-Modal) Synchrony." *Speech Communication* 44 (2004): 43–53.

Greenblatt, Stephen. *Shakespearean Negotiations: The Circulation of Social Energy in Renaissance England.* Berkeley: University of California Press, 1988.

Greimas, A. J., and Jacques Fontanille. *The Semiotics of Passions: From States of Affairs to States of Feeling.* Trans. Paul Perron and Frank Collins. Minneapolis: University of Minnesota Press, 1993.

Grosz, Elizabeth. "Feminist Futures?" *Tulsa Studies in Women's Literature* 21.1 (2002): 13–20.

———. *Time Travels: Feminism, Nature, Power.* Durham: Duke University Press, 2005.

Hagendoorn, Ivar G. "Some Speculative Hypotheses about the Nature and Perception of Dance and Choreography." *Journal of Consciousness Studies* 11.3/4 (2005): 79–110.

Hall, Marcia. Introduction. *The Cambridge Companion to Raphael.* Ed. Marcia Hall. Cambridge: Cambridge University Press, 2006.

Halpern, Andrea R. "Mental Scanning in Auditory Imagery for Songs." *Journal of Experimental Psychology: Learning, Memory, and Cognition* 14 (1988): 434–43.

Halpern, Andrea R., and Robert J. Zatorre. "When That Tune Runs through Your Head: A PET Investigation of Auditory Imagery for Familiar Melodies." *Cerebral Cortex* 9 (1999): 697–704.

Halpern, Andrea R., et al. "Behavioral and Neural Correlates of Perceived and Imagined Musical Timbre." *Neuropsychologia* 42 (2004): 1281–92.

Hammerstein, Elieser G. "Heimat-Attachment and Return to the Native Place: Experiences with the Behavioral Biology of Migrants." *Human Ethology Bulletin* (June 1997): 3–5.

Harré, Rom. "The Discursive Turn in Social Psychology." *The Handbook of Discourse Analysis.* Ed. Deborah Schiffrin, Deborah Tannen, and Heidi E. Hamilton. Oxford, UK: Blackwell, 2001. 688–706.

———. "Introduction: The Second Cognitive Revolution." *American Behavorial Scientist* 36 (1992): 5–7.

Harré, Rom, and Grant Gillett. *The Discursive Mind.* London: Sage, 1994.

Harré, Rom, and Luk Langenhove, eds. *Positioning Theory: Moral Contexts of Intentional Action.* Oxford, UK: Blackwell, 1999.

Harré, Rom, and Peter Stearns, eds. *Discursive Psychology in Practice.* Thousand Oaks, CA: Sage, 1995.

Harris, Paul L. *The Work of Imagination.* Oxford, UK: Blackwell, 2001.

Harrison, Allan G., and David F. Treagust. "Conceptual Change Using Multiple

Interpretive Perspectives: Two Case Studies in Secondary School Chemistry." *Instructional Science* 29 (2001): 45–85.

Hart, F. Elizabeth. "Embodied Literature: A Cognitive-Poststructuralist Approach to Genre." Richardson and Spolsky 85–105.

———. "The Epistemology of Cognitive Literary Studies." *Philosophy and Literature* 25.2 (2002): 314–34.

Hart, George L. *The Poem of Ancient Tamil: Their Milieu and Their Sanskrit Counterparts*. Berkeley: University of California Press, 1975.

Hassin, Ran R., James S. Uleman, and John R. Bargh, eds. *The New Unconscious*. New York: Oxford University Press, 2005.

Hauser, Arnold. *The Social History of Art*. Vol. 1. Trans. Stanley Godman. New York: Vintage, 1957.

Hayles, N. Katherine. "Constrained Constructivism: Locating Scientific Inquiry in the Theater of Representation." *Realism and Representation: Essays on the Problem of Realism in Relation to Science, Literature, and Culture*. Ed. George Levine. Madison: University of Wisconsin Press, 1993. 27–43.

———. "Desiring Agency: Limiting Metaphors and Enabling Constraints in Dawkins and Deleuze/Guattari." *SubStance* 30.1/2 (2001): 144–59.

Haywood, Eliza. *Love in Excess*. 1719–20. Ed. David Oakleaf. Toronto: Broadview, 2000.

Hebdige, Dick. *Subculture: The Meaning of Style*. London: Routledge, 1979.

Heider, Fritz, and Marianne Simmel. "An Experimental Study of Apparent Behavior." *American Journal of Psychology* 57 (1944): 243–59.

Hemingway, Ernest. *A Farewell to Arms*. New York: Scribner's, 1929.

———. "Hills Like White Elephants." 1927. *The Complete Short Stories of Ernest Hemingway*. New York: Scribner's, 1987. 211–14.

Herman, David. *Basic Elements of Narrative*. Malden, MA: Wiley-Blackwell, 2009.

———. "Cognitive Approaches to Narrative Analysis." *Cognitive Poetics: Goals, Gains, and Gaps*. Ed. Geert Brône and Jeroen Vandaele. Berlin: Walter de Gruyter, 2009. 79–118.

———. "Cognitive Narratology." *Living Handbook of Narratology*. Ed. John Pier, Wolf Schmid, Jörg Schönert, and Peter Hühn. Berlin: Walter de Gruyter, 2009. 30–43.

———. "Dialogue in a Discourse Context: Scenes of Talk in Fictional Narrative." *Narrative Inquiry* 16.1 (2006): 75–84.

———. "Genette Meets Vygotsky: Narrative Embedding and Distributed Intelligence." *Language and Literature* 15.4 (2006): 375–98.

———. "Histories of Narrative Theory (I): A Genealogy of Early Developments."

The Blackwell Companion to Narrative Theory. Ed. James Phelan and Peter J. Rabinowitz. Malden, MA: Blackwell, 2005. 19–35.

——. Introduction. *Narratologies: New Perspectives on Narrative Analysis.* Columbus: Ohio State University Press, 1999. 1–30.

——. "Multimodal Storytelling and Identity Construction in Graphic Narratives." *Telling Stories: Building Bridges among Language, Narrative, Identity, Interaction, Society and Culture.* Ed. Anna de Fina and Deborah Schiffrin. Georgetown: Georgetown University Press, forthcoming.

——. "Narrative: Cognitive Approaches." *Encyclopedia of Language and Linguistics.* 2nd ed. Vol. 8. Ed. Keith Brown et al. Amsterdam: Elsevier, 2006. 452–59.

——. "Narrative as Cognitive Instrument." Herman, Jahn, and Ryan 349–50.

——. "Quantitative Methods in Narratology: A Corpus-Based Study of Motion Events in Stories." *Narratology beyond Literary Criticism.* Ed. Jan Christoph Meister. Berlin: Walter de Gruyter, 2005. 125–49.

——. "Regrounding Narrative: The Study of Narratively Organized Systems for Thinking." *What Is Narratology? Questions and Answers regarding the Status of a Theory.* Ed. Tom Kindt and Hans-Harald Müller. Berlin: Walter de Gruyter, 2003. 303–29.

——. "Scripts, Sequences, and Stories: Elements of a Postclassical Narratology." *PMLA* 112 (1997): 1046–59.

——. "Stories as a Tool for Thinking." *Narrative Theory and the Cognitive Sciences.* Ed. David Herman. Stanford, CA: Publications of the Center for the Study of Language and Information, 2003. 163–92.

——. "Toward a Transmedial Narratology." *Narrative across Media: The Languages of Storytelling.* Ed. Marie-Laure Ryan. 47–75.

——, ed. *Narrative Theory and the Cognitive Sciences.* Stanford, CA: Publications of the Center for the Study of Language and Information Publications, 2003.

Herman, David, Manfred Jahn, and Marie-Laure Ryan, eds. *Routledge Encyclopedia of Narrative Theory.* London: Routledge, 2005.

Hernadi, Paul. "Literature and Evolution." *SubStance* 30.1/2 (2001): 55–71.

Higgins, John. *Raymond Williams: Literature, Marxism, and Cultural Materialism.* New York: Routledge, 1999.

Hirschfeld, Lawrence, and Susan Gelman, eds. *Mapping the Mind: Domain Specificity in Cognition and Culture.* New York: Cambridge University Press, 1994.

Hogan, Patrick Colm. "Beauty, Politics, and Cultural Otherness: The Bias of Literary Difference." *Literary India: Comparative Studies in Aesthetics, Colonial-*

ism, and Culture. Ed. Patrick Colm Hogan and Lalita Pandit. Albany: State University of New York Press, 1995. 3–43.

———. *Cognitive Science, Literature, and the Arts: A Guide for Humanists*. New York: Routledge, 2003.

———. *Empire and Poetic Voice: Cognitive and Cultural Studies*. Albany: State University of New York Press, 2004.

———. "Literary Universals." *Poetics Today* 18.2 (1997): 223–49.

———. *The Mind and Its Stories: Narrative Universals and Human Emotion*. Cambridge: Cambridge University Press, 2003.

———. "Of Literary Universals: Ninety-Five Theses." *Philosophy and Literature* 32.1 (2008): 145–60.

———. "The Possibility of Aesthetics." *British Journal of Aesthetics* 34.4 (1994): 337–49.

———. "Shakespeare, Eastern Theatre, and Literary Universals: Drama in the Context of Cognitive Science." *Shakespeare East and West*. Ed. Minoru Fujita. Richmond, UK: Japan Library, 1996. 164–80; 189–90.

———. "Toward a Cognitive Science of Poetics: Ānandavardhana, Abhinavagupta, and the Theory of Literature." *College Literature* 23.1 (1996): 164–78.

———. *Understanding Nationalism: On Narrative, Neuroscience, and Identity*. Columbus: Ohio State University Press, 2009.

Hogan, Patrick Colm, and Lalita Pandit. Introduction. *Cognitive Shakespeare: Criticism and Theory in the Age of Neuroscience*. Ed. Patrick Colm Hogan and Lalita Pandit. Spec. issue of *College Literature* 33.1 (2006): 1–13.

Holcroft, Thomas. *The Adventures of Hugh Trevor*. 1797. Ed. Seamus Deane. Oxford University Press, 1978.

Holland, John, et al. *Induction: Processes of Inference, Learning, and Discovery*. Cambridge, MA: MIT Press, 1986.

Holland, Norman N. "Where Is a Text? A Neurological View." *New Literary History* 33.1 (2002): 21–38.

———. "The Willing Suspension of Disbelief: A Neuro-Psychoanalytic View." *PsyArt: An Online Journal for the Psychological Study of the Arts* (22 January 2003). http://clas.ufl.edu/ipsa/journal/2003_holland06.shtml. Accessed 16 February 2006.

Hopkins, Gerard Manley. "Pied Beauty." *The Major Works*. Ed. Catherine Phillips. New York: Oxford University Press, 2002. 132–33.

———. "The Woodlark." *The Major Works*. Ed. Catherine Phillips. New York: Oxford University Press, 2002. 122–23.

Horace. *Satires, Epistles, Ars Poetica*. Cambridge, MA: Harvard University Press, 1991.

Howarth, William. "Some Principles of Ecocriticism." Glotfelty and Fromm 69–87.

Hubbard, Edward M., and V. S. Ramachandran. "Refining the Experimental Lever: A Reply to Shanon and Pribram." *Journal of Consciousness Studies* 10.3 (2003): 77–84.

Hughes Claire, and Robert Plomin. "Individual Differences in Early Understanding of Mind: Genes, Non-Shared Environment and Modularity." Carruthers and Chamberlain 47–61.

Hume, David. *Works*. Vol. 3. London, 1777.

Hume, Robert D. *Reconstructing Contexts: The Aims and Principles of Archaeo-Historicism*. Oxford: Oxford University Press, 1999.

Hutchins, Edwin. *Cognition in the Wild*. Cambridge, MA: MIT Press, 1995.

———. "How a Cockpit Remembers Its Speeds." *Cognitive Science* 19 (1995): 265–88.

Ingarden, Roman. *The Literary Work of Art: An Investigation on the Borderlines of Ontology, Logic, and Theory of Literature*. Trans. George C. Grabowicz. Evanston: Northwestern University Press, 1973.

Isaac, Anne R., David F. Marks, and David G. Russell. "An Instrument for Assessing Imagery for Movement: The Vividness of Movement Imagery Questionnaire." *Journal of Mental Imagery* 10 (1986): 23–30.

Iser, Wolfgang. *The Act of Reading*. London: Routledge, 1978.

Jackendoff, Ray. *Consciousness and the Computational Mind*. Cambridge, MA: MIT Press, 1987.

———. *Semantics and Cognition*. Cambridge, MA: MIT Press, 1983.

Jackson, Frank. "Epiphenomenal Qualia." *Philosophical Quarterly* 32 (1982): 127–36.

Jackson, Tony. "Issues and Problems in the Blending of the Cognitive Science, Evolutionary Psychology, and Literary Study." *Poetics Today* 23.1 (2002): 161–79.

Jahn, Manfred. "Cognitive Narratology." Herman, Jahn, and Ryan 67–71.

James, Henry. *The Portrait of a Lady*. 1880–81. New York: Penguin, 2003.

Johnson, Barbara. "The Frame of Reference: Poe, Lacan, Derrida." Muller and Richardson. Baltimore: Johns Hopkins University Press, 1988. 213–51.

Johnson, Mark. *The Body in the Mind: The Bodily Basis of Meaning, Imagination, and Reason*. Chicago: University of Chicago Press, 1987.

Johnson, Samuel. "Life of Cowley." *Criticism: The Major Texts*. Ed. Walter Bate. 1952. New York: Harcourt, 1970. 217–18.

Johnson, Steven. *Everything Bad Is Good for You: How Today's Popular Culture Is Actually Making Us Smarter*. New York: Riverhead Books, 2005.

Johnson, Susan, Virginia Slaughter, and Susan Carey. "Whose Gaze Will Infants

Follow? Features That Elicit Gaze-Following in 12-Month-Olds." *Developmental Science* 1.2 (1998): 233–38.

Johnson-Laird, Philip N. *The Computer and the Mind: An Introduction to Cognitive Science.* Cambridge, MA: Harvard University Press, 1988.

Johnston, Kenneth G. *The Tip of the Iceberg: Hemingway and the Short Story.* Greenwood, FL: Penkevill, 1987.

Kable, Joseph W., et al. "Conceptual Representations of Action in the Lateral Temporal Cortex." *Journal of Cognitive Neuroscience* 17 (2005): 1855–70.

Kailasapathy, K. *Tamil Heroic Poetry.* Oxford, UK: Clarendon, 1968.

Kalidasa. *The Abhijnanasakuntalam of Kalidasa.* Ed. M. R. Kale. Delhi: Motilal Banarsidass, 1969.

Kaplan, Stephen. "Environmental Preference in a Knowledge-Seeking, Knowledge-Using Organism." Barkow, Cosmides, and Tooby 581–98.

Kaufmann, Walter. *Tragedy and Philosophy.* New York: Doubleday, 1968.

Kazin, Alfred, ed. *The Portable Blake.* New York: Viking, 1968.

Keats, John. "The Eve of St. Agnes." *Complete Poems.* Ed. Jack Stillinger. Cambridge, MA: Harvard University Press, 1982. 229–39.

———. *Isabella. Complete Poems.* Ed. Jack Stillinger. Cambridge, MA: Harvard University Press, 1982. 184–98.

———. Ode to a Nightingale." *Complete Poems.* Ed. Jack Stillinger. Cambridge, MA: Harvard University Press, 1982. 279–84.

Keen, Suzanne. *Empathy and the Novel.* Oxford: Oxford University Press, 2007.

———. "Strategic Empathizing: Techniques of Bounded, Ambassadorial, and Broadcast Narrative Empathy." *Deutsche Vierteljahrs Schrift* 82.3 (2008): 477–93.

Keene, Donald, ed. and trans. *Anthology of Japanese Literature to the Nineteenth Century.* New York: Penguin, 1968.

———, ed. *Lady Han* and *The Reed Cutter. Twenty Plays of the Nō Theatre.* New York: Columbia University Press, 1970. 129–45; 147–64.

———, ed. *Love Suicides in the Women's Temple. Major Plays of Chikamatsu.* New York: Columbia University Press, 1990. 131–60.

Kevles, Bettyann Holzmann. *Naked to the Bone: Medical Imaging in the Twentieth Century.* New Brunswick: Rutgers University Press, 1997.

Kiparsky, Paul. "On Theory and Interpretation." *The Linguistics of Writing: Arguments between Language and Literature.* Ed. Nigel Fabb et al. New York: Methuen, 1987. 185–98.

———. "The Role of Linguistics in a Theory of Poetry." *Essays in Modern Stylistics.* Ed. Donald C. Freeman. London: Methuen, 1981. 9–23.

Kirk, Robert. "Zombies." *The Stanford Encyclopedia of Philosophy (Fall 2003*

Edition). Ed. Edward N. Zalta. http://plato.stanford.edu/archives/fall2003/ entries/zombies.

Klein, Richard. G. *The Human Career: Human Biological and Cultural Origins.* 2nd ed. Chicago: University of Chicago Press, 1999.

Klemenz-Belgardt, Edith. "American Research on Response to Literature: The Empirical Studies." *Poetics* 10 (1981): 357–80.

Knapp, Steven, and Walter Benn Michaels. "Against Theory." *Critical Inquiry* 8 (1982): 723–42.

———. "Against Theory 2: Hermeneutics and Deconstruction." *Critical Inquiry* 12 (1987): 49–68.

Knobe, Joshua, and Jesse Prinz. "Intuitions about Consciousness: Experimental Studies." *Phenomenology and the Cognitive Sciences* 7.1 (2008): 67–83.

Kosslyn, Stephen. *Image and Brain: The Resolution of the Imagery Debate.* Cambridge, MA: MIT Press, 1994.

Kosslyn, Stephen, et al. "Imagining Rotation by Endogenous versus Exogenous Forces: Distinct Neural Mechanisms." *NeuroReport* 12 (2001): 2519–25.

Kotchemidova, Christina. "From Good Cheer to 'Drive-By Smiling': A Social History of Cheerfulness." *Journal of Social History* 39.1 (2005): 5–37.

Kövecses, Zoltán. "Metaphor, Universals of." *The Cambridge Encyclopedia of the Language Sciences.* Cambridge: Cambridge University Press, forthcoming.

Koyré, Alexander. *From the Closed World to the Infinite Universe.* Baltimore: Johns Hopkins University Press, 1958.

Kraemer, David J. M., et al. "Sound of Silence Activates Auditory Cortex." *Nature* 434 (2005): 158.

Kripke, Saul. *Naming and Necessity.* Oxford, UK: Blackwell, 1980.

Kuhn, Thomas. "Robert Boyle and Structural Chemistry." *The Scientific Enterprise in Early Modern Europe.* Ed. Peter Dear. Chicago: University of Chicago Press, 1997. 212–36

———. *The Structure of Scientific Revolutions.* 3rd ed. Chicago: University of Chicago Press, 1996.

Kunene, Daniel P. *Heroic Poetry of the Basotho.* Oxford, UK: Clarendon, 1971.

Lakatos, Imre. "Falsification and the Methodology of Scientific Research Programmes." *Criticism and the Growth of Knowledge.* Ed. Imre Lakatos and Alan Musgrave. Cambridge: Cambridge University Press, 1970. 91–195.

Lakoff, George. *Women, Fire, and Dangerous Things: What Categories Reveal About the Mind.* Chicago: University of Chicago Press, 1987.

Lakoff, George, and Mark Johnson. *Metaphors We Live By.* Chicago: University of Chicago Press, 1980.

———. *Philosophy in the Flesh: The Embodied Mind and its Challenge to Western Thought.* New York: Basic Books, 1999.

Lal, P., ed. and trans. *Toy Cart* and *Ratnavali*. *Great Sanskrit Plays, in New English Transcreations*. New York: New Directions, 1964. 339–76.

Langacker, Ronald W. *Foundations of Cognitive Grammar*. Vol. 1: *Theoretical Prerequisites*. Stanford: Stanford University Press, 1987.

Latour, Bruno. *Pandora's Hope: Essays on the Reality of Science Studies*. Cambridge, MA: Harvard University Press, 1999.

Lave, Jean, and Etienne Wenger. *Situated Learning: Legitimate Peripheral Practice*. Cambridge: Cambridge University Press, 1991.

Lawler, Andrew. "Tortoise Pace for the Evolution of Chinese Writing?" *Science* 300.5620 (2003): 723.

Lears, T. J. Jackson. "The Concept of Cultural Hegemony." *American Historical Review* 90 (June 1985): 567–93.

Lee, Hermione. *Virginia Woolf*. New York: Knopf, 1997.

———. "Virginia Woolf's Essays." Roe and Sellers 91–108.

Lee, Penny. " 'Feelings of the Mind' in Talk about Thinking in English." *Cognitive Linguistics* 14.2/3 (2003): 221–49.

Lehmann, Sandra, and Micah M. Murray. "The Role of Multisensory Memories in Unisensory Object Discrimination." *Cognitive Brain Research* 24 (2005): 326–34.

Leitch, Vincent B., and Mitchell R. Lewis. "Cultural Studies." *The Johns Hopkins Guide to Literary Theory and Criticism*. Ed. Michael Groden, Martin Kreiswirth, and Imre Szeman. Baltimore: Johns Hopkins University Press, 2005.

Leslie, Alan. "ToMM, ToBY, and Agency: Core Architecture and Domain Specificity." Hirschfeld and Gelman 119–48.

Levin, Janet. "Qualia." *The MIT Encyclopedia of the Cognitive Sciences*. Ed. Robert A. Wilson and Frank C. Keil. Cambridge, MA: MIT Press, 1999. 693–94.

Levine, Joseph. "Materialism and Qualia: The Explanatory Gap." *Pacific Philosophical Quarterly* 64.4 (1983): 354–61.

Levinson, Stephen. "Pragmatics, Universals in." *The Cambridge Encyclopedia of the Language Sciences*. Ed. Patrick Colm Hogan. Cambridge: Cambridge University Press, forthcoming.

Levi-Strauss, Claude. *Tristes Tropiques*. Paris: Librarie Plon, 1955.

Lewis, David. *Counterfactuals*. Cambridge, MA: Harvard University Press, 1973.

Liu, Hsieh. *The Literary Mind and the Carving of Dragons*. Trans. Vincent Yuchung Shih. New York: Columbia University Press, 1959.

Liu, Jung-en, ed. and trans. *Chien-nu* and *Chang*. *Six Yuan Plays*. New York: Penguin, 1972. 83–113; 159–87.

Lord, Albert. *The Singer of Tales*. Cambridge, MA: Harvard University Press, 1960.

Love, Glen A. *Practical Ecocriticism: Literature, Biology, and the Environment.* Charlottesville: University of Virginia Press, 2003.

Macksey, Richard, and Eugenio Donato, eds. *The Structuralist Controversy: The Languages of Criticism and the Sciences of Man.* Baltimore: Johns Hopkins University Press, 1972.

Manes, Christopher. "Nature and Silence." Glotfelty and Fromm 15–29.

Mann, Thomas. *The Magic Mountain.* 1924. Trans. John E. Woods. New York: Knopf, 1995.

Mansfield, Katherine. *Katherine Mansfield's Selected Stories.* Ed. Vincent O'Sullivan. New York: Norton, 2006.

Marks, David F. "Visual Imagery Differences in the Recall of Pictures." *British Journal of Psychology* 64 (1973): 17–24.

Marshall, David. *The Figure of Theater: Shaftesbury, Defoe, Adam Smith, and George Eliot.* New York: Columbia University Press, 1986.

Martindale, Colin. "The Pleasures of Thought: A Theory of Cognitive Hedonics." *Journal of Mind and Behavior* 5 (1984): 49–80.

Martinovitch, Nicholas N. *The Turkish Theatre.* New York: Theatre Arts, 1933.

Marx, Karl. *Capital.* Vol. 1: *A Critical Analysis of Capitalist Production.* Ed. Frederick Engels. Trans. Samuel Moore and Edward Aveling. New York, 1867.

———. *Economic and Philosophic Manuscripts of 1844.* Ed. Dirk Struik. Trans. Martin Milligan. New York: International Publishers, 1964.

May, Theresa J. "Greening the Theater: Taking Ecocriticism from Page to Stage." *New Connections in Ecocriticism.* Ed. Ian Marshall. Spec. issue of *Interdisciplinary Literary Studies* 7.1 (2005): 84–103.

Mazel, David. "American Literary Environmentalism as Domestic Orientalism." Glotfelty and Fromm 137–46.

McCarthy, Geoffrey. "Physiological Studies of Face Processing in Humans." *The New Cognitive Neurosciences.* 2nd ed. Ed. Michael S. Gazzaniga. Cambridge, MA: MIT Press, 2000. 393–409.

McCloskey, Michael. "Naïve Theories of Motion." Gentner and Stevens 299–324.

McConachie, Bruce. *American Theater in the Culture of the Cold War: Producing and Contesting Containment, 1947–1962.* Iowa City: University of Iowa Press, 2003.

———. *Engaging Audiences: A Cognitive Approach to Spectating in the Theatre.* Houndmills, UK: Palgrave, 2008.

———. "Using the Concept of Cultural Hegemony to Write Theatre History." *Interpreting the Theatrical Past: Essays in the Historiography of Performance.* Ed. Thomas Postlewait and Bruce A. McConachie. Iowa City: University of Iowa Press, 1989. 37–58.

McMillan, Dorothy. " 'Dr.' Baillie." *1798: The Year of the Lyrical Ballads*. Ed. Richard Cronin. Houndmills, UK: Macmillan, 1998. 68–92.

Menand, Louis. "Dangers Within and Without." *Profession 2005*. New York: Modern Language Association, 2005. 10–17.

———. *The Metaphysical Club: A Story of Ideas in America*. New York: Farrar, Straus and Giroux, 2001.

Merleau-Ponty, Maurice. *Phenomenology of Perception*. Trans. Colin Smith. London: Routledge and Kegan Paul, 1962.

Mervis, Carolyn B., and Eleanor Rosch. "Categorization of Natural Objects." *Annual Review of Psychology* 32 (1981): 89–115.

Miall, David. *Literary Reading: Empirical and Theoretical Studies*. New York: Peter Lang, 2006.

Miller, Barbara Stoler. Introduction. *Love Song of the Dark Lord: Jayadeva's "Gitagovinda."* New York: Columbia University Press, 1977. 3–66.

Miller, George, and Philip N. Johnson-Laird. *Language and Perception*. Cambridge, MA: Harvard University Press, 1976.

Miller, J. Hillis. "The Triumph of Theory, the Resistance to Reading, and the Question of the Material Base." *PMLA* 102.3 (1987): 281–91.

Mills, Linda. "Narrative Therapy." Herman, Jahn, and Ryan 375–76.

Milner, Andrew. *Re-Imagining Cultural Studies: The Promise of Cultural Materialism*. London: Sage, 2002.

Mitchell, Jason P. "The False Dichotomy between Simulation and Theory-Theory: The Argument's Error." *Trends in Cognitive Science* 9 (2005): 363–64.

Mithen, Steven. *After the Ice: A Global Human History*. Cambridge, MA: Harvard University Press, 2003.

Modell, Arnold H. *Imagination and the Meaningful Brain*. Cambridge, MA: MIT Press, 2003.

Moreh, Shmuel. *Live Theatre and Dramatic Literature in the Medieval Arab World*. New York: New York University Press, 1992.

Moschovakis, Nicholas R. "Topicality and Conceptual Blending: *Titus Andronicus* and the Case of William Hacket." *College Literature* 33.1 (2006): 127–50.

Mullan, John. *Sentiment and Sociability: The Language of Feeling in the Eighteenth Century*. Oxford, UK: Clarendon Press, 1988.

Muller, John P., and William J. Richardson, eds. *The Purloined Poe: Lacan, Derrida, and Psychoanalytic Reading*. Baltimore: Johns Hopkins University Press, 1988.

Munro, Alice. "Wild Swans." *The Beggar Maid: Stories of Flo and Rose*. New York: Vintage, 1991. 57–67.

Murray, Micah M., et al. "Rapid Discrimination of Visual and Multisensory

Memories Revealed by Electrical Neuroimaging." *NeuroImage* 21 (2004): 125–35.

Murray, W. A. "Donne's Gold-Leaf and His Compasses." *Modern Language Notes* 73.5 (1958): 329–30.

Nagel, Thomas. "What Is It Like to Be a Bat?" *Philosophical Review* 83.4 (1974): 435–50.

Nehamas, Alexander. *The Art of Living: Socratic Reflections from Plato to Foucault.* Sather Classical Lectures 61. Berkeley: University of California Press, 1998.

Nelson, Cary. "Always Already Cultural Studies: Two Conferences and a Manifesto." *Journal of the Midwest Modern Language Association* 24.1 (1991): 24–38.

Nersessian, Nancy. "Conceptual Change in Science and Science Education." *Synthese* 80 (1989): 163–83.

——. "Kuhn, Conceptual Change, and Cognitive Science." *Thomas Kuhn.* Ed. Thomas Nickles. Cambridge: Cambridge University Press, 2003. 178–211.

Ngũgĩ wa Thiong'o. *Moving the Centre: The Struggle for Cultural Freedoms.* London: James Currey, 1993.

Nicholson, Marjorie Hope. *The Breaking of the Circle: Studies in the Effect of the "New Science" upon Seventeenth-Century Poetry.* Rev. ed. New York: Columbia, 1960.

Nietzsche, Friedrich. *On the Advantage and Disadvantage of History for Life.* 1874. Trans. Peter Preuss. Indianapolis: Hackett, 1980.

Nizami, Ganjavi. *Leila und Madschnun.* Trans. Rudolph Gelpke. Zurich: Manesse, 1963.

Nussbaum, Martha C. *Upheavals of Thought: The Intelligence of Emotions.* Cambridge: Cambridge University Press, 2001.

Oatley, Keith. *Best Laid Schemes: The Psychology of Emotions.* Cambridge: Cambridge University Press and Paris: Editions de la Maison des Sciences de l'Homme, 1992.

——. "Simulation of Substance and Shadow: Inner Emotions and Outer Behavior in Shakespeare's Psychology of Character." *College Literature* 33.1 (2006): 15–33.

Oberhuber, Konrad. *A Masterpiece Close-up: The "Transfiguration" by Raphael.* Cambridge, MA: Fogg Art Museum, n.d.

Okada, Hitoshi, Kazuo Matsuoka, and Takeo Hatakeyama. "Individual Differences in the Range of Sensory Modalities Experienced in Dreams." *Dreaming* 15 (2005): 106–15.

Ong, Walter J. *Orality and Literacy: The Technologizing of the World.* New York: Methuen, 1982.

Opland, Jeff. *Xhosa Oral Poetry: Aspects of Black South African Tradition*. Cambridge: Cambridge University Press, 1983.

Orians, Gordon H., and Judith H. Heergwagen. "Evolved Responses to Landscapes." Barkow, Cosmides, and Tooby 555–79.

Origgi, Gloria, and Dan Sperber. "Evolution, Communication and the Proper Function of Language." Carruthers and Chamberlain 140–69.

Oyama, Susan. *Evolution's Eye: A System Views of the Biology-Culture Divide*. Durham: Duke University Press, 2000.

Page, Ruth. Introduction. *New Perspectives on Narrative and Multimodality*. New York: Routledge, 2009. 1–13.

Palmer, Alan. *Fictional Minds*. Lincoln: University of Nebraska Press, 2004.

———. "The Middlemarch Mind: Intermental Thought in the Novel." *Style* 39.4 (2006): 427–39.

———. *Social Minds in the Novel*. Columbus: Ohio State University Press, 2010.

Pandit, Lalita. "Caste, Race, and Nation: History and Dialectic in Rabindranath Tagore's *Gora*." *Literary India: Comparative Studies in Aesthetics, Colonialism, and Culture*. Ed. Patrick Colm Hogan and Lalita Pandit. Albany: State University of New York Press, 1995. 207–33.

———. "Emotion, Perception, and *Anagnorisis* in *The Comedy of Errors*: A Cognitive Perspective." *College Literature* 33.1 (2006): 94–126.

Paster, Gail Kern. *The Body Embarrassed: Drama and the Disciplines of Shame in Early Modern England*. Ithaca: Cornell University Press, 1993.

Pavel, Thomas G. *Fictional Worlds*. Cambridge, MA: Harvard University Press, 1986.

Penfield, Wilder, and Herbert Jaspers. *Epilepsy and the Functional Anatomy of the Human Brain*. Boston: Little, Brown, 1954.

Perelman, Chaim, and Lucie Olbrechts-Tyteca. *The New Rhetoric: A Treatise on Argumentation*. Notre Dame, IN: University of Notre Dame Press, 1969.

Peretz, Isabelle, and Robert J. Zatorre. "Brain Organization for Music Processing." *Annual Review of Psychology* 56 (2005): 89–114.

Persson, Per. *Understanding Cinema: A Psychological Theory of Moving Imagery*. Cambridge: Cambridge University Press, 2003.

Petrinovich, Lewis. "Darwin and the Representative Expression of Reality." *Darwin and Facial Expression: A Century of Research in Review*. Ed. Paul Ekman. New York: Academic Press, 1973. 223–56.

Philippi, Donald L. *Songs of Gods, Songs of Humans: The Epic Tradition of the Ainu*. San Francisco: North Point, 1982.

Phillips, Dana. *The Truth of Ecology: Nature, Culture, and Literature in America*. Oxford: Oxford University Press, 2003.

Piaget, Jean. *Le structuralisme*. Paris: Presses Universitaires de France, 1968.

Pickering, Roger. *Reflections upon Theatrical Expression in Tragedy*. London, 1755.

Pinker, Steven. *The Blank Slate: The Modern Denial of Human Nature*. New York: Penguin, 2002.

———. *How the Mind Works*. New York: Norton, 1997.

Piper, David. *The Illustrated History of Art*. New York: Crescent Books, 1991.

Plantinga, Carl. "Film Theory and Aesthetics: Notes on a Schism." *Journal of Aesthetics and Art Criticism* 51 (1993): 445–54.

Poe, Edgar Allan. *The Collected Tales and Poems of Edgar Allan Poe*. New York: Modern Library, 1992.

Pope, Alexander. "An Essay on Criticism." 1711. *The Critical Tradition: Classic Texts and Contemporary Trends*. Ed. David H. Richter. New York: St. Martin's, 1989. 199–208.

Porro, Carlo A., et al. "Primary Motor and Sensory Cortex Activation during Motor Performance and Motor Imagery: A Functional Magnetic Resonance Imagery Study." *Journal of Neuroscience* 16 (1996): 7688–98.

Potter, Jonathan, and Margaret Wetherell. *Discourse and Social Psychology*. London: Sage, 1987.

Prather, S. C., John R. Votaw, and Krish Sathian. "Task-Specific Recruitment of Dorsal and Ventral Visual Areas During Tactile Perception." *Neuropsychologia* 42 (2004): 1079–87.

Pratt, Mary Louise. *Toward a Speech Act Theory of Literary Discourse*. Bloomington: Indiana University Press, 1977.

Premack, David, and Verena Dasser. "Perceptual Origins and Conceptual Evidence for Theory of Mind in Apes and Children." Whiten 253–66.

Pribram, Karl. "Commentary on 'Synaesthesia' by Ramachandran and Hubbard." *Journal of Consciousness Studies* 10.3 (2003): 75–76.

Prince, Gerald. *A Dictionary of Narratology*. 2nd ed. Lincoln: University of Nebraska Press, 2003.

Pugh, R. Kenneth, et al. "Cerebral Organization of Component Processes in Reading." *Brain* 119.4 (1996): 1221–38.

Pukui, Mary Kawena, and Alfons L. Korn. *The Echo of Our Song: Chants and Poems of the Hawaiians*. Honolulu: University of Hawaii Press, 1993.

Putnam, Michael C. J. *Virgil's "Aeneid": Interpretation and Influence*. Chapel Hill: University of North Carolina Press, 1995.

Pylyshyn, Zenon. "Is the Imagery Debate Over? If So, What Was It About?" *Language, Brain, and Cognitive Development*. Ed. Emmanuel Dupoux. Cambridge, MA: MIT Press, 2001. 59–82.

Rabinow, Paul, ed. *The Foucault Reader*. New York: Pantheon, 1984.

Racine, Jean. *Phèdre*. *Théâtre Complet*. Vol. 2. Ed. André Stegmann. Paris: Flammarion, 1965.

Ramachandran, V. S. "Behavioral and Magnetoencephalographic Correlates of Plasticity in the Adult Human Brain." *Proceedings of the National Academy of Sciences* 90 (1993): 10413–20.

———. *A Brief Tour of Human Consciousness: From Impostor Poodles to Purple Numbers*. New York: Pi Press, 2004.

Ramachandran, V. S., and Sandra Blakesle. "Hyper-Normal Stimuli and the Quest for the Neural Basis of Artistic Universals." Getty Research Institute, Los Angeles, November 2002.

———. *Phantoms in the Brain: Probing the Mystery of the Human Mind*. New York: Morrow, 1998.

Ramachandran, V. S., and Edward M. Hubbard. "Synaesthesia: A Window into Perception, Thought and Language." *Journal of Consciousness Studies* 8.12 (2001): 3–34.

Richards, I. A. *Principles of Literary Criticism*. New York: Routledge, 2001.

Richardson, Alan. *Mental Imagery*. New York: Springer, 1969.

Richardson, Alan. *British Romanticism and the Science of the Mind*. Cambridge: Cambridge University Press, 2001.

———. *The Neural Sublime: Cognitive Theories and Romantic Texts*. Baltimore: Johns Hopkins University Press, 2010.

———. "A Neural Theater: Joanna Baillie's *Plays on the Passions*." *Joanna Baillie, Romantic Dramatist: Critical Essays*. Ed. Thomas Crochunis. London: Routledge, 2004. 130–45.

———. "Rethinking Romantic Incest: Human Universals, Literary Representation, and the Biology of Mind." *New Literary History* 31.3 (2000): 553–72.

———. "Studies in Literature and Cognition: A Field Map." Richardson and Spolsky 1–30.

Richardson, Alan, and Ellen Spolsky, eds. *The Work of Fiction: Cognition, Culture, and Complexity*. Aldershot, UK: Ashgate, 2004.

Richardson, Alan, and Francis Steen. "Literature and the Cognitive Revolution: An Introduction." *Poetics Today* 23.1 (2002): 1–8.

Richardson, Samuel. *Clarissa; or, The History of a Young Lady*. 1748. Ed. Angus Ross. New York: Penguin, 1985.

———. *Selected Letters of Samuel Richardson*. Ed. John Carroll. Oxford, UK: Clarendon Press, 1964.

Ricks, Christopher. *Keats and Embarrassment*. Oxford, UK: Clarendon Press, 1974.

Rizzolatti, Giacomo, and Laila Craighero. "The Mirror-Neuron System." *Annual Review of Neuroscience* (2004): 169–92.

Rizzolatti, Giacomo, Leonardo Fogassi, and Vittoriao Gallese. "Neuropsychological Mechanisms Underlying the Understanding and Imitation of Action." *Nature Reviews Neuroscience* 2.9 (2001): 661–70.

Roach, Joseph. "Culture and Performance in the Circum-Atlantic World." *Performativity and Performance.* Ed. Andrew Parker and Eve Kosofsky Sedgwick. New York: Routledge, 1995. 45–63.

Roe, Sue, and Susan Sellers, eds. *The Cambridge Companion to Virginia Woolf.* Cambridge: Cambridge University Press, 2000.

Rogoff, Barbara. *Apprenticeship in Thinking: Cognitive Development in Social Context.* New York: Oxford University Press, 1991.

Ronen, Ruth. *Possible Worlds in Literary Theory.* Cambridge: Cambridge University Press, 1994.

Rosen, Robert. *Essays on Life Itself.* New York: Columbia University Press, 2000.

Rossini, Paolo M., et al. "Corticospinal Excitability Modulation to Hand Muscles During Movement Imagery." *Cerebral Cortex* 9 (1999): 161–67.

Rousseau, Jean-Jacques. *Emile; or, On Education.* 1762. Trans. Alan Bloom. New York: Basic Books, 1979.

Rubin, David. *Memory in Oral Traditions: The Cognitive Psychology of Epic, Ballads, and Counting-Out Rhymes.* New York: Oxford University Press, 1995.

Ryan, Marie-Laure. *Possible Worlds, Artificial Intelligence, and Narrative Theory.* Bloomington: Indiana University Press, 1991.

Sacks, Oliver. *An Anthropologist on Mars.* New York: Knopf, 1995.

———. *Lectures on Conversation.* Vols. 1 and 2. Ed. Gail Jefferson. Oxford, UK: Blackwell, 1992.

Said, Edward. "Bookless in Gaza." *Nation* 23 September 1996: 6–7.

Sandars, Nancy K. Introduction. *The Babylonian Creation. Poems of Heaven and Hell from Ancient Mesopotamia.* New York: Penguin, 1971. 11–17.

Sathian, Krish. "Visual Cortical Activity during Tactile Perception in the Sighted and the Visually Deprived." *Developmental Psychobiology* 46 (2005): 279–86.

Sawday, Jonathan. *The Body Emblazoned: Dissection and the Human Body in Renaissance Culture.* London: Routledge, 1995.

Saxe, Rebecca. "Hybrid Vigor: Reply to Mitchell." *Trends in Cognitive Sciences* 9.8 (2005): 364.

Scarry, Elaine. *Dreaming by the Book.* New York: Farrar, Straus and Giroux, 1999.

———. "Panel Discussion: Science, Culture, Meaning Values." *Unity of Knowledge: The Convergence of Natural and Human Science.* New York: New York Academy of Sciences, 2001. 233–57.

Schank, Roger C. *Tell Me a Story: A New Look at Real and Artificial Memory.* New York: Scribner's, 1990.

Schauber, Ellen, and Ellen Spolsky. *The Bounds of Interpretation: Linguistic Theory and Literary Text.* Stanford: Stanford University Press, 1986.

Schegloff, Emanuel A. "Notes on Conversational Practice: Formulating Place." *Studies in Social Interaction.* Ed. David Sudnow. New York: Free Press, 1972. 75–119.

Schiffrin, Deborah. *Discourse Markers.* Cambridge: Cambridge University Press, 1987.

Schiller, Gertrud. *Iconography of Christian Art.* Greenwich, CT: New York Graphic Society, 1971.

Scholl, Brian, and Patrice D. Tremoulet. "Perceptual Causality and Animacy." *Trends in Cognitive Sciences* 4.2 (2000): 299–309.

Schore, Allan N. "Attachment and the Regulation of the Right Brain." *Attachment and Human Development* 2.1 (2000): 23–47.

Searle, John R. *The Rediscovery of the Mind.* Cambridge, MA: MIT Press, 1992.

Shamay-Tsoory, Simone G., Yasmin Tibi-Elhanany, and Judith Aharon-Peretz. "The Ventromedial Prefrontal Cortex Is Involved in Understanding Affective but Not Cognitive Theory of Mind Stories." *Social Neuroscience* 1.3/4 (2006): 149–66.

Shapin, Steven. *The Scientific Revolution.* Chicago: University of Chicago Press, 1996.

Shapin, Steven, and Simon Schaeffer. *Leviathan and the Air-Pump: Hobbes, Boyle, and the Experimental Life.* Princeton: Princeton University Press, 1989.

Shearman, John. *Only Connect: Art and the Spectator in the Italian Renaissance.* Princeton: Princeton University Press, 1992.

Sheehan, P. W. "A Shortened Form of Betts' Questionnaire Upon Mental Imagery." *Journal of Clinical Psychology* 23 (1967): 386–89.

Sheets-Johnstone, Maxine. *The Primacy of Movement.* Amsterdam: John Benjamins, 1999.

———. *The Roots of Power: Animate Form and Gendered Bodies.* Chicago: Open Court, 1994.

———. *The Roots of Thinking.* Philadephia: Temple University Press, 1990.

Sherzer, Joel. "Poetic Structuring of Kuna Discourse: The Line." *Native American Discourse: Poetics and Rhetoric.* Ed. Joel Sherzer and Anthony C. Woodbury. Cambridge: Cambridge University Press, 1987. 103–39.

Sherzer, Joel, and Anthony Woodbury. Introduction. *Native American Discourse: Poetics and Rhetoric.* Ed. Joel Sherzer and Anthony C. Woodbury. Cambridge: Cambridge University Press, 1987. 1–16.

Shore, Bradd. *Culture in Mind: Cognition, Culture, and the Problem of Meaning.* New York: Oxford University Press, 1996.

Siddons, Henry. *Practical Illustrations of Rhetorical Gesture and Action, Adapted to the English Drama . . .* 1807. London, 1822.

Sidney, Sir Philip. *Selected Prose and Poetry.* Ed. Robert Kimbrough. 2nd ed. Madison: University of Wisconsin Press, 1983.

"Sinbad the Sailor and Sinbad the Porter." Trans. N. J. Dawood. *Tales from the Thousand and One Nights.* New York: Penguin, 1955. 156–67.

Singer, Tania, Daniel Wolpert, and Christopher D. Frith. "Introduction: The Study of Social Interactions." *The Neuroscience of Social Interaction: Decoding, Imitating, and Influencing the Actions of Others.* Ed. Christopher D. Frith and Daniel Wolpert. Oxford: Oxford University Press, 2004. xiii–xxvii.

Sitter, John. "Touching Satire." American Society for Eighteenth-Century Studies. Montreal, Canada, 31 March 2006.

Slovic, Scott. "Nature Writing and Environmental Psychology: The Interiority of Outdoor Experience." Glotfelty and Fromm 351–70.

Smith, Craig, and Leslie Kirby. "Affect and Cognitive Appraisal Processes." *Handbook of Affect and Social Cognition.* Ed. Joseph Forgas. Mahwah, NJ: Lawrence Erlbaum, 2001. 75–92.

Smith, Eliot, and Diane Mackie. "Intergroup Emotions." *Handbook of Emotions.* 3rd ed. Ed. Michael Lewis, Jeannette Haviland-Jones, and Lisa Feldman Barrett. New York: Guilford Press, 2008. 428–39.

Smith, Greg. *Film Structure and the Emotion System.* Cambridge: Cambridge University Press, 2003.

Spenser, Edmund. *The Faerie Queene.* 1590–96. Ed. Abraham Dylan Stoll and Carol V. Kaske. Indianapolis: Hackett, 2006.

Sperber, Dan. *Explaining Culture: A Naturalistic Approach.* Oxford, UK: Blackwell, 1996.

Sperber, Dan, and Lawrence Hirschfeld. "Culture, Cognition, and Evolution." *The MIT Encyclopedia of the Cognitive Sciences.* Ed. Robert Wilson and Frank Keil. Cambridge, MA: MIT Press, 1999. cxi–cxxxii.

Spiller, Elizabeth. *Science, Reading, and the Art of Making Knowledge, 1580–1670.* Cambridge: Cambridge University Press, 2004.

Spivak, Gayatri Chakravorty. Translator's preface. *Of Grammatology.* Trans. Gayatri Chakravorty Spivak. Baltimore: Johns Hopkins University Press, 1976. ix–lxxxvii.

Spolsky, Ellen. "Cognitive Literary Historicism: A Response to Adler and Gross." *Poetics Today* 24.2 (2003): 161–83.

———. "Darwin and Derrida: Cognitive Literary Theory as a Species of Post-Structuralism." *Poetics Today* 23.1 (2002): 43–62.

——. "Elaborated Knowledge: Reading Kinesis in Pictures." *Poetics Today* 17.2 (1996): 157–80.

——. "Frozen in Time?" Rev. of *The Literary Animal: Evolution and the Nature of Narrative*, ed. Jonathan Gottschall and David Sloan Wilson. *Poetics Today* 28.4 (2007): 807–16.

——. *Gaps in Nature: Literary Interpretation and the Modular Mind*. Albany: State University of New York Press, 1993.

——. "Narrative as Nourishment." *Toward a Theory of Narrative Acts*. Ed. Frederick Luis Aldama. University of Texas Press, 2010. 37–60.

——. Preface. Richardson and Spolsky vii–xiii.

——. "Purposes Mistook: Failures are More Tellable." "Cognitive Approaches to Narrative" panel, annual meeting, Society for the Study of Narrative, Burlington, VT, 2004.

——. *Satisfying Skepticism: Embodied Knowledge in the Early Modern World*. Aldershot, UK: Ashgate, 2001.

——. "Toward a Theory of Embodiment for Literature." *Poetics Today* 24.1 (2003): 127–37.

——. "Why and How to Take the Wheat and Leave the Chaff." *SubStance* 30.1/2 (2001): 178–98.

——. "Women's Work is Chastity: Lucretia, *Cymbeline*, and Cognitive Impenetrability." Richardson and Spolsky 51–83.

——. *Word vs. Image: Cognitive Hunger in Shakespeare's England*. Houndmills, UK: Palgrave, 2007.

Stafford, Barbara Maria. *Good Looking: Essays on the Virtue of Images*. Cambridge, MA: MIT Press, 1996.

——. "Romantic Systematics and the Genealogy of Thought: The Formal Roots of a Cognitive History of Images." *Configurations* 12.3 (2004): 315–48.

Stanzel, Franz Karl. *A Theory of Narrative*. Trans. Charlotte Goedsche. Cambridge: Cambridge University Press, 1984.

Starr, Gabrielle G. "Cavendish, Aesthetics, and the Anti-Platonic Line." *Eighteenth-Century Studies* 39.3 (2006): 295–308.

——. "Ethics, Meaning, and the Work of Beauty." *Eighteenth-Century Studies* 35.3 (2002): 361–78.

——. *Lyric Generations: Poetry and the Novel in the Long Eighteenth Century*. Baltimore: Johns Hopkins University Press, 2004.

——. "Poetic Subjects and Grecian Urns: Close Reading and the Tools of Cognitive Science." *Modern Philology* 105.1 (2007): 48–61.

Stearns, Peter. "Emotion." *Discursive Psychology in Practice*. Ed. Rom Harré and Peter Stearns. Thousand Oaks, CA: Sage, 1995. 37–54.

———. "Extending the Agenda of Cultural Research." *Chronicle of Higher Education* 2 May 2003: B7–9

Stearns, Peter, and Carol Stearns. "Emotionology: Clarifying the History of Emotions and Emotional Standards." *American Historical Review* 90 (Feb. 1985): 13–36.

Stefan, Katja, et al. "Formation of a Motor Memory by Action Observation." *Journal of Neuroscience* 25 (2005): 9339–46.

Stein, Barry E., and M. Alex Meredith. *The Merging of the Senses.* Cambridge, MA: MIT Press, 1993.

Sterelny, Kim. *Thought in a Hostile World: The Evolution of Human Cognition.* Malden, MA: Blackwell, 2003.

Sternberg, Meir. "How Narrativity Makes a Difference." *Narrative* 9.2 (January 2001): 115–22.

Sterne, Laurence. *The Life and Opinions of Tristram Shandy, Gentleman.* 1759–67. New York: Penguin, 1978.

Stevens, Catherine, and Shirley McKechnie. "Thinking in Action: Thought Made Visible in Contemporary Dance." *Cognitive Processing* 6 (2005): 243–52.

Stevens, Jennifer A. "Interference Effects Demonstrate Distinct Roles for Visual and Motor Imagery During the Mental Representation of Human Action." *Cognition* 95 (2005): 329–50.

Stevenson, Richard J., and Trevor I. Case. "Olfactory Dreams: Phenomenology, Relationship to Volitional Imagery and Odor Identification." *Imagination, Cognition, and Personality* 24 (2005): 69–90.

———. "Olfactory Imagery: A Review." *Psychonomic Bulletin and Review* 12 (2005): 244–64.

Stewart, Susan. *Poetry and the Fate of the Senses.* Chicago: University of Chicago Press, 2002.

Storey, John. *Inventing Popular Culture: From Folklore to Globalization.* Malden, MA: Blackwell, 2003.

Sutton, John. "Animal Spirits and Nervous Fluids" *All in the Mind.* Australian National Broadcasting. 29 April 2003.

———. "Porous Memory and the Cognitive Life of Things." *Prefiguring Cyberculture: An Intellectual History.* Ed. Darren Tofts, Annemarie Jonson, and Alessio Cavallaro. Cambridge, MA: MIT Press, 2002. 130–41.

Tabbi, Joseph. *Cognitive Fictions.* Minneapolis: University of Minnesota Press, 2002.

Talmy, Leonard. *Toward a Cognitive Semantics.* Vols. 1 and 2. Cambridge, MA: MIT Press, 2000.

Tan, Ed. "Emotion, Art, and the Humanities." *Handbook of Emotions.* 2nd ed.

Ed. Michael Lewis and Jeannette M. Haviland-Jones. New York: Guilford Press, 2000. 116–34.

Tanner, Tony. *Jane Austen*. Houndmills, UK: Macmillan, 1986.

Taylor, John. *Cognitive Grammar*. Oxford: Oxford University Press, 2002.

Thagard, Paul, and Ethan Toombs. "Atoms, Categorization, and Conceptual Change." *Handbook of Categorization in Cognitive Science*. Ed. Henri Cohen and Claire Lefebvre. Amsterdam: Elsevier, 2005. 243–54.

Thoreau, Henry David. *Walden and Civil Disobedience*. Ed. Sherman Paul. Boston: Houghton Mifflin, 1960.

Tillyard, E. M. W. *The Elizabethan World Picture*. New York: Vintage, 1959.

Toulmin, Stephen, and June Goodfield. *The Architecture of Matter*. Rev. ed. Chicago: University of Chicago Press, 1982.

Tsur, Reuven. *Toward a Theory of Cognitive Poetics*. Amsterdam: Elsevier-North Holland, 1992.

Tuan, Yi-Fu. *Space and Place: The Perspective of Experience*. Minneapolis: University of Minnesota Press, 1977.

Turner, Henry. *The English Renaissance Stage: Geometry, Poetics, and the Practical, Spatial Arts, 1580–1630*. Oxford: Oxford University Press, 2006.

Turner, Mark. *The Literary Mind*. New York: Oxford University Press, 1996.

Tye, Michael. "Qualia." *The Stanford Encyclopedia of Philosophy (Summer 2003 Edition)*. Ed. Edward N. Zalta. http://plato.stanford.edu/archives/sum2003/entries/qualia.

Uttal, William R. *The New Phrenology: The Limits of Localizing Cognitive Processes in the Brain*. Cambridge, MA: MIT Press, 2001.

Valmiki. *Srimad Valmiki Ramayanam*. 3 vols. Trans. N. Raghunathan. Madras: Vighneswara, 1981.

van Peer, Willie. "Towards a Poetics of Emotion." *Emotion and the Arts*. Ed. Mette Hjort and Sue Laver. New York: Oxford University Press, 1997. 215–24.

Vermeule, Blakey. "God Novels." Richardson and Spolsky 147–66.

———. *The Party of Humanity: Writing Moral Psychology in Eighteenth-Century Britain*. Baltimore: Johns Hopkins University Press, 2000.

Virgil. *The Aeneid*. Trans. Robert Fitzgerald. New York: Knopf, 1992.

Vygotsky, Lev S. *Mind in Society: The Development of Higher Psychological Processes*. Ed. Michael Cole, Vera John-Steiner, Sylvia Scribner, and Ellen Souberman. Cambridge, MA: Harvard University Press, 1978.

Wagner-Martin, Linda, ed. *Ernest Hemingway: Seven Decades of Criticism*. East Lansing: Michigan State University Press, 1998.

Waley, Arthur. *The Nō Plays of Japan*. London: Allen and Unwin, 1988.

Warner, William B. *Licensing Entertainment: The Elevation of Novel Reading in Britain, 1684–1750*. Berkeley: University of California Press, 1998.

Wasserman, Earl R. "The Sympathetic Imagination in Eighteenth-Century Theories of Acting." *Journal or English and Germanic Philology* 46 (1947): 264–72.

Waugh, Evelyn. *Men at Arms*. 1952. Harmondsworth, UK: Penguin, 1964.

Wehrs, Donald. "Moral Physiology, Ethical Prototypes, and the Denaturing of Sense in Shakespearean Tragedy." *College Literature* 33.1 (2006): 67–92.

Weisberg, Deena Skolnick. "The Creation and Comprehension of Fictional Worlds." PhD diss. Yale University, 2008.

Werth, Paul. *Text Worlds: Representing Conceptual Space in Discourse*. London: Longman, 1999.

Wertsch, James V. *Voices of the Mind: A Sociocultural Approach to Mediated Action*. Cambridge, MA: Harvard University Press, 1991.

West, Shearer. *The Image of the Actor: Verbal and Visual Representation in the Age of Garrick and Kemble*. New York: St. Martin's Press, 1991.

Westling, Louise H. *The Green Breast of the World: Landscape, Gender, and American Fiction*. Athens: University of Georgia Press, 1996.

Whiten, Andrew, ed. *Natural Theories of Mind: Evolution, Development, and Simulation of Everyday Mindreading*. Oxford, UK: Blackwell, 1991.

Whitworth, Michael. "Virginia Woolf and Modernism." Roe and Sellers 146–63.

Williams, Raymond. *Communications*. 2nd ed. London: Chatto and Windus, 1966.

———. *Culture*. Glasgow: Fontana New Sociology Series, 1981.

———. *The Long Revolution*. Harmondsworth, UK: Penguin, 1965.

———. *Marxism and Literature*. Oxford: Oxford University Press, 1977.

———. *Problems in Materialism and Culture: Selected Essays*. London: Verso, 1980.

Wilson, Timothy. *Strangers to Ourselves: Discovering the Adaptive Unconscious*. Cambridge, MA: Harvard University Press, 2002.

Wittgenstein, Ludwig. *Philosophical Investigations*. 3rd ed. Ed. G. E. M. Anscombe and Rush Rhees. Trans. G. E. M. Anscombe. Oxford, UK: Blackwell, 1953.

Woloch, Alex. *The One vs. the Many: Minor Characters and the Space of the Protagonist in the Novel*. Princeton: Princeton University Press, 2004.

Woolf, Virginia. The Diary of Virginia Woolf. 5 vols. Ed. Anne Olivier Bell. London: Hogarth Press, 1977–84.

———. *Jacob's Room*. 1922. London: Hogarth, 1976.

———. *The Letters of Virginia Woolf*. Vol. 2. Ed. Nigel Nicholson. London: Hogarth Press, 1975–80.

——. *Mrs. Dalloway*. 1925. San Diego: Harcourt Brace, 1981.

Woolner, Alfred Cooper, and Lakshman Sarup, eds. and trans. *Vision of Vasavadatta. Thirteen Plays of Bhasa*. Delhi: Motilal Banarsidass, 1930. 37–70.

Yabe, Hirooki, et al. "Time May Be Compressed in Sound Representation as Replicated in Sensory Memory." *NeuroReport* 16 (2005): 95–98.

Yathharth (The Truth). Giriraj Music and Media Exim. 2002.

Yoo, Seung-Schik, et al. "Neural Substrates of Tactile Imagery: A Functional MRI Study." *NeuroReport* 14 (2003): 581–85.

Zeki, Semir. *Inner Vision: An Exploration of Art and the Brain*. Oxford: Oxford University Press, 1999.

——. "A Theory of Microconsciousness" Lecture, "Recherches/Mixites: Arts-Sciences-Technologies" seminar, IRCAM, Paris, 25 April 2003.

Zhang, Minming, et al. "Multisensory Cortical Processing of Object Shape and Its Relation to Mental Imagery." *Cognitive, Affective, and Behavioral Neuroscience* 4 (2004): 251–59.

Zunshine, Lisa. "Eighteenth-Century Print Culture and the 'Truth' of Fictional Narrative." *Philosophy and Literature* 25.2 (2001): 215–32.

——. "Rhetoric, Cognition, and Ideology in Anna Laetitia Barbauld's 1781 *Hymns in Prose for Children*." *Poetics Today* 23.1 (2001): 231–59.

——. "Richardson's *Clarissa* and a Theory of Mind." Richardson and Spolsky 127–46.

——. *Strange Concepts and the Stories They Make Possible: Cognition, Culture, Narrative*. Baltimore: Johns Hopkins University Press, 2008.

——. "Theory of Mind and Experimental Representations of Fictional Consciousness." *Narrative* 11.3 (2003): 270–91.

——. "Theory of Mind and Fictions of Embodied Transparency." *Narrative* 16.1 (2008): 65–92.

——. *Why We Read Fiction: Theory of Mind and the Novel*. Columbus: Ohio State University Press, 2006.

CONTRIBUTORS

MARY THOMAS CRANE is the Rattigan Professor of English at Boston College. She is the author of *Framing Authority: Sayings, Self, and Society in Sixteenth-Century England* (1993) and *Shakespeare's Brain: Reading with Cognitive Theory* (2000).

NANCY EASTERLIN is a University Research professor in the Department of English at University of New Orleans. She is coeditor of *After Poststructuralism: Interdisciplinarity and Literary Theory* (1993) and author of *Wordsworth and the Question of "Romantic Religion"* (1996) as well as numerous essays employing a biocultural (evolutionary-cognitive) approach to literary criticism and theory. She is currently completing a book entitled *What Is Literature For? Biocultural Theory and Interpretation* (forthcoming).

DAVID HERMAN, who cofounded the Project Narrative initiative at Ohio State University and served as its inaugural director, teaches in OSU's English Department. He has authored, edited, or coedited a number of studies on aspects of narrative, including a forthcoming volume on the history of consciousness representation titled *The Emergence of Mind.* The editor of the *Frontiers of Narrative* book series and the new journal *Storyworlds,* both published by the University of Nebraska Press, he was recently awarded a research fellowship from the American Council of Learned Societies for his 2009 project "Storytelling and the Sciences of Mind."

PATRICK COLM HOGAN is a professor in the Department of English, the Program in Comparative Literature and Cultural Studies, and the Program in Cognitive Science at the University of Connecticut. He is the author of eleven books, including *Cognitive Science, Literature, and the Arts: A Guide for Humanists* (2003) and *Understanding Indian Movies: Culture, Cognition, and Cinematic Imagination*

(2008). He is the editor of the forthcoming *Cambridge Encyclopedia of the Language Sciences*.

BRUCE McCONACHIE is the chair of theatre arts at the University of Pittsburgh. His cognitively inflected publications include *American Theater in the Culture of the Cold War: Producing and Contesting Containment* (2003), *Performance and Cognition: Theatre Studies and the Cognitive Turn*, coedited with F. Elizabeth Hart (2006), and *Engaging Audiences: A Cognitive Approach to Spectating in the Theatre* (2008). With Blakey Vermeule, McConachie coedits the book series, "Cognitive Studies in Literature and Performance" for Palgrave. A former president of the American Society for Theatre Research, he is also one of the coauthors of *Theatre Histories: An Introduction* (2006).

ALAN PALMER is an independent scholar living in London. His book *Fictional Minds* (2004) was a cowinner of the MLA Prize for Independent Scholars and also a cowinner of the Perkins Prize (awarded by the International Society for the Study of Narrative). His articles have been published in the journals *Narrative*, *Semiotica*, and *Style*, and he has contributed chapters to a number of edited volumes, including *Narrative Theory and the Cognitive Sciences* (2003) and *Contemporary Stylistics* (2007). He is an honorary research fellow at the Department of Linguistics and English Language, Lancaster University.

ALAN RICHARDSON is a professor of English at Boston College. A scholar of Romanticism, his books include *The Neural Sublime: Cognitive Theories and Romantic Texts* (2010), *British Romanticism and the Science of the Mind* (2001), and *Literature, Education, and Romanticism: Reading as Social Practice, 1780–1832* (1994). He has published general essays on cognitive literary criticism in *Mosaic* and *Philosophy and Literature* and is coeditor of a special issue of *Poetics Today* entitled "Literature and the Cognitive Revolution" and of the volume *The Work of Fiction: Culture, Cognition, and Complexity* (2004).

ELLEN SPOLSKY is a professor of English at Bar-Ilan University in Israel. She is a literary theorist with an interest in the connections among philosophical and biological theories of culture as explored in cognitive cultural theory, iconotropism, and performance theory. She is the author of *Gaps in Nature: Literary Interpretation and the Modular Mind* (1993), *Satisfying Skepticism: Embodied Knowledge in the Early Modern World* (2001), and most recently, *Word vs. Image: Cognitive Hunger in Shakespeare's England* (2007).

G. GABRIELLE STARR is an associate professor of English at New York University. She is the author of *Lyric Generations: Novel and Poetry in the Long Eighteenth Century* (2004) and of articles on Aphra Behn, Daniel Defoe, Margaret Cavendish, and the materialist tradition of aesthetics in the English eighteenth century. She has also published work on cognitive science and its implications for close reading. In 2003, she received a grant to study neuroscience from the Andrew W. Mellon Foundation and is at work, with the collaboration of neuroscientists Nava Rubin and Ed Vessel, on an fMRI project on art and the brain.

BLAKEY VERMEULE is an associate professor of English at Stanford University. She is the author of *The Party of Humanity: Writing Moral Psychology in Eighteenth-Century Britain* (2000) and *Why Do We Care about Literary Characters?* (2010). She is currently at work on a third book called "Transformations: How Literature Solves Problems in Cognition and Evolution." She coedits a series on cognitive approaches to literature and performance published by Palgrave.

LISA ZUNSHINE is the Bush-Holbrook Professor of English at the University of Kentucky, specializing in eighteenth-century British literature. She is the author, editor, or coeditor of nine books, including *Bastards and Foundlings: Illegitimacy in Eighteenth-Century England* (2005), *Approaches to Teaching the Novels of Samuel Richardson* (2006; coedited with Jocelyn Harris), *Why We Read Fiction: Theory of Mind and the Novel* (2006), *Acting Theory and the English Stage, 1700–1830* (2008), and *Strange Concepts and the Stories They Make Possible: Cognition, Culture, Narrative* (2008). In 2007–8, supported by a Guggenheim fellowship, she was a visiting scholar in the Department of Psychology at Yale University.

Cleland, John, *Fanny Hill*, 287
Clement, John, 107, 317n9
Code, Lorraine, 308
Coetzee, J. M., *Disgrace*, 272–73
cognitive aesthetics, 115, 276, 289–91;
    and close reading, 325n10
cognitive approaches to literature, 1, 61,
    176, 292; and cultural historicism,
    210, 211–22; and deconstruction,
    210; and ecocriticism, 210; and femi-
    nism, 210; and gender studies, 210;
    and history of moral philosophy, 210;
    and literary aesthetics, 210; and nar-
    rative theory, 210; and other literary-
    theoretical approaches, 210, 213; and
    poststructuralism, 292–310
cognitive competition, as historically
    contingent, 235
cognitive cultural studies: boundaries
    between various subfields of, 3–4;
    goal of, 3, 85; as grounded in the
    work of Raymond Williams, 5–8; and
    historicizing, 235; history of, 5; and
    literary realism, 23; and other literary-
    theoretical approaches, 5–6, 116
cognitive ecocriticism, 3, 22–23, 233–34;
    and ecocriticism, 257–60; and evo-
    lutionary psychology, 259–63; and
    journey narratives, 266–70; and liter-
    ary realism, 264; and narratives of con-
    finement, 270–72; and nature-culture
    dichotomy, 263–64, 265–66; and place
    attachment, 272–73; and pragmatism,
    258; and wayfinding, 257–74
cognitive evolutionary psychology,
    158; and cultural historicism, 115–33;
    and cultural studies, 28, 121; and eco-
    criticism, 22, 115, 259–63; and per-
    formativity studies, 121; and theory of
    mind, 205; and wayfinding, 260–63
cognitive historicism, 3, 26–27; and cog-
    nitive science, 61; and cultural change,
    62; definition of, 61–62, 67–68
cognitive linguistics, 35, 115, 158
cognitive narratology, 3, 21, 85, 155–
    75; definition of, 151; and discursive
    psychology, 155–58
cognitive neuroscience, 115, 158, 277,
    281

cognitive poetics, 4
cognitive postcolonial theory, 231–33;
    and human universalism, 231
cognitivism, 160, 165. *See also* first cog-
    nitive revolution
Cohn, Dorrit, 319n17
Coleridge, Samuel Taylor, 214
Comrie, Bernard, 312n4, 313n13,
    313n18
conceptual blending theory, 4. *See also*
    conceptual mapping
conceptual change: and cognitive stud-
    ies of metaphor and analogy, 103–14;
    and metaphysical imagery, 111
conceptual mapping, 115, 140–43
connectionism, 239
contextual historicism, 4
Cooper, Arthur, 312n5, 313n22, 313n25
Cooper, Astley, 75
Copernicus, Nicolaus, 103
Cosmides, Leda, 313n2, 323n14, 326n5
Crane, Mary Thomas, 25–26, 31, 61,
    103, 210, 310, 316n2, 317n13,
    318n1
Croft, William, 313n13, 313n18, 321n22
Cruse, Alan D., 321n22
Culler, Jonathan, 333n8, 333n21
cultural hegemony, theories of, 134–37;
    and cognitive science, 138–50; and
    cultural models, 139, 142; and
    epistemology of embodied realism,
    141–45; and organic intellectuals,
    135–36, 143, 145, 148; and particu-
    late theory of culture, 144, 145; and
    social schemas, 142–43; and universal
    primitives, 143
cultural historicism, 115
cultural studies: and cognitive cultural
    studies, 7–8; definition of, 7
culture: and cognitive science, 84, 139;
    and modular theory of cognition, 295–
    96; works of art as engines of, 85
Curry, Sue, 324n1
Cytowic, Richard E., 332n46, 332n49

Damasio, Antonio, 243, 320n9, 325n2
D'Andrade, Roy, 144
Darwin, Charles, 15, 30, 235, 292, 297,
    300, 305–9, 326n2; *The Descent of*

and embodied transparency, 131–32; and emotionology, 162, 168–73; evolutionary history of, 240–43; felt by actors on stage, 130–31; functionalist account of, 241–43; and narrative therapy, 173; neurobiological account of, 239–40, 245; as related to cognition, 237–38; as response to literature, 245–50; and structure of feeling (Williams), 138; as studied by non-Western literary theorists, 232; universalist view of, 250–52; and wayfinding, 261–62

empathy, 23; and cognitive postcolonial theory, 231–32; and universalism, 38, 231

empirical studies of literature, 4

Engel, Johann Jacob, 128

Engell, James, 329n16

Engholm, Scott, 312n11, 312n14

The English Theophrastus, 133, 319n15

Epicurus, 317n8

Esrock, Ellen J., 31, 234, 235

Euclid, *Elements of Geometry,* 113

Evola, Vito, 35

evolutionary literary theory, 67. *See also* Literary Darwinism

facial expressions, 65–83; and biological determinism, 66; and cultural norms and expectations, 66–67; and "display rules," 67; of liars in works of fiction, 115, 124–28; and theory of mind, 65

failures: as conducive to storytelling, 24, 92–93; and critique of metaphysical idealism, 293; of mind reading, 77, 79, 80; and modular theory of cognition, 88–89, 294–95

Fanon, Frantz, 60, 313n31

Feldman, Jerome A., 315n6

feminist criticism, 5, 210

Fielding, Henry, 115; *Tom Jones,* 28, 116, 124–25, 127, 128, 133

Finch, Ann, 266, 269

first cognitive revolution, 156, 159–60

Firth, Raymond, 312n5, 313n11

Fish, Stanley, 200–202, 299–300, 305, 323n13, 333n10, 333n13

Flanagan, Owen, 320n9

Flower Drum Song (Rodgers and Hammerstein), 149

Fludernik, Monika, 174; *Towards a "Natural" Narratology,* 151

fMRI, 327n2. *See also* brain imaging

focalization, 164, 165, 183–84

Fodor, Jerry, 295, 315n3

Fogassi, Leonardo, 318n5

Fontanille, Jacques, 321n27

Foote, Samuel, *A Treatise on Passions,* 130

foreshadowing, as a literary universal, 43, 54

Forster, E. M., *Aspects of the Novel,* 216, 218–19

Foucault, Michel, 104, 105, 303–6

four elements, 105

four humors, 105

Fowles, John, *The Collector,* 270

Freccero, John, 114

Freeman, Anthony, 159, 320n9

Freeman, Donald, 316n2

Freeman, Walter J., 315n5

Freud, Sigmund, 297, 303, 305

Frijda, Nico, 238

Frith, Christopher D., 363

Frye, Northrop, 46, 296

Galati, Dario, 314n2

Galen, 316n6

Galilei, Galileo, 103, 107, 108, 109, 317n9

Gallagher, Catherine, 121

Gallese, Vittoriao, 318n5

Gardner, Howard, 320n9, 320n14

Garfinkel, Harold, 160, 320n18

Garman, Michael, 313n27

Garrick, David, 130, 131, 133

Gathercole, Susan, 313n27

Gay, Penny, 319n17

Geertz, Clifford, 185

Genette, Gérard, 155

Gentner, Dedre, 110, 111, 112, 316nn4–5

Gentner, Donald R., 316n4

Ghosh, Amitav, 232

Gibson, James J., 139, 315n15

Gilb, Dagoberto, 232

Gildon, Charles, *The Life of Mr. Thomas Betterton,* 130

Lakoff, George, 24, 25, 103, 104, 107, 108, 135, 139–46, 165, 313n12, 315n19, 316n1, 316n4
Lal, P., 312n10
Lamarckism, 69
Landenwich, Sarah, 312n11
Langacker, Ronald, 165, 321n35
Latour, Bruno, 317n14
Lavater, Johann Kaspar, 71
Lave, Jean, 320n17
Lawrence, D. H., 94, 218
Lears, T. J. Jackson, 136
Lee, Hermione, 322n2
Lee, Penny, 321n27
Leitch, Vincent B., 311nn3–4
Leslie, Alan, 323n9
Leucippus, 317n8
Levin, Janet, 173
Levine, Joseph, 321n30
Levinson, Stephen, 35
Lévi-Strauss, Claude, 296, 303, 311n2, 333n15
Lewis, David, 179
Lewis, Mitchell R., 311nn3–4
line length, as a literary universal, 58
literacy, 62
Literary Darwinism, 313n1
literary texts, and tellability, 92
literary universals, 3, 16–17, 37–60, 67, 133, 210; and absolute vs. statistical universals, 42; and antiuniversalism, 38; and colonialism, 38; and cultural construction, 253; and cultural differentialism, 38; and culture and history, 40, 50, 251, 253; definition of, 42; empirical study of, 51–60; and hegemonic absolutes, 39; history of study of, 35; and indexical vs. nonindexical universals, 50; and nontechnical correlations, 43; and a pattern of encoding, 54–55; and a pattern of maximizing relevance, 52–54, 55–56; and pseudouniversalism, 17; and racism and ethnocentrism, 60; and rehearsal memory, 57–60; and repertoire of techniques, 43; and schemata defining literary types and subtypes, 44; and standard line lengths for poetry, 56–60; and study of emo-

tions, 250–52; and the threshold of forced attentional focus, 55–56; and typologies, 49–50
Liu, Hsieh, 312n5
Liu, Jung-en, 312nn9–10
Lock, Andrew, 320n3
Lord, Albert, 313n16, 313n28
Love, Glen, 233, 325n7, 327n11
Love Letter from the Licensed Quarter, 47
Lucretius, 317n8

Machiavellian reasoning, 20, 214–16, 222–27, 230; definition of, 215; and flat vs. round characters, 216–21; and the mastermind character, 222, 223–24; and round literary work, 221–22; and theory of mind, 215–16; and tropes of reflection, 222
Mackenzie, Henry, 128
Mackie, Diane, 326n14
Manes, Christopher, 326n4
Manley, Delariviere, 122
Mann, Thomas, *The Magic Mountain*, 20, 226–30
Manohra, 46
Mansfield, Katherine, "The Little Governess," 23, 268, 269
Marks, David F., 328n3
Marron, Orley, 316n23
Marshall, David, 319n17
Martindale, Colin, 289–90
Martinovitch, Nicholas N., 312n8
Marx, Karl, 60, 137, 297, 305, 313n17, 313n31
Mathiak, Klaus, 329n11
Matsuoka, Kazuo, 328n4
May, Theresa, 271
Mayr, Ernst, 67
McCarthy, Geoffrey, 314n1
McCarthyism, 147
McClosky, Michael, 107, 317n9
McConachie, Bruce, 5, 24–25, 26, 32, 61; *American Theater in the Culture of the Cold War*, 145–50
McLean, Mervyn, 312n5, 313n11
McMillan, Dorothy, 314n7
Mead, Margaret, 66
MEG, 327n2. *See also* brain imaging